Back in the Day

Also by Melvyn Bragg

FICTION

For Want of a Nail
The Second Inheritance

The Cumbrian Trilogy:
The Hired Man
A Place in England
Kingdom Come

The Nerve
A Christmas Child
Without a City Wall
The Silken Net
Autumn Manoeuvres
Love and Glory
Josh Lawton
The Maid of Buttermere
A Time to Dance
A Time to Dance: the screenplay
Crystal Rooms
Credo
The Soldier's Return
A Son of War
Crossing the Lines
Remember Me . . .
Grace and Mary
Now is the Time
Love Without End

NON-FICTION

Speak for England
Land of the Lakes
Laurence Olivier
Cumbria in Verse (*edited*)
Rich: The Life of Richard Burton
On Giants' Shoulders
The Adventure of English
12 Books that Changed the World
In Our Time
The South Bank Show: Final Cut
The Book of Books
William Tyndale: A Very Brief History

Melvyn Bragg

Back in the Day

A Memoir

SCEPTRE

First published in Great Britain in 2022 by Sceptre
An imprint of Hodder & Stoughton
An Hachette UK company

1

A CIP catalogue record for this title is available from the British Library

Hardback ISBN 9781529394450
Trade Paperback ISBN 9781529394467
eBook ISBN 9781529394474

Typeset in Sabon MT Std by Palimpsest Book Production Limited,
Falkirk, Stirlingshire

Printed and bound in Great Britain by Clays Ltd, Elcograf S.p.A.

Hodder & Stoughton policy is to use papers that are natural,
renewable and recyclable products and made from wood grown in sustainable
forests. The logging and manufacturing processes are expected to conform
to the environmental regulations of the country of origin.

Hodder & Stoughton Ltd
Carmelite House
50 Victoria Embankment
London EC4Y 0DZ

www.sceptrebooks.co.uk

To my grandsons
Arthur and Eric

The past is never dead
It is not even past.

William Faulkner

Author's Note

This is a memoir of my early life, the lives of my family and friends and of the town of Wigton in which I lived.

I have written about some of these events before in fiction. My past and the town have been subjects to which I've returned many times. I wanted to revisit it in a chronicle drawn from memory. There are misrememberings, I'm sure, and now and then a patch of embroidery to make sense of a scene. But I have tried here to follow the most forceful of the memories and allow that to dictate the book, which in the first half makes it more of a series of impressions in no strict order, when I was finding my way.

There then comes a crisis, a time when I had to rebuild my life and discover how I could hold it together. To find a way to gather up the pieces.

This is the personal experience of someone who feels very lucky to have been alive in such a place at such a time.

Chapter One

I was brought up in a house of lies. The lies were intended to be kind. Some lies help. Through time some lies become as powerful as truths, like an implant in your body that comes from the body of someone else but becomes part of you. Maybe some lies make your life better, even stronger. But many lies only appear to be benign. 'Evasions' would be a kinder word but, looking back, 'lies' seems more truthful.

I could feel the lies. Even then, even young. Now they seem like small corpses buried along the way.

There was a mystery in the house, so hidden you could not see it or hear it but you could sense it. That sense of lying hung around the house like a wraith of smoke. Once or twice there would be a mild cruelty from one of the adults. Do you know who you really are, little boy, only child among the chair legs and the clutter of people?

If I were caught lying, I would be punished.

The lies have lost their sting over the years, but the scars remain, to be scratched, sometimes almost affectionately. Surely there was no harm done. Surely little if any was intended – and isn't it the intention that causes the wound? But a cast of mind, a view of the world was partly formed in that childhood web; and the adult world would have its own lies, lying in wait.

There is a photograph of my grandmother, Mrs Gilbertson, sitting in the yard on a sunny day. Photographs of such as her were rare in her time. Days sufficiently sunny to haul out an armchair were few. She sits, wide-hipped and large, a Victorian matriarch. In the few Victorian and Edwardian snaps I have seen of her family all of them wear stern expressions, as if the moment was too important to trivialise. Or perhaps to show that they were as worth consideration as anyone else who had achieved the status of being photographed. Mrs Gilbertson, often stern, is here at ease, almost smiling, as I like to remember her. She was the great love of my mother's early life, a figure of impregnable respectability.

She died when I was six. She was laid out in a coffin on a sofa that dominated the largely unused parlour. There was also an unused piano. The sofa was flanked by two matching chairs decked with doilies to protect them against those who so rarely sat in them. A print of *The Haywain* decorated the mantelpiece. I was allowed to go and see her on my own. After a while I grew unsure about this death. Her face was just as it had been, just as white, the cheeks very pouchy. It became unbearable just to sit still and do nothing. I stood up, glanced around the empty room and looked over the edge of the coffin. With the index finger of my right hand I poked her smooth white plump cheek. I think the finger left a dent.

There was also a report from about the same time of my grandmother sitting on her chair, this time in the kitchen, crying out, 'Don't hit the boy!'

When my father set out to clip or smack me I would – I was told – scurry under my grandmother's chair, which was all but wedged in a corner. I could get through the gap but my dad couldn't and I doubt he would have dared to try. This was not abuse. It was the sudden and quickly passing loss of temper of someone back home for a few days, raw from his experiences in the world at war. And I'm sure I was spiky towards this intruder who had come back from war and in some way taken over my role.

Later he gave me his creed. Never be a coward. Respect those who are less fortunate. You are better than no one. But no one is better than you. He told me he had heard that in a sermon during the war and never forgotten it.

He could tug me in like a kite whenever he had a mind. This makes him seem severe: he wasn't. He was strong. He enjoyed telling us about his past – as a boots boy, as a boy farm labourer, and some of his misadventures in the air force. He made his past seem happy by laughing at what had happened along the way.

But there were other times. One of his sisters told me – when I was eight and stayed with her for a week while my parents moved house – that one farmer he worked for was so mean that she and her sister feared that Stanley, my father, would starve. The sisters, Elsie and Mary, worked on a nearby farm. On Sundays, she said, they would walk the 'few miles' to see their brother – on Sunday afternoon he would be 'free' – and take him food they had saved throughout the week. His lodging was in a loft space in the barn. 'We just sat and watched him eat,' Elsie said. 'His bit of a room was well away from the house.' There was a second parcel handed over 'to keep him going'.

His temper, though quickly over, made me wary of him but no less respectful and no less loving, a word never uttered in that house except in popular songs. He was a good father however much I annoyed him in the early years. Boys were hit by men at that time. If a friend of my dad's caught me out of order, he would feel perfectly entitled to clip my ear. If a teacher was met by disobedience he would cane you, and if you told your father (which would be a foolish move), he would inevitably say, 'You must have deserved it.' My father, like his father, was strong, hot-tempered at times, but a kind man and with pacific qualities that were to be tested to the limit.

Most disturbing of all, my grandmother – 'Don't hit the boy!' – was not my grandmother at all; she was not my mother's real mother. This was never said but I'm sure I could sense the fracture.

I did not discover the truth of this until I was into my teens.

Mrs Gilbertson, as well as having her own children, fostered others. My mother was one such. Unacknowledged. The main – though not the only – source of the lies. My mother had been fostered out very early on. She insistently referred to Mrs Gilbertson warmly as 'Mother'. But now and then, a slip of the tongue and something would be said, quickly covered up but there, a question with no answers.

Her real mother appeared in my life only a handful of times when I was . . . ten? Twelve? We would sit at either end of the kitchen table, the two of us, abandoned by my embarrassed mother, and attempt a conversation. There was always half a crown, once or twice a ten-shilling note, as she left. Who she was, where from, what she did, how she lived – none of that was explained. When I was seventeen, she died. The news washed across me, leaving, I thought then, no trace.

But these brief moments remain – remembered or misremembered. I wish I had known her. I wish she had known me. Now, as I write this, I think about her more than ever. I miss not having known her. She must have endured great sadness. I hope I am wrong. I hope she gathered strength to find a better life than the cruel morals of the time had imposed on her. Which was that she had to leave the child in the town and herself leave the town and find work elsewhere. She went over the border into Scotland.

From a small place of five thousand people and twelve buildings for Christian worship.

My mother was dutiful and I remember that when Belle – I was finally told her name – grew old and weak, she offered to take her in, come and live with us. But it was too late and Belle declined.

My mother was illegitimate, a bastard, a word of historic damnation, spoiled goods from birth. Fostered, she must have felt branded. She left school at fourteen and eventually found work in the clothing factory.

I regret that years ago I did not ask some of the older women in the town about the young Belle. And why did I not set myself to find out who my 'real' grandfather was? Many would have known. I can't understand why I was not curious until recently. Perhaps because my mother was always so emphatic that Mrs

Gilbertson was 'Mother'. Her husband was dead so there was no 'Father' but the house did not lack men.

What I realised too late was that those in the town who chronicled its lives would have been fully aware of the story and the players over two or three generations of this not uncommon tragedy. Belle left the town. But him? Her – what can we call him? Not 'lover' – or was he? Was he forced to act against his better self? Was he already married, or under the lash of parents who thought Belle not good enough? (The evidence would be plain to see. After all, as people would have said, she had 'got herself pregnant', a bewildering application of the Virgin Birth.) Or was he just weak and with enough money to pay Mrs Gilbertson for her services?

But while Belle had left the town, he presumably had stayed. What if he had other children? Were there half-brothers or -sisters, by their daily presence dumbly taunting my mother, and also shadowing me throughout my childhood? Very possibly. At the least there would be remarks and recognitions my mother would have learned to weather, while I had never been told a thing. How strong she must have been. She was clever, observant, emotionally focused. She must have sensed, must have heard whispers, which said, 'This is your father,' or 'That is your half-sister, half-brother.' She must have found a way to absorb it and to insulate me. Legitimacy was imperative in that small town at that time.

For me, now, it is uncomfortable, even unbearable in retrospect, to realise that to many of the townspeople you were someone other than you thought you were. Was your best friend your half-brother? That younger dark-haired girl who resembled your mother and you looked at so intently: was she your half-sister?

There was a kind of *omertà* in the town, a code of silence, as far as I was concerned.

I now think I remember glances intent and knowing. I want to track them down, these absent relatives, even if they are dead. But somehow I have inherited *omertà* or, in English, 'Let sleeping dogs lie.' A fear that what had been borne for so long would flare into life with complications too hard to bear at a time when nothing could be done. The danger of much worse embarrassment and pain was surely the most likely outcome and best avoided for all our sakes. Or have I become so cocooned in lies that I prefer to avoid the truth? Or afraid of its outcome? Last year I did make an effort. The agency I contacted said there was too little evidence to go on and, besides, all the key 'players' (their word) would be dead. Which just spurred me to try harder and then to decide against it. I was looking for my own benefit only. It was selfish. It was too late.

Maybe I was not meant to know. Unanswered questions can become comforting speculations. As I grow older, I look for answers in memory, as I do in writing this book, rather than research. The unknown, in so many ways, draws you into veiling mists and there can be peace in that.

But I still 'see' them now when I go to Wigton: unacknowledged kin from a parallel universe.

But where's the damage in a habit of lying if it does not bring hurt? But it does. It always does, if only to the liar himself. 'Mrs Gilbertson was Mother to me,' said my mother.

'Don't hit the boy!' she said to my father.

I cannot remember him once hitting the boy.

Chapter Two

This book is embedded in Wigton, which is one of its leading characters.

From an early age the town became a theatre, a stage for ever-changing dramas. I saw its cast on the streets and each one played his or her part, from boys in clogs shod with iron caulkers that sent out sparks when you kicked them hard on the sandstone kerbs, to men in polished riding boots and jaunty trilbies, cheerfully grinning at life; from the perpetually hungry children with the melancholy of the undernourished to the comfortably replete, straining waistcoat buttons all but bursting. Two factories kept the workers off the streets.

There were the unemployed, observing the place like natural philosophers, on the dole, leaning against pub walls, hands dug deep into pockets, clocking the world and spitting into the gutter until opening time. Often blamed because they could find no work, long numbed and damned by persistent rejection, bruised wives sometimes, not splitting on them. Respectable men nodding and waving confidently in their Redmayne's suits, double-breasted, professional men calmly patrolling their domain; working women in black, old at forty, glad to greet each other and add to the daily story; other women more aloof, dressed a cut above, nodding selectively. Salami-thin degrees of class. Streets plagued with scruffy, ragged-arsed, rampant young boys and some of the bolder girls in constant motion with hoops and skipping ropes, racing around the central maze of the town, able to tack through its tortuous pathways effortlessly, only rarely exposing themselves to the two main thoroughfares – King Street and High Street.

There were entrances and exits from every alley, and slits between buildings, down which children slid into tiny yards or ran into other winding lanes. We lived on that stage, hugger-mugger, no escape, interwoven narrow passages from one street to another, like a plot that held together the daily drama, perfect for community and infection. Curious dwellings left over from previous centuries, minuscule decaying houses up stone steps marooned, like homes in fairy stories, others down cellar steps into basements once deliberately kept damp to help the weavers of a previous century. There were rooms spanned like an arched bridge across a narrow street, high up; and quaint shops as individual as their proprietors who lived above them.

The town was our globe. Little to keep children in those cramped quarters. The streets were our living rooms. Often it was meal-by-meal shopping and, for grown-ups, for stopping and talking, turning gossip into dramas, gossip as a script topped up every day. The word 'community' is sometimes drowned in too sweet a nostalgia. Not here. Not then. The town was an inexhaustible subject for its clannish inhabitants.

Funerals proved this. Blinds were drawn on all shop windows when a hearse passed by. People stood silently still. Men took off their hats or caps. One of their own was passing, the town a lesser place now.

A few people from country houses, so grand they seemed a different breed, would pop into the town to shop. Some made a point of saying a decent 'hello'; others nodded rather extravagantly. There were yet others who fancied themselves, whose appearances and posh twang you saved up for mimicking. There were people you steered clear of, occasionally a stranger, beguiling or dangerous. Mostly we were looking out for and finding the rhythms of the ordinary, of appearances and disappearances, growing and ageing, the constant flow of women out to shop attached to small children too young for school. Plenty of schools in waiting, and places of worship, and Mr Cusack's Palace Cinema – three films a week and a children's matinee on Saturday mornings.

There was the undercurrent, persistent, largely ignored. A swathe of families who had not cast off the disablements of a nineteenth-century Dickensian poverty. Their half-starved children would wear old plimsolls at school with no socks even in midwinter, crusts for breakfast. Free milk at school was the real breakfast. They had been hammered into the most menial tasks well before the First World War, adrift often on the dole at best in the mid-wars' national nervous breakdown, fodder again in the Second World War and even now, in the dawn that was the National Health Service, they were still stuck. Somehow they seemed to be left out, not yet chosen for the new council houses with inside lavatories, gardens and three bedrooms on the new estates that were beginning to encircle the town. Many were still without access. Aspiration was too exhausting. The crushed nature of their history seemed to prevent them from taking the first step on the post-war ladder.

Men from the workhouse drifted down from their Station Hill home to haunt the town in daylight, like ghosts hoping to find a place to rest. And there were the lame, the 'slow', the very old and very ill, still, most of them, cared for by family inside already crowded houses, brought out for the sun or a small event, to disappear again into what a visitor would see as the irredeemable drabness of the central cluster of the old town.

The town was swept by TB just after the war. My mother and I both caught it. Like many others, as a child I slept in the same bed as my mother. Diseases spread rapidly, especially in those cramped central streets and in houses almost empty of Things: no carpet, few chairs, maybe a bust sofa from a sale or a friend. But they were still game, these poverty-stricken families. Proud Wigtonians. Passionately patriotic. Still up for wars, and eager to be drawn into the town's common events, hopeless to others, but not to each other, under the waves but refusing to drown. There were no beggars in the town, but at that time there were always tramps. Crippled by the war, looking for peace, passing through.

There were war heroes – four unshowy men highly decorated for outstanding bravery in the trenches of the Somme – and there were 'bad 'uns'. Petty thieves, sometimes worse, one or two not unknown to Durham jail, often looking for trouble. Looking for a fight, trying to find money to drink enough to become drunk; scavengers, poachers, apparently aimless but somehow preserving old ways of surviving deprivation. These were to be avoided save by those like my mother who had been to school with their mothers.

As a shot of the exotic, there were the nuns from the big convent attached to the Catholic church. They dressed like the Virgin Mary in the stained-glass windows of St Mary's Anglican Church. They usually moved around the town in pairs or leading crocodiles of shaven-headed orphans who had their strict home in the Roman Catholic settlement. The lines stepped off the pavement for the professional men known to the nuns, or for rich farmers with fine sports jackets, blooming with weathered health, now and then sporting a flowing silk pocket handkerchief and a smart waistcoat, on their way to a whisky, to team up with the men who knew about horses. Horses and pony traps, more common in the mid-forties than the few uniformly black cars and heavy ungeared bicycles. Most people walked. The streets were made for walking.

Chapter Three

My grandmother's many relatives became mine. Uncles, aunts, numerous cousins were part of who I was and mostly welcomed by me as kindly people. This would be up to the age of seven. Perhaps to find a way through undeclared confusion, I had contracted an occasional habit for lying. I look at it now in much the same category as measles – my mother said she made sure I contracted measles because it 'got rid of them' – or chickenpox, or the plague of boils I had in 1946, proud daily counting, fifteen on one leg, eleven on the other, or whooping cough, again supposed to be a blessing in disguise. Some disguise. The racket I made ricocheted through the house, like bursts from a machine-gun. And there was at the age of six or seven that bout of TB, which I don't remember.

Lies crept in. Sometimes they were tolerated – I went through a patch of telling non-'relatives' that I was a twin. He was a boy from the circus I had seen. I worked out an independent life for us and I would consult him about certain matters. It didn't last long. My invention was small change compared to the reality. Such was the urge to load me with relatives that it appeared half the townspeople were to be known as 'aunty' or 'uncle' or just 'related'. It could be suffocating; it could also be part of a surveillance system.

'Everyone knew everybody.' Child surveillance was constant and omnipresent. You were rarely further than two or three enquiries – 'Have you seen . . .?', 'Where was he?' – before you were discovered. I did not realise then that the effectiveness of that system also guaranteed a sensation of total liberty – on the streets and alleys and in the fields. I believe that this was common for centuries in crowded working-class communities. It was a community strength. Unfortunately it also acted as an intelligence service.

Then there were real lies. I had started school early, aged four, since my father was in the war. I loved it. The mighty rocking horse in the corner of Form One, the sandpit beside it, the vast 'picture' of God just as he should be – a kindly-looking old man with snowy hair and beard – and Miss Ivison, the teacher, old-fashioned in her long black dress even in our tiny experience, with a broad Cumbrian accent, and a long wooden pointer that jabbed at the multiplication tables we chanted every morning – number verses, doggerel that will never be erased, 'Four times four is sixteen, five times five is twenty-five, ten times ten is a hundred.' She had a method for teaching us to read that she would not reveal, and when, much later, I asked her how she did it, 'I have my own ways,' she said, and that was all she said.

But most of all, even at that age, the boys played football in the school yard. When a ball could be found, never a 'proper' ball, just anything round would do, a game would start up, in a street, in twilight, into the dark.

A year or two later when my father came back from the war, football was one of our mutual interests.

There were few ways I could impress my father who overwhelmingly impressed me. I lied about football at school. Every Friday – I can't believe I had the nerve to be so flamboyant – I told him of a goal or two I had scored or, on a good day, three. He seemed very pleased. In fact in real life I just about managed to be between useless and average.

My father was a member of the Lion and Lamb quiz club, which met in that pub on Sundays from opening time at noon to a reluctant move to dinner at about 1.30 p.m. So was Mr Purdham, a local man from a poor home who had become a battleship commander in the war. He returned to the town to serve the two-year stint of teaching that was part of his heroically won place in a teacher-training college and decided to stay. He was headmaster of the infant school.

When the subject of football games came up, he 'put my father right'.

Soon afterwards my father suggested we walk down to the railway station. Our house at that time was in a yard off Station Road. It was as near nirvana as I could envisage. Trains, steam, the Meccano-style bridge over the tracks on which you could stand and let the train pass under you once or twice, letting out steam to bathe you in a mysterious warm cloud. A little later, when I knew about such things, I saw this as an equivalence of Jesus Christ's ascension into Heaven. And there was my uncle – not – Uncle John, who worked there as a porter and would let me do odd jobs.

Halfway down Station Road there were the police station, a row of police houses, and the local court. On that walk my father stopped and pointed to it and asked me if I knew what it was. I said I did. And what happened to people who told lies? I can't remember my answer but I knew instantly that he meant football. I froze. What happened to people who lied, he said, if the police found out – as they always did – was that they would be arrested and locked up in prison. He pointed out the police station. They could stay there a long time. I never forgot it. He must have known I lied only to impress him yet that did not count. He never mentioned it again.

Match reports stopped for ever more. And for months at least I thought I was going to Hell and nothing could prevent it. Hell was already real. Sunday school had seen to that. Now Hell was inside Wigton police station, just down Station Road.

In the period this book spans I lived in three places. I remember very little of the first one. It was a two-up one-down in a yard at the bottom of Union Street, where my mother was born. One of a huddle of four, which shared a washhouse and an outside lavatory, it was a typical house in the town at that time. The rent was low, the only thing my father could afford. We lived there from my birth for about a year and a half. Then came my grandmother's house, my mother's old home, in Council House Yard off Station Road, into which my mother and I moved after the war began. It was a big place, called a council house because it had been purchased by the council. Finally, when I was eight, we moved into a flat above the pub where my father became its tenant landlord.

There were three rooms downstairs in Station Road – the parlour in which a piano proudly stood, unopened, the floor covered with linoleum and boasting a small carpet; the kitchen, the main room, coal fire puttering, the wireless, a table for food and games – ludo, tiddlywinks, cards, Monopoly – or cutting out Christmas decorations, again a linoleum floor, a prodded rug in front of the fire; and the back kitchen, with a big sink, an oven that connected to the kitchen, flagstones. Plopping gas mantles downstairs; upstairs a lamp or candles.

All these rooms seemed vast to me as a child – we could even play football in the back kitchen. The washhouse was outside the back door in a small yard, which also housed a coal shed and the lavatory with its chemical bucket. Lavatory paper was a wad of neatly cut squares from the newspaper, strung up and hung on a nail. On the other side of a wall was Toppin's Field, strewn with cows being fattened up for their butcher's shop. Also in the big field there was the clothing factory, Redmayne's, where my mother had put in a seven-year stint making buttonholes until she was dismissed when she married, as was the way.

There were already a family and two lodgers housed in that council-house space when we arrived. All the upstairs rooms had been subdivided. Yet when my father went off to the war it made more sense for my mother to move back into the 'big house' than stay in the damp confinement of Union Street. And I could be babysat by my grandmother while my mother went out to work.

My father had an easygoing side to his character and when he came back after the war he seemed to settle well enough. He had been brought up in a family of eight children – his father was one of sixteen – always in constricted quarters. He knew the strategies and manoeuvres required to find space and avoid anger and claustrophobia. But, like my mother, he was always keen to get out of the house. After the war, when he came back from work in the Rayophone factory, he would soon find a good excuse to go out. He found part-time jobs in a pub or with a bookie. He had been born twenty miles away to the west among the coalfields and only came to Wigton in his teens. He was soon settled and 'well liked' – or so grown-ups would not tire of telling me.

As for my mother, the town immersed her. She was forever checking it. She became one of its unofficial chroniclers. She took on the role with zeal in a town in which there were those prepared to see her as a blemish, the inheritor of shame, a figure fallen far below the High Standards exacted by Those Who Mattered. She dug into the present, perhaps, to make the past bearable.

She also looked to me to bring her information every time I set foot outside the house. Nothing was too trivial. She took this seriously and made sure I was accurate, even in matters such as the coats or hats or, in season, the dresses the women or girls had been wearing. These were often difficult for me to remember.

When she was ninety, at the onset of a five-year stretch of Alzheimer's, I decided to give her a birthday party. As far as I knew she had never had one. I invited about twenty friends of hers and we had lunch on the terrace of the Underscar Hotel, which looks full over Derwentwater, according to Wordsworth the jewel of the Lakes. It was said that the Lancashire industrialist who had built the magnificent house that became the hotel chopped down all the trees that blocked his view of a house across the lake in which his mistress lived.

It was almost unbearably hot on that day. The view reached deep south into the Lake District, so detailed under the unclouded sky. I decided I would say a few words about my mother and made notes because from the initiation of the idea there was a doubt. She hated show. She hated being picked out. But she was ninety.

About two sentences in, I caught her gaze, straight on me, hard. But I had to go on. After about six sentences she turned to her best friend, Jean Morrison, and said, very clearly, so that it seemed to ring around the crystal air and reach across the valley, 'I always wanted a girl.'

I proposed the toast and sat down.

She joined forces with the girls she had met at school and the women with whom she worked at Redmayne's clothing factory. As a girl she went to Sunday school and joined the Guides and the cycling club; her bicycle took her to village dances within a radius of about a dozen miles. Though she had a pleasant voice she resisted efforts to lever her into the choir in St Mary's – she did not like the dressing-up part of it. With friends, she was at the church gates at every wedding that walked down the aisle on a Saturday afternoon from the altar to the west door. When sacked for matrimony by the factory she took up cleaning houses in and around Wigton. She did not smoke, rarely drank and never swore. She could be resolute and obstinate in her opinions, never loudly expressed. She was thought to be good-looking, black hair, slim, good teeth. It is a fair guess that she knew the name of everyone in the town. When I fibbed to her she saw through it instantly.

She would sometimes pick up the pieces. Once when I was about thirteen and had a gang of five, I got carried away and said that my mother had made all of us black masks so that we could be like Zorro. No one believed me but the more they objected the more pig- headed I became and promised the masks by that afternoon.

Somehow through the panic my mother understood the situation and found some old blind material, which had been used for the blackouts in the war. We rushed to cut it into five face masks but the material would not co-operate. Finally she shook her head. My days were done, I thought. The gang – my own gang! – would throw me out. I was inconsolable. I remember all that in detail but the consequences I feared so painfully are wiped out. I was soon with my friends again. Perhaps they knew it was a lie or just too ambitious so had invested nothing in it.

The lies did not entirely go away: now and then years afterwards I would hear myself deliver a whopper and defend it insanely, knowing that the recipient knew as well as I did that it was not true. And there were the white lies, mini evasions, small boasts that would trouble me afterwards, often for months. It was as if it had been branded into me or, rather, had seeped in from the false relationships in that early house. Finally they faded away and only reappear at upset times, a cry from the past.

Chapter Four

Andrew was a fixture in the Station Road house. He had been another of my grandmother's foster children. About my mother's age and a terrible boaster. I hate to write 'liar' because he seemed to me, even as a boy, to have suffered too much, but he did lie. And he was a petty thief. While my father was in the war, Andrew was for some reason exempt. He kept on his tough, unskilled, dirty bottom-rung job at the polluted Rayophone factory.

Like millions of others, Andrew was used as a basic replaceable cog in the industrial machine. Born to receive no sympathy, employed without mercy, used up, then thrown away. He had a permanent nasty smoker's cough – cigarettes and the factory air. His face was sallow. He carried no excess weight. His hair was black and flat, always soaked in Brylcreem. His voice was loud, his accent broad, his tone assertive. He banked on my mother's lifelong loyalty to stay in the house. She cooked for him, washed his clothes and the Brylcreem-soaked pillows, treated him like the orphan he was and the brother he had seemed to be, and she would hear no criticism of him. My father proved his profound affection for her by tolerating this. He could not stand Andrew and saw right through him. But Andrew came to the table.

He worked shifts at the factory in a twenty-four-hour cycle and at set times of day and night: 10 p.m. to 6 a.m., 6 a.m. to 2 p.m., 2 p.m. to 10 p.m. He had lived in Mrs Gilbertson's house in Station Road since he was a baby and was the only one who had never left. He had his own chair in the kitchen where he sat and sometimes read the *News Chronicle* after my father had finished with it. He accompanied his reading with harsh exclamations. The two subjects on which he held forth most frequently were football, about which he was fanatical, and politicians, whom he hated and mistrusted, every one. To Andrew, my father was the intruder.

His promises to me were wild. A gramophone, a billiard table, a trip to Newcastle to see Newcastle United. Of such riches there was no end, and again and again I believed him. When I was small – three or four – and my father was away, as I thought winning the war, Andrew would sometimes suddenly grab hold of me, lift me up in front of him and shake me as he smiled and repeated, 'Who wants a shave, then? Who wants a shave?' This was a rare break in his taciturnity. He would lower my face to his and rub the stiff black bristles of his chin against my face so that I shouted out in pain-pleasure. His bristles reminded me of the yard brush. My grandmother and my mother, alarmed at the screams, would tell him to stop. He always did. I've no recollection at all of abuse or any sexual groping. That was not his way. He was just unbearably lonely, not a bad man, a man all but cemented in lonely hurt.

He was strong, like my father, like all the men who came to the house, strong through hard, repetitive physical work, in all cases work that had begun when they were boys of seven or eight and ordered to 'help'. He was in a long tradition of men and women whose menial toil made England rich at the cost of stunted lives.

Inside the house he had his own space. When my mother's male 'cousins', as she told me they were, bicycled the six miles from where they lived to leave their bikes in our yard and go to the Saturday-night dance, he would make a point of contradicting them, in his harsh tones. I now see it as showing off his greater closeness to my mother and me. Silent, though, when my father was there.

It was my father who, years on, when we had moved into our third and final house in Wigton – a flat above the Black-A-Moor pub – finally fed up with his petty thieving at the till, told my mother and me that Andrew must go. I was thirteen at the time. I became hysterical. My father – persuaded by my mother, I suspect – relented for a few months, then suddenly Andrew left and took lodgings elsewhere. I was not told the reason. Thieving again, I suspect. I remember no hysteria this time.

There was joy in him. An inner secret imaginary life, perhaps his real existence. In the loft above what had been a stable in the yard behind the pub that my father took over as a tenant landlord when I was eight, Andrew kept budgerigars. He had dozens of birds. They were not for show but for him. He had been given the loft entire by my father and he had caged the whole space cleverly. He went up an unsteady ladder into a world of colour, movement, birdsong and total delight enhanced by his own transformation. He loved those tiny delicate birds. He would clean out the cages scrupulously, move the birds around by some system of his own, make chirping noises as he laid out seed on his fingers, take one gently now and then in his big shovelling hands and stroke it with his thumb, examine it, even peck a little kiss on its head before letting it go. To see him among the birds was like seeing the first film in technicolour. A place of fantasy hidden in the northern town, with its sense of secrecy. It was almost magic as Andrew lost himself among the lovely little birds, yellows, blues, greens, flitting from perch to perch as if to display themselves to their fullest advantage for the eyes that feasted on them. Now and then Andrew would turn to me and smile. Once or twice he would tell me to hold out my index finger and place a bird on it. I stood as stiff as a sentry to earn its trust, but it soon lifted and flew away. Andrew would smile again. Sometimes he had three or four on his fingers.

There was a day, a Sunday afternoon, when one of them escaped. The trapdoor above the ladder must have been left ajar. Andrew noticed and slid down the ladder. I followed, picking up on his panic and fear. In front of us was the Sunday desert of Market Hill; ahead the road to the baths by way of the big gasometer; to the left was an alley which led to Toppin's Field. He chose that and ran – I remember being amazed by how fast he ran – into the yard where he pushed himself onto the wall, hoicked me up with him and scanned the field, inhabited by a few almost stationary cows.

'She's ower yonder! They'll git her!'

I followed him as best I could. We sped past the allotments, Andrew's eyes focused on the small beautiful yellow bird, which had made for the roof of the West Cumberland Farmers' building – a warehouse. There she sat on the peak of the roof, head swivelling around, so out of place under the heavily clouded grey sky, the trees shedding the last leaves of autumn.

'Put your foot against that,' he pointed to the drainpipe, 'and push hard.'

Andrew shinned up the drainpipe and was quickly onto the roof. He began a slow crawl towards his pet, chirping a little, holding out one hand as if he had seed to offer. I stood back and watched, my heart in my throat. Andrew's upset at the danger the bird was in became mine. I dared not say a word as he traversed the roof, ever closer to the beautiful little bird.

Then, suddenly, it flitted away.

Andrew made a cry and scrambled across the rooftop to survey the fields and thin woodland that trailed down to the railway line.

'We've lost her!' he shouted – not to me, not to anyone. He slithered down the roof, swung himself from the gutter, dropped to the ground and headed off again at full speed.

We searched in the Stampery, a little clutch of houses on their own. We went down to the railway line. But she had gone. We searched until I was tired and the light was beginning to fade. Then he turned back.

I had never seen him cry. I do not think I had ever seen a man cry. Andrew's silent tears were unstoppable.

'They'll murder her. They're helpless,' he said. 'Some crow, some sparrowhawk, they'll peck her to bits. Poor little bugger,' he muttered, again and again. 'Poor little bugger . . .'

Without looking at me, he set off back, through the field, avoiding the men in their allotments. Some of them would have witnessed his rescue attempt. When I got to the stable and went up the ladder, the trapdoor was shut and wedged. I could not get into the loft.

Chapter Five

I like books that describe the place in which they are set. When I was about sixteen the English teacher asked us to write an essay about 'Our Town' – this was the title of a play by Thornton Wilder. We put it on. I have never forgotten the takeover effect *Our Town* had on me. Wigton, I thought, was like that.

Wigton is an ancient market town tucked into the north-west of England, on a rise of land between the mountainous northern ranges of the Lake District and the rich soft fertile Solway Plain just south of Hadrian's Wall, where the Romans had fought one of their fiercest enemies, the Celts. Mr Scott, who taught my mother and myself, liked to give out the high points in the town's history. To the west was a strip of sea, the Solway Firth, in which English armies had been drowned, attempting to take a short surprise route across the sands to Scotland and failing to beat the speed of the incoming tide. A mile outside the town to the south was Old Carlisle, an unexcavated Roman camp said to have housed a thousand cavalry, where we played whole summer's days among the mounds and pathways from ancient times. To the north, but still inside the town, were the two factories – one, the clothing factory, almost exclusively staffed by women, the other by men – that provided for much of the workforce. The High Street had been established by Norsemen over a thousand years ago. When we learned of that at school all the boys wanted to be Vikings.

It was a small northern town, its industries characteristically planted next to spectacular countryside. The five thousand or so inhabitants lived largely, like myself in my early months, in insanitary slums. When I was born, a month after the start of the

Second World War, there were twelve functioning churches, chapels or meeting houses, pillars of the town. God ruled. On Sundays the town was as silent as a tomb. Public life was inside the houses of God. At one stage I went to church three times every Sunday. Despite the great decline in churchgoing after the First World War, chapels and churches still drew substantial congregations in their Sunday best. Shops closed, play frowned on. Parables and references to biblical events were not uncommon in common speech.

The Roman Catholic church, convent and school were a separate and powerful force. So were the Methodists, the Congregationalists, the Quakers and various Salvationists and Rechabites, and, above all, the Anglicans in a church first established in the Middle Ages, rebuilt just over a couple of hundred years ago as an unobtrusive Georgian classic.

The exceptional feature of the town was the grand Georgian house on top of Highmoor Hill, with its three miles of iron railings that had penned in a herd of deer. The First World War had seen most of the railings taken for active service. The marvel of its tower, visible for miles around, still remained. It was a tall Venetian bell tower – a copy – a much-cherished eccentricity, evidence of a previous owner's passion for Venice. It was planted in the middle of the elegant Georgian roof as if carefully lowered there by a monster crane. Or it could have been a phallus erupting out of the buttoned-down English country house. It was a proud beacon to the townspeople through the day, and when lit by the moon at night there was something Gothically poetic about it. Highmoor, the exclamation mark of home to many of those returning to the town.

There was, unusually for such a modest town, a swimming-pool, which was a prized possession for all of us. The workhouse, tucked well away from the town centre next to the cemetery, was on the northern edge of the town. A traditional Victorian covered market, plumb in the centre next to St Mary's, attracted salesmen from as far away as Newcastle for Tuesday sales. There were functions there, too, and dances, as there were in the Drill Hall, the Temperance Hall and the Congregational Rooms. On market days the town was thrang – busy – with cattle, sheep, pigs, who had their own auction rooms. All this crowded into the heart of the old town. When Slater's Fair came it set up on Market Hill, opposite the Black-A-Moor Hotel, near the centre of the town. It became its heartbeat for a week.

To me Wigton was a place of infinite variety. There were choirs, church and town, a silver band, football, rugby, cycling, cricket, tennis and bowls clubs. Darts, snooker, a Reading Room, fourteen pubs or drinking dens (a front parlour run by the women of the house, with a fire and two barrels of beer and two or three illicit bottles of spirits); four banks, above which were flats where the managers lived. Doctors and solicitors also lived in the town, as did most teachers and councillors, although in my boyhood they were moving out. Dogs of many breeds, two of which had won at Crufts. Pigeon men who sent their birds to France, knowing they would home their way back. The owners checked the flight time it took at the Vaults pub. There was illegal but still popular cockfighting, hare coursing, ferrets to hunt down rabbits.

I feel as if I am listing books from the Old Testament. The Chronicles of Wigton. I still feel pride in it. In memory now this diversity of largely working-class activities is vivid. I am in awe at the extensive and complex web spun from so little by men and women who refused to be worn down by their deadening work and poor wages. The factories kept the town afloat. The many hobbies pursued kept it alive.

The house in Council House Yard was fronted by a big cobbled space that served as the place to dry washing for the whole of Station Road. On Monday mornings the women came with their sheets and shirts. To a small boy on a misty day it could seem like an army of ghosts and become another playground. The yard also housed the Fire Brigade, manned by volunteers who were summoned by a hooter that wailed over the town with a wartime insistence. They came out of factories and wood yards and shops on foot or on their bicycles as the hooter urged them on to swing down Station Road and stylishly swerve into our yard. Heroes!

In the corner of the yard was a shed for the man who swept the streets, Mr Stoddart. He also kept an illicit shop open in Water Street on Sunday evenings – the only one that would sell single cigarettes. There was an estate agent, a stablebox, and one house, ours, once privately owned, then bought up cheaply by the council and let. The yard also housed the town library, supervised by Mr Carrick, the town clerk, the town's historian and author of stories or 'teales' in the dialect. He himself liked to choose dialect words in his conversational speech, which was always delivered in a clear and stately manner.

He made sure I had at least one, often two books every Friday night and inducted me into that group to whom the library became a necessity.

In our backyard there was the usual washhouse, coal shed, and the WC. The Winston Churchill. The lav. The only space that guaranteed privacy. The paper or comic was taken there to be read in peace.

The bath was brought from the washhouse into the kitchen, the heavy black kettle boiled up to secure a hot scrubbing. I had a bath once a week. The dirt accreted could be so adhesive you needed a stiff brush to scrape it off. A clean shirt was put out on Sunday and that, too, had to last for a week. The exposed parts – hands and face, particularly behind the ears – were cleaned morning and night. Hair was washed with soap.

No one like us in the 1940s had a fridge, running hot water, a washing-machine, a vacuum-cleaner, a telephone, gramophone, a car, fitted carpets, electricity or central heating. We shopped for the day's meals, dinner and supper, carefully, consulting our ration books. There were hot-water bottles (pot or rubber ribbed). Messages were sent by word of mouth. I can't remember us ever feeling sorry for ourselves.

Our family was lucky. I was aware of that from those I knew in Water Street, the poorest street in the town. I had evidence that we were lucky. There was always food on the table, no feeling of poverty. Many – often the big families – were really poor: children went hungry; there were hand-me-down or charity clothes and shoes, raids on turnip fields and orchards for food, and rakings of the town for empty lemonade bottles, which, returned, gave you twopence. When any Water Street friends came to ask me if I wanted to go out and play, as a matter of course my mother gave them a slice of cake or a jam sandwich.

People's parents and their parents' parents had gone together to school, church, chapel, the wars, the seaside at Silloth, on a trip to Keswick, shared memories of the elephants in the circus walking down High Street, floods next to the railway station, the big fire that wiped out the tannery at the top of Water Street.

We thought we were well enough off. After the war both my parents worked – my father at the factory that employed mostly men. He, unskilled, worked on the machines; he also took on a couple of part-time jobs. My mother, later, worked on the post in the mornings and then cleaned houses. We wanted for nothing we wanted.

There was still a heavy presence of dialect even though Education Acts, the influence of the BBC and the insistence of schoolteachers and ambitious mothers over the years that we should not speak 'common' like 'that' was eroding it. It held on in what could still be called the 'lower class'. It was the sound of their loyalty to the town and their place in it. When I spoke it I felt comfortable, in a tribe, one of us. It was the sound of our identity.

Despite the discouragement, we held on tightly to the dialect words, which were speckled by contributions from India (the army) and Romany (the gypsies who wintered behind the cemetery). Those who aspired to a posh accent were traitors or show-offs. If you inherited it, that was acceptable. If you came from a working-class background and assumed it, you were suspect or scorned. 'We speak a language that the strangers do not know' was the Wigton boast, and for the least well-off, it was a comfort and a refuge, and, I found, a clan.

There were thousands of local words. In Wigton a girl was a lass or a mort, a man was a gadji, a river a beck, a cow a ku, a stone a staine, an oak a yek, a cane a yebby, swimming trunks were dukers, frightened was flait; thous and thees predominated as the local accent leaned into the local dialect, a horse could be a grey or a hoss, one was yan, going was gangen, to deek was to look, baary was good, sek a baary mort, ower yonder was over there, mang nix was say nothing. It was warm, guttural. One reason I am reluctant to use it is that I do not want those who do to continue to be exposed to mockery, which they had always been to some extent but ever more so as BBC English standardised speech.

The class 'system' – as far as it impinged on me as a boy – did not seem to be oppressive. As kids we thought we were first class. The middle class, as I saw them, were few and floated above the rest of us. But they were more confined. They lived seemingly untroubled by the daily grind. To me as a boy they could have been a different tribe, looking like us, outwardly acting like us, unthreatening, like *Homo sapiens* among the Neanderthals, often amiable but always different. Yet the close intermingling in the various clubs and communities meant that there was only rarely a hard line between them and us. War had blunted many of the edges. The slow embrace of peace brought with it a general gratitude that 'all that' was behind us. But now and then we had to tread carefully. Snobbery was ineradicable. The divisions between the classes could still run deep.

There were the great events. Wigton Horse Fair coincided with the autumn half-term and filled the town with stallions, ponies, Shetlands, mares, Shire horses, hunters . . . The gypsies would come and trade; the boys, flamboyantly dressed, would test horses by riding them bareback up and down High Street. I wanted to be a gypsy even more than a cowboy. The Blue Bell pub next to our Council House Yard had its own yard where the men would take the big horses after walking them in from the surrounding villages and wash their hoofs, perhaps replait and decorate the manes, brush up their coats before taking them to the street and up to Hope's Auction. The town swirled with local farmers, horse-breeders and farriers, buyers from far and near; pools of knowledge were exchanged in the bars. The streets were bespattered and stinking, but no matter to us. It was as if a town from cowboy pictures had stepped out of the screen.

I would like to claim that my father – who knew about horses – took me into the heart of the auction to point things out. But it was not like that. He left me to navigate my own way around the place. Nor would I have wanted his assistance. I wanted to fly around on my own on no one's leash or with one or two pals. I wanted to be heady and free with it all, the bidding, the 'showing' and selling, the pungent stinking sense of a place made new. The horse sales had been in Wigton for ever and surely would last for ever more, as reliable as Bonfire Night and the Market Hill fair.

Chapter Six

Lies were not confined to the house. In my teens, it gradually became disturbingly clear that I had been swaddled in layers of lies about the world I lived in. It was painful to face up to that. Such was the force and certainty with which these ruling views had been presented. Early convictions had a knotweed grip, comprised as they were of some truth, some prejudice, some myth, some misunderstanding and misinterpretation and some point-blank lies. Above all, they painted a virtuous, brave, gentle, knightly, stainless civilising picture of Us and Our Empire.

How powerfully we clung to those stories of past glories. And as we too, we thought, had suffered over time – invasions, exploitation and serfdom – surely we had earned some of the praise we heaped on ourselves. We were unconquerable in battle and unique in our fair and never-failing traditions. There were even matches called England's Glory.

These imperial views were unassailable throughout my childhood. They pinked the mind and dominated a spinning globe. They were to crumble like reluctant and mountainous icebergs, collapsing very slowly, cracking and finally crashing into an ocean of disbelief and confusing shame. Yet that shame was succeeded by the question – as I went out into the world – why should it be my shame? I had had nothing to do with it. Nor had any of my friends. My father and mother were as unprejudiced and unrepressive as it was possible to be.

But did my generation and the next and the one after have to carry for ever a new white man's burden – of the unforgiving past? We could still think England was the best country in the world, free, and getting better: just look at the new council estates. But now a new history was edging in. We had done unforgivable wrong. It was like the curse on Cain. There seemed no end and no cure: apologies were offensive. It was unsettling – Elastoplast over open wounds, which merely drew closer attention to injustice and barbarity. As the decades went on, what had been good about the country was scarcely even whispered, a source of shame, almost a secret, refused admission to the pride once felt.

And in its way, the church of my childhood, once beyond criticism, seemed as I grew older to shed its grand original purpose, its authority, its sacred rituals and also be diminished and challenged, even discarded.

My father's youngest brother and sister were in the choir of St Mary's, and when the call went out for more trebles I was press-ganged into it at six. I wore a long black cassock, buttoned from neck to ankles, and a pleated white surplice, like an oversized dress shirt. We prayed in the vestry before processing into church and then we were On!

The choral singing took me into another sphere. To be immersed in a choir was to lose yourself in something finer. Singing can take over your mind. The music and the voices weave around your brain transforming it, and you become part of this organ-accompanied community of sound. Your own voice disappears. I would feel that God and all Heaven were listening. We were on His side. It was a state unlike any other. Being yourself ceased to exist. It was weightless and free. Out of ordinariness singing implanted passionate faith, a dimension never forgotten, leaving for ever a sense, a trace of the existence of another world now all but impossible to reclaim.

Mr Mitchinson, the choirmaster and organist, was, as his father had been, an electrician. At the Thursday-night choir practices he rarely took off his overcoat. He was a distinguished-looking man, slim-faced, thin grey hair. He carried his tuning fork like a baton. He was unforgiving, however cold the night, and we would go over the lines until he was satisfied, whatever time it took. He was a favourite with one or two of the grown-up girl choristers and we noticed that but said nothing. He was respected and, we could tell, good.

Singing in the choir was a steady earner. You got fourpence for every time you attended (choir practice, the Sunday-morning service, matins, and Sunday-evening service, evensong) and sixpence was docked if you failed to turn up. We queued up in the vestry every quarter for our pay. A wedding could fill it out by up to a shilling a head.

The downside of church was sin. It was planted in my mind early on. I became obsessed by my sinfulness. It was the most damaging feature of my religion. At times I felt I was knee deep in it – I was being sucked into a swamp by it – unable to escape. For what? A swear word. A small lie. Failure to say prayers. Faults so puny but the sin promised punishment so real. Once the virus of sin has crept into your mind, it is impossible to get rid of it.

During my early years I was a blind believer. Not fanatical but unquestioning. Yes to the Virgin Birth; to Jesus's physical Ascension into Heaven; yes to miracles; yes to the Resurrection; to angels, archangels, cherubim and seraphim and all the company of Heaven; and the power of prayer. The goodness of God was unarguable despite his biblically reported acts of revenge and destruction. Christ was perfect and an example you must always follow and always fail to meet. It was a toxic, head-spinning mix. When late adolescence rose up against this castle of conviction it was at first resisted. For instance, when we argued among ourselves, I had a theory that God could have planted a unique seed in Eve that went into other women for ever after. Therefore wicked sex was unnecessary. Faith healers who came from America even to Carlisle proved that the lame could walk again, the blind see. The tomb could have been sealed for three days in such a subtle way that Christ might have breathed again, made a recovery from the cross and been restored back to life when the tomb was opened. Heaven was in the songs and in dreams. We just knew it was there. But the conviction could not withstand the taunting and the reasoning that were soon to turn on it. Puberty and the age of doubt were followed by adolescence and the Age of Reason and new prison doors opened.

No God. No Resurrection. No Virgin Birth. No miracles. No faith. No structure, no certainty. But what remained was the sense of the ultimate mystery of why and how we were here.

Meanwhile there was the dressing up in ankle-length black button-up cassocks and the white surplices. The procession on festival occasions from the west door to the east in the darkened church where the altar pointed east towards the birthplace of Christ! We glided down the nave; we floated in our sacred garments to join the cross on the altar on our certain way to Heaven. The centrepiece of the stained-glass window above the altar pictured Jesus Christ seated among a crowd of children and underneath the words 'Suffer the little children to come unto me and forbid them not for theirs is the Kingdom of Heaven.'

Each of us in the choir carried a candle and we sang as we processed and the congregation sang with us. It was a spectacle. Those assembled in church were an audience, men in best suits, women, too, in their best. It was an occasion like going to a play.

We were led by Len, who carried the cross. He was a man's age, whispered to be 'backward', a young teenager's height. He said very, very little, wore double-strength bottle-bottom spectacles and waited in the vestry after every evening service to see if a boy or two remained whom he could chase around the big table. Some of us thought it was a game: he was not difficult to outwit. If an adult chorister came back into the vestry he would say 'Now stop it, Len!' Len would lose his agitation immediately and sidle away.

At the altar, the choir, who had been processing in twos, parted like the Red Sea and we went to our separate places, still singing, while Len stood still as a rock until the vicar signalled that the time had come for him to carry the cross to its niche.

In the forties and fifties, the choir was strong in our church and in many of the others. We, who were thought to be below the salt of much culture, were taught to sing magnificent anthems, to chant psalms, to learn hymns by heart. Yet at home when 'classical' music came on the wireless on the Third Programme I and many I knew turned it off instantly, as if fearing infection. It was not for us.

Class beat culture. Culture came in brands dictated by class, class accents and a sense of entitlement, which was excluding and meant to be. But classical music flowed into the church of St Mary's, under Mr Mitchinson, who challenged us to take on the four-part harmonies of some of the greatest composers and the centuries-old chanting of the psalms and the prayers – simple-seeming lines of beauty. This experience, year in year out from six to fourteen, has always been a reminder of what had been true for so many like us long ago, our equality before music and a rich inheritance.

There was also the language: the readings were from the King James Bible, based on William Tyndale's poetic prose, and those rhythms, words, phrases, shapers of our tongue, rang around the church and in the school assemblies week in, week out. Like the music in St Mary's, it was the untutored part of an education, free for all who had ears to hear.

For choirboys the church was also a playground. We arrived early for choir practice on Thursdays to set up opposing armies, and from the trenches of the pews we bombed each other with devoutly embroidered hassocks. We dared each other to climb up the wonky ladder to the belfry. Outside the church, the old grave-yard was still there, mouldering away, sinking into the earth, sprouting weeds – a few trees out of control – perfect for games of chasey and hide and seek, especially on dark nights . . .

I can't remember being given more than the mildest rebuke for those antics. What did provoke rage happened during a sermon.

There was a man called Johnny King. He was deaf and dumb. He worked in Redmayne's as a cutter. Tall, ramrod, always turned out in a well-cut suit. He lodged with Mrs Blair, who had a cottage in a cluster of houses known as the Stampery. Mrs Blair was a friend of Grandma Gilbertson. I would take messages to and fro between them.

It was from Mrs Blair that I learned how to do deaf-and-dumb language. The five vowels on your left hand followed by much clinching of fingers and thumbs for the rest.

I taught it to Eric and William and a couple of others in the choir. For a while it became a craze. Especially useful to while away long sermons. Unfortunately, because we had not fully mastered the language and sometimes could not make out the signs from the other choir stalls, which faced our own in the chancel, the exchanges at one evensong became extravagant. We sought help in loud whispers and wild semaphore. The tenors whispered to us to 'calm down'; the congregation coughed politely; the women in the choir tried not to laugh.

The vicar kept turning round from the height of his pulpit at the imminent pandemonium on the front two choir stalls. Mr Mitchinson rose from the organ. The vicar's pause, his glower, even his headshaking had no effect. Discreet laughter in the congregation became less discreet.

Suddenly the vicar stopped talking, came down the pulpit steps, strode across to me and, quite loudly, said, 'Go to the vestry. I will see you later.' He went back to his sermon. Me to my shameful isolation in the vestry.

I was suspended for a month.

The Church of England ran a youth club, as did several of the other churches and chapels. Ours was called the Anglican Young People's Association – the AYPA. We had our own marching song:

AYPA advance
On through the years.
Honour shall crown thy name
Uphold thy standards.
1 – 2 – 3 – 4
Pride of our Pioneers
AYPA.
To tell the world that
We are here to STAY!

We met in the Parish Rooms early on a Wednesday evening. These rooms held upstairs a hall for dances and dramatics (there was a small touring repertory company, which brought its plays to the town for a few weeks every autumn), for rummage sales and the Christmas fair.

Downstairs was for meetings of organisations such as the AYPA.

It was run by a group of people, gentle people – mostly married, men and women in their twenties and early thirties – who went to church regularly. We had quizzes, we spun the plate, we sang a lot and debated: three people in a balloon, a doctor, a scientist and a vicar – which two would you throw out? People from the town who had been abroad came to show us their photographs of Foreign Parts. Mr Donnelly, the painter and decorator, went to the Alps every year and his photos of peaks and skiing showed us another world. People who had record collections brought them along – with a gramophone – to demonstrate the quality of this or that composer. I remember an argumentative evening when I tried to 'prove' that Mario Lanza was better than Beniamino Gigli – I had minimal evidence. I thought the speaker was being snobbish. I got very heated.

A former vicar, the Reverend Rex Malden, came with his photographs. He was a devoted photographer. His subjects were the people of Wigton, especially those who came to church, and he would go through the whole routine. He would set up a dark room in a small anteroom and explain the process from the lenses in the camera to the final photographs. That needed some sleight of hand but he managed. He set up a photographic club in the town with Mr Scott, another devotee, the headmaster of the infant school. With loans from his collection of cameras, and unlimited enthusiasm, he taught a generation of boys. We liked him because he did not act like the vicar when he was at the AYPA. And we knew the people in the photographs.

We went on trips to the Lake District and walked through the woods to Watendlath. All this was organised with calm and selfless decency, unappreciated at the time, by Kenneth Rumney and his wife Jean, Fred Sinton and his wife Agnes, and Isabel Parker, all believers in doing good at the expense of their own leisure. There seemed to be more time. Was it that there was so much less for us to do, to see, to visit, no car, no television, no discos, or had the legacy of two world wars and an economic nervous breakdown between those wars, which left most people living on tight rations, encouraged this move of 'helping the kids' in such ways?

Nor was it without its hot and racy side. We invited AYPA clubs from the nearby towns to an 'evening' – and we in return went there. We debated (sometimes political topics of the day – 'We believe that we are all equal' or the three men in a balloon one) – and finally there would be dancing to gramophone records . . . the valeta, the quickstep, Three Drops of Brandy – jiving was still in the distance as far as Wigton was concerned. Difficult now to believe how exciting those meetings were! When the record started you went across the room and said, as if you were in a grand ballroom in Park Lane, 'Could I have this dance?' Afterwards you led the girl back to the seat from which you had plucked her.

There was also what just might be called early intimations of sex. A group came from the seaside fishing town of Silloth one night and we played a version of Musical Chairs where – I can't remember how – boys sat in a circle and you got a girl on your knee when the music stopped. I was about thirteen at the time.

Erotic longings were registering through a thicket of confused sensations. To know what you 'did' and how far you could 'go' got in the way of what you could 'do'. Especially in the Parish Rooms. One night the decision was taken for me.

She sat on my knee. Though she came from Silloth, ten miles away, she went to the same school as me – the Nelson Thomlinson Grammar School – but she was a couple of years older. She was a star athlete, way out of reach but now on my knee and for the forfeit she had to kiss me!

Even now, sixty-seven years on, I have a powerful memory of it, though words are inadequate. Sensations overwhelm them as they often do. Some words are like petals that drop off the flower the moment you touch them. The physical sensual experience still sends its message into the present. I had never known anything remotely like it. It was a full, lingering, warm kiss. I am sure she had breasts and I am sure they were pressed against me – maybe I thought they got in the way. I wanted it never to stop. But the music started on the scratchy record and up she got and left me and went around in the circle and never landed on me again. God!

The next Saturday I set off for Silloth on my bike. I had heard that she lived in West Silloth, a place of intricate sand dunes made for golf and illicit encounters. I could have been in a desert. I got there in the late morning and combed it for about two hours without a sign of her. I got parched. I was in something near agony. Hope finally subsided: sense crept in. But there were two options left. I biked around a nearby estate. I biked around the town. No sign.

On the Monday, feeling weak, I went across to her at playtime. She threw me a smile, I think, and waved me on. I retreated. Outside the AYPA and the Parish Rooms she was back in the old hierarchies. Was I too young for her? Or was I just hopeless at kissing?

Chapter Seven

When I try to characterise my father I find it confusing. There is overall warmth, admiration layered with a sliver of fear. He had come back from the war into the Station Road house, displaced me in my mother's life and taken over in ways I wanted to challenge. Even at six or seven? Especially at six or seven when you are on red alert about the play of family power and the priorities of affection – who's in? Who's out? We were a trio embedded in a group in a house that found coexistence, largely, in evasion.

Shows of affection in the house between the three of us were so rare that I can remember none. I cannot remember us ever doing anything in threes. Loving public display, even in domestic, supposedly private spaces, was not encouraged. 'Don't be so soppy!' 'Don't moan!' 'Keep your feelings to yourself.' These were the messages. This, I think, was not just a feature of working-class households or families. After the Second World War – and between the wars as well as further back – the English across the spectrum thought that strong feelings should be repressed: to express them was embarrassing and a mark of weakness. Men hugging each other? Kissing even relatives on both cheeks?

There could be a nod or a smile of approval from him or sympathy, but even those were not to be over-emphasised.

My father had been the oldest boy in a large family. There were two families. He was in the first, of four. After his mother's early death, his father Harry married again, and again there were four children.

Harry himself came from an even bigger family. They had lived on the edge of Bassenthwaite, the most northerly lake. That big but not spectacularly exceptional number of children scaled out across Cumberland. The boys went into the army – six of them joined up, five for the First World War – then onto the land or to the west coast for the coal mines. The girls went into service – all seven of them. My father's father began at thirteen scaring crows, then worked as a farm labourer, moved to the west to the better wages in the coastal industrial belt. He went into the army in 1914, returned to the mines, suffered a bad accident in a pit disaster and finally found work as Wigton's park keeper.

Hannah, his second wife, said to their youngest daughter that she would never have 'got through without Stan'. He was twelve at the time. She was a spirited young woman but by the time they began to raise a second family in a damp cottage on a farm where her husband was both labourer and groom to the Shire horses, his temper seems to have frayed. His anger, which could sometimes pass like a flash, was a terrible thing if you were caught in it. Stanley, Hannah said, was the only one who could 'handle' him. Often by persuading his stepmother to extract sixpence from the housekeeping purse, sufficient to send him off to the pub for a pint. Then, the report was, they would pull back the rugs and dance on the flagstone floor, singing and clapping to make the music, the rhythm for it. I suspect this did not happen frequently, but the memory dug in.

Harry was proud of his employer's horses. There's a photograph of him holding one of those grand Shire horses at the Wigton Horse Show – each matching the other for the smart turn-out.

I remember him clearly. As my father was away in the war, my grandfather became a substitute. In the late thirties, as well as being the Wigton park keeper, he also did other jobs for the council and worked without a holiday for the rest of his life. The reward was the house. By that time the first family had left 'home' and lived in at their workplaces.

The council had decided to build a new house for their park keeper – just outside the ornamental gates. It was such a fine house!

There were two doors to the sitting room, an amazing feature, unknown in the family's past, verging on 'posh'. This spacious room accommodated a piano, a three-piece suite, a cupboard, one drawer of which was a 'ratching' drawer, packed with odd bits and bobs that the grandchildren could ransack in the search for something discarded but still seductive to a child. There was a dining table with six chairs. Upstairs, three bedrooms and a box room. By bunking up, these rooms could sleep Harry, Hannah and four young adults. The house stood in its own plot of land.

Harry was a good gardener. Many men in the town at that time were capable of bringing home fresh vegetables and in quantity from their allotments. The garden of Park House became my grandfather's allotment. He grew basic vegetables – potatoes, carrots, runner beans, beetroot, onions – and rhubarb. From the garden to the plate in a couple of hours. He was most proud of his potatoes – the largest of the crops. He would take you to see and admire them as they pushed aside the soil, breaking free to fill the pot. Eating out as a family was unknown and unthinkable, both for his family and, later, for mine.

He kept hens and, because they entertained him, he had a few bantams. He liked to give his grandchildren their tiny eggs. When needed he would wring the neck of one of the chickens, hang it on a post and later bring it in to be plucked, gutted and roasted. For Hannah's sake he kept a space free for a lawn and another patch for a flower bed. In the next field the owner had lent him a small plot of land next to the hedge against the park and here he built a shed for his pigs, which, when butchered – he could do that himself: he had been a butcher for a while after his pit accident – provided ham shanks, bacon and sausages for some months.

He was handy, like so many of his generation. He could build a wall or a wardrobe, fix an electrical fault, paper a room or paint it as required by Hannah. She baked all of the bread, scones, biscuits, cakes, rock buns, teacakes, and cooked all of the meals for what, at one stage, was a boisterous and numerous family.

From the Park House porch she sold lemonade delivered in crates every week by Arnison's, the local lemonade factory. She could darn, stitch, sew and turn a cuff and a collar. If it had been pointed out to her that this displayed a marvellous range of talents ceaselessly employed with little room for rest or error, she would have brushed the compliment aside. Running the house was what she did. As well as recipes for food there were recipes for illness, sometimes from herbs gathered from round about the fields. Harry, for all his talents, was banned from this and deemed to be a useless man, which satisfied her pride. It kept a sort of balance of power. He respected her role, she his.

If you think this seems too idealised, then you would be mistaken. It was common. Those houses of many children, small means and hard work were the foundational pillars of a society that took the working class for granted and valued it not. There were tens of thousands of working-class women, many of whom had started life in service, who made a sufficiency out of slim pickings, who thrived where today we would starve, made plain life undull. There is more. There was also at that time dedicated churchgoing, child-rearing, and time over, somehow, which in retrospect baffles me and speaks of clever organisation. Time to have time for everyone. My grandmother was rarely fussed. Rarely rushed. I discovered when I was about fifteen that Hannah was not my 'real' grandmother. I remember precisely the moment: one of my father's sisters told me when I was on holiday at her house, she was standing at the front door. I did not break step. Hannah was to me as Mrs Gilbertson had been to my mother, and nothing could or would ever mar that. That both my parents had 'false' mothers did not strike me as exceptional.

My grandfather could get a tune out of anything but he was best on a melodion. The little squeezebox was like a toy in his big hands, but the broad fingers could hit the right tiny white buttons as from time to time we would sing along. Songs that had always been around – 'The Skye Boat Song', 'Loch Lomond', 'When Johnny Comes Marching Home', 'Tipperary', on they went, a hoard. Harry's children from the second marriage – Wilson, Fred, Irwin and Margaret – were or had been in the choir. The piano stood in the corner unused after the war. The lid was closed. Fred, the fourth child of the second marriage, who had played it, had died as a result of an illness contracted during the war and none of the others had had the heart to take it up. Fred had also played the organ at St Mary's as a stand-in. The polished, unplayed piano was his memorial.

My grandfather's second family was light years away from his own upbringing. Wilson was in local government and a skilful craftsman at marquetry. Irwin, who had been to the grammar school, left at sixteen. He qualified as a draughtsman through night school and spent a lifetime at Tate & Lyle. Margaret, who was a soprano at St Mary's for many years, worked in a shop, then stayed at home and devoted her free time to helping in the church. Harry would go there only in exceptional circumstances. He said the war had cured him of all that.

The four tennis courts in the park were free; Irwin, Wilson and, later, I played tennis there alongside schoolteachers, the doctor. Irwin played for the town's rugby team, which Wilson was key in organising – Hannah washed the team's kit for every game. I will for ever see my grandfather in the armchair to the left of the coal fire, taking out a stick of black twist and cutting off a thin slice with his large pocket knife before prodding it into a small pipe for his evening smoke. He always carried a knife. A single blade sharpened repeatedly. We all carried knives then, men and boys. Sometimes – as when I joined the Scouts – multi-purposed clunky things that could have done damage to a horse, never mind taking a stone out of its hoof. And, like other Scouts, I carried a long-bladed sheath knife. Knives were not used in fights – that came later. Harry had a trick that always got me. He would show me the knife in his hand, then take it to his mouth and pretend to swallow it. He was very convincing.

In that house he must have felt throned in bounty. In the other armchair there was Ned, the lodger, who processed the town's rubbish in what had been the fire station in Council House Yard. I cannot remember Ned saying a single word. The box room had been turned into his bedroom.

The small pipe was characteristic. Harry had been brought up and remained austere. I remember him saying that the problem nowadays was that 'people eat far too much'. Only later would it dawn on me that the championing of small portions came from a background when that was all there was on offer. The single small pipe. No alcohol, if no money for it. Working clothes and a Sunday suit the total wardrobe.

He was slight but strong. His blue eyes sparkled out of a countryman's ruddy face, which still bore the scars from the pit accident: the right cheek was twisted up towards the place in his skull that had been badly fractured. He hobble-walked at speed. One time he borrowed a bike from one of his sons to pedal the half-mile or so uphill to the town. My father saw him walking at his usual speed pushing the bike and when challenged he said he had no time to stop and get on it.

He said things we – his children and grandchildren – cherished. 'And the Lord said unto Moses – go forth! And he went fifth and was disqualified.' And the only comment I remember from his time soldiering in the First World War was 'Always keep your feet dry.'

He was fearless. As I witnessed. Bicycles were banned from the park. Some of the older lads on boring summer evenings, especially Sundays, would rove the town on their bikes looking for trouble. There was a circular lawn just beyond the ornate entrance gates to the park. It was bordered by municipal flowerbeds, which my grandfather forced me to weed whenever he could catch me. One of the perils of going to the park was that he would find me a job. The path around this lawn was ideal for pretending to be on a motorbike and racing flat out, the bike leaning into the flowerbeds all the time, sometimes crushing the sacred municipal flowers, sometimes even speeding over the finely mown grass.

One night half a dozen of the lads invaded the park with their bikes. I was with a friend nearby among the swings, the banana slide, the roundabout. The gang swept in like bandits and took over. What I next saw was my grandfather, coming across from the bowling green, which he would have been giving a final seeing to, cap on, sleeves rolled up, intent, as if blinkered. The lads – mid-to-late teens – took no notice at first. As he drew nearer he began to shout at them to 'Git out! Git out! Git out!' I felt afraid for him.

He came at his usual speed-hobble and they, too, seemed to speed up, making motorbike noises as they swung around the path. He went straight onto the path and forced them to slow down. Some stopped. Most dismounted and held their bikes as if to charge at him with them. Even now as I write this – seventy years on? – I feel dry-throated. Some of those lads were rough. Should I help? I was too small and too scared. But he was so outnumbered. They yelled at him and swore. You could feel their desire to defy him. He stood his ground, planted there, and repeated, 'Out! Out! No bikes in the park! Out!' He barred their progress on that narrow path. I'll never know what swung them away, but at a moment like a flock of birds suddenly switching direction, they did turn away, mounted their bikes, still shouting defiance, and went out through the gates, onto Park Road, and up into the new council estate. He called me over to help tidy up the flowerbeds.

Chapter Eight

The park had been created to the west of the old town by the River Wiza, about half a mile from its centre. It was generously landed. There was room for the hundreds of people and scores of floats that filled it on carnival day in the summer, with space left over for carnival sports – the sack, the egg and spoon, wheelbarrow and three-legged races and a few short dashes. The floats drew up at one end of the sward, like covered wagons in a western. The fancy dress was judged beside the tennis courts. The committee inhabited the shelter next to that circle of lawn and gave each child a sixpence. The band parked themselves on a convenient strip of land near the refreshment tent beside the old town pump, which had long before been displaced from the middle of the town by a fountain and become merely an ornamental embellishment to the park.

There were swings for small children into which they could be virtually locked for safety, open swings for the older and bolder, which could be forced higher and higher until the chains threatened to snap, and the American swing, a plank with sitting slots engined by a willing slave at each end who, again, tried to make it go so high that it would buck dangerously. There was a roundabout, which you could spin faster and faster before you dared each other to jump on. Finally the magnificence of the banana slide. It took a hammering. As soon as we could we ignored the sensible steps up to the little cabin at the top and climbed up the structure that held the whole thing together or we walked up the slide itself before coming down headfirst on our backs. As often as we could we rubbed the surface with the dead ends of old candles, which our clothes polished to make a much faster run. It was built for safety to tame us: we tried to untame it. Best of all was to go down so fast that you shot off at the end, which I remember doing once in a sort of dive and landing on my face and spread hands, leaving a mess of scratches and splodges of blood. I raced across to Park House. There was a scolding and repair work from my grandmother.

Park House was safety. It was out and out a family house and I was part of that family, inserting myself unselfconsciously and feeling every grain at home. The second, the 'new' family – Irwin, Wilson, Margaret – seemed quite happy to have this minor around, like a late-dropped last child or a mascot. Most of all Hannah let me 'help' her in the kitchen: all thumbs while peeling the potatoes, rolling the pastry, being allowed to run my index finger around the rim of the sugar-streaked bowl after she had decorated a cake.

Treating the park as the Wild West did not go down well with my grandfather but luckily he spent a good deal of his time behind the privet walls shielding the bowling green. If he saw me, I would be conscripted to help him there: trim the edge of the green, carefully pull the light roller, weed the banks sloping down to the green itself, which was as smooth as a billiard table. He treasured it and would even give a slight nod when visiting teams said it was one of the best greens in the county.

The bowling green was free. So was the putting green, although you had to give a returnable deposit on the club and the ball. It was a time when, depleted by war, the country made the most of less. The park in all its aspects thrived, and was well kept by one austere and proud man. It catered for different generations, giving them unprecedented free opportunities.

In the various scenes that resurrect the park there were the floats, usually scenes from books and films recreated for the carnival. They were staged on coal lorries, the Co-op lorry, Walter Wilson's lorry, Redmayne's lorry, tractors with trailers – twenty or more of them, decorated secretly the night before, freely lent for the day. They moved in solid procession through the town before reaching the park, and drawing up in a circle waiting to be judged, guardians of this annual feast of celebration. There were children in fancy dress and adults also who were game to join in; the stars were the morris dancers, thirty-six girls dancing to the town's band and 'The Hundred Pipers'. 'Like little angels,' the mothers said, 'they'll never be as happy as this again. It makes you want to cry.' The procession stopped at three places in the streets for the crowd to watch them have their moment – gentle, decent, inclusive, a show without show; there was applause and the children smiled shyly. The carnival portrayed a town easy with itself, together without strain throughout a thronging Saturday afternoon.

I remember long summer-holiday mornings when two or three of us drifted around looking for nothing more than happy diversion. No more than half a dozen children in the park. A feeling of infinite time. We basked in the place and had time to drift, time to feel that mornings had no end, that there was and would always be this soul's ease in the world. We could play football on the least cultivated part of the biggest sward of grass, or cricket, with the bottom of the trunk of a tree being the wicket, or putting without leaving a deposit if my grandfather was in a good mood or we had done some useful jobs for him. We feasted on that park. But even here, in this other Eden, you had to watch out for his temper, which could be absent for weeks and unruffled by numerous offences against his sense of what should be: then he would crack.

Overlooking the bowling club, within its privet walls, there was a large, dangerously rickety structure, once a general clubroom, now used as a storeroom. It backed onto a narrow, tantalising copse.

My grandfather had made sure that climbing the trees in that strip of woodland was difficult. Lower branches had been lopped off. But if you got onto the roof – forbidden at threat of Hell and sensibly so, it was a creaking shifting patchwork of cowboy building – you could lean out, jump and grab an upper branch.

That was good enough. But the glory was that because the trees were so close-packed, you could go from tree to tree around this small forest feeling that you inhabited the world of Tarzan.

If Harry spotted you in the wood, it ignited his full-voiced rage. If he spotted you on the roof, he was after you. As he was, one morning, and I was the prey.

He came around the side of the bowling green at full throttle, legs and voice. I slithered off the roof and ran back into what I thought was the legal refuge of the swings, roundabout and the banana slide. But he followed me. I swerved across to Ma Powell's field, over the gate marked PRIVATE, and across the bridge over the Wiza. When I turned he was already over the gate. At the top of the field I went through another gate, which led into a lane beside Wigton Hall and doubled back to the road. Looked back. I can recall the panic. He had never turned on me before. It was frightening. What had been sparked by a desire to protect me from my own stupidity and a fury that his laws were being broken had turned into a manhunt.

On the West Road, but he was still there. I am sure that now I was near a spasm of terror. He was an angry man and I was a panicky boy.

All down West Street. Past the British Legion, past the fountain in the centre of the town, now busy enough with shoppers, into King Street. People, small children, everyday activity.

But he was still there, regardless, and closing in. Past pubs and shops and banks and onto Market Hill where I lived in the flat over the pub. By now I was running for my life.

Fortunately the pub was open. I ran through and up the stairs into the bathroom, which had a bolt on the inside. My grandfather's voice at first overcame my father's attempt to calm him down and I moved to the window out of which I could have dropped onto the corrugated roof of the Gents and picked my way into next door's garden.

But the noise of the voices abated, then stopped, followed by a knock on the bathroom door.

My father stood there, as I remember, trying not to smile. 'He's very mad at you. He told you not to do that. It's dangerous and he's responsible. You'll have to come down and face him and say you're sorry. And you won't do it again. Come on.'

I could have liquefied. But there was no running away now.

My father turned, walked down the stairs and took it for granted I would follow him. Which I did. My grandfather was alone in the Darts Room, motionless. I had never seen anyone so angry. There were no smiles from him. In front of him was a gill of bitter. I kept my distance and eventually heard a voice saying, 'I'm sorry.' It was mine. My grandfather remained motionless and my father tapped my shoulder. I went out, out of the Darts Room, out of the pub, and ran as fast as I could across Market Hill in the opposite direction to the park.

The family system depended on obedience. Obedience was enforced by respect or fear. If the first did not serve, the second came in. The town was held together by this. The gentleness I often noticed and experienced in the town was dependent on the harshness just under the surface. Drink could rip it off as easily as a blanket being pulled off a bed. The deeper you drilled, the more brutal it became. The great and difficult aim was to make sure that the layers of kindness, friendship, communal care were persuaded to stay intact, cover a repressed hurt reality that could be unleashed as violently as a nightmare.

Chapter Nine

When I was about eight we moved – less than a hundred yards from Council House Yard – to the pub, the Black-A-Moor, in which I lived until I was eighteen.

I was sent away while my parents made the move. I don't know how my father persuaded my mother to take on a pub. She was as near as made no difference teetotal. But my mother's temperance was to become an asset. The Black-A-Moor was run down and dilapidated. It had no customer base. The old lady who ran it was tired, on her own and past it. You had to walk the extra stretch to get to it, just out of the central core of the town. It was the last pub on the way to the Catholic church and the East End – in the mid-nineteenth century so notorious for its fighting and uproar among weavers who lived there that the militia was sent from Carlisle to quieten it down. The magistrate concluded that 'Wigton men fight each other just for the love of fighting.'

Dad had helped out in pubs after work. He had been in service, briefly, as a boy in the mines for a while, then on the land, in a steel mill in Scunthorpe just after the war where my mother refused to stay for more than a fortnight because the best he could manage for the three of us was a single lodging room. At school when he was twelve he had won a scholarship limited to the parish schools in the north-west of England: this would have taken him to a boarding school in Liverpool but it could not be afforded. His cleverness and knowledge were masked by his amiability. One of his brothers, Wilson, who had worked on the same site as my father, was forever telling me how popular he was. I grew up knowing that whatever I did I could never be as well liked as my father. It became something like envy.

The move to the pub was a handcart and rapid affair. The previous tenant left early on the Monday morning. We went in later that morning, opened at 11.30 a.m. and the pub was under way. Furniture was going out and coming in as the first pints were pulled. My parents were encircled by their work, the barrels of beer in the cellar, dozens of bottles, beers and some spirits in the bar, on the shelves. The crushingly small kitchenette was off the kitchen itself, which was part of the pub. I was sent out of the way.

My mother escorted me across the road to Market Hill. This was once the people's place for markets and fairs. By some sleight of hand on the part of the council, it had become the bus station, red double deckers sweeping in around the hill to park and wait in one of the three lanes. The buses were busy morning till night with passengers from the west coast to Carlisle through the many byways and the barely navigable lanes of that part of Cumberland. Cheap, reliable, a boon. She asked the conductor to see me to Whitehaven – about forty miles away – and make sure I got off and joined the right bus queue for the villages to the west. I needed a bus that would stop in Rowrah – she emphasised the name – where my father's sister Elsie lived. It was half-term. It was my first holiday. The brown cardboard suitcase was too big. I sat upstairs at the front wondering what Whitehaven looked like. I was captivated by the bold evidence of heavy industry along the coast road taken by the bus.

With her husband and two children, Aunty Elsie lived at number 1 Station Road, next to the railway line in a two-up two-down. Irwin, her older son, and I slept in the same single bed, head to toe, a pillow at each end. The pisspot was under the bed. Rowrah was a small industrial village, a few strips of cottages. The feature was the quarry. There was one pub in which Elsie worked as a barmaid. John, her husband, was on the coal wagon. John drank.

Aunty Elsie said, 'John doesn't understand people who don't drink.' Occasionally, on a Saturday night at the pub, he would sing hunting songs in a rather tremulous tenor voice.

Elsie and her sister Mary – who had landed up in a neighbouring village – had been close to my father. Elsie shared his easygoing intelligence. She read unceasingly, novels chiefly – the library was just a couple of bus stops away. On fine days she would walk deep into the countryside. My mother admired Elsie's knowledge of flowers and herbs. John, her husband, was her second cousin. She was always, as I saw (and in these compact spaces you missed very little), easy and gentle with John, treating him caringly, knowing he needed it.

He was rarely without a sufficient helping of beer. Elsie had that lightness about her, time for people's foibles and shortcomings. In what could have been a cramped, tethered, loveless existence, she made warmth, humour and a sweet mockery. Like her sister Mary, she had been put into service at fourteen. I never heard her complain of it; by contrast Mary, once she got going, was devastating about their condition. She had been badly bruised by servitude.

There was a gang of boys in the village, mostly sons of miners, and we played together. They were a tough lot. There was a very narrow ledge at the bottom of the railway bridge wall. The dare was to edge across it, clinging to the top of the wall as a train approached and went under you. We faced each other, competed with each other, went into the woods and built a camp. One day we went to the seaside a few miles away, shivered on the beach at St Bees near Windscale, which made polonium for nuclear bombs, forced ourselves into the frozen sea and shivered again while we ate homemade sandwiches that had been wrapped in greaseproof paper but still somehow collected sand.

When I got back to my new home, the move was complete. We had a flat to ourselves, upstairs. I had my own bedroom. My window looked out over Market Hill to the fields and the tower. It was to be my principality for ten years. There was a single bed. Lino. A wardrobe with shelving. And that was that until later on my father bought a small bookcase at a sale, a table and a chair. Then it doubled as a study. Andrew had the bedroom next door and had to walk through mine to get to his. The room had been partitioned.

On the same landing there was a bathroom, big for the time, converted from a former bedroom when the Black-A-Moor had been a hotel and half a dozen men would sleep in that room. At that time they had to go downstairs and into the backyard for the lavatory. My father now worked in part of the bathroom. A chest of drawers provided his desktop and he would stand there smoking, 'doing the books', entering the previous day's trade in the copperplate handwriting he had been taught at the school in Bromfield. It was the village where his father had had his dream job working with Shire horses, until the farmer fell on hard times and he was 'let go'.

Dad began to make a small profit. He would show me the figures. I liked to scan them for the pleasure of seeing such columns of neat numbers come out correctly. On Saturday mornings he would take money to Martins Bank and occasionally let me go with him. Once he showed me his savings – about eighty pounds. Added to this was 'interest'. Money, he explained to me, 'for doing nothing'. I remember being dumbfounded. For doing nothing!

My father, who had drunk in his day, had all but given up drinking. He never drank when he was working in the pub. If he went out – to a hound trail or the races – he would have a drink or two but when he came back he sat on the public side of the bar to have another. The reason for this decision was, he told me, because he never wanted to be accused of giving the wrong change under the influence of alcohol.

In the period known as 'after hours', when the pub had closed, especially at weekends when the helpers came into the kitchen after tidying up, washing and polishing the glasses and sweeping out, he might have a bottle of light ale, to be sociable with the others who were allowed to drink 'after time' (10 p.m.) as long as the drink was not paid for. One of the great attractions of the job to my father was that not only was he his own boss, he could not be fired unless he broke the law or failed to keep in credit with the local brewery, from which he had to buy all his beer and spirits and even the cigarettes. Spirits were not splashed around in the Black-A-Moor save on high days and holidays. It could more accurately be described as a beer house. But above the front door was written, on glass, 'Stanley Bragg, Prop. Licensed to sell Ales, Wines, Spirits and Tobacco'. 'Wines' must have referred to sherry.

The beer – mild, bitter, porter – came in big hooped wooden barrels, accompanied by the light infantry, dozens of bottles of pale ale, milk stout and Guinness. It was delivered from Workington Brewery, eighteen miles away, every Thursday. One of the draymen was Billy Ivison, who played for the Workington Town Rugby League side and also for Great Britain. Whenever I was not at school on a Thursday I would hang around just to see him and 'help'. The man who worked with him was called Stan. My father's name. I saw that as a miraculous coincidence.

The two of them offloaded the barrels, opened the cellar trap-door on the front of the pub, tested the ramp, roped the barrels and carefully slipped them into the cellar. Then they hoisted them onto the wooden rails where they rested until my father went to 'tap' them. This unplugged the beer. Instantly he attached the nozzle of the long black rubber hose that snaked up through the ceiling into the bar. He would then go up to the bar, draw through one or two half glasses to make sure the beer was not cloudy.

Usually the draymen arrived in the late morning and we gave them dinner. That – on holidays – was my job. I would go to the fish-and-chip shop next to the fountain run by a Spanish brother and sister, Manuel and Jose. I would bring back a fish and portion of chips each. They ate in the kitchen, which in the evenings turned into the pub kitchen, but we still used it as if it were a normal kitchen. Curious what you remember. I laid the table, salt, vinegar, bread, butter, best plates. I displayed the meal carefully, as if I were a squire serving a knight. Once I must have said something like 'It's fish and chips again.' Stan said, 'It's the way you've set them out that makes all the difference.' I have never forgotten that. Compliments were rare. I watched Billy Ivison carefully while he ate.

And when they left, Dad would always point out how gentle Billy Ivison was. He was about the same height as my father – five foot seven or eight – but so broad, unfat, lithe, and 'just an ordinary fella', my father would say triumphantly. Yet to see him on the rugby field, as we did when we could take the bus to Workington, was to see a wonderful, thoughtful athlete, unshake-able whatever the power of the tackle. 'He's just so good!' my father said.

To call such a man 'just an ordinary fella' was deeply felt praise.

My father had come back from the war rather beer-fat but he never worried about it. He played bowls when he could find the time. Every morning he walked up the street at about ten, a time when for all his previous adult life he had been at work. I believe this interval of leisure gave him enormous satisfaction, made him feel free. Back by eleven thirty to open the pub (twelve on Sundays), close at three (two thirty on Sundays), open again at five thirty (seven on Sundays), close at 10 p.m. (every night), 365 days a year. He smoked heavily and would walk up King Street, cigarette between his stained forefinger and middle finger, scan-ning the street as if it were his estate. Streets seemed public property to many people in the town. Especially those who lived lives of intense cohabitation in the critically confined housing.

Although the hours he put in at the pub were probably the longest and most demanding he had known, the mid-morning stroll up King Street, to the fountain and then along the High Street, took him into a different world. He would tell me about it.

This was what gents could do, he said, like the lovable toffs in P. G. Wodehouse, which both of us enjoyed; the peak of their privilege, he thought, was to do what others could not do at certain times. Strolling about the mid-morning town, taking note of the business of the day as if he were above all that . . . I'm sure that was a finer thing than any holiday could ever have been.

He took only two holidays that I know of: three days in Blackpool, another three in Leeds. The holiday in Blackpool was taken with reluctance when I was eleven. Holidays for me were visits to relatives for a week or, as I grew older, a week at the Butlin's in Ayrshire with my mother. We went three years on the trot. It was beyond Hollywood.

There were rows of neat, brightly painted chalets – I shared one with my mother. The vast, glamorous open-air swimming pool was so cold that when I first dived in I thought I had been electrocuted. The roller-skating rink, the table-tennis hall, the daily competitions between 'Houses' – York versus Lancaster – which defined where you enjoyed your mass breakfast, dinner and supper . . . concerts, contests, the spectacular playground, running, running, dances every evening, a square-dance night with costumes provided, coaching at cricket, one morning a march to Robert Burns's Cottage, in army style, singing all the way.

Unbelievably, all of it FREE! We were all equally housed, equally fed, equally entitled to all the entertainment. The National Health Service, nationalised industries and to me then the nation-wide Butlin's were the Holy Trinity of my post-war Britain.

You were urged to enter competitions – from the knobbliest knees to the Young Tarzan. I was hoicked into the latter by the Redcoat girls, who scooped up a score of us, told us to take off our jumpers and shirts and vests and stand on the stage in the theatre, arms outstretched, chest pumped up, following instructions in the hope of discovering a muscle. Got nowhere. Unfortunately, all of us were photographed. My mother took mine home. I dreaded the day anyone found it, although she swore she had put it in the bottom of a drawer.

Then there was the singing contest. I thought I had a chance in the juniors with 'I Believe'. But a boy from Edinburgh turned up, one of those blessed with a perfect treble voice, and sang 'At The End Of The Day'.

There was boxing, where I dislocated my thumb on the iron head of a lad from Melrose. I needed a bandage. There's a photograph of the bandage with myself attached, dressed as a cowboy for the square-dance night. My mother, beside me, is dressed as a cowgirl, I presume. They taught us as we danced. The caller: 'Three steps forward, three steps back, bow to your partner, take her waist, swing her around and off we go, dozy doe for a dozy doe.' We'd danced together since I was eight. I now see how much that might have mattered, probably did matter, to my mother. No other boy I know of danced or shopped or just walked up the street with his mother. I now think that her shame, especially in the first part of her life, was like a wound that would never heal. It did. And I was part of the cure. Odd as it might seem, I was proof of her legitimacy. Now I realise that, I can conjure up the process.

At Butlin's, there was love at first sight. Three times. There was a Snow White beauty from Newcastle. I would have been about twelve, she about twenty with jet-black hair, clear skin and, more than anything else, the smile, the fun. She taught me to roller-skate on the second day. I thought I became something of a skater over the next couple of days and showed off until, tactfully but still causing a minor heartbreak, she made it clear she had done with me now and preferred to roller-skate with this tall fella from Sunderland.

There swung into my ken two girls from Kilmarnock. Near enough my age. One blonde, one dark. They worked as a couple. Fell for the blonde on Sunday, Monday and Tuesday until square-dance night when she turned up in a bonnet and inexplicably all warm feeling drained away. I regrouped around her dark-haired friend to the bewilderment of all three of us. We kept up a penpal correspondence for about four weeks. Nothing seemed impossible.

I knew that money had been paid up front – seven pounds for the week for my mother, three pounds ten shillings for me – but that transaction was above my comprehension: all I knew was that Butlin's was my oyster. An effortless and thrilling egalitarianism – the only control was in the hands of handsome young men and women wearing red jackets and white skirts or trousers, the young Redcoats, who would usher and cheerfully bully us through the day. The adults among us were sympathetic to discipline and mass movement, provided it was good-natured and in a good cause – wars and factories had cultivated that. The Redcoats collected the young together round the camp as they led us into the dances and concerts. One of them would hammer a big bass drum, and we all sang,

> 'Come and join us,
> Come and join us,
> Come and join our happy throng.'

Boom! Boom! Boom!

We were Pied Piper-led and we loved it. Just as we were jerked out of sleep by the Tannoy belting out the song:

> 'Wakey wakey! Wakey wakey!
> Rise and shaky!
> Remember Rip Van Winkle slept a long, long time,
> When he woke he was old and grey, so –
> Wakey wakey! Wakey wakey!
> It's going to be a glorious day!'

Even when it rained stair rods. And out we would stream to the food halls. In the evening the Tannoy would announce, 'The wee 'un's greetin' in Chalet Forty-five, Row N,' and the alerted parent would haul down to the prefabricated holiday huts where a Redcoat would be at the door.

It seemed then, it seems now, an innocent time. It seemed then, it has seemed since, a warm and brilliant organisation of pleasure for families, who would save up money for a holiday not conceivable before.

There would have been fights, I am sure, though I didn't see any, but there were bars. There might have been thieving, although very few had much worth stealing. There may have been abuse, although it was a time when communities exercised a strong sense of patrolling their boundaries. But for children, for me, that was beneath the surface and the surface was like being in a film. We ran around, unbelievably privileged, in this Scottish film-set camp-site, next to a freezing sea.

For years, I kept the badges. A highland piper in a kilt playing the bagpipes with AYR and the year engraved on it. I came back to our town with just the touch of a Scottish accent and a yearning for roller skates.

Then there was Blackpool.

My father's excuse was that he had done enough travelling in the war. Eventually my mother must have managed to persuade him that he needed to spend some time with me. It was unthink-able that the three of us should go, just as it was out of the question that we would all go to a café. He was convinced the pub would be in danger of anything from spontaneous combus-tion to mass looting if he spent time away and, besides, what was there to do in Blackpool?

At first he tried his best. He was helped over the hurdle of not being in the Black-A-Moor by the Illuminations. We went in autumn and stepped out of the dark northern nights into the full force of more than a million coloured light-bulbs. They orna-mented the tram that glided along the front, chasing away any gloom, with the magic of electricity. All over the town we were escorted by loops of light-bulbs strung along the road, mostly swaying in the west wind off the sea, sweeping upwards across the streets, connecting the sea to the emblazoned theatres, spiral-ling into fanciful shapes or bulb-painted scenes from *Snow White and the Seven Dwarfs* and other famous films. Lagoons with glittering waterfalls of flickering white bulbs, pubs interlaced with red, yellow and blue lights.

Blackpool Tower, Lancashire's answer to Eiffel, dressed up to the nines, soared above the orgy of light. Blackpool was designed to make you say, 'Look at that!' or 'How did they do that?' and 'Wow!' It was unpretentious Installation Art before the term had been stolen for High Culture. And everywhere there were songs in the air. Blackpool flaunted itself, one in the eye for old blackout or gas-lit ration-book Britain, bringing glitter and glamour to the thousands of workers who came, town by town, from the north-west, for their week beside the sea. It was a domestic Empire of Fun implanted on the north-west shore of a battered England. And working class to the last inch.

That gave it its surging cohesion. Of course there were gradations – the slightly better-off, perhaps even shopkeepers, skilled working class, the semi-skilled, and on it went – as everywhere else, fine sliced until there was no one left save those who could not afford a holiday. But the working class made it theirs.

Some men in the town – a sizeable number – when asked where they were going for their holidays, would say, 'I'm just taking days,' and put on their best suits and walk a little around the streets before taking a bus to Carlisle. You would see them in Wigton, seeming strangers marooned in their own town. Andrew was one of those.

Back on the front at Blackpool it was excitement at what was still the novel and sumptuous idea of a family holiday in a place designed for pleasure. The morning walk along the front was a promenade, a cavalcade of leisure, an appreciation of the Sea Air, a week of which would surely clear the lungs of the thick sticky fug of heavy industry. We were a congregation so pleased to be part of this extravaganza. That it was all but class exclusive now seems part of its originality and its grandeur.

Peep shows on the pier, a penny a peep, saucy – What The Butler Saw. Fortune tellers, little fairgrounds on the piers, street criers on the front selling the shows for which Blackpool was so famous, flaunting stars from radio, film, and even America.

My father liked the morning stroll. He was always easy chatting to strangers and here, plumb centred among his own kind released from the jaws of work, he must have been in his element. We would stop and sit on a bench and soon I'd scoot off onto the sand or with sixpence, even more, to spend at one of the crowds of games built to seduce you along the piers. When I came back he would be talking away, cigarette in his left hand, left leg over right, relaxed, talking unfailingly to men about football or the day's news, and comparing experiences in the different towns, perhaps, but mostly, I guess, it would be 'chat of the day'. What he liked most was to let conversation follow a path it set itself, drift without apparent aim. After that we would find somewhere to eat (we would have had our full but silent breakfast in the B-and-B), then make for the South Beach − the mechanical monsters made to provoke screams of fear and a passing touch of hysteria.

Dad wasn't struck by these engines of entertainment. He paid for my rides on the Great Roller Coaster, the Ghost Train, the Twin Rocket, but it was not as much fun as it promised. I was being watched, where I wanted to let loose. And there were no pals. Still, no complaints. But it lacked the intimacy of the fair that came to Wigton. The scale was from another world and meaty with prospective boasting about the Amazing Holiday in Blackpool.

On the second night we went to a football match to see the then fabled Blackpool internationals Stanley Matthews and Stan Mortensen. When we went to Carlisle United together I would be passed over the crowd, like other kids, and sit almost on the touchline. In Blackpool I stood on the terraces. I expect my father found a way to gain height or hoisted me up on his shoulders, but it was a distant spectacle. And I could never be sure I was really following Stanley Matthews and Stan Mortensen and, besides, Blackpool wasn't my team.

The Winter Gardens, which seated three thousand, claimed us for one night of its spectacular show − galleons sank on the stage, acrobats from foreign countries whirled through the air and northern comedians rocked the pleasure dome. But I could tell that all was not well with my father. At night in our two single beds he kept the light on to read. I went to sleep the moment my head hit the pillow.

On the fourth day, the morning, out of the five we had booked in for, after breakfast − 7.30–9 a.m. − we set out for the stroll, passing the bookie where Dad placed his daily bet.

He was so bored. Even I, then, who would have struggled to understand the condition, could see and feel the numbing glaze in his eyes, his gestures – all of these were a perfect fit for the later award of the word 'bored'. He had left me, that was plain. Most of all, he wanted to leave Blackpool and get back to where he could talk to the men who came into the bar and be in a world of companionship rather than play the custodian of the boy.

On the front I paused to look in the window of a shop. I was transfixed by a bright yellow polo-necked pullover, which occupied the centre of the window display. I cannot remember before then being in the slightest degree interested in clothes. You had your best suit – or I had and others like me had. Often called your Sunday suit, which, when you threatened to grow out of it, was, generally at Easter two years later, handed on to a cousin, or replaced and relegated to school wear. This was at the unblazered national school before the arrival of the Grammar School Blazer. I was lucky, I realised later. Because my mother had worked in the clothing factory, she got my clothes cheaper than the shop price. I think she paid for the materials and a pound or so for the labour and a friend of ours would knock them up. There might be an old pair of trousers (short pants) and a jacket for mucking about in and there was neither fuss nor fad about any of it. Those were the clothes we wore. Just as what was put on the table was the food we ate.

But this bright yellow polo-necked pullover!

It was the sort of thing worn by the boys whose families brought the fair to our town, the Slaters, whose small touring fair was eventually to settle and winter in the town. The boys had long hair, wild scarves around their necks, floral shirts – all out of reach and out of the question but a hovering inspiration. This yellow polo-necked pullover was right up there with the Slaters. There was lust involved. Dad spotted that. 'If I bought it for you,' he said, 'could we go back today instead of tomorrow?' I imagine, and I think correctly, that when I looked up at him I saw his genial expression edging towards agony – three days already!

I nodded. We went into the shop. I pulled it on over my shirt and tie and vest. He bought it. In next to no time we were on the train, up to Carlisle, the bus to Wigton, across Market Hill to the Black-A-Moor where my mother took one look at my magnificent prize new garment, which made me feel as cocky as the Slater boys, who could leap on and off the fastest turns of the speedway and have as many goes on the dodgems as they ever wanted.

'You can take that off for a start,' she said.

I never saw it again.

Chapter Ten

After school, Dad worked as a boy labourer on a farm a few miles away from his home on the west side of the county. The only time he mentioned his miserable employer, a well-off farmer, was to tell me about the time they were at a horse show. A friend of this farmer asked him to look after his horse for most of the day. A big Shire horse. My grandfather had loved working with them and Dad had picked up how to deal with them.

This meant trotting him every now and then, feeding him from the bag of oats, giving him yet another brush down, talking to him. 'I was there for nearly five hours,' he said. 'The man who hired me was a very tall man in a tweed suit that looked scarcely worn, with a silver watch chain across his waistcoat. When he came back to claim his horse, he gave me half a crown. It was a fortune. As soon as he was out of sight, my boss, who looked scruffy by comparison, came up and said, "How much did he give you?" I showed him the large silvery glistening half-crown coin. He took it. "You work for me," he said. "Never forget that."'

His sisters moved across the county to the shores of Ullswater, one of the biggest of the lakes, to an extensive country house. They sent him a note saying the house needed a boot boy and when they came home for their four-day holiday they would take him back with them.

Work in that house defined my father's view of what he called the 'real' gentry. He was spare with anecdotes about himself or I was too shy or too stupid to ask him direct questions about his past. But in this instance he spoke of Lady – forgotten the name. She was recently widowed. As the boot boy he had a

66

range of chores but boots and shoes came first. After one morning's riding, the elder daughter, about sixteen and in a foul temper, came in, hoicked off her very muddy boots, threw them at my father – then about fifteen and small for his age – and said, 'Clean these right away!'

He threw them back at her and said, 'Clean them yourself,' and walked off.

Her complaints led both of them into Lady –'s writing room. When Stan refused to say what had happened, the girl's mother guessed, challenged the truth out of her daughter and secured a tearful confession. Dad reported her judgement like a gospel. She said, 'You will apologise to Stanley. You will clean your own boots today and for the rest of the week. You will never again behave like that. Stanley, I admire you for not being a sneak.' He treasured that remark.

But what he most remembered was the food. Mary, his older sister, worked in the kitchen and aided and abetted him when he spotted a chance to make a criminal raid on a tray of scones or teacakes or biscuits. Cakes were a grab too far. 'I couldn't believe there was that much food. When they had a house party I would nip into the kitchen just to see the food! The food! Great big platters of lamb or beef and game, sometimes venison, mountains of vegetables, every kind you could think of, and then the puddings! Just the smell could make you feel full. I'd never seen such food! So much food, so MUCH!'

When bad luck hit the house the servants were dismissed. After a stint in the steel works he drifted across to Wigton to work as an unskilled machinist in British Rayophone. This made the transparent paper wrapped around certain cigarette packets and other objects of desire. It was shift work: 6 a.m. to 2 p.m., 2 p.m. to 10 p.m., 10 p.m. to 6 a.m. Your shift changed every three weeks. The factory closed down for a week in summer to be overhauled and cleaned. It had a tall chimney that belched out chemically sickly rancid smoke. An industrial challenge to Highmoor Tower. When the wind was in the wrong direction, the smoke swept over the town and became known as the Wigton Smell.

The war. The return. The factory again for two or three years. Then the chance to be 'my own boss' and the winning of the tenancy to the pub that no one else wanted, the Black-A-Moor. Workington Brewery, who owned it, just hoped to see if anyone could prop up a place on its last legs.

Suddenly he was not subject to orders. He was running his own work life. He was almost liberated: still a tenant, even though a landlord. So when he walked up street he took in the small shops and let it cross his mind that one day in some future he ought to be able to buy one and be wholly his own man. I don't think he felt he had moved up a class – that was not his cast of mind. What he wanted was independence.

He was free from class envy. He was settled in his skin, secure in the place he had been allotted, unwilling to waste life on unchangeable regrets, too self-confident or proud to want to climb the social ladder. If my father ever used the word 'class', it would be as in working class, linked to 'ordinary people'.

I think he saw himself as he saw many in the factory, in the pub, on the street, as decent – a favourite word – as well as ordinary. That was enough. That was good. There was a life there.

The word 'class' was also used as praise – 'He/she's first class.' I think he saw the best of his peers as first class, especially when they had started from nothing. Often sportsmen, most of whom came from a background not dissimilar to his own. Though playing sport had not been a part of his own education, he was captivated by it. Batting averages, bowling feats, footballing magic, boxing skill, and horses, studying the form in the morning, putting the bet on at midday and then the buzz of expectation. In the pub he collected bets – always small, often intricate – and was on the 'bookie's run'. It was illegal in those days to carry bets publicly through the streets, but a nod and a wink. Bets would be collected from some of the pubs by the bookie's assistant and smuggled up street under the nodding gaze of the complicit policeman. His daily (save for Sunday) bets were minor skirmishes with chance, a part of his mental workout. When once I asked him how the gambling was going, 'Holding my own,' he said, and turned the question away. 'Holding my own.' He smiled when he said that. His smile defined his character – generous, laughing at himself, a little hidden.

As he strolled up King Street, there could be a musing on which shop he might actually buy if he had the money to put down a first payment on a freehold property. Free. The word 'freehold' was a powerful dream, perhaps the more powerful because whatever calculation he made he knew he might never get there. This was part of a leisured stroll. Over the years he mentioned this and his listing of shops in the street so often that I learned them by heart.

There was Smith's just up on the left, a double-fronted outfitters now in its second lengthy generation, a miracle of survival even then when sturdy suits were in demand. The owner, Bewsher, had taken over from a father who had prospered and sent him to a local boarding school, which had cut him off from his friends in the town. When Bewsher came back he sought out new friends. He would find some time in the afternoon, about two o'clock when trade was slow, to come down street to Dad's pub for company. A large, clever, sad man who always wore a black trilby, indoors and out. Drank whisky mac. He was bald. Unusually he lived not above the shop but in a nearby village, a substantial house with several acres, inherited from his father. My father said, 'There was nothing he didn't know. It was a privilege to listen to him.'

Next up was Ivinson's fruit and veg and flowers, too cramped, too small, too cold with the draught from the back room where things were kept 'fresh' and the back door left open to the alley, which looped past the Parish Rooms. Henry Ivinson was kept going by dreams of what he would do with three fields belonging to his wife. He wore a brown overall and gloves against the cold, summer and winter. Small shops, small profits, a living and a life.

Just along from Bewsher's shop was the Spotted Cow, snack bar and ice creams, dependent on the milk round, which entailed a dawn or pre-dawn rising. No temptation to my father – he'd had enough of that. It was owned by the father of my best friend William. Then Danny Pearson's general grocery shop, again, like Ivinson's, a corridor of a shop with not enough full-time work for two. Danny's daughter, Cilla, who was lame with a club foot and never very well, helped out, kept the till and engineered extremely thin-sliced ham.

A few doors on was Miss Peters's sweet shop. White-haired and always well dressed, with a jewelled brooch at the throat of her blouse, Miss Peters sat in her parlour beyond the massed jars of her shop of sweets, the door open so that she could see who came in after the doorbell tinkled. She had inherited her shop and seemed quite content for it to be frozen in the pre-war age. My father said that he had never seen Miss Peters outside the shop. My father had dream designs on Miss Peters's shop. It would, he thought, just suit Ethel nicely: easy opening hours and children would always want to buy sweets. The shop had two floors above it, each with three windows across.

As he went up the street, he would sometimes calculate how he would save for a mortgage for one of the shops. It would be the summit of independence to own one and to be part of the parade that had calmly seen Wigton through its difficult wartime days. Shop to shut at 6 p.m. Five-and-a-half-day week. Wednesday early closing. There was a perfect life to be had here, for both of them, he would say to my mother.

Next, Johnston's shoe shop, est. 1850 by George Johnston and passed down to a George Johnston ever since, its windows spread out, the longest stretch of any shop in the town. It was where the farmers bought their boots and wellingtons, their children bought their sensible shoes, and their wives, on the shopping expeditions, could also find themselves catered for. The Johnston family was doubly famous for the shop and its success, and the breeding of Basset hounds, which showed and won at Crufts.

Later, near the turn of the twentieth century, the then George, just a few years older than myself, long-jawed, proud to retain his Wigton twang, interested in Burgundy red wines, was for several years a judge at Crufts, the British Premier Dog Show. One year he caused a sensation. He chaired the judges and selected a whippet – the working man's dog – as the champion of champions. There was surprise and some outrage in the national newspapers, but George stood firm. It was, he was quoted as saying, 'the perfect dog' and he had 'never seen the like'.

By now my father had walked about halfway up the south side of King Street to Water Street, cramped and damp and often splattered with the shit from the cattle being driven from the Auction Fields down to the railway station. That short street held a hundred and forty-two households – flats, cellars, occasionally a whole house rammed up, rented, inhabited by the some of the poorest. They were miserably maintained.

On the corner was Ronnie's the Hairdresser. Dad always stopped in for the crack. The two other barbers in Wigton had bare rooms, a sink, a mirror, the operating chair and that was it. Ronnie made efforts. A couple of bashed-up but comfortable sofas had been acquired; there was a heap of old movie magazines, some years out of date – several copies of *Titbits*, the *National Geographic*, wilting copies of magazines on dogs and horses, a few comics – the *Beano*, the *Rover* – and now and then an almost up-to-date newspaper left behind by a customer; and there was a small coal fire. It was cosy. You just popped in – if you knew Ronnie well enough – to fill in a bit of time and have a smoke in the warm, sometimes a good argument, even if you left without a lock being shorn. Ronnie didn't mind. He liked the company. He liked the talk.

He was the younger brother of my mother's best friend, so Dad had a connection. Ronnie's family lived in a small flat up steep stairs above Bell's, another butcher's. Like his father, Ronnie had had polio. He walked with two sticks and great difficulty. The shop was organised with rails to aid his draining disability, which he totally, utterly ignored. He lumber-loped around the rails with agile stoicism and non-stop engagement in the talk while he clipped away. He had done his training in Carlisle. He had practised in the town on his friends, old and young, including me, free.

He played drums in a dance band – more of a trio, not the best band in town but they would be hired for the smaller dos. He married, had a son, finally got a car, which was a risk to all in his way but he never crashed too badly. He would take up fads. One was to go camping with his two best friends who worked at the factory. They arranged it for four of the days in the summer week that the factory was locked down for 'refurbishment'. They were set for Keswick in the Lake District, about sixteen miles away. A tent was borrowed from Mr Donolly, pots and pans and a Primus stove were found, three sleeping bags were created and a tarpaulin for the groundsheet. It was to be the real McCoy.

It poured down. It pelted and slashed and sluiced down. The lakes in the Lake District gorged on the bursting streams, which flung themselves wantonly down the mountain. There were reports on the wireless of floods.

Ronnie made the decision that they would camp in the parlour, the second of the two rooms on the first floor. The tent was put up, Primus stove activated and – no cheating – save for lavatory excursions, they stayed in their camp for four days, which became the story in Ronnie's shop for some weeks to come. They lied about walks they had taken, about boat trips, pub outings, battling with the elements. It was a cabaret.

Ronnie liked to be in the fashion so he would offer haircuts styled after the film stars of the day, but what you got mostly was short back and sides. His famous catchphrase as the customer was about to leave was 'Anything for the weekend, sir?'

As soon as foreign travel became cheap enough, Ronnie and his two pals were off to Spain to return bursting with phrases and news from that new world of sun and wine – 'That's what they all sup over there. Wine! You just snap your fingers – they bring it to the table!' '*Gracias!*' and '*Adios*' figured heavily in the vocabulary for a while. 'Siestas' were greatly admired. My father thought the world of him.

There was an incident in the shop involving my father, which I heard about from Ronnie himself.

It was a fine Saturday morning. I must have been seven because we were still in Council House Yard.

It was a time to drift around the street after the Saturday matinee at the Palace. A time to 'be' Zorro or Tarzan or any number of cowboys and just roam around, putting in time before dinner.

I was in the High Street when a stranger asked me if I could direct him to the church. He had heard that it was a beautiful church. He was dressed like a gentleman. His face was rather pink, kindly-looking, his manner was gentle.

Proud to be his guide, I took him along to St Mary's. He asked me to show him the inside. There was a woman cleaning in the altar space, but no one else was there. It was deeply still, as always when empty, a stillness that subdued and rather overcame me.

I had told him I was in the choir and he seemed very interested. Did I wear robes? Yes. Could he see them? Yes. Flattered, I led him into the vestry and put on the cassock, not buttoning it, and the fresh white surplice. He wanted to take a photograph and asked me to stand away from the window. Then he fussed around me and suddenly, violently, I was almost felled with panic. I remember tearing off the surplice, throwing off the cassock and when he tried to stop me, shouting out. What I shouted I don't know. But I remembered the woman at the altar and shouted again, and then I fled.

Over the wall, down Church Street into King Street, into Council House Yard. My father was there. I cannot have been wholly incoherent, though I was, as my mother later said, 'in a state'. I tried to say what had happened.

Ronnie concluded the story later for me and to everyone else in the shop. He trembled as he talked. His voice could be dramatic, even rather camp. 'Stan just came in,' he said. 'Ooh, God, I thowt.

Ooh, God. I was shaving this fella, a stranger, a nice enough lookin' fella, quiet. "It was *you*, wasn't it?" Stan said, and came right across to us. Honest to God I thowt he was going to have the razor out of my hand and slash his throat. Stan had a terrible temper on him. I was scared stiff and I was innocent! He rips the cloth off the fella and pulls him out of the chair and I thowt he would throttle him. "You dirty bastard," he said. He half carried him across the shop and slammed him against that wall. The place shook. Bottles dropped off the shelves. The fella was saying, "I did nothing. Don't hurt me. I did nothing! You're hurting me!" He was squealing. Just squealing. I thowt Stan would kill him.

'Then he just stood back. And he said quietly, "Get your jacket. Get your coat. And get out of here. If I see you in the town in an hour's time I won't be accountable for what I'll do to you."

'The fella couldn't git out fast enough. Somebody said he ran down to Market Hill and just jumped on a bus that was waiting to go. There was folk come in by then to find out what had gone on. None of us knew what to say. Stan went out without another word. Not one other word. I had to sit down, I tell you. I couldn't trust myself to shave another face all afternoon.'

Perhaps on a normal morning my father would have time to cross Water Street and go past another pub, the Vic, and on to the saddler's. He liked to step inside now and then, to talk horses. And there was something about the ripe smell of polished leather in the shop that was, faintly, addictive. It was owned and run by a Captain Wood, who lived outside the town in Bromfield, the village in which Harry had worked as a labourer and groom. Stanley as a boy had come to know him, largely by doing odd jobs. Now he could meet the man across the counter, face to face. Captain Wood's shop was a destination for the local landed gentry and the rich farmers. Hunting was his passion, the hunting set was his life and, through him, Stanley would listen to the details of that web of gentry and rich farming contacts, which spread for several miles in all directions outside the town.

The most ornamental and spectacular figure who came into town was Miss Parkin, who would ride into Wigton, side-saddle, from her fine house, Braithwaite Hall, about a mile and a half away. Sometimes she was with her bloodhounds. She shopped from horseback. She leaned down and handed her basket and list to a shop assistant and sat patiently until she was served. Miss Parkin was greatly appreciated. She welcomed chat. Stan's conversations with her and other morning strollers made the town more layered, giving him more to think about as he stood, as he often did later, alone at noontime in an empty bar when he let his thoughts float up like smoke from his cigarette.

When he turned back towards the pub to meet the 11.30 a.m. opening time, he would, as Ethel did, feel that there was a sufficient world in the town. He had only dipped his toe in it on that morning's stroll, but the shops and buildings continued up and down King Street and off into New Street and Water Street, West Street. Its rival was High Street, the oldest part of the town. All these streets had their histories. Trades, crafts, churches, chapels, schools, slums, a few fine houses. Over time he noted it all and savoured it in his morning outings and talked it over with Ethel.

Those privileged hours let him into a place he could adopt, his first settled community, which had faced two world wars and a blitzing depression and come through – as he saw it in those mornings – still with a strong sense of itself. Most of those who lived there were nowhere near rich, most without wider opportunities, but there was an air of settlement he thought. Or perhaps he had caught this from his wife, whose deep entrenchment in the town fascinated him. So he, too, now rested in the old town, an ordinary man, at home.

Now and then he called up his most familiar line of poetry 'A man's a man for a' that'.

Chapter Eleven

Both my parents had dark hair, my father's combed and brushed to the going standard – a firm parting on the left, the merest touch of a quiff, a dab of Brylcreem to hold it in place and save any further bother for the rest of the day. He had a round face, dark brown eyes, a smile never far away, and a strong nose. He took no exercise save the walk up the street and the regular ups and downs to the cellar. Later on he would take up bowls. He was easy in his manner, his left hand rarely far from a cigarette, so cheap to buy in the war, never pushing himself, always more of a stroll than a walk, enjoying interruptions. Another consequence of war was his false teeth. As he described it, 'A few of us got fed up with the dentist so we went down and had the lot out under gas.' His false teeth were splendid, compared with the widespread collapse inside the mouths of many of our customers. As a boy I was never easy seeing them in the glass he used to soak and clean them in. They looked like a specimen.

Ethel – who disliked her name (and was not up for a second to be deflected from this view even when, much later, I told her that Ethel or Aethel was a royal name in the early Middle Ages) – was thought of as a bit of a beauty. I gathered that most emphatically from reports of her refusal to enter any of the regular beauty contests that came around – even best-looking mother or best-looking landlady. She would have none of it. Many years later, at Butlin's, to which my mother took my elder daughter, she was persuaded by that very insistent daughter to enter the 'Glamorous Grandmother' competition. 'And she won!' my daughter announced triumphantly, the moment they got off the train at Carlisle. 'And she got a prize! It's a silver cup!' She had previously won a cup at the baths for coming first in a two-lengths backstroke race. Ethel loved swimming. The baths was a cheap luxury for local children. Nearby towns had none. I saw a photograph – she wore a floral swimming cap crammed with small multi-coloured plastic petals. She liked to dive in from the top step.

She met Stanley through the cycling club. Sunday expeditions could take them across the neck of England, often following the Roman Wall, east to the seaside resort of Whitley Bay about sixty miles away. Or they would go south through the Lakes to Shap Fell, the mountain wall fortress that had cut off Cumberland and Westmorland from the south for centuries. They biked to the country dances, my mother and her friends often as not in long dresses they had 'run up' for themselves. Dad had a shot or two on the public tennis courts down in the park under the encouraging support of his younger half-brothers. My mother walked around the town all her life, and incessantly. It was her greatest pastime. I have her small diaries with their frugal reports. By far the most common being 'went for a walk' to Highmoor, around the Syke, through the Show Fields, which were alongside the River Wiza, to the cemetery, to Standing Stone. 'Went for a walk . . .' The pub curtailed that but only a little. After closing time at 3 p.m., or on a quiet day, she would once again rove around Wigton, forever revisiting, reaffirming, round by the baths, up Stony Banks, through Crozier's Field into Highmoor, by Bird Cage Walk and the Shade Walk up to the cemetery . . .

She would talk about the town to Dad and me, mostly in the form of news bulletins. Her knowledge of Wigton and its people came to be an advantage when she unexpectedly agreed to move to the pub. She did not disapprove of pubs – she said later – and she saw how much Stanley wanted it and had said they could make a 'good shot' at it. He said they could get a decent living out of it and have a place of their own to live in. But pubs had never featured in her life. She only very rarely agreed to join Stanley on a Saturday night when some men would take out their wives for an hour or two. Now she was pitched into the middle of it and landed with a working schedule tied to 365 days a year.

Hard work had never bothered her. When as a girl she came back from school, her job was to 'clean through' the house on Station Road. A little older and she washed out the ladies' lavatories, part of a sturdy Victorian pairing, MEN and WOMEN, red brick outside, imitation marble inside. They stood at the entrance to Council House Yard. This secured a small cut in the rent.

She took the exam for the Thomlinson School – the girls' grammar school – and, according to the headmaster of the national school (he later taught me), she ought to have 'walked' it. 'It has always puzzled me,' he said. There is a school group photograph that includes her at the time. She is scowling and looks almost wild, gypsy-like, and angry. Maybe she was not up to it on the day. Maybe the teacher, Mr Scott, had overestimated her ability. But there is another way of looking at it.

The Thomlinson School at that time was fee-paying. Unlike the national and Catholic schools, it was uniformed and drew largely on the better-off from Wigton and around the villages, only a few of whom my mother would have encountered at the Guides, the swimming-pool, the cycling club, Sunday school. I think it quite likely that she did not want to go. She was very conscious of the pack she ran with and always loyal to it. Then there would be the expense. The uniform, the satchel, the special clothes for sport.

Illegitimate girls, bastards – the words were never far away when she was young – had no place getting above themselves. You came out of Union Street, where your mother was registered and where you had found your first house. Union Street kids did not go to the Thomlinson School. I think that her self-confidence – as distinct from her self-reliance and determination to brave the world – only began to take root when she took up with my father. Stanley, from west Cumberland, never out of work, handsome, strong, must have seemed perfect. Not only was he safe, but foreign to the town and therefore initially unaware of the early fault and well able to bat off any hint of harsh judgement. And he had family. Real family. A stake in the place. Down in that lovely house by the park. They embraced her, although I overheard her say later, 'They terrified me at first, all of them just looking me up and down. But then they couldn't have been nicer, especially Mary and Elsie.'

She was born in 1917 and her mother was eased out of the religiously enwrapped town a couple of months on. The pieces were left for my mother to pick up. It was a tight town that practised prejudice. Forgiveness might be preached from every pulpit and intoned in all the prayers, but judgement ruled the houses. It was essential to a feeling of superiority, which oiled certain necessary wheels. Illegitimacy was not uncommon, but familiarity did not breed mercy. 'It's not the child's fault. It's him and her, them I blame.' But blame stained the child and I am sure that my mother as a girl would have known and felt it.

The word 'bastard' was too forbidden and exciting to be resisted by the cruel children who enjoyed tormenting those they thought to be weaker. Such a sore word! And you could say it without it counting as swearing. Some would have done. And Ethel could not deny it. They must have been stabs of icicles to her heart. And to whom could she turn, who would give her the comfort she needed? Mrs Gilbertson perhaps, but however affectionately the hair was stroked it could not be denied. And bastards were bad. That was undeniable. Sooner or later that badness would 'come out' and the wickedness would be plain for all to see. Just a very few tormentors were all that was needed for the whispering to turn to torture.

She endured it. I was her closest observer, from the time I was aware, and I never saw any sign of her flinching. She never lost her temper on that issue, or any issue, though I can remember one dramatic loss of temper when she found out that a much bigger boy, a neighbour, was regularly bullying me. She grabbed my arm, led me, and in front of people found him in King Street.

He was as big as she was and tough. She told him, loudly and publicly, that if *ever* he hit me again he would regret it. 'You won't set Stan on me?' he asked.

'You'll have me to deal with.' She pointed her finger at him. 'You'll have me to face.' She stepped up close. She paused, then concluded, 'Hit him just once more if you dare. Your mother and father should be ashamed of you.'

'You won't tell them, Ethel, will you?' She left him beside a little knot of unsympathetic spectators.

I never saw her cry.

But she did much more than absorb the blows. She made illegitimacy the springboard of her character. She made a place in the town to show that it didn't matter and she belonged.

When she left school at fourteen, she had a nine-month stint as a 'Cracker Packer' at Carr's biscuit works in Carlisle. She clocked on at eight, took the bus for the eleven-mile journey when it was dark and biked when it was light. The Cracker Packers shovelled thousands of Carr's Cream Crackers into tins and boxes to be delivered not only over the county but as far as London and, in the war, to the Front, when the 'girls' would often slip greetings between the biscuits: 'Come back safe' and 'We're thinking of you.'

After nine months a job she had put her name down for, at Redmayne's the clothing factory, became available and she worked there until she was twenty-two.

The parting present was either a prodded rug or a box of fish knives. The prodded rug, hard-wearing, colourful, would have served the flagged kitchen in Station Road very well. These rugs were simply made. A close netting of string was hung behind the front door. Next to it was a box of matchbox-sized bits of cloth of many colours. And there was a bodkin. You prodded a bit of cloth into the net and in time it became a colourful, serviceable rug. Some women made elaborate scenes and patterns and sold them or gave them to charities to be sold on. It would now be called 'folk art'. Some of them are inventive and dazzling. But at that time a prodded rug was just a prodded rug. My mother plumped for the fish knives.

Once, she opened the box to show us the two ranks of slender, funnily shaped fish knives and tuning-like forks. She then shut the box and, to my knowledge, she never opened it again. When we moved to the pub the fish knives came with us and could be found when I poked around in a bottom drawer in the chest of drawers in the bathroom, which served as my father's desk. When they left the pub so did the fish knives. When next I stumbled on them they were rusty, never having been used and now unusable. I asked her, finally, when she was in her nineties, why she had chosen the fish knives. She was in the hospital, bright on that day and managing a conversation almost as before. So why choose the fish knives seventy years ago? She swung her head from side to side, as shy young girls do when asked a question that threatens to embarrass them. Then she looked up, smiled, I swear, mischievously, and said, 'Swank.'

She spoke of working in the crowded factory, more a sweat shop, down Station Road with nothing but affection, save in one instance when a particularly strict supervisor was there for three years. 'He would be in before us in the morning, jacket off, sleeves rolled up, his horrible greasy ginger hair stiff with Brylcreem. He would march up and down between the machines and try to stop us talking. "I will not have talking." So we sang. He went mad. The madder he went the louder we sang. He reported us to Mr Redmayne, who came to the factory himself and said he had no objection to talking, still less to singing, because it "aerates the girls' lungs".'

I remember the women coming out of the factory on warm summer evenings and linking arms across the virtually trafficless Station Road and singing their way up King Street. They got the songs from the wireless and it took only a handful of hearings to secure them. My mother was happily embedded in that. She found the close support of lifelong friends. You put up with the work because that was what you did. On Friday night the small brown pay packet was handed over to Mrs Gilbertson, who returned two and sixpence for spending and put aside another two and sixpence for savings. The rest went towards her 'keep'. Her biological mother paid a fostering sum every fortnight by postal order.

For a while after my mother and I had moved back into Council House Yard, where I could be left safely, and when my father was in the war, she worked for the post office. Her job was to deliver parcels to the farms and hamlets beyond the boundaries of Wigton – about ten miles a morning up and down a few hills. 'It could be a bit grim on a dark winter's morning, especially when it rained.' For this she was provided with a bulky bicycle, fronted by a disproportionately big basket. Even without the heaped-up parcels the bike 'weighed a ton'. On good days she loved it – the bicycling in the well-farmed countryside, thick hedgerows packed with birds' nests, copses, fields well stocked with cattle, horses out of the stable as the dawn chased away the dark. People in the outlying places could be kind: two or three fresh eggs, a boon in a time of strict rationing, and now and then a small ham shank. Letters were given her to take across the valley which, she said, made her feel useful. She would be back in the house by seven thirty, eight at the latest, to make breakfast and, as a few years passed, see me off to school. Then on certain days back to the post office for two hours' 'sorting'.

After that she would go out to clean houses. Before I went to school and then in the holidays I would sometimes go along with her. It gave Grandma Gilbertson a rest and I was company, I suppose, somehow shoring up her position – not only a cleaner but a mother.

The best houses in the town belonged to tradesmen. One to a butcher, another to an ironmonger. These were, by the almost rock-bottom standard of most of the central cottages, well built, three bedrooms at least, indoor bathroom, a separate kitchen, a parlour-sitting room, even a garden. The wives would likely have been at the same national school as my mother, though not often at the same time, and some went on to the high school, but when you included Girl Guides and the numerous church youth clubs, there was a common equality of social background that may have softened any social difference. Hard to know. My mother never commented and all I remember is an easiness.

The women who sought help were generally under-occupied and unemployed so there was a certain aspect of show in it or the cleaner was company, or possibly any feeling of rank was not on my child radar. I think there was, more often than not, good manners, an unspoken acceptance of the rungs on the ladder and a determination not to rub in the differences. Most importantly, my mother, I think, was now secure. Well married, to a good man from a good family, with a child, and above all, those eight years in the factory with scores of women interdependently working on the making of clothes, a regiment in its way of mutually supportive working women who made the best of it and built up what became a lifelong solidarity: this had anchored her to the town. She was liberated from any feeling of being a misfit.

The house she most liked to clean was about two miles out of the town. I sat on the pillion seat over the back wheel, now and then reminded to keep my legs stuck out away from the back wheel as she pedalled steadily on her heavy old bike with no gears. We went down to the East End, past the rubbish tip, alongside the location for another of the council estates that were beginning to surround the town, on to Kirkland, past the grand house inhabited by Barbara Wilson, devoted to hunting, whom sometimes we spotted exercising her horses, past three farms set well back from the narrow road, and after a right-angled turn, we freewheeled at speed down the steep hill – and there it was: Greenwood.

It belonged to Mrs Cavaghan, the most glamorous and magnificent woman I had ever seen. Even now, more than seventy years on, her lustre remains. She was tall, large but not at all fat – golf kept her fit. Her hair was blonde, bountiful, heaped back, heavy yet flowing. Her voice was rich, musical, and different from any I had heard – now it is easy to say it was 'county', 'gentry', 'upper', but then it seemed to me unique, aristocratic but wholly friendly, merry, a smile in it. It was clear even to a boy that her fondness for my mother was genuine and she took full pleasure in her company. My mother liked her very much at the time, and for ever after: the dark and the blonde, the slim almost slight and the full even voluptuous, without any patronising on one side (I am certain my mother and I would have sensed it) or servility on the other.

Whenever Mrs Cavaghan was in bed, lying in or mildly ill with, say, a light touch of flu, or a hangover (as I worked out, much later), I was allowed to take up a pot of tea, cup and saucer and a plate of biscuits to her bedroom at 10 a.m. It was a cave of wonder. The huge bed in which she was central, a silk – it must have been silk – dressing-gown carelessly slipped over her night-dress. Heaped-up pillows, heavy dark golden-tasselled red curtains only half drawn, painted cupboards the like of which I'd never seen. They were decorated with flowers and plants I never knew existed. There was a disturbing dishevelment of clothes on the floor at the foot of the bed. The wallpaper was even more luscious than the cupboards, more like paintings with birds of all shapes and sizes. And also on the walls there were real paintings, draw-ings, mirrors, candles . . . The nearest comparison I had was a picture book of Aladdin's Cave at school. I had never seen, never dreamed a room like that existed, and she lay there as if it was just another day, smoking a cigarette, thanking me as if climbing the stairs had been Everest. I would have been about seven. I was smitten.

Her husband, an officer in the local regiment, had been killed just after the outbreak of war. His photo, showing him so grand in his uniform, stood single and splendid in a large silver frame on a small table beside her bed. A crowded ashtray was its only companion.

She had two children, a girl a year older than me, a boy a year younger, Annette and George. Both of them went to the local school, although at a certain age – eight? nine? – they were to disappear to boarding schools.

While they were in the house, it was the best playground imaginable with the best playmates. George was reckless, up for anything, charging around the farm, which was attached to the house, like a frisky young bullock. He would climb to the top of a mountain of bales in the Big Barn and leap off the top daring us to follow, which we did. He would go into a far field with a stick and foolishly provoke the cattle until they turned on us and we ran for our lives. What he most wanted to be was a soldier-hero as his father had been. The ambition filled him with an insatiable restlessness to grow up, get out into the world and Show Them – whoever and whatever They were. Though the youngest of us he was in many ways our leader until he erupted into a temper about – what? The cause was often trivial or unclear but the temper was controllable only by his mother, who would leave the house calling, 'Georgie! Georgie!' and stride around the estate until she found him to bring him home.

Annette was a beauty. We all knew that at school although I cannot recollect us ever saying as much. We didn't do that. Like her mother's and George's, her hair was blonde, wavy, almost curly, profuse, her face pretty in a way that was singular at the national school, her amiability matchless. Of course I had a passion for her – who didn't?

Mrs Cavaghan was generous with the house. For my mother, although the most she might ever have said was that Greenwood was 'lovely', it was as near perfect as made no difference. It stood alone all but a mile from the nearest neighbour. A double-fronted Georgian house, deeply laid back from the unintrusive road, sheltered by a garden that was well kept by Gustav, the Polish driver. Behind it was the farm, beside it a copse featuring a decaying summerhouse – ideal for hide and seek – beyond it the barns, the hens, a thriving piggery, and beyond that fields of cattle.

For my mother the prize was a dining room with a table seating twelve, which she polished until it was a mirror. And then the silver. For me it was the size of the place, especially the two staircases. The two staircases were somehow intoxicating. You raced up one, along a substantial corridor and down the other to land in a different part of the house; you could go up a third flight of much narrower stairs, which led to what must have been attics and servants' quarters, now neglected and sensational to play in. Especially when there were parties. Whenever there was an event, a birthday for Annette or George, Christmas or term ending or it seemed to me any old excuse, Mrs Cavaghan would welcome all George and Annette's friends from school and across the county and round about to occupy the whole place – to race up and down the stairs, discover the three bathrooms made for 'kiss and run', explore the attics made for innocent naughtiness, pound through the large drawing room, steam in and out of what to most of us was a vast kitchen, a table groaning with sandwiches, rolls, cakes, fruit and nuts, and lemonade. We were at a royal feast.

Like several of the wealthy farmers at that time in the small planetary villages, hamlets and isolated estates circling the sun of Wigton, Mrs Cavaghan (my mother refused the invitation to call her by her first name: she, as I remember, managed the relationship without having to use any name at all) liked to come into the town. There were the market days, and people came in from a wide radius with vegetables for sale at one designated strip of street, there for centuries, outside the Anglican church.

The farmers would come in to buy and sell their cattle, sheep, pigs and horses. The women would shop in the numerous specialist shops, and there were the pubs – Mrs Cavaghan and her friends went to the Crown and Mitre, directly opposite the church.

Throughout the war the pubs boomed. Mrs Cavaghan would be driven to the pub by Gustav, enter the saloon bar with a swirl of anticipation and drink gin. Annette and George came along from time to time and slept or played in the large Alvis, being brought pop and crisps at intervals. Sometimes Mrs Cavaghan would ask that I join them, and I took them round the gas-lit town, up its dark alleys into its web, as if I were showing off the city of Rome to wide-eyed barbarians. Then we'd race back to the car to find Gustav near distraught. On one occasion he ordered me to go home.

My mother did not like Gustav. I don't know how I knew but I knew. There were also such people in the town, on the streets as we went shopping or walking, whom she did not acknowledge or somehow deftly spurned. Perhaps they knew her 'secret' father and were ready to put her down or perhaps she sensed them to be 'not very nice'.

The Wigton Morris Dancers were not beery men dressed to the nines in knickerbockers and ribbons, treading medieval measures with the hearty banging of sticks and Heys! and Hos! The Wigton Morris Dancers were girls, generally about ten or eleven. There would be at least thirty-two of them, sometimes more. The town band led the morris dancers, who, for as long as people could remember, were the chief feature of Wigton's carnival. My mother's association with them over the years wove her into the town like nothing else. She herself had been a morris dancer.

She trained the girls for five weeks beforehand, in the road leading to the West Cumberland Farmers' warehouse. It was a straight road for a good distance and guaranteed to be free of traffic after five thirty. That was a convenient time for the girls. It was inside the old town, across from the police station and the factory, next to the football field.

She had taught them when she worked at Redmayne's and afterwards when she worked in the pub. They were almost all children whose mothers she had known for years, more often than not from working with them in the factory.

The required costume could be difficult to afford. All of them had to wear a white dress, which the factory girls could run up, white socks and black shoes. The shoes could be a struggle for some of the families, the poorest in the town, whose children longed to be in the morris dancers and whose mothers promised them they would be. The girls had a slim elastic band around each wrist and ankle hung with small silver bells, which made a sound like the tinkling of a gentle waterfall over rocks as they walked. When they danced it was a sweet rippling cascade. They wore a laurel wreath of white ribbons in their hair and all the dancers had a white handkerchief with a bell sewn into each of the four corners.

In such a remote place, in a working-class celebration, you might have expected the dancers to be rough-hewn and clumsy. Not these dancers. They could have been maidens dancing before a medieval monarch. The dance was courtly and elegant. The contrast with the rumpety-thump of the carnival could not have been greater. They floated in from an earlier age. Those who watched, especially the women, appreciated that elegance, that courtly daintiness. It just showed you what could be done, they said.

The movements, as in many ancient dances, were quite simple. The tune was 'The Hundred Pipers', which was played by the silver band when the procession stopped for their performance.

These slight white figures, in rain and sun and grim clouds, took so much pride in being part of the morris dancers. And so much effort went into the immaculate turn-out of two or even three in a family. The crowd looked on with equal pride, the mothers on the pavement watching intently and applauding as loudly as they could, sisters and even brothers arrested in admiration as these three dozen girls in classic formations bent forward in a bow with their handkerchiefs in their right hands, left hands on their hips, went first to the left, then the bow to the right, then bending back with the handkerchief cast over a shoulder. Effortlessly quartets would join together, right hands high, fingertips touching, bells shivering, dancing in a circle first one way then the other, until the music progressed and they slipped back into the original classical formation.

It took two or three weeks to get all of them into the way of it. Another fortnight for polish. The more experienced girls taught the newcomers. They practised in groups, and gradually they came together, and sang the song 'with a hundred pipers an' a', an' a', a hundred pipers an' a'', which drilled them and made the sweetest sound as it swept gently across the fields. In those rehearsals my mother walked alongside them, anxious but quietly encouraging, picking out names to praise. I liked to go with her and watch. Sometimes when there was a gap I was put in as a substitute.

They always had a final dress rehearsal the night before the carnival. Jack Atkinson, who played in the pub, came along with his accordion; Mr Ingrams, who used to be in a Guards band, tall as they make them, brought his trumpet and played the melody. It rang across the fields. I walked to one side of them, practically in the gutter by the hedge.

The mothers came for this rehearsal and the older sisters who had been dancers in their day. The women stood in a line, backs to the hedges; many crossed their arms in judgement, tightly holding in their deeper feelings.

The trumpet sounded, the accordion gave a warm accompaniment, the girls set off, bells jangling and jingling, a crush of sweet sounds. My mother left them alone. She stood halfway down the narrow road, near the mothers. I stood a few yards away. When the girls finished the dance she walked along the line of them, telling each by name how good they had been, how good they would be the next day.

One woman, painfully thin, who had known very hard times but still shone with hope, had taken on four children, two of her own, two of her late sister's. She worked as a part-time cleaner at the auction. Her husband, unskilled, worked, like Andrew, at the factory. She had served her time at Redmayne's and there was help with the material. Making up the dresses was not too difficult. The socks and shoes were the problem and took several weeks. They saved, they even borrowed.

She was weeping.

'They're beautiful, Jess,' my mother said to her. 'You've made them all look beautiful.'

The woman nodded. 'There's no bonnier lasses in all England, is there, Ethel?'

'You made them look lovely. You did such a good job.'

The woman wiped away her tears with her sleeve and straightened up. 'I wouldn't have missed it for the world, Ethel. I'd have given my right arm for this.' She crossed herself.

So came the day – behind the band, which led the parade. Down High Street, around the fountain into West Street and into the park, clenched in concentration, dancing their hearts out. They loved it; the street-packed crowd loved them. There was cheering and clapping. They were the stars, however ingenious and mighty the floats, however boisterous the comic characters. Carnival Day in Wigton belonged to the morris dancers.

They would ask my mother as she went up street and time approached, 'Can I be a morris dancer next year, please, Mrs Bragg?' All of them would turn up, then some fall away and the rest became part of the history of the town.

From then on, over the years, wherever she went in the town my mother was greeted by children who as they aged never forgot and saw their children dance too and remembered rehearsing on those evenings and her firm teaching down at the West Cumberland Farmers, when they were young and innocent and the world was a dream.

Chapter Twelve

My mother's time to walk up the street was in the afternoon. Now and then I went with her.

As she stepped out of the pub, directly in front of her was Market Hill, a sloping space once given to 'the people of Wigton'. In her youth it was the pitch of the twice-yearly Slaters Fair. It was the hub and gaudy dynamo of the town, crowded with sway boats, the speedway, dodgems, noisy music, roll-a-penny stalls, clanking slot machines, children's roundabouts, a duck shoot, a big hammer to hit the spring that jetted the ball up to ping the top and win a prize, smaller stalls up side-streets.

When the buses took over Market Hill the council moved the fair to the edge of the town, to the Show Fields beside the river. My mother still missed the fair being part of the town itself. It had been so dramatic. Colour, cries of happiness, the town streaming into it to wander round and talk to the fair people in the daytime and at night to enter a harmlessly brash, coloured other world, especially when darkness came and hundreds of light-bulbs gave the night town glamour. It had never been the same outside the town, she said. Yet they would all walk down from the pub after closing time for the last hour of the fair on a Saturday.

I suspect that much of my mother's strolling through the afternoon town would have been a form of dream walking. She would make the few daily purchases of food but her mind would be scanning and musing on the town, chronicling her way, which she passed on to me as if it was important that I should be kept fully informed.

As she turned uphill into King Street, she would glance up at the large houses perched on a shelf above the hill: one of them, for centuries the old grammar school, now the home of two spinster sisters. She liked the image of children hundreds of years ago in the town being housed and taught there; it added to the rootedness of the place and just to pass it by was enough for her to feel the rootedness of the town.

Plaskett's Lane, which led up to Toppin's Farm and was around the corner, was regularly splattered with evidence of sheep and cattle being driven to and from the market. Beyond the farm was the field in which the Redmayne's factory had been built, and that, too, daily delivered images from her past. Halfway up Plaskett's Lane, John Willie Stuart, whose left leg had been amputated at the knee and replaced with an iron rectangle, had a stable for his pony and the flat cart with which he went about his scrap business. He talked in the roughest dialect and loudly. He would come to the Black-A-Moor for a pint of mild before his dinner and sometimes stay on, despite his fierce wife coming into the bar and demanding his return home. At times she brought his dinner to the pub on a plate, set it on the bar counter and walked out not saying a word. 'He would just eat away,' my mother said. 'He was bothering nobody.' Scenes like these were never far from the surface of her mind. She wanted to be reminded of her past or perhaps she could not help the constant flow of images, voices, incidents, as she strolled, looking about her, making sure all was as it should be. The town was under her skin, lined her mind, which was always fully charged with curiosity and memory and a seeking of reassurance.

She liked the walk up the street past Tickle's Lane, partly because the name never failed to raise a smile and also because of the broken-down wall, which was its street boundary. It was the gathering place for some of the men from the workhouse who would walk the mile or so into the town to sit and look at the people and the traffic and talk. She always felt sorry for them.

She would say hello and one or two would eagerly return the greeting. She had a dread of the workhouse.

A few of the men would use their knives to carve small boats or a horse, even a bird, out of a stray bit of wood, which they would hand over to the more curious and bolder children. The few cottages on Tickle's Lane – owned by one of the shopkeepers in King Street – were known to be exceptionally poorly maintained and people could not wait to get out of their mouldy and crumbling grip, but the rents were very low, as they had been at the bottom of Union Street.

Next, the bus station office and, beside it, a small pothouse, one of only two now left in the town. It had likely been there for possibly two hundred years. Two barrels of beer in the front room of a cottage, a fire, a cosy place for a few elderly drinkers. The landlady also took in washing and was not always in attendance, but the regulars served themselves and put the few pence into a dish on the table. Ethel always liked to catch up with Mrs Dixon, the landlady, who was full of detailed news about even the most minor movements on the street. Mrs Dixon was one of the few people as interested in detail as she herself was.

As if built to challenge, oust and even emphasise the contrast between one century and another, slap next door there was the vast and still splendid Victorian red-brick Blue Bell Hotel, where Stan had worked when shifts at the factory allowed. It was the big yard behind the hotel that the men who walked from the villages with Shire horses used for making final preparations for the sales.

Across the road was where Jack McGee banged his big drum – Boom! Boom! Boom! – at the corner of Water Street and sang hymns and spoke of Hell and hallelujahs on Saturday nights. His wife Jane took a collection. After the prayers they marched back to the Salvation Mission – boom, boom – to count the takings, which Jack later put to good use in the Vaults. It was enjoyable but my mother could never stop her gaze flitting to Jane, a 'sad little thing', she said, who always had to walk behind Jack's flat cart even when he collected scrap round about the town and the nearby villages.

From being with her so much and so closely, I believe I came to understand her thoughts. I know that part of her drifted up that town on those lazy afternoons with a purpose: to experience it? To enjoy it? It was not a mournful expedition to shore up the past. She had sealed the past. This was the expedition of a connoisseur. This was her gallery, not pathetically standing in for something lost or missed, but something that rewarded revisiting and closely examining, looking for and noting any change – as others go again and again to a favourite composer or museum or author.

The greetings often no more than the merest 'How are you?' or 'Hello' to everyone she passed by. The purchase of cakes in her friend Jeannie McGuffie's shop where the smell of newly baked bread took her over for those waiting minutes. Shops like old friends. Noel Carrick's sweet shop with its stock so well laid out in the big window. Noel, a Catholic whose son was a priest, so neat at the door waiting to chat to the next customer who turned up. So well turned out, trousers never baggy, clean white shirt. Stan, she said, could never be as smart as that.

The Co-op with the men in their brown coats and so unhurried, her Co-op number printed on her mind, the cheapness of it without shoddiness, a fine line she and others were grateful for. The women chatting while parcels were wrapped in brown paper and tied up with string, while ration books were checked and the coupons clipped off. Such modest actions fitted the air of unprofiting honesty about the place, which she appreciated, nobody shouting, nobody rushing, your place secure, time to exchange opinions.

When she came to Meeting House Lane she had much to take in. Like many of the lanes in the town, it was approached through an arch, a mini-tunnel over which a room was perched like a crow's nest. She never failed to look carefully down that lane and even if the glance itself took mere moments, the experience took her down a deep shaft of memory and pleasure. Because there was Joe Cusack's Palace Cinema. There she had gone as a girl to permitted matinees and as time went on and wages were earned, at least one film a week. It brought her wonder, the magic of musicals, heroes, stars and happy families, dancing in the streets, ordinary good people winning, kitchens that were out of this world, beautiful houses, and a spellbound feeling, in the dark, huddled alongside a hundred or more, all transfixed by the light and the story and the dreams on the screen. They were people like her. It gave her other lives, even, rather strangely, other people to talk about, like new friends.

Outside in the street, the naming of the shops reassured her of the security and continuity of the town, looking at the window displays, seeing the real world through a thin plane of glass, accessible, hers to have or hope for, part of her daily life.

In the cinema she felt an unaccustomed peace, a happiness without any stress, floating into wide-awake dreams. It fed her imagination; it gave her personal histories and lovely bubbles of unattainable ambition. It was here that inspired a quiet act of boldness. For it was here, in her twenties, finally settled in herself, that after seeing *Ninotchka*, with Greta Garbo and Melvyn Douglas, she decided on my name. A name as alien to Wigton as Tyrannosaurus Rex.

Further down the lane was the original Meeting House – a small dark room, the oak beams sagging – the home of the Salvation Army, where still the old stories of Christian Soldiers, Christ's Army, were told with conviction. Messages from another world they seem now, another planet. But her affection for the Sally Army never wavered. She had gone there as a child to the children's club, as I was to do, and watched transfixed as mere pinpricks in cardboard were projected onto a screen and came out as cockerels, horses, swans . . . They sang, 'I'm bobbin', bobbin', bobbin' like a tiny little robin. Jesus saves! Jesus saves!' Somebody would play the harmonium. In their pub my parents welcomed the sober, serious, Victorian-dressed-and-bonneted Salvation Army women, who came into the den of drink on busy Saturday nights to sell the *War Cry* and *Young Soldier*.

Opposite the Meeting House a long low cottage had been taken over by a former Traveller's family. The man of the house, Sean, painted studies of the town and made useful pocket money from it. The Wigton Dramatic Society got him to paint the scenery in exchange for tickets.

Along past Stoddart's hardware, more Stan's territory than hers, like Dodd's electrical goods, the steps up to the offices of the *Wigton Advertiser*, Tilly's bread shop, Messenger's news-agent's, and the fountain. This was a memorial column funded by George Moore. Mr Scott told all his pupils that George Moore was Wigton's Dick Whittington who had left the town a penurious boy and returned with a fortune from London to build a castle-home just outside the town and erect this memorial monument to his wife. About thirty feet tall, and tapered like an Egyptian pillar, it was topped by Pre-Raphaelite iron plaques, gilded from base to peak, guarded by four lampposts, railed all around save for two gaps for drinking basins for both people and horses. Men on the dole would lean against the railings in the dull hours, suck, chew tobacco and spit, sometimes a fair distance. Charles Dickens had stayed at the pub opposite the monument, the King's Arms, and been particularly taken with the spitting.

To the west of the fountain, the street led past substantial houses and the old Mechanics Institute building; a few hundred yards further down there were the park, the Show Fields, and one of the new estates. To the east was King Street and on from there to Carlisle, the county town where my mother would some-times go on an afternoon of intensive window shopping. Sometimes she would take me along, seeding a lifelong aversion to shopping.

South from the fountain, the High Street pointed to the fells and the lakes. High Street was the original settlement of Wigton. My mother and myself and hundreds of other children were taught at school, by Mr Scott, that this was where the Norsemen settled more than a century before the time of William the Conqueror. They made smallholdings along the High Street. These backed onto what were called, then and now, 'The Crofts'.

She had never forgotten such snippets of history – it gave the town distinction, she thought. It gave her a sense of belonging to somewhere special. Mr Scott had been her favourite teacher. He had given her *Alice's Adventures in Wonderland*, which she still had, alongside the King James Bible, presented for good attendance at Sunday school by the will of Philip, Lord Wharton.

Mr Scott was a verger at the church, an enthusiastic photographer who developed all his own pictures and taught others to do the same. He married a woman too stout to kneel at the altar rail for communion but allowed to stand. 'A class or two above me, I'm afraid,' he would say of his wife proudly. Their son, whom they sent to a local public school, got into Oxford, went into the war and was reported dead but never found in the desert during the campaign against Rommel in Africa. Mrs Scott never recovered. If the hymn containing the lines 'lone and dreary, faint and weary, through the desert he would go' were to be included in a service, she would not go to church.

It was a quicker walk back but difficult not to stop and talk. For many of the women, the street was where conversation prospered. These afternoon outings could be like a country dance, going from one partner to another, seemingly without end. Ailments were a staple. Imminent weddings, recent funerals and births were a regular fixture. The doings of governments and the sayings of politicians were low on the list, if on the list at all. The chronicles of the town were regularly updated. Flashpoints in the life of the monarchy were always good for a comment. All the juiciest scraps and rumours of the day would be woven into the tapestry.

But pace had to be maintained to make the tea before opening time. Middleham the butcher, whose two sons worked in the slaughterhouse in Church Street – she had paused once outside it, on a walk with her best friend, and seen the pistol go into the ear of the tethered cow, seen the front legs buckle, its head fall forward, its heavy body slump down dead. 'How could they do that?' The girls ran away never to return. The connection between the execution and the meat on the table was too hard to bear. For some weeks she had tried to do without meat, but when there was nothing else on offer, hunger made the decision.

Past Bowes the chemist, whose son had also gone to the local boarding school. He was lost when he came back for holidays. He had no friends in the town yet he haunted it. You couldn't help being sorry for the lad, my mother said, as he roved about, looking for what he had been made to abandon. Sometimes sending them away didn't work, people said, and it was an odd business at the best of times. Why have them in the first place?

Past the tunnelled entrance to Church Street, the dog's back leg of a street, the centre of the medieval town, a shortcut to school, and down to Water Street.

Water Street had a special place in Ethel's heart.

You had to make a decision about Water Street. Most people avoided it, fearful that it stood not only for poverty and disease but also therefore for violence, a common slur.

Water Street was the high road from the auctions to the railway station, and on auction days either Patchy or Kettler could earn good cash money by driving the cattle through the streets. The first of these, where they evacuated much of their bladder and intestinal loads, was Water Street. It was, sometimes twice a week, slathered with steaming shit. In summer it was clouded with bluebottles and midges and a predatory host of insects. Most Wigtonians voted with their feet, which took them up Church Street or King Street itself rather than risk Water Street.

Its poverty was plain to see in the ten or so post-war years before demolition slowly began as people were moved to one of the new council estates on the southern edge of the town. Yet some regretted leaving it. They missed the intense neighbourliness of Water Street and life in the centre of the town.

It was a place with its own ways. In the bigger families the boys had to get out of the front room on Fridays onto the street while the girls had their bath, and on Saturday the girls were ejected while the boys soaked themselves. There were men there who could mend anything. Just after the war a plague of TB swept down the street, like something from the Old Testament.

My mother would not hear a word against Water Street. Water Street to her was full of people who helped each other out. They were friendly and open and didn't give in. Most of them had the meanest jobs, for which they got the meanest wages, the men and boys digging trenches for the new houses and ditches for road maintenance, brickies if they were lucky, the women in service or cleaners in the bigger shops or in Redmayne's factory, doing the heavy lifting or, put bluntly, the dirty cleaning at the men's factory. They kept the town working. They were nice people, Ethel would say, sometimes with that subdued, set-faced anger that unmistakably signalled 'no more to be said'.

Her character, like that of my father, was cemented in a visceral sense of equality. She had time for the better-off, for the more educated, for the influential, but not if they thought it gave them the right to look down on Water Street.

I think now that, just as she had been fostered, she in turn fostered parts of the town. She applied a special inclusiveness to her manner and in her acts to those on the margins of exclusion. She reached out as she thought Mrs Gilbertson had reached out to her.

She always paused at the end of Water Street, to look along it, seeing if she could spot anyone. Keeping an eye on it. And then back to the pub, satisfied, fed as full of observations, impressions, reflections as if she had read a selection of lines and thoughts by the finest authors.

Chapter Thirteen

There were four decent-sized rooms in the flat above the Black-A-Moor Hotel. One, my parents' bedroom, must have been the bedroom of landlords over the generations. As mentioned, another had been turned into two for me and Andrew by means of a plywood partition. The third room, which became a bathroom and my father's workroom, could have accommodated at least four, possibly six, beds, when it was a hotel, as could the fourth, which stayed, petrified, for three years as an unused parlour until my father gave up asking the brewery to make any changes and funded its transformation himself. By then my mother had had enough of the ship's galley scullery and the 'public' eating place in the pub kitchen. The parlour was turned into a kitchen and sitting room, glorified with G Plan furniture, which seemed to me glamorous, luxurious, a pleasure just to look at, a shiny sideboard part of the G Plan set, carpets, an open fire, a G Plan table that could seat six if the side flaps were employed. The piano remained.

There was a stable and lavatories in the backyard.

The hotel, now known for what it was, a pub, stood four square in sandstone halfway down Market Hill. To the left of it were two houses also in sandstone, the predominating building material in the town, to the right a high wall and above that the old grammar school, now a house with a fine orchard and garden. I suspect that when I walked along the high wall outside the bathroom to slip out of the flat unseen I was one of its sole observers. The rich orchard had apples and pears, gooseberries, strawberries and even cherries. It was too close to rob.

There was a deep front to the pub that cut it well off the road. I had to sweep that front every morning, just as all other business fronts in the town were swept. My father was strict about work and the job had to be done meticulously, all the dirt steered into the gutter to the bottom end, guided into a shovel and binned. My greater problem was the timing. The school buses doubled up to carry general passengers. Before they went to school, they would drive in from Silloth and Aspatria and the intermediate country villages to unload their passengers opposite the pub on Market Hill. The schoolchildren would stay on board and gawp. If I got my timing wrong, or the bus was early, I would be in full glare of a busload of grammar-school pupils of all ages. When I grew older I knew some of them would be looking and commenting or working out comments for later and I burned. This went on for years.

In the backyard a stand-up Gents, generally stinking, which I swilled out every morning. My father did the separate men's lavatory. After four years of sharing our 'family' bathroom with the female customers, Dad and his friends built a Ladies under the corrugated roof that sheltered the bicycles. The narrow yard sloped up to the stable where Andrew kept his budgerigars. For a while a sagging old punch bag hung under the corrugated roof.

My father was unfussed about where he lived. My mother was grateful for the newly furnished flat but she would have been much more satisfied to live in a 'real' house with an upstairs and a downstairs, and a garden backing onto other gardens. That would have been slotted an ordinary life. She did not complain but alluded to it now and then. She had hard learned to mask her private longings. When rarely she admitted her dreams it was lightly done, drained of envy or regret, just one of those things.

One of my father's first acts when they moved into the pub was to teach her to pull a pint. The four mahogany-handled pumps on the oak bar were fed by thick black rubber pipes, which holed through the floor into the cellar and nozzled into one of the barrels. Ale – the cheapest drink; mild dearer; bitter ('A pub is always judged on its bitter,' one of my father's customers once said – I thought it very wise); and porter – the darkest beer, a stout unfavourably compared with Guinness, which was then available in our pub in the bottle but not in the barrel. To draw a clear pint you had to tilt the glass about thirty degrees towards you and pull slowly and steadily so as not to excite too much froth. The froth level was the mark of a good pint. Too deep and the customer was short-changed, too shallow and it looked and therefore tasted too flat. After that first vital pull, the glass was straightened by degrees until it came to attention ready to be served with the white rim of froth as neat and tidy as a vicar's dog collar.

Much the same principle applied to the bottled beer. As I grew older, another of my jobs before school was to make sure the shelves were filled with bottles to plug the gaps left by the previous day's sales. The bottles were in wooden crates of twenty-four, handles at the sides, to be taken steady up the eleven cellar steps into the bar, wiped down and set out in a neat formation.

My father would rinse out the pumps every morning. He put their nozzles in a bucket of water in the cellar and drew through until the water was clear in the glass.

While he did that, early on, my mother cleaned and polished the four pub rooms – bar, Darts Room, Singing Room and kitchen. In winter four grates were cleared, four fires laid, crumpled paper and kindling. Another of my jobs was to make sure there was a steady stack of kindling available in the cellar. As time went on and it could be afforded my mother would have part-time help in the mornings at weekends. Her attitude towards Mrs Greenop, who lived five doors down the hill, was solicitous. She didn't want Mrs Greenop to do the dirtier work; on the other hand, none of it was particularly clean. She sought to find a way through this.

By eleven thirty the pub was ready for custom. Very few turned up save for Alfred. At eleven thirty-one most weekdays Alfred, who lived in one of the small terraced cottages across the road, would be in for his pint of mild. Elevenpence. He sat next to the fire, winter and summer. Never took off his cap. His hands shook and he needed both of them to guide the glass to his mouth. 'Shell shock,' my father said, when I plucked up the nerve to ask. 'There's a few like that. He was in Burma. The war's still in his head.' After two pints he would go up street to the café where his sister worked. She gave him his dinner.

There was a morning when only my father and I were in the pub after Alfred's stumbling exit. We sat in the bar. Occasionally my father would open up.

'I don't know how he keeps on going,' he said. He leaned against the clock end of the bar. I stood at the other. 'What some of them went through.' He paused and looked at me as if to size up whether I was up for what he had to say. He spoke steadily, never looking at me, giving me a complicated message he was determined I should hear.

'There's other lads, the three Fell brothers, all came back. In the First World War they got the Military Cross and bar for outstanding bravery at the battles of Ypres and the Somme. I heard them talk about it once. You could hardly credit what they'd been through. Forced to wade through deep mud, while the German machine-guns just ripped the line to pieces. Walking on the bodies of their mates who had been mown down in front of them and provided – their words – "stepping stones". Another Wigton lad, a stretcher-bearer, was ordered to go out to no man's land to fetch in the wounded, and when he said it was a death trap, their commanding officer – another Cumbrian fella – took out his pistol and said he would shoot him if he disobeyed. Another local, a sniper, was caught by the Jerries and the tendons in his legs slashed so that he was crippled for life. We wouldn't have done that.

'No plan but to go on and be shot. And they obeyed orders,' my father said quietly, looking away from me. 'They obeyed orders because they were serving their country and the King. Was it worth it? You had to believe it was.' I remember him pausing for a long time. 'They were honourable, decent men, just ordinary men. Some of them were heroes, but who cares now? They walk down the street carrying all that inside them – keeping in the terrible things they saw. How do they live with it? I don't know how they do it. Your mam worked at the post office with one of them.'

We sat for a while in silence, until the door opened and a stranger came in wanting a quick drink while waiting for the bus for Carlisle.

I have never got that talk out of my head.

Later one or two would pop in for a short stopover before or after shifts or to punctuate the idle drift of a day on the pension or to put in time waiting for a bus. The slow midday custom picked up at weekends.

Dad would by then be leaning against the polished oak bar. The bar was narrow, the only furniture a long settle in front of the window, which could seat four at a pinch. There were photographs of hounds above the fireplace and at one end of the bar a softly ticking clock surmounted by a rearing horse, which Dad had bought from the previous proprietor, Mrs Archibald.

I wonder what else he thought about when he was alone in the noonday bar. He liked to size people up. He also liked to study form in the racing pages. But there would be longueurs. He told me on one occasion that his ambition had been to become a village schoolmaster. Did he still dream of that? I know how much he liked discussing issues in the news – was he framing unspoken conversations? Where did he go to, alone in the bar, just gazing ahead? In which decade did he travel? Did he, like the rest of us, lead other lives so many that they satisfied him without ever being revealed? A day-dreamer, then. Content in wherever his mind took him, glad to have the time to roam.

The bar faced south and on fine days the sun would light up the motes in the air. The reflections from the sparkling ranks of glasses on the shelves that faced the window gave an ethereal depth to the place. As time went on his back suffered from those hours of standing behind the bar and he would wear a heavy belt. He bought a high stool he had spotted in a sale. He enjoyed looking in on the sales now and then and rarely failed to turn up with a 'bargain', which my mother rarely failed to consign at a tactful later date to the cellars or the stable.

One of the most lasting memory pictures I have is of him standing leaning against that bar, the pub empty, myself having run down the stairs or, younger, slid down the banister, glancing at him as I went out. He would usually turn to me with a kindly smile. That was all. But the picture in the bar held me, its ancient solidity and the association with a past beyond the pub itself when men came together as now to pass the time, to seek and find company and warmth, and in their number and companionship a dignity often denied them. To be part of the world with others of their kind. And that smile – no slickly assumed mask, just a from-the-heart smile, which showed the man he was, contented in his own thoughts.

It was a smile sometimes replaced by a small nod of greeting, which met each customer. It said – we can make something of this life, we are all in this together; the way is to see it through together; it was recognition.

His smile was like my mother's use of the word 'nice'. To her it was not a sign of a limited vocabulary but a bedrock word for all occasions. It meant kind, pleasant, uncomplaining, friendly, generous, helpful and, above all, untainted by any form of meanness or snobbery. It was an affirmation of the struggle many people in the town had to keep bread on the table, clothes on their children's backs and still find the means within themselves to think outside their often constricting needs. Nice was even better than good. The smile said – let life flow.

Though not without critics and not themselves without critical thoughts of some others, Ethel and Stan were well thought of in Wigton.

Now that he had become a fixture in the town, my dad began to absorb it, although it would never be in his blood. His 'home' was the mining and farming region to the west. When he took over the pub he was more aware than he had ever been that it was his wife whose background put people at their ease. She was deep in the town's detail. When he looked out over Market Hill there would be none of the surge of memories Ethel brought to the scene.

The tall terraced houses that dominated it were blanks to him. To Ethel they were alive in her memory. What he could see beyond the hill to the baths and beyond to Highmoor Tower raised no feelings, save perhaps that he was fortunate to have arrived at such a comfortable place. He was entering his forties, lucky to be where he was, confident he would make a good fist of the pub, waiting for the men who would come into the bar and talk, complain, sometimes confess when alone, drawn in by his openness and talent at talking to anyone or leaving them be if they preferred their silence to his company.

The pub began to fill some time after six o'clock and on colder and wetter days the fires more than earned their keep. Men would come into the bar – men only – principally to dry out their sodden clothes. Some had worked all day on the roads or on the steadily increasing number of building sites on the new council estates and private estates. A number of them had come over from Newcastle for the well-paid work and would stay for five and half days, often in poor lodgings, the shared back room of a decaying terraced house. So the fire, especially in the bar – which roasted that small room in no time – would shiver them into life. You could see the steam come off their scarred jackets; their trouser legs would be comfortingly scorched. The cool beer lightly anaesthetised them.

As night came the bar filled up. Weekends had their own character. But through the week the clientele, which grew steadily over the years, would turn up at their regular times for their regular drink. From all of these men there was the satisfaction of seeing their usual beer pulled, their customary bottle opened without a word needing to be exchanged.

Most came in after eight o'clock. There were a fair number of factory workers, and those who worked in the small shops and businesses that furnished the town. They knew each other. The talk wound through an endless story: mostly comment on something that had happened in the town. Sport had its place: arguments about the merits of boxers, footballers, cricketers, detailed analysis of team averages, fights won on points or by knockout, not only goals scored but general effectiveness on the field – the sort of close analysis not unlike that applied to academic studies.

The Robinson brothers were regulars in the bar. They lived down the hill in the East End, next to the terraced cottage where their parents still lived. They were a confident, handsome family, skilled men, four brothers, taller than most of their contemporaries, two of them good singers. They had the gift of disagreeing without provocation. Like my father they loved to talk about matters of the day and ideas. Like him they respected the 'no religion, no politics' – which they interpreted, correctly, as no party politics. Personalities were different: they could be taken on. So the virtues and limitations of Attlee were discussed, Macmillan was examined. Most of all what governments had done and what they had failed to do was ever recurring. 'They should have done . . .'; 'Why did they do . . .?'; 'What point is there in the atom bomb?' That was a fierce one, and a regular. On other topics 'Our kid could draw better than that Picasso . . .' Television had not yet netted a mass audience. Radio comedians were quoted to provoke a few laughs. Films, 'pictures', were in the mix, gangsters, cowboys and action movies leading the field.

But most of the talk grew out of the moment among themselves. The Robinson brothers were masters at this. One of them would pick up what somebody had said or they had read, something they wanted to tease out, the origin or age of the world, the significance of a reference to some report of a newly discovered tribe in the Amazon – all these and so many other topics were energised by the chat and chaffing of the moment, the laughs that could be raised, usually by catching each other out or by reaching back to a particularly embarrassing moment. Conversation on the hoof. The day he fell off the scaffolding but landed in a bank of sand, the night he had been so drunk he had gone to someone else's (similar, it was admitted) terraced house, opened the door (typically unlocked) and settled himself in front of the fire, hard to wake up. But most of all nothing so dramatic, just the ebb and flow of the day, the sameness and the change that make up a companionable world. The all but imperceptible tides of time.

Mr Johnston, his wife and son lived in a fine sandstone semi-detached next to the pub. Mr Johnston was in insurance. He had a dog and gave it two walks every evening. The first was to his field, inherited from his father, up Stony Banks next to the baths and permanently let off. He liked to walk by way of Tenters up to his field, lean on the wall, smoke a cigarette and look across the field to the Church of St Mary's, the Auction Fields and the Nelson Thomlinson Grammar School. 'Very well located,' he would say of his field. 'Its day will come.'

His other walk, which his wife thought was a walk up the street, took him the ten yards to the bar of the Black-A-Moor. Two gills of bitter and a gin and peppermint filled out the hour and a half. Mr Johnston liked to talk about world affairs. His wife disapproved of him going into pubs. He had his place standing at the corner of the bar furthest from the fire.

The town in that post-war decade had its corps of drifters. Kettler was the most famous. Service in Italy in the war had destroyed any appetite he had ever had save for drink. He lived alone in a basement in Union Street, comfortably furnished from leftovers at the sales, where he lent a hand and could make a pound or two on a good day. Like all the basements his was damp but nothing that a heap of coal could not overcome. The coal was free, a good sack secured by helping Mr Bell, one of the coal merchants, to tidy up and hose down his yard and his lorry early on Saturday. He subsisted on almost but not quite stale bread, collected in the late afternoon, baked that morning by Mr Johnson, to whom Kettler also lent a hand when needed. He liked tripe and sometimes sausages from Arthur Middleham, a butcher who had been at school with him. He helped Arthur's sons at the slaughterhouse now and then.

There was the dole, the tips for driving cattle after the Tuesday market down Water Street to the railway station; and there were dominoes. Kettler fancied himself at dominoes. A penny a drop but it added up. Or play for a pint. On bar-empty days, his pint of ale in front of him, the cloth cap rather jauntily set back from a deeply furrowed, leathered face with sceptical blue eyes and a ripe, sprouting magnificent purple nose way beyond repair, he would challenge my father to a game and they could play for an hour or two. At closing time, Kettler would saunter up street looking for a comfortable wall to lean against with his pals and watch the world go by.

There was a man called Nigel who, like the chemist's son, and Mr Scott's son, had been sent off to a local public school. He had landed up in the Colonial Office, which took him to Nigeria. He spent all his leave in the town, much of opening time through the afternoon on the settle in our bar. He was always dressed in what my mother called a 'fitted suit', razor creases, clean shirt, highly polished shoes. He stayed with his sister. My mother was sorry for him. 'He's just lost himself,' she said. 'He used to be such a nice little lad.' He drank two or three bottles of pale ale, finishing with a stiff gin and tonic. He liked talking to my father and was happy to answer any queries about Nigeria, other parts of Africa, the customs, the colonial service. He spoke sadly and his face had a melancholic cast, accentuated by an unsuccessful fair moustache on his upper lip, his flatly brushed thinning fair hair scarcely covering baldness. He wore rimless spectacles for reading and came with the *Daily Telegraph*.

Charles Spencer was an alcoholic. He was the youngest son and the black sheep of a local wealthy farming family, charming, dressed like a country gentleman, the expensive tweed jacket, the flamboyant silk handkerchief flowing from the top pocket, brown brogues. Sometimes he wore a fawn waistcoat. He had a permanently red, almost scarlet, face and a rather desperate look mitigated by a sweet smile. He had been well educated: he was well read and loved to compose elaborate sentences with as many polysyllables as possible. My father enjoyed his company and when only one or two others were in the daytime bar, to Charles's delight he would tease out of him the books he had read and his opinions on matters of moment. When the family declined and Charles became anxious about spending money, my father would hand him a beer or two on the slate to see him through the afternoon. So it toddled along until one day the news came that he had fallen badly, hit his head on the pavement and died the next day.

Tom Mix had renamed himself. He was called Harold Long. He worked for the council digging ditches, repairing roads. Tall, lean, once handsome now grizzled, he supped two pints of mild every workday early evening on his way home. He had seen the cowboy Tom Mix at the Palace Cinema, been transfixed, and copied him. He spoke with an American drawl – 'pardner', 'howdy', 'I'll mosey along'. He had bashed a black trilby hat into a sort of Stetson. He had been born and brought up in Wigton. He had a severely disabled daughter. People said he was marvellous with her. He had married a handsome dark-skinned woman, who had worked in the fair that visited Wigton twice a year. Tom Mix had persuaded her to leave the fair. They had a second daughter as dark as her mother, who won beauty contests at the town carnival from an early age.

The Roman Catholics used the pub. Down the hill from the Blackie there was the comprehensive Catholic settlement. Church, school, orphanage, sports field, and a convent with about twenty-five nuns.

There were pubs in which Catholics were not welcome.

On Thursday nights, after their choir practice, some of the all male Catholic choir, three or four of them, would stroll the couple of hundred yards up the hill to the bar of the Blackie. They had changed clothes between work and the choir practice and would be noticeably smarter than the majority of others. As a group they were confident and full of often challenging opinions, which my father loved to hear, sometimes take on, sometimes agree with. Two of them played football for the town; one was an outstanding swimmer and helped Wigton to a respectable place in the local league. They liked to sing. Just before they left and without much encouragement, they would harmonise one or two popular songs of the day, and then it was back out into the town, often walking a mile or so to the new council estates on the outskirts.

At my father's funeral many years later the church, St Mary's, Anglican, was packed. Members of the Bowling Club formed a guard of honour and carried the coffin. This was at the end of the nineties, but shops drew their blinds, traffic was diverted or stopped until the cortège reached the boundary of the old town.

As I came out of the church with my mother I saw, across the street, a group of men. They wore dark suits, white shirts, dark ties and stood in a line directly opposite the west door of the church.

They were the Catholics who had come into the pub. They would not come into the church but they had organised themselves and taken time off work to be there, just across the road, to see the coffin loaded into the hearse, led down the street by the undertaker before being driven away. It would go down the High Street, pass the fountain, down King Street, people on the pavement all the way, past the Black-A-Moor and then pass the Catholic Church, outside which, we were told, some of the nuns had lined up to see him on his way.

On Saturday nights three or four labourers – bachelors – from the farms a mile or two away would ride into the town, in all weathers, park their bikes under the corrugated roof in the backyard, lodge themselves in the warm bar and tank up until they either set off homewards or walk themselves and their vehicles up to the Market Hall and, as it was late, get a reduced ticket entry for the last hour of the dance.

One of them was Jack Relph, a large man, country-faced, almost raw with the weather, a hand that grasped the pint as if it were an eggcup, pebble glasses and a permanent smile, even though his never-to-be-taken-off greatcoat might be soaked or breeding icicles. He would always call me 'cousin'. 'We're related, you know,' he would say.

'Jack's related to everybody,' was Dad's contribution, as he pulled the pint of 'mixed' – mild and bitter, and then he would say, 'Specially for you, Jack.'

Jack came early so I might well have been in the bar for the first hour or so after opening time. As I grew older, twelve, thirteen, Dad would let me mind the bar at dead times – between six thirty and seven thirty on a weekday evening, when one or two regulars at most might be there and wouldn't object to being served by the landlord's son. He had taught me how to pull a pint and pour a bottle and I knew the prices. Often the total custom was the two men, friends who lived together across the hill. They, like others in the town, had been blasted by the war, again in Burma. They sought out quiet times. They murmured to each other on the settle, seeking no other company, and after a nod when the pints were handed over, nothing more was expected or desired from me. Another couple came in but less regularly, Joseph and Arnold. Arnold was bald, always in a heavy coat, said little; he'd come back from the war and been unable to face life alone. His friend, Joseph, looked after him.

On one evening, they were there, and so was Tom, a small man – as many working men were in those days – from a cottage down the road. He said very little but would smile and nod at points in the conversations. He was quiet, married, bringing up two children, a regular. Two evenings a week was all he could afford. He drank two gills of ale and liked to stand towards the end of the bar, near to the door, perhaps so that people went past him when they came in and left him to his own company.

I was alone behind the bar. He pushed his glass forward, nodded at me and smiled. 'Another?'

'Yes.'

'About time,' I said. 'You've been standing with that for nearly half an hour.'

I had not noticed that my father had come into the bar. I felt a heavy blow on my shoulders – I would be almost as tall as him then – but he lifted me clear off the ground and took me out of the bar, across the narrow corridor and into the empty Darts Room.

He shook me violently before he set me on my feet. 'You will go back into the bar and apologise.' He could scarcely get the words out. He himself was shaking with an anger I had never seen or could have imagined. 'Say you're sorry. You insulted that man. He's a good man. Say it was a stupid thing to do, and say you will never do anything like it again. And you won't.'

He let go of my shoulder and pushed me towards the door. I was a breath short of bursting into tears of fear and shame. I did what Dad had told me. Perhaps Tom nodded. Nothing was said. I went back into the Darts Room. My father was smoking.

'Upstairs, and stay there.'

The fierceness in his words was a lash.

Chapter Fourteen

The Darts Room was as made-for-purpose as the bar. As you walked in the door you faced the dartboard above the fireplace. On either side of the colourful circular board was a slate with a ledge for the chalk that was used to mark the score: the two slates were for the two sides, either singles or teams. The scoring was always backwards. You needed a double – a narrow band on the outer rim of the board – to get into the game and a double to finish. Most one-to-one games started from the number 301, which had to be chiselled down to the last double. Best to start with double twenty: then, say, in the same pitch of the three arrows you were allowed, you might get treble five (the trebles were a narrow inner ring) and a loose shot, just a five. Score sixty. Score left on *your* board therefore 241. Next man up.

There were darts provided in a box on the mantelpiece. Three or four sets of three, only one with the feathered flights, the others plastic-flighted but, according to those who used them, just as well balanced. The more devoted players brought their own darts, usually in a wallet in an inside pocket, pulled out with a touch of pride, always feather-flighted.

In front of the dartboard was a rubber mat the regulation eight feet distant from the board. On either side wall of the room were leatherette sofas and narrow iron-legged tables served by chairs that just managed to keep out of the flight zone. Again, like the bar, it was mostly men, usually men waiting their turn for a game. But not all. There were men who did not fancy the bar, thought the kitchen a little too posh and the Singing Room either completely empty or too noisy, and to them the darts were free entertainment. At weekends there might be women there when the pub was crowded.

The darts enthusiasts did not share a style. Some leaned forward so far they looked as if they would fall over – but they gained a foot or two. Others stood as upright as guardsmen, four-square, perfectly balanced, as they saw it, faced smack on to the bullseye, red in its tiny circled enclosure mid-board. Others stood sideways, as if their darts were in some way arrows in a long bow. They shot or pitched with body facing the window, head swivelled around to the board. I liked to watch them and would imitate the best of them when the pub was empty.

The dedicated darts players played for drinks. Best out of three for a pint. Seasoned customers stepped back. Gullible, hopeful or young challengers stepped up and usually paid for it. When the dedicated played each other there was only rarely a side-bet. Or they would practise. Happy to spend half an hour or even more seeing how often they could hit treble nineteen.

The three Pearson brothers moved from pub to pub. They would usually start up street at the Lion and Lamb and work their way down. Charlie was the oldest. He worked on the buses as a driver, and attributed the family's skill to their mother. 'She could pitch! Mother had a great eye!' John was the best player. David, who worked on the dustcart, was erratic but, as Charlie said, 'He could be a match winner.' He had a temper and could flare up. People would be wary around David.

Tom Johnston became the first waiter in the Darts Room. He was a slightly built man, who had boxed successfully as a bantamweight in the army. He carried a chair leg when he went home on Saturday nights, which could be rowdy in the town. He walked across the middle of Market Hill, up some rarely used steps in the far corner, a shadow among the shading trees, then past Ivinson's field, past the pig auction and to his alms cottage beside the church. The Johnstons could have fallen out with the Armstrongs, the Pearsons, the Graveses or the Coulthards. Tom took no chances.

He loved waiting on, collecting the tray from the stable-door half-bar that Dad had put in on the corridor side. He would carry a quantity of pints, halves, bottles and the occasional 'small', unspilled, through a cluster of men. 'Watch up! Let the dog see the rabbit.' He always wore a brown waistcoat, shirt sleeves rolled up, jacket on a hook in the pantry.

After Tom retired, Jack Waters took over. Jack was Irish. He worked on a farm a couple of miles away and lived in a tied cottage with his wife and children. The job – evenings, Fridays and Saturdays – suited him perfectly. He was paid cash. Dad gave all the waiters drinks after closing time (a landlord could not be 'had' by the law for giving drinks to friends in his own premises – which is where the double use of the kitchen came in handy) – and, like Tom, he revelled in the job. He was also exceptionally strong and devoted to my father.

Then there was Josh Parker.

He and my father had worked together at the factory. Their backgrounds were close enough for cousinship. His eldest daughter, Isabel, a few years older than me, was as measured and lovely as could be imagined. She was an infant-school teacher and chairman of the group that ran the AYPA. When there were spats she always unpicked the knot and, scarcely raising her voice, sorted us out. In previous days the word 'wise' would have been thought appropriate, but even by the early fifties, it had fallen out of common complimentary use and if employed at all it was a sneer – 'wise-guy'. I knew two of her brothers, Reggie who worked on the post all his life, and Ian, given 'Tich', who was in our first skiffle group on the double bass (tea chest, broom shank, twine – surprising what a strong bass line he could get out of it). He went into the army and made it his career.

Josh was a superlatively good darts player. Good-looking, always tidily dressed, quiet spoken, totally unflashy. He was just – good. Everybody knew it. Now and then one of the Pearsons would challenge him – best out of three for a pint – but it was rarely much of a contest. He was not infallible. He could miss like anybody else. It was his consistency. He had a dartboard behind the door of their new council-house kitchen and word was he practised every day.

He liked to throw fluently, seemingly without pause between the arrows, hesitating only when the backwards arithmetic gave him a problem. In big matches – against other pubs – when Dad sat in the Darts Room, Josh would tip him the nod and Dad, sitting behind him, would quietly scroll down to score for him. 'Ninety-three,' Dad would all but whisper. 'Go for treble twenty. Right. Single seventeen. Good. Double eight to finish.'

By far the biggest games were run nationally by the most popular paper of the day, the *News of the World* (its boast: 'All human life is here'). The paper ran a nationwide darts competition, which started in the most remote corners of the kingdom and, after months of town knockouts, county knockouts and regional knockouts – all carefully reported – gathered towards the final with a glittering trophy and big prize money.

The last sixteen contestants always met at a lunch for the grand final in London. Josh asked my father to go to London with him. Both men wore suits, white shirts, ties and polished shoes. They were to be put up at a small hotel next to the arena.

It was, Dad said, as crowded and exciting as a boxing bill. There was an MC in a red coat, brandishing a microphone as big as a stick of rhubarb. At one end of the hall four dartboards were set up, floodlit. The players were allowed a supporter on the front row, behind them. Some of the finalists had brought a fan club from their pub. Josh seemed not a bit nervous. Dad loved being in the middle of it all.

It came down to the semi-finals. Josh had just squeaked through in one of the games, but played well enough for the bookies to make him joint favourite.

301, best of five games, two-all with Josh's throw and the chance to clinch it to the final. He stood so elegantly, Dad thought, just a tad side on, his concentration so intense you could feel it. His throw.

Double top, first arrow, forty. Another twenty. Swerve to nine-teens. Another double. Ninety-eight scored. '203 to go,' Stan whispered. Josh's opponent, a slender, pale-faced lad from Norwich, stood up: 114, 182 to go. Josh had the advantage of the first pitch: 103, 102 to go. Josh was flying. Ninety-six, the Norwich lad. Ninety-three left, Josh had the chance to win the game. He glanced at Dad and again started with a double top. Sixty-two to go. Double twelve. Josh's arrow sank into the middle of double twelve. 'Double seventeen,' dry-throated Dad whispered. Double seventeen it was, smack in.

A voice said, 'Four on the board. Next man.'

Dad had got it wrong. Should have said double nineteen. The Norwich lad polished it off. Josh shook his hand. My father, I am certain, shrank with shame . . .

For ever after, when I would come across Josh – or Mr Parker, as I called him – in the streets, he would always, always, always stop me and smile gently and say, 'You know, I think I could have been English champion that night. But nineteen, seventeen. It's easy done . . .'

He only rarely came into the pub again and then with a sad politeness, just for the one drink in the bar. My father never forgave himself. Nor did Josh.

Chapter Fifteen

'He has a lovely voice,' my mother would say. 'He wanted to do nothing but sing. He sang from the day I knew him.'

Kenneth lived with his mother and father above his father's butcher's shop at the bottom of New Street between Sheddy Pape's painting and decorating shop and the Primitive Methodist church a few yards from the police station. As children, Ethel and Kenneth, the Staintons and the Wallaces and sometimes the Toppins girls, would play together on light evenings in and around the pool of empty pavement and road that bordered the police station and the law courts. Skipping games for the girls, boys would bring a ball – a worn-out tennis ball would do – and it would be hurled against the side of the church to set off a game of tag. My mother was fond of Kenneth.

'When he was a boy Kenneth would come to play with us but his heart wasn't in it,' she said. 'He was in the school choir and sometimes they would give him a solo. That was as near as I saw him happy. He was such a lovely lad, a bit cissified but not a cissy. His father had him working in the back of that butcher's shop from the moment he left school. With his voice he should have been trained. We were in the same form at the national school, and on the last day of term Miss Tate would ask him to sing and he'd be off like a lark. Christmas was perfect for him, although they spoiled him. He got too many presents. We got an orange and a sixpence. He got toys. Nobody minded save him. He wanted us to share them. Even as a boy he had that lonely streak in him and he wanted to be part of the rest. He could see that all his presents set him apart . . . He never seemed to have anybody special. He would sing or whistle as he walked. People did in those days.'

Kenneth was rather short, with a bush of curly black hair, a pale face, rather podgy, and a mouth seeking out a smile, hoping it would be returned. My mother always smiled a little sadly when she talked about Kenneth. 'Tucked away in the freezing back of that shop, chopping up those carcasses. I'm sure he didn't like it but he wouldn't complain. He wouldn't be allowed to. I think he sang a solo once, when he was in his early twenties, at Carlisle covered market in a county choir competition. Wigton won a prize through him, and the write-up in the *Carlisle Journal* said he had "a voice to match the great Joseph Locke". He carried that mention around with him, I believe, in his wallet. Some of the lads were inclined to make fun of him. He was so serious about it. Most of all he liked songs from operas; he would try to explain them first before singing them. He had been given a gramophone when he was a boy and there was a second-hand shop in Carlisle that sold the records he liked.'

Kenneth used to hang around the Singing Room in the pub on Friday or Saturday nights. It was one of the few dedicated Singing Rooms in the town. There was a piano, which Geoffrey, who worked as a clerk in the council, would play. It was agreed that he was very good but he tended to get carried away with his chords and elaborations, which could leave people behind. He seemed to be using it for practice. His boyhood interest in the piano had lapsed and the company in the pub got him back to it. But it didn't last. A two- or, on Saturdays, a three-hour stint was too much, even though the money was handy.

Jack Atkinson took over with his accordion. Jack, self-taught, had a gift for the buttons and keyboard of the hefty squeezebox he slung across his chest. The way he could pick out a tune sometimes after no more than a few bars being hummed or whisperingly sung never ceased to be admired.

He sat on the piano stool. The piano lid, shut, was a useful shelf for drinks. Frances, a friend of my mother's since they had been in the Guides together, was the waitress for that room. Single, quite large, buoyant, the Friday and Saturday nights gave her a social life.

The room was full by about eight o'clock. There would be a few like Kenneth hanging around in the corridor, leaning against the railings of the staircase to our flat. These were barred at the bottom by a small wooden gate, not locked, merely snecked. As the evening drew on, the Singing Room could become so packed that Frances had some difficulty threading her way through, the tray held high. 'Excuse me, please. Excuse me, gentlemen, please.' A bit like a refrain of whatever song was being sung.

What most liked best were songs that all of them knew. Scottish airs, Irish ballads, songs from the war and from school, even the occasional hymn if it had some 'go' in it, and songs of the day – 'Cruising Down The River', 'If I Was A Blackbird' (which gave some men the opportunity to show off their whistling) – picked up from the wireless. But the old ones always turned up trumps. 'Over The Sea To Skye', 'Loch Lomond', 'Galway Bay', 'I'll Take You Home Again, Kathleen', especially when the Irish lads were in, 'Tipperary', 'Bobby Shaftoe', 'Coming Round The Mountain'. 'Abide With Me' near the end, if church men were in. When the Robinson brothers were there it would be 'The Two Wigton Mashers', 'The Horn Of The Huntsman' and 'John Peel' as a rouser, punctuated with loud 'Halloos!'. There were Al Jolsons, especially 'April Showers' and 'Swanee', other songs from American films, 'Singin' In The Rain', 'Don't Eat The Daisies', and old tub thumpers 'I've Got A Loverly Bunch of Coconuts', tear jerkers – 'We'll Meet Again', 'The White Cliffs of Dover'. Out they all rolled. It was endless, this flow of song from the Singing Room.

The singing would often draw me to look over the banisters. Kenneth would hover just outside the door, nervous, even a little frightened, waiting for something to tell him it was his moment. He was careful not to turn up every Saturday, but when he did come he would stand outside the Singing Room door grasping his half of mild, and people passing by him would say, 'Giving us a song tonight, Kenneth?' and 'What you got for us tonight, Kenneth?' My mother would come out of the bar and by her mere presence reassure him, take his glass, shepherd him into the room when there was a pause, while Jack put down his accordion, drank some of his Guinness and lit a cigarette.

Kenneth, still suffering from a hornet's nest of nerves, would go in and make his way across to Jack, who liked him, which settled him.

'What's it to be? "Danny Boy" or "Violetta"?' ' "Violetta".'

Jack nodded, put his glass on the piano, drew out the accordion and played a few introductory chords, which brought some hush.

Then Kenneth's nerves fled. He planted himself next to Jack, his gaze set just above the thirty or more people now poised to hear him as they had heard and appreciated him before. He paused and then he began.

His voice was sweet, soaring, and powerful, a tenor unstrained and untrained, something pure about it as he made the song his own and took over the room. The other rooms quietened down while Kenneth sang. There was in him the gift to make many of the customers feel good about themselves, and the simple melody sung with such unselfconscious passion reached into them. Applause came from all the rooms in the pub and he looked at his audience, or rather he blinked awake and saw them and his smile was itself worth waiting for.

Now and then somebody would say, 'Give us your "Ave Maria", Kenneth. Give us "Ave Maria".'

And he did. Whenever he did, Ethel would again come to the door to listen more closely. Stillness spread through the pub. People listened intently. And when he finished, high, long drawn-out, perfect in volume and pitch, there were cheers.

Then, he knew, his time was up. He would seek out my mother. 'Was it all right, Ethel?'

'You were very good, Kenneth. Better than some that have been trained.'

'Are you sure, Ethel?'

'I'm sure, Kenneth.'

Then she went back into the bar.

He would be too fired up to stay and take up the offers of a drink. After a few minutes he would leave and go the long way home, down the hill and turn into the Shade Walk, a lane that led to the West Cumberland Farmers and then trickled between the allotments and one of the narrow rivers that flowed through the town. It would take him home with the guarantee of meeting no one, being so late, dark or sometimes under moonlit star-speckled skies. In front of him was the factory throbbing work, lit up against the night like a pleasure cruiser.

'Violetta' and 'Ave Maria' and their reception at the pub rang through his head, like bells chiming out his triumph. He hummed them, whispered them and finally, when he came to the stretch of lane between Toppin's Field and the field in which the Wigton Harriers played their football, he could be sure that he was safe. Unable to contain himself, once again, and in full voice, he sang 'Violetta' and 'Ave Maria' to the fields and to the sky. The men going to and fro from the factory would smile and pass it on – 'Kenneth was singing to himself again, in the dark.'

His voice was full of joy. The songs soared. In that freedom and solitude he sang for the love of singing and found his audience in the cosmic amphitheatre.

Chapter Sixteen

We would get tea out of the way and the kitchen tidied up before opening time at five thirty. Tea was the big meal. We all three, or four, depending on Andrew's shift, would sit down together. Breakfast and dinner were a relay.

Until my father had saved enough money to install a kitchen upstairs, we made do for our own use as well as the customers' with what we'd found in the pub kitchen. A big wooden table, four wooden chairs, a few old easy chairs, the fire with an oven beside it and, just off the kitchen, a pantry that would have suited a small boat. Two was a crowd. A sink, corner shelves for crockery and tins of things, and the cooker.

The old kitchen had its own distinct clientele. Harry Crookhall's wife Lily and her mother set a style matched by Mrs Hill, who was the housekeeper for Wigton Hall and came down through the town on Saturday and Sunday evenings to take 'her' seat beside the fire and drink port and lemon. Lily Crookhall and Mrs Hill were out of the ordinary in a pub such as the Black-A-Moor. You would have expected them to make for the Crown or even the Crown and Mitre. Harry brought them in.

Harry was well off, a successful accountant, permanently cheerful. I don't know why or how he landed in our pub, but he was a fixture from early on. He would hang his jacket on a peg next to the clock in the bar, reveal a fresh shirt with arm bands and gold-looking cuff links and dive in. He would take no pay. He came on Friday and Saturday nights. He liked to work in the bar and was quite happy to be in charge of washing, drying, cleaning and polishing the used glasses, which came in increasing numbers on those two evenings. My father liked to get to the heart of people, what made them tick. But Harry was a puzzle. He could and did work the pumps and serve the customers, but the role he had cast for himself was of being helpful while his wife and her mother drank safely in good company in the next room.

Lily, Wigton born and bred, was always done up to the nines, a magnificent arrangement of blonde hair, perfect make-up and perhaps most surprising of all, given her looks and Harry's means, as pleasant and easygoing a woman as you could hope to meet.

Her mother – who had also been born in the town – had married a successful grocer and been comfortably widowed for more than ten years. She was still handsome and mischievous, never backward in coming forward in any chat or chaffing. They had their regular seats and their regular drinks: sweet sherry for Lily, Tio Pepe for her mother. They neither offered to buy drinks for others nor accepted offers of drinks being bought for them. Both of them smoked du Maurier. People looked forward to seeing them.

Mrs Hill was enigmatic. Nobody knew whether there was a Mr Hill. Wigton Hall was the grandest house of the town. Early Victorian with Tudor references, walled garden, lawns, fruit, orchards, a cottage for the gardener. Mr Mumdio lived there. He managed and had substantial shares in the Rayophone factory, which seemed to resist recession mainly, the workers thought, because of low pay, no unions and the lack of competing jobs in the town.

He was a magnificent-looking man, especially for a town in which so many of the working men were of average or below average height. While the more prosperous dressed and comported themselves conventionally, Mr Mumdio, well over six feet, shoulders always thrown back, was beautifully booted and suited, no great mixer, kept himself to himself, save for the wealthy cronies with whom he went to stay. They would come to the Hall for dinner. He was best known for an illegitimate son in the town, every bit as tall and vivid as he was, wholly unacknowledged. Unperturbed, he walked through the town like its emperor.

Mrs Hill, always dressed in dark colours, a bit prim, fingers carrying two or sometimes three rings on each hand, small, slim, a woman not to be taken lightly, but as the evening wore on she loosened up, told stories, even bought drinks for her favourites. But not to be escorted. She walked home alone.

There was a bookie who made the kitchen his port of call and sat beside Mrs Hill; there was Sheddy Pape who kept the paint shop in New Street and had been my father's best man; Ronnie the barber came when he felt fit enough to manage it. Strangers would gravitate towards it as the friendliest, least demanding room, and perhaps there was something about it that still carried the character of the time when the kitchen was the hub of the place, when business was less busy. Sometimes, on a quiet night, the Robinsons would come in bringing a domino board with them. My grandfather, who had stopped drinking when he moved to Wigton – too expensive, the pubs too far from home – would put on his suit and hat on Sunday nights and walk the mile or so through the town to enjoy the crack and the two or three free bottles of stout provided by his son. Cathy, who had worked at the factory with my mother, was the waitress for the kitchen. She was single and, like my mother, she was teetotal. From life with her parents in a religiously minded house, the pub was a blessed release. She particularly liked to listen to the gossip from Mrs Hill, with her edited tales of the doings in Wigton Hall. It also attracted Bert Toppin, a butcher and Wigton farmer who had had his eye on Cathy for some years.

After the Coronation, when television came in, my father put one in a corner above the sofa. It was only on in pub hours through the week, if requested. Never in the evening at weekends.

It was the last pub in Wigton to retain a kitchen in fact and in name. The Crown and Mitre had a saloon bar, as had one or two others. The Crown had a private bar, the Kildare had a lounge bar. My mother liked 'the kitchen' and resisted any attempt to change the name.

On weekday afternoons after tidying up, she would sit on a small stool in front of the fire and go through *Woman's Own* and *Woman's Illustrated* carefully. She was wrapped up in the lives of blameless, handsome doctors, nurses, lawyers, bankers, the boxes of chocolates, the neatly turned stories, which always ended blissfully and chastely. Or she would use the pub kitchen (before the Great Leap Upstairs) to talk when someone dropped by for tea, just as if it were a normal room. On nights when trade was light, she would join the few in the kitchen and feel at home. She made the kitchen serve her.

She had settled in. Against expectation. She had followed Stan's wishes. To her surprise, the fears she thought she might have at such public exposure were not difficult to beat away. Although she had only rarely and rather awkwardly visited pubs, the fact that this was equally her home and full of Wigton people gave her the confidence she needed. Stan said that from the beginning. 'The lettering on the door says my name only but that's what the Brewery demands. It's fifty-fifty. It's ours: we both work here.' And the kitchen soon became as comfortable as your old shoe.

She blossomed. For it was here also that the full impact of all the friendships and connections she had made so disinterestedly along the way was felt. Stanley would say, 'It's Ethel they come to see,' and smile, his head inclined a little to one side, the smile that brought out the best in him, she thought, the smile that made her smile back. Because, although she would never admit it, she began to see that it was true. It added to her sense of being part of the place and she would think of this, secretly to herself, and enjoy the pleasure it brought her.

It was 'Ethel and Stan's'. Her old girlfriends and work friends would drop in to this oddity of a kitchen either between opening hours or at a quiet time, just to be comfortable in her place. Her looks helped her. There was extra for a new dress now and then, for regular visits to the hairdresser and time to make up before she went downstairs to serve in the pub. Every day was to some degree a look-your-best day and it suited her.

In the afternoon, when her friends came, she did not offer drinks. She would make a pot of tea and there would be biscuits, scones, maybe a cake. It was all ordinary. Just ordinary. As near as 'just like everybody else' as she would ever get. She blossomed.

When Mrs Askew – who had lived three doors up from her in that first year in Union Street – mentioned that she was looking for someone to take over the Christmas Club, my mother, to her own surprise, said that if no one else could be found she would do it.

It was a pernickety job. People contributed as much as they could afford every week – from a shilling to, at tops, half a crown. This was entered in a book and signed by the giver and the recipient – in this case my mother. Two weeks before Christmas this was totted up and presents were selected from a Gift List provided by the operating company to whom my mother had regularly sent her accounts. Sometimes I went with her on her rounds.

We went into houses, lit by gaslight after dark, often cosy. There was talk of the town, while I looked around or played with the children in the other room or just sat and listened as my mother enjoyed a brief encounter. I remember nothing self-pitying. Even when the conversation could be a roll call of ailments. On the whole, over many generations these people had made the best of meagre pickings and rare opportunities and out of them constructed a world well set in friendship and stoicism.

Over the years my mother became something of a messenger, through the twisting alleys, into the small yards, patient as arthritic fingers ratched in a purse for the coins, having to go against her nature and refuse hospitality 'or I'll never get round everybody.' She carried notes or verbal messages from one to another. It could have been awkward, but she took to it.

More unexpectedly, she agreed to be treasurer of the recently formed Labour Party. Wigton was in a rural constituency in which the Tories fought the Liberals, while Labour kept out of it and built up its base on the industrial west coast. The post-war Labour government, led by Clement Attlee, had embraced nationalisation and set up the National Health Service, which declared that all citizens of whatever age or background would be given medical care, freely, wherever they were, 'from the cradle to the grave'. This miraculous creation with one bound prised the condition of the majority of people out of a near-medieval medical dependency.

Mrs Bell had approached her. She was the chairman of the Party. She was married to a postman who kept a flock of geese in a garden beside their cottage down a lane opposite the cemetery. Mrs Bell was the supervisor of school dinners in the two large prefabricated huts that served the schools – save the Catholics, who made their own arrangements. She was large, always well dressed, cheerfully acknowledged to be 'bossy but fair' and an entertaining contrast to her rather modest husband, whose life was spent on parcels, letters, fattening his geese and growing basic vegetables for the table. He would deliver occasional songs or monologues on socialism at the meetings.

Mrs Bell came clean about her dilemma. No one else was up for being the treasurer. Handling other people's money was too much of a worry. There would be subscriptions, payments for the use of the Temperance Hall for meetings and, as time went on, all manner of payments to be correctly sorted out.

'You run the Christmas Club,' said Mrs Bell, beaming across the kitchen table where they met for the showdown after closing time one Wednesday afternoon. After a well-pitched paean to the virtues of the Labour Party, Mrs Bell continued, 'You're in a responsible position in this public house. Everybody knows you.' She took a bite of the lemon sponge cake and a sip of tea. 'You're not sure? It's going to be a new world, Ethel. A whole new world! Will you join us? We need a thriving Labour Party in Wigton.'

It was not easy. She had always voted for the Liberal candidate, as Stanley had done . . . But it was different now, surely, since the war, since the National Health. Mrs Bell's invitation had forced her to think.

She was stirred by the idea of a New World. Although she had friends of all political persuasions and none, although she bore no resentment whatsoever towards the wealthy Mrs Cavaghan, and although her best friend Mary Price, and others she met in the cycling club and around the place, came from Conservative-voting families, and she would never dream of taking against them one iota for that, there was rooted in her heart a conviction that everyone should be given an equal chance in life, that no one should suffer ill health because of a lack of money, above all that ordinary people should have their 'say'. Mrs Bell had found a source of conviction that had often been acted on but rarely declared. Now, for reasons she had not faced up to before, my mother found that the answer was already formed . . . but one final question.

'Do you think I can do it?'

'I have not the slightest doubt.'

Ethel nodded and smiled, a little, not entirely comfortable with the compliment.

'Thank you.' Mrs Bell's relief was undisguised.

'Now then. This kitchen,' said Mrs Bell, scanning it approvingly, 'could be the perfect place for our committee meetings. I know that the Temperance Hall will give us the space for the more general meetings but *this* would be just right for the five of us on the committee. There's you,' she nodded at Ethel, to be sure, 'John Housby, Freeman Robinson, Jamie Holliday . . . he's deputy chairman . . . and me.'

Ethel took her time. 'Does it have to be every week?'

'No – once a fortnight at the very most. For between one and two hours.'

Ethel allowed a pause to grow.

'My own house is too far away from the town.'

'I understand.'

'John works from home mainly and hates any disturbance.'

'Yes.'

'Jamie?'

'Jamie's house is too small . . . and then the children . . . same with Freeman. So that just leaves you.' Mrs Bell's tone switched to bright and businesslike.

Ethel hesitated. 'There's Stan to consider.' As there was no response, she went on, 'He doesn't encourage political talk in the pub. Are you sure there's nowhere else?'

'Sure.' Mrs Bell was not prepared to make a concession at this stage.

'I'll talk to him. I can't commit until I've talked it through with him.'

Mrs Bell nodded, not trusting herself to question why a husband ought to be consulted. She herself never did.

Ethel laid it out after closing time when just Stan and she were in the kitchen, tea, a sandwich.

'What makes you want to do it?' was his first question.

'I don't know,' she said. 'Except that I know I want to.'

'It could make things awkward.'

'I can see that.'

She sat on the small stool in front of the fire, looking at the embering of the coals, nestling her cup of tea in both hands. 'I'd like to do this, Stan.'

He lit up another cigarette.

She had not asked him for much. And she had not objected to the pub. She worked seven days every week, largely out of sync with the lives of her friends. She made no complaints.

From their early days she had shone for him: the mixture of wariness and boldness, the challenge and the armour. She could be so lovely when she let herself go. Her smile could rock him. But he had realised early on that it was partly because he was an outsider that she inclined to him, that and the family he brought in tow, a family housed and openly interconnected as family should be. Before long they had started going steady. He thought he had made an enviable conquest.

As he looked down on her, crouched over the last warmth from the day's fire, intent, it seemed, on the glances of flame, her back to him, absorbed in the moment, he felt a surge of friendship and love for her.

She had always been an attractive girl and young woman but it had been coloured by a little nervousness, provoking but aloof. Now, in her early thirties, a sureness had emerged. Her hair was still dark, her features slimmed down from the early days of their courtship. High cheekbones, dark brown eyes like his own, the pale skin and a smile that broke through any defence. He felt lucky, which he did not express often enough, proud to be with her, which he did not express at all in words and would not do so now.

'I suppose I could argue that there are two kitchens,' Stan said. It amused him that on such a subject he was talking to the back of her head. 'This is a licensed kitchen in opening hours. Then it's our own kitchen outside opening hours . . . I could argue that a private meeting was nobody's business but our own; I can see no objection to that part of it. If some of them objected to it being the Labour Party we would lose a few customers . . . but it's our own business who we have around out of hours. Do you think they could come soon after three o'clock closing and be done at five at the latest, giving us half an hour to tidy up for opening?' She was silent. His words were like a spell that must not be broken. He continued, 'John works from home, doesn't he? He could make the space for a meeting out of hours here if he wanted to. Freeman and Jamie will be on shifts at the factory, but you could work around the shifts. Mrs Bell would always be there! And you wouldn't have far to go, would you?'

She turned her head and, after a moment, gave him a most beautiful smile. He felt like a king.

Some years later, with pride, he told me how he had fixed it.

Chapter Seventeen

My father liked to gamble. Cards, dominoes, horses, football –
with the coupons regularly checked out against the results on a
Saturday afternoon at 5 p.m. – and dogs.

As far as I was aware he rarely if ever punted more than he
could afford to lose. But, still, it's a fair bet that he lost more
than he won. Having been a part-time bookie he would know
that. It didn't stop him.

It spiced up his day. It seemed the key to a fantasy of riches,
though I'm not sure about that. He did it for the love of doing
it. To beat the system. He believed that if he studied form closely
enough and exercised his own mathematical method, it would
come right. When it failed he would retrace his steps to work
out where he had miscalculated or, more usually, find excuses –
the unfavourable drop of the dominoes, a disappointing cut of
the cards, soft going at Kempton Park, ground too hard at
Cheltenham, loss of form on the football pitch or by a jockey,
unexpected emergence of a new 'flier' at the dogs. He knew that
chance was the greatest enemy but he thought he could beat it.

My father almost always appeared calm and relaxed. People
took to his easygoing character, his unassertive ability to take
up a conversation with all comers. Yet, when gambling, he was
rarely far from intense, with his calculations of each-way bets,
doubles, without three, the miraculous picking of a triumphant
outsider . . .

Hounds gave his gambling habit and his love of sport most of
the play it needed. These were trail hounds, bred off hunting
dogs but leaner, faster, bred for speed. Depending on age and
gender they would cover five to ten miles of high fell country in

a circuit laid down by two trailers, each one leading a bundle of rags, a drag scent of paraffin and aniseed, which inspired the dogs to chase it as if it were a fox. The men who laid down the scent for the trail would meet miles out in the country and each took on half the course with one of them finally approaching the slip at the starting line when anything up to forty or fifty dogs would be held by their collars, already breathing in the toxic scent, barking, straining, howling to go. They could be followed by the human eye for some distance and then by binoculars as they scaled the sides of steep fells, leaped over stone walls and gates, and soon thinned out to a string of hounds on the horizon, racing at an unbelievable pace, like mythical animals pursuing the invisible.

The meets would begin in the fields of supportive farmers. As well as the dogs there would be the bookies chalking the names and the odds on their boards, calling them out in a continuous patter. There would be a van with tea and sandwiches. That was it. In the middle of what a stranger might describe as 'nowhere'. To the hound men these fells, wide open but complex, were a prize in themselves: cherished.

Hound trailing was strongest in the north-west of England's fell lands in Cumberland and Westmorland, with a dip into Lancashire, and a slender reach across the border into Scotland and over to Northumberland. It was a sport for working people, men and women. Some called it 'the poor man's horseracing'.

All you needed was a dog. Many working people kept a dog and so to keep a trail hound was not an excessive cost. The feeding might be a bit above normal. They were amiable creatures. Standing on their hind legs and putting their paws onto the shoulders of their masters they could easily reach five feet or more. They needed a brisk walk of a few miles most days.

The organisation of these meets was not easy. It depended on widespread goodwill. A number of farmers had to give their permission for the trails to go across their fields. Sheep, horses and cattle had to be cleared away, farms had to be adjoining so that a continuous trail could be laid. On the main field where the meet was held, tracks had to be available for cars and vans. These and other necessities had to be negotiated by volunteers every time. There were rosettes for the first six over the line, certificates, modest prize money, and the local paper lassoed in to supply coverage.

The hounds were celebrated among their owners and the devoted number of admirers. League tables were published in the *Cumberland News*. The feats of stars – Black Diamond and Perivale – attracted weekly publicity. To be the owner of a winning dog was someone to be. The owner, who could be a labourer, a brickie, a farmer's wife or daughter, glowed as the big red rosette was pinned to the collar and led around the winner's ring. Dog talk was good.

The thrill was in the finish. The course would have been chosen so that the leading dogs would be in full view over the last mile. They would gallop furiously down a steep fell or gasp up from a valley. As soon as the owners saw them, their whistles would begin to blow, the names of the dogs were called out, howled out, flung through the air to pull their dog to the finishing line, shrill even shrieking excitement ringing around the fells.

It was an exhilarating cacophony. But inside the noise were thirty or forty individual whistles, calls, tones, each clearly aimed at one of the dogs. Not entirely unlike an orchestra tuning up. It is a marvel that such a wall of noise could be so individuated and that such a crowd of people at the finishing line could sustain the link between themselves and a tired dog, who had spent so many miles chasing an imaginary fox.

The first six seized the glory of the rosettes and the prize money, but after them . . . the gaps would grow between the finishers, some too tired, some that would never win. They trickled in, as still the whistles blew, names were called out, though fewer and fewer until only one or two were left and then no dogs came and their owners set out across country to bring them home.

The problem for many of the hound men in Wigton – which was a thriving centre for the sport – was transport. Just a few miles could be biked or walked. A lift from the few cars in the town able to house a lean, large hound was not common. The local taxi might be shared and cram in three or four at a pinch. But it was costly.

My father decided to lay on a bus. There were two single-decker buses in private ownership in the town, which could carry up to thirty with dogs.

He talked to them, talked to the hound men, worked out how many passengers they needed to make the job worth their while, did his calculations and arrived at a viable average that would benefit the coach owner and be within the means of these men. If, over a month, the coach people were out of pocket, he made up the difference. It rarely came to that but it closed the deal. It was not without risk but he took it and after the first year it was self-financing. He paid himself no fee.

When there was a profit he put the money into the Wigton Hound Trailing Association fund. The extra trade in the pub from these buses was modest. Some of the men would drop in for a drink beforehand. Mostly they collected together at the far end of Market Hill waiting for their bus and, when it returned, led the dogs back through the town to their kennels.

Dad seemed to see it as an obligation. He liked these people. He enjoyed organising. The finicky listings of who could or could not come, for example, did not drive him mad.

For every week he had to let all the trail men know which meet they were headed for, sign up a number of sure customers, tell them the times of departure and return and set the fare dependent on the distance.

In the late mornings, when the bar was empty, he was happy to stand there, cigarette coiling and wasting into smoke between the index and middle fingers. After placing his bets on the horses, he would work out the numbers for the Hound Trail Bus, making allowance for the inevitable percentage who would fall away and counting on those who never signed up but always came along at the last minute. With the hounds, he was in among it, part of it, listening to the owners, learning every step of the dogs' progress, sympathising and, soon, being asked for advice, because they knew he remembered things. At one stage he owned two hounds. Neither won a thing.

The Vaults was the pub of the pigeon men, where the clock was kept into which was fed the arrival times of these amazing long-distance homing pigeons; the Lion and Lamb was the pub of Carlisle United, which played in the Third Division North. It too laid on a coach for home and away games on Saturdays. The Crown and the Crown and Mitre drew in the farmers, especially on auction and market days, and when there was a dance on in the Market Hall nearby. The Crown specialised in 'lock-ins', for which the owner, a former policeman, was never bothered by the law. The British Legion – a sort of pub by night time – was the place for snooker and billiards. The Blue Bell had a big yard where farm labourers from the countryside could park their bikes and the decent thing was to have one or two drinks there to start off the evening. There was a period when the football team changed in the back room of the Station Hotel. The Kildare was for the better-off, and unless you were at some point in the proceedings going to switch to shorts – whisky, gin, sherry, rum – you could feel out of place. And the Blackie – as the Black-A-Moor Hotel was often referred to – sometimes even two early evenings a week as well as on Saturday afternoon in season, was where the men with the hounds congregated, walking to the pub through the streets and lanes, with their prized hounds on a short lead and a thick leather collar – the dogs were strong and took some holding. The men moved through the town to join a posse of like-minded men, plainly and warmly dressed against the weather in well-worn, battered clothes, buoyed by the baying of their hounds, spurred on by dreams of glory.

Chapter Eighteen

Fights just broke out. One minute there would be singing, then a crash as glasses hit the floor and chairs turned over and two men would be at each other. Poor nutrition, the sudden fast intake of alcohol, festering grudges, old rivalries, honour – a frenzy of fury given its chance, or badness for no reason, but the need to hit out.

They had to be cleared out quickly without the fight spreading to other rooms. Dad would be out of the bar, Jack Waters first there from the Darts Room; one or two others helped, steering the men into the narrow passage – still flailing – Dad trying to talk them down, 'Now then, lads, there's no need for that', and with Jack Waters pushing them towards the front door. Heave! Heave! 'Come on now, lads – outside – come on now, lads.' Push them out, tumble down the steps into the street, door slammed, locked.

The sound of drunken men at each other could be frightening. That my mother might be involved . . . But my father locked the bar having shepherded Frances and Cathy in to join my mother.

I tried to control it. I would be reading in bed or listening to the wireless. The weekend noise, especially on Saturdays, could shake the place, but the sound of a fight was always distinctive and I would jump out of bed.

The top landing led down with six steps to the hairpin bend, eleven steps further down into the pub. That was all lit up. The landing steps would stay in the dark unless I switched on the lights, which I never did.

My voodoo (while I was hanging over the banister to watch it all) was that if I went up the six steps the fighting would subside.

If, as often happened, it broke out again into a second or third phase with people getting really hurt, then I would have to go down the six steps and start again. It was shocking as well as frightening. It seized me in a spasm of helplessness. Would they lay into my father and mother?

Up and down; fixed on the fight; blood, swearing; wanting so much for it to be over that it was beyond prayer.

Suddenly they were outside.

There were two streetlights opposite the pub, one on Market Hill, the other on the road to the baths. I'd run back into my room and draw open the curtains. There was enough light to watch them hammer away, encircled by a small group who had nipped out to be close, nine or ten of them. It was still frightening, still shocking, but at a distance a spectator sport.

The external noises were curses and gasps. Inside the Singing Room Jack was immediately back on his accordion. Dad was pulling pints. My mother, Frances and Cathy were in among the customers, pretending all was well. My mother hated it.

It took about two years for my father to clear the pub of these Saturday-night brawls. The Blackie was not uniquely targeted, but for a while it was the most vulnerable, partly because there was something of the last-stop saloon about it – post Blackie and on the way to the East End there were no more pubs. That gave it an edge. The buses swept into Market Hill just opposite and thirsty punters who had come to sample Wigton's celebrated range of pubs often went to the Black-A-Moor for their first drink and would return for their last before the bus back.

The Wigton attitude to strangers was polarised. Most customers welcomed the fresh blood. Some strongly resented this invasion of another tribe. Most resented were those from the city of Carlisle, ten miles away, whose pubs by some quirk had been taken over by the government in the war and, uniquely in the United Kingdom, were state-controlled. This had two consequences: the beer was well maintained and rather cheaper, and the pubs were generally thought to be dull and characterless.

Wigton lured men from Carlisle with reports of singing and, at weekends, the Good Times when you could skip from one pub a few yards along to the next up King Street and along the High Street.

The most violent Carlisle fight in our pub began in the Darts Room where a Wigton regular took exception to a pair of Carlisle men who had appropriated the seats of himself and his pal while they had gone out to the backyard lavatory. Jack Waters told my father that he had had his eye on these two boyos from the start. Big lads, 'They were full of themselves,' he said in the kitchen later, after the pub had closed and they had settled down for a round-up of the night. I had come downstairs by then in pyjamas and dressing-gown to join them and listen. It was allowed because of what had happened. 'One of them said something,' said Jack. 'He had taken offence to being asked to give up his seat. Then all hell broke loose.'

As time went on and these events recurred, though with lessening regularity, there was no pattern. It could be offence at the way one man was judged to be looking at another man's wife or friend. It could be 'language'. 'Language' in front of women was rarely pardoned, and 'We'll have none of that', 'Who are you telling?', 'We'll have none of that here.' 'Why don't you f——k off!' That was enough. Either in the room itself, or in the narrow corridor to the backyard, there could be a mere brushing of arms, a clumsy attempt to get past someone, and——! A hard look, a misinterpreted shrug, an indisputable slight, sometimes a straight challenge – 'I'll see you outside.' Honour!

On that night Jack had tackled the Carlisle lads and somehow pulled them, with a bit of help, and pushed them into the corridor. Dad had come out of the bar and they had begun to eff and blind. One of them swiped at Dad and caught him smack in the right eye. Dad went for him but Jack pulled him back. The same man tried to get behind the bar where Ethel, Cathy and Frances were. Jack, who had been following the usual 'heave-ho' tactic, went mad. He pummelled and heaved them violently to the front door, followed by my father, who ignored Jack's shout – 'You stay inside!' – as he tumbled out with the two of them into the rain. My father went after him but by that time Jack was across the road on Market Hill itself, knocking 'ten bells' out of them both. 'It was,' said my father later, appreciatively, nursing his eye, 'a thing of beauty. A sight to behold. He felled them.'

Both the Carlisle men retreated. One of them shouted, 'We'll be back next week!'

'Good,' said Jack. 'And don't forget!' He watched them limp away, came back to the door and said, 'Ethel all right?' She put a bandage ('It's nothing') around the bleeding knuckles of his right hand. He accepted a whisky and ginger from my father to go with his habitual free drink, which was a half of porter, and, after the round-up in the kitchen, got his bike from under the shed for the two miles back to Micklethwaite, the road ahead barely illuminated in the sluicing rain by the small yellow battery light between the handlebars.

There were men who went out looking for a fight and invariably found one. Usually at the dance after the pubs had closed, but often enough in the pubs themselves. Some battles were in the backyard, way beyond throwing out, and they could be serious. Never knives but everything else. Some when rival families happened to hit the same pub after first drinking elsewhere. Almost always Saturday nights when there was money still left from Friday's pay packet and, for most, no work in the morning. Some came to the boil after simmering all week in the factory, on the building site, or in the house – it could be brother against brother – powered by too much alcohol and in some cases years of generational violence inside the family, boasting of it, 'hard' families. They knew the magistrates well.

Some pubs rarely saw violence at all, because the tone and class of the pub made it clear that it did not welcome the poorer, rougher, aggressively roving elements, or because they had been barred. Being barred was the way that landlords policed their clientele. It was not an easy transaction, as my father found.

Those who had been thrown out on a Saturday night came around on Sunday morning smack on opening time, twelve noon. One or two of them would have been to church, some still heavily hung-over, others had scrubbed up and bitten through a raw onion. These instant penitents were uniformly sorry, did not know what had got into them, it'll never happen again, Stan, no offence. They would stand at the half loose-box door into the corridor – taking advantage of the zero or low turnout in the pub at twelve noon on a Sunday – and mutter their excuses and apologies. I would watch and listen over the banisters unseen. Some of these were the town's toughest characters. Some of them asked to see Ethel, who knew their mothers. Dad would have none of it. He had worked out the sentence. He was very patient, and polite, and used their Christian names.

He explained his policy: a two-months bar for being reluctantly involved. A three-months bar for starting it. A six-months bar for starting it, foul language and trying to stir up a riot.

Most finally accepted, which was not to say that they would not be back in a Sunday or two to plead their cause once again. Some were threatening. Dad always seemed easy in himself. Smoking, talking quietly and explaining why he'd had to do it. He knew they would change, he said, in time. I never saw him being attacked on a Sunday morning but now and then I felt it was a close thing.

I followed every moment of that Jack Waters fight. It stood out. By then I carried an old walking stick, which was partly a weapon and partly had a magical function. As the noise swelled, I believed I could judge whether it was to be a violent night. If I moved the walking stick up to the top of those six steps then, despite the loud shouting and singing below, this would indicate a fight-free night. When the noise grew, as I thought, threatening, and Jack would leave the Darts Room to help Frances in the Singing Room, then the stick would come down the six stairs nearer to possible action, possibly preparing for action but most of all in some magical way, I believed, averting any uproar. Then when Dad called, 'Last orders, gentlemen, please. Last orders, please,' and finally 'Time, gentlemen, please. Time, please,' I could just about relax and, after a few more minutes to make sure, go back to bed to read, to listen to the wireless. There were times, many times in the early months before my father cleared the pub, when I was eight or nine, when I was blank with fear about what 'they' would do. And I was rightly afraid of what one or two of them might do to me when I was walking up the street. 'Tell your father.' A threat.

As time went by and the pub's reputation for intolerance grew, gradually disorder diminished. I think I quite liked the subterranean noise, but only quite. Saturday night was a time for me to get out.

When they discussed the fights, especially of Wigton men against each other, it was my mother, tense, sipping a Britvic orange juice, who led the apologists. 'They're good enough lads, underneath all that,' she would say. 'They've never had anything.'

The gathering was against her.

'That's no excuse.'

'That's just an excuse.'

'He's nasty, Ethel. He's just nasty.'

My mother would let that point of view roll in – 'Bred in them', 'Only way is to lock them up', 'Bring back hard labour.' Then she responded.

'That would only make it worse,' she said. She would glance at Cathy and Frances, who were not keen to join in. Jack Atkinson, more often than not the key witness from his pivotal seat with the accordion in the Singing Room, could contribute effectively but he was not on her side.

'It isn't always their fault,' she maintained. 'Some of them have this reputation and there's them will goad them. Take them on and be a hero. Maybe most lads have come in for a quiet night but they don't get a chance.'

'Two onto one and using their feet?'

'They get plenty of chances but they won't take them,' said Jack Atkinson. 'Reggie is just vicious.'

'They can't always be in the wrong,' my mother said firmly. 'His mother couldn't be nicer. She's had to bring them up in a place not fit to live in.'

'Others manage.'

'But there's good in some of these lads,' my mother would say this quietly, rather desperately, wanting those around her to believe what she so strongly believed to be true. 'There's good in them. It just has to be found.'

Perhaps there was a silence or my father would find a diversionary tactic to take his wife out of what could become a firing line. The talk would move on.

My father followed boxing. In Carlisle covered market there was boxing once a month on a Monday night and we rarely missed it. My cousin Geoff would often come along. He was the oldest of five boys, had been trained locally as a boxer – as a lightweight, never beaten at his own weight – left school at fifteen to work for a builder and later spent a couple of years extra to his national service in the RAF. Dad was very fond of him, particularly his pluck, a sense of fearlessness and the way he laughed any troubles away. Geoff and myself would put on the boxing gloves (training gloves, big puffy things, soft as pillows). He was a couple of years older and it was no contest but he let me down lightly, swaying away, stepping aside as I slung useless hooks and jabs that rarely landed. On the boxing Mondays we would get the money for a bag of monkey nuts at Ivinson's, catch the bus to Carlisle and come back talking of nothing but boxing and home to bed, head to toe in my single, Geoff up early to catch the first bus to his home village six miles away.

Sometimes Dad and I would stay up until two or three in the morning to hear a particularly important fight from America – especially one featuring Joe Louis or any British fighters. One Monday Randolph Turpin came to Carlisle as part of an exhibition tour when he was middleweight champion of the world. He had beaten the glamorous Sugar Ray Robinson against all odds.

We fought in the streets, we fought in the fields, we fought in the playgrounds. You never surrendered. At the infants school, Scopie Alison was cock of the walk, and in my last year I was encouraged to take him on. Scopie was one of four brothers, all of whom were to play rugby for the town, and it was easy to refuse though difficult to make it seem that I wasn't chickening out. I think I made an attempt at some sort of friendship with Scopie. He knew what I was about. Everyone knew he would 'batter' me.

There were other fist fights between gangs. Short. Cut and run. The fight I remember clearly was a little later, when I was at the national school, aged about ten. The cock of the Roman Catholic Junior School and I were fixed up for a fight after church on a Sunday night. I have no recollection of how this came about. We met under the first street lamp on Market Hill next to the road. When I stood facing him I distinctly remember that I felt no inclination to fight him, no animosity, no anger so it was pointless. I did not want to hit him. I did not want him to hit me.

But a deal had been made. We squared up, one of us led with a left. The other responded and then some sort of contest took place. He was far more up for it than I was, and as far as I could guess – in the opening few minutes – sharper and stronger with very bony knuckles. After a while I 'boxed defensively' – only pausing to square up now and then under the lamps, then went slowly backwards down Market Hill towards the Gents lavatory and the public telephone, which was all but opposite the entrance to the Black-A-Moor. And there the fight stopped. I had clearly lost. He most likely asked, 'Give in?' If so, I might have nodded. He went home. I went across the road fingering a growing lump on my forehead . . .

Sometimes in the early years on Fridays or Sundays when the pub had been busy enough but not at full stretch, I would wander downstairs to the bar after closing time.

Dad would be counting up the takings. He let me help. Little towers of twelve brown pennies. Two towers of halfpennies to match each penny tower. Sixpences piled up to make five bob, threepences neatly stacked in piles of eight, shillings ten. Notes were Dad's responsibility. He would then open his account book and, in neat copperplate handwriting, enter the takings of the day, compare them with the takings on the same day a week and then a year before. In the back of the book was the list of those barred: name, date barred, date allowed re-entry. Fourteen in year one, nine in year two, then a plunge to four: soon after that it ceased to be an issue.

We would talk about fighting. I had seen how he dealt with the customers, all the time hoping he would sail into them and knock them flying, as Jack Waters did.

But it was always push, talk, get them out, bolt the door, let them settle it on the street.

For whatever reason, I said that if it came to a fight between Andrew and my father, I would back Andrew. We were standing by the till. I had little idea of the distrust and dislike my father had for this false brother of his wife, how he resented the lock of her loyalty to give him a lodging and a run of the place far beyond sense or reason. He was soon to find evidence for what he had suspected for some time – Andrew was a thief.

When I said that to him about Andrew, something I now know to be utterly untrue, he merely smiled – I can still see it – and said, 'So you think that, do you?' 'Yes,' I uttered, eagerly, and continued to pile up the coins.

It was only later, much later, I appreciated how strong my father was. How strong to stand up to those mostly younger men who turned up penitent but still near to anger on a Sunday morning. So skilfully to shovel a clump of wrestling, pushing, semi-drunken strong bodies out of the pub. To endure the occasional taunting and muttered threats as he walked up street. To hold the centre without losing his self-control or the respect of those who knew him well.

It was a tolerance, intelligent, forgiving, hard won and hard held on to. It was in its way a view of the world arrived at through a testing life. As time went on I saw it more and more clearly and admired it more and more keenly.

I wish I had told him.

Chapter Nineteen

In the first half of the ten years between moving into the pub and leaving Wigton, I would get out into the town as often as possible. Until I got a bike I ran everywhere. Away from the pub as if I had to escape, back to it because at the end of the day there was nowhere else to go. My surest way to get to sleep was to imagine I was in the middle of a desert in America and had to build and stock a self-sufficient fortress incapable of capture.

In the town I felt free.

In those ten years the old town was very slowly draining away and reshaping itself in estates, council and private, as the better-off sought a better life, like a ring of planets around the sun. The town, though, still kept its coherence between my childhood after the Second World War and my exit from it. Family names, small businesses, old houses, street names and many lanes had been there for centuries and were slow to yield to change. It was stuck in history, a mid-century capsule of a small northern English town running into the country, farms opening into the town itself, full of ancient dialect words and inter-married families, a web closely spun. An England that had been, and still was, but was irreversibly beginning to alter.

For me, it was all there needed to be.

School took up much less time than playing, starting at the infants' school.

At the infants' school, built in smart red brick just after the First World War, staffed by six strict teachers, the time spent in class was far less than the daytime left over for playing in the town. Add weekends and thirteen weeks' holiday a year, and playing beat school hollow. And even at the school between nine and three thirty there were three 'playtimes', one, the dinner break, long enough to organise games that could go on for days. Then back to the three Rs, chanting simple poems and tables, to being drilled and being controlled.

The cane might have been a 'help', certainly among the boys. I never saw a girl get the cane. We could be whacked even for a minor disruption – on the bottom, through thick short pants, which was OK, or on the palm of the hand, which stung to your tear ducts that had to be sealed.

Our teachers – all covering the same general spread of subjects – were Miss Ivison, Miss Steele, Miss Moffat (who also read stories from the Bible), Miss Young, Mrs Bennet, Mr Purdham, class six. And Mr Scott the headmaster.

The old national school, to which we all transferred when we were ten, was Dickensian, bleak, four classrooms for boys and girls, two concrete playgrounds that continued the separation of the sexes begun in the infants' school. We sat in blocks of boys on one side, girls on the other. We played clothes-ripping games of football on the concrete, where you had to slide tackle, dive if you were a goalie, ignore bloody knees, British Bulldog, Montykitty and any number of chase games. When we peeped across at girls they were skipping or calmly huddled together, always talking. What did they find to talk about?

The school was near freezing in winter.

Mr Brown, a large, non-Cumbrian, gentle man with tightly crinkled black hair, caught me as I fell when I was about nine. I had become unable to function – to read, to add up or to write. I would start at the top left-hand corner of the page and end up on the bottom right-hand corner. I could not control it. Partly, I suspect, caused by the disabling embarrassment of my new wire-rimmed national-health specs. However carefully I smuggled them on when lessons began and whipped them off the instant it was playtime, the dented bridge of the nose and the line from nose to ear could not be hidden.

I was unbearably ashamed and too easily lost my temper at the taunts – 'Four Eyes'. Or perhaps the collapse was to do with the pub in the early years and its Saturday night violence.

I realised years later that Mr Brown nursed me through. One way he did this was by telling me that when he asked boys what they had done at the infants' school 'some of them said they were in your gang'. He made that seem an achievement. In other ways that good teachers have, he began to restore my confidence.

Most of all he put me in a school play, a story of Robin Hood and the Sheriff of Nottingham. *Robin Hood* was one of the few books I possessed and I could all but recite it by heart. Over the years I made bows and arrows from slender branches and used them until they broke. I was to play one of the outlaws, Will Scarlett, with two or three lines to speak. But Robin Hood caught – was it mumps? – something that knocked him out. Mr Brown asked me on the day before if I knew Robin Hood's lines. I said I thought I did.

He asked me to be Robin Hood. He said he knew I could do it.

It was performed in the Market Hall at the end of the summer term. My parents came. They applauded. 'Have at thee, varlet! Drop that sword!' I did it without the specs. My father had a word with Mr Brown afterwards, who told him (which he passed on to me) that I could do well but just needed a bit more confidence. Who knows what difference such small exchanges make, but I entered Mr Brown's class as an inexplicable (to me) mess and went 'up' at ten to Miss Tate's, ready to take the scholarship for the grammar school. Due to Miss Tate's forceful methods, almost all the class was shoved through. Thanks to recent legislation, the grammar school was free of all charges.

The Nelson Thomlinson Grammar School, established almost four hundred years previously, was a great opportunity. But it was also the beginning of stepping away from the old town.

I had always sought out friends with the desperation of an only child whose parents had no time for him. I was fortunate in the safe haven always available at my grandfather's house in which his youngest children – Irwin and Margaret – were only a few years older than I was. But even they were not the same as 'best friends': those who would play with you whatever, those who would remain lifelong friends. Without these I could not secure my own ballast. To be alone was a given, to be managed; to be close to others was a necessity. However kind my parents were, the pub and its 365-day demands blotted up their time and most of their energy. I did not expect more attention than I was given. I was lucky to get what I got. I accepted and much later came to appreciate being alone. But in the early years in the pub there was a need, almost a panic, especially on Saturday nights, for friends. One or two would be enough, boys with whom I felt unalone and guarded from the disturbances of solitude, which could suck me into a weird distress.

I needed friends so close I could lose myself in them. I sought them out.

It might seem calculating now but I had no idea at all then that that was what I was doing, or why. It just had to be like that. One way and another I put a gang together.

When we were about ten, set-gaps were the rage. One of us – William, Mike, Eric, Geoff, Robert – did something difficult, like jump across what looked like a narrowish but deep stretch of the river and the others had to follow – that was the set-gap – or something silly, like hop along the top of a narrow brick wall. There were no prizes or penalties. We just moved on, soaked, bruised or intact. These tests could be a little worrying when you had to swing across a fragile lower branch of a tree or hold your breath until you were fit to burst – timed by Eric, who had a second pointer on his watch. Eric was the mathematician, the slightest of us all, and even as a boy the word 'elegant' could have been used even though his background was no different from ours.

The River Wiza, the biggest of the rivers and streams that ran through the town, was a gift. On the West Road, barely out of the town, one empty field led to another as the river twisted its way from the fells to the sea. Building a dam was always an option even though we knew that by the next morning it might have been destroyed by one of the men from the factory downstream that needed the water. It was good to see the river turn into a little reservoir. We could swim there or, if we found or had pulled off suitable branches, try to make a raft.

When we got bored we played football. William had a full-size football, which he sometimes remembered to bring along; then it disappeared. It was his younger brother's turn to have it. So we used a tennis ball. Three-a-side, two-a-side, even one-a-side until well into the dark.

A year or two on we decided to track the river to its source. We stopped when it went under a road. The road seemed to break the spell. We switched to following the river towards the sea and followed it well out of the town until we were too far from Wigton to get back in good time.

There was a sharp bend in the Wiza in Ma Powell's field, just beyond the bridge that led into the park, with a sandbank on one side about five feet high. One day, rather aimlessly, we hacked into it with the sharpest stones we could find and quickly made progress. The next day those who could turned up with an old shovel or poker and dug in. We soon had a space we could creep into. The idea was to make a cave at the end of the tunnel and, later, to hack out another tunnel, which would have a secret exit into the field. This took some time, but the fine summer holiday was made for it.

Eric's father had come out of the war smitten by the power of German engineering, and Eric pointed out that there were serious engineering challenges here. We drew on films such as *The Wooden Horse*, in which British soldiers dig a tunnel out of a German prison camp.

We brought stumps of candles to light up our tunnels and bits of old carpet to sit on in the cave. We built an ammunition dump for the stones easily collected in the shallows of the river and tried and failed to make a fire at the far end of the cave, which continued to grow by the day. At one stage it could fit in three at a pinch. Others kept guard. It took most of the holiday.

We went home looking like sandmen.

There were worries. The first was when Geoff, the tallest, got stuck in the tunnel, gasped and panted for help and had to be dragged out by his feet. We worried it might wreck the tunnel. Geoff's father had come north from Wigan as a master tailor at Redmayne's. Perhaps that made Geoff difficult for us to fathom. He was always game but said very little so you never quite knew where he stood. After his near thing, we sat outside the cave and talked things over. What was it for? This stumped us. Micky suggested we could use it for days on end, camp there. Micky was all for pushing things to the limit. Some of his set-gaps were scarily dangerous. Eric suggested we extend it into a wide network. We were tired; there were no takers. All of us thought it would be a grand fortress but we didn't have an enemy. And how could we disguise the increasingly large hole that gaped blackly out of the sandbank and was sure to be spotted by a factory man or anybody just strolling along by the river of an evening? We solved that, we thought, by patting the dug-out sand into a thin camouflaging wall inside the entrance. We thought it looked effective. But how could we disguise the escape hole we had made in the field? We had to be sure that people did not accidentally fall into it. We did that by finding large branches and strewing them across the hazardous hole. But inquisitive cows were always a threat.

What was it for? I suggested it might be a tomb but that didn't get very far. A tomb, Eric pointed out, needed at least one dead body. Micky suggested we could store or hide things there, but we couldn't think what to store or where to find anything worth hiding. It had been dug, we were fed up with it. The holiday was coming to an end and we needed to find a purpose. Fill it in, said William. That's the safest thing. It got no votes.

It could be our headquarters, yes, but it was a long way to come for a meeting and what would we talk about? And we would never be able to wangle a way to sleep in it.

A torrent solved the problem. A strong, tree-bending downpour that lasted for days, brought hail, raised the river level high, and it seemed would never stop. When it did we went to inspect our work.

The cave was flooded. It was impossible to crawl in. The false wall had been swept away. The branches over the hole in the field had been scattered. Now it was just a hole full of dirty water.

'Even if we'd had a stone fight,' Eric said, 'it would have been useless as a fort.' We had spent almost all the summer holiday on it.

Just down the river, above the stretch where it had been straightened and deepened for the factory, was a steep little wooded rise, which was perfect cover for a raid on Dr Goldsburgh's orchard. This was reported to be enormous.

We had some form at robbing orchards. There was an orchard in the old Crofts belonging to Joseph Johnson, the bread and pie maker. The wall was high but we could give one of us a leg up to see if it was safe. If so, another and perhaps, depending on our forces, a third, could be hauled up, lie flat on the wall top and then drop down, grab as many apples and pears as possible, carry them stuffed up our jumpers and race back to the wall. Mr Johnson almost caught us once and, as we hauled Eric up the wall, he shouted out, 'I know you! I know you! I'll tell your fathers! I'll tell your mothers! I'll catch you one of these days!' Our names rang across the orchard, like sentences of death. We avoided passing his shop for some time. We did not have much of an appetite for those apples or pears.

I can remember no feelings of guilt. Curious, because by then – about twelve – I was already deep in High Church Anglican Sin and Guilt, and earnestly called out, 'Forgive us our trespasses,' every night in the Lord's Prayer before bed. In church I chanted the general confession in as firm a voice as I could muster so that God would get the message and shift away the Everest of guilt that had been built from the terrible sins of the previous week.

But there was no guilt in robbing orchards.

I knew it was stealing but (I know not how) perhaps the fact that we were taking a risk – to be caught, reported to our parents, to the school, to the police, and marched off to the magistrate's court at the bottom of New Street – made it OK. It was a morality of our own that took precedence over the Ten Commandments.

It was never discussed.

The Dr Goldsburgh operation was to be a big one.

We recced it: that steep uphill scramble, the only approach, was hindered by a mass of what we called thorny bushes and weedy little trees that made it difficult to get through without making a noise. We attributed to Dr Goldsburgh, who lived in what we thought of as a magnificent long house on West Street just opposite the end of the Crofts, the cunning of a mastermind. As far as we could find out, his orchard had never been raided. We were finding out why.

The only possible way into it was further barred by a tall fence – stout posts and high chicken wire. Beyond that, a ditch.

We crept back down more noisily than when we had made the approach and decided not to give up. The barrier proved the riches that were waiting for us.

'We could dig under that netting,' said Eric. 'Tried and tested.' Wise.

We took shovels. All five of us went.

The posts had been driven in deep but we kept at it until there was a space big enough even for Geoff.

It was twilight, but we could make out a paradise of an orchard. The house appeared empty save for a few small internal lights. They were threatening enough in the shadowing evening.

Leaving the shovels behind, we kept to our plan, which was not to grab and run this time, but to creep on our bellies, like we'd seen Red Indians do in a film, crawling through a wood to take the American cavalry by surprise. We would then have good time to fill our pockets and pullovers as never before. It was not easy going and we began to worry that our mothers would kill us over the state of our clothes.

When the lights came on, big, beamed down the garden, we froze. From terror not tactics.

Then the voice, a deep, posh, angry voice, like the Voice of God; 'I've been waiting for you, you little beggars!' His dog, a friendly Labrador – but how could we know that? – barked loudly, continuously. The doctor's words and the barking dog worked where light had failed. We shot back to our hole, slithered through, a progress accelerated by the sound of Dr Goldsburgh and his lion of a dog barking insanely, both of whom were so close that afterwards we swore we could feel the dog's breath down our necks and the doctor's hands reach out for our feet as we dived under the chicken wire.

We heard again 'I'll catch you, you little beggars!' And again. But we got through, down to the river path and then we ran and ran and ran like hell.

Our final raid was on Mrs Barnes's orchard. Mrs Barnes had a beautiful apple orchard. Come autumn they burned like baubles on a Christmas tree. You could taste them just by looking at them over the hedge. The glitch was that Mrs Barnes lived next door to my grandparents. More than that, my grandmother deeply admired Mrs Barnes, and my young uncles, Wilson and Irwin, were intrigued by her son, Adrian, an English teacher at the grammar school in Carlisle to which he travelled in a sports car. Its maintenance consumed most of his weekends. He was exceptionally friendly.

Mrs Barnes's house stood alone and splendid in its own grounds. When her late husband, a solicitor, had bought it, Park House had not been built and her house stood next to open fields, near, but not too near, the ornate tall gates that led into the park.

My grandmother gave Mrs Barnes a hand now and then when the regular cleaner was unavailable. The old polished furniture, the paintings on the walls – 'Beautiful scenes from the Lake District,' she reported – the thick carpets, silver-framed photographs, a piano, shelves stacked so tidily with books . . . and Mrs Barnes, mild, warm, friendly, always asking if my grandmother 'needed' anything, always happy to chat. And she was so 'well spoken', my grand-mother said, almost reverently; her voice was refined, polite; there was nobody else she knew who spoke like that. And she looked so distinguished, silver hair parted in the middle and gathered in a loose bun, her face only slightly weathered from the time she spent in the garden, very pale blue eyes, no make-up and clothes that denoted her status, several cuts above.

'I could go in that house every day,' Hannah, my grandmother, would say, when the subject of Mrs Barnes surfaced. 'And I could just sit down and listen to her talk.'

An event in the history of Park House, which I witnessed and cherish, came from words that, one calm day, had floated through my grandmother's open sitting-room window and reached the ears of Mrs Barnes and a visiting friend, a professor of English. The words were my grandfather's dialect and uninhibited accent. He had just come into the room and he began in mid-sentence.

'Siste! On a yet like yon ower yonder and thowt nowt could brek it!'

A little later the professor and Mrs Barnes turned up at the front door. When Hannah saw them on the step she thought something was wrong and knew it for certain when Mrs Barnes said, 'This is Professor Keely, Mrs Bragg. He'd very much like to meet your husband. May we come in?'

'And I had that old pinny on,' she reported later.

'Herbert!' The proper Christian name came out as a fearful signal. 'We have visitors.'

Harry came in from the kitchen, shirt sleeves rolled up, no collar, waistcoat open, cheap shapeless trousers. He nodded to Mrs Barnes.

'You must think me very rude, Mr Bragg, but my friend would like to talk to you.' It was not a sentence that gave Harry any confidence.

'This is Professor Keely.'

Once more Harry confined himself to a nod.

'He was fascinated when he heard how you talked.'

Harry and Hannah looked at each other for the merest moment and his look said, 'What have I done wrong?' and hers 'They think we're savages.'

Professor Keely had interviewed many country people for his study on dialects of the North and he was used to suspicion and incomprehension.

'Mr Bragg, I just overheard you talk,' he said. 'Your accent is so pure, and what I heard of your vocabulary is Old English and Norse, a perfectly preserved example. I know this may seem intrusive but could you find an hour or two to let me interview you for a book I'm writing?'

The moon could have crashed through the ceiling. Hannah's face was red with embarrassed astonishment. Harry took it in his stride and kept his dignity and then: 'Aa've been telt that afoor. In't waar. A teacher.'

'That's what I am.'

'So Aa can't larn thee nowt.'

'Oh yes you can, Mr Bragg. If you could spare me some of your time – oh! Yes, you jolly well can! I should be most grateful.'

Hannah looked at her husband as if he had turned into an oracle and it was not welcome. Then Harry smiled broadly. 'Well. Aa'll be buggered.'

'Herbert! Language!'

'Sorry.'

But the smile remained. More importantly so did Mrs Barnes, and Hannah's shame was somewhat salved. But she never forgot that, in a moment of triumph, Harry had 'showed off our bringings up'.

For a couple of evenings, Harry went across to Mrs Barnes's house and allowed himself to be interrogated. At first it was embarrassing, and his throat would threaten to choke. The professor was such an odd specimen. But as Harry's wariness dissolved he saw that underneath he was normal enough and a real scholar. He didn't let a word pass. So Harry relaxed and talked of the meetings rather proudly.

On the day he left, Professor Keely came to say goodbye. His thanks were easily seen to be genuine. He gave Harry a small padded box, 'For your trouble. What you said could make a chapter of its own. I'm very grateful. If there ever is a book, I'll certainly send you a copy.'

'I enjoyed it when it got gaan.'

The parcel contained a pipe. It was too big for Harry: it would take too much tobacco to fill it. It was put in the drawer where they kept old photographs. The story became family folklore.

So when the night arrived to raid Mrs Barnes's orchard I was reluctant.

'You yella?' Geoff. Eric also gave me a hard look. There were only the three of us – Geoff to help me through the hedge, Eric to be the lookout and me to get the apples. I knew the orchard better than the other two. It stood to reason.

But would my grandmother or Mrs Barnes be looking out of an appropriate window at an inappropriate time? Just one glance would nail me. The consequences didn't bear thinking about.

The operation was the slickest we had carried out.

Even so when next I went to Park House and my grandmother said – in a tone I could not read (was she angry, was she upset in any way, would she ever let me help with the baking again?), 'Mrs Barnes said she would like to see you the next time you came down. Now come here.'

I went towards her, pre-flinching, but all she wanted was to scrub my face and neck and dampen my hair down to a flat and inhuman neatness and shuffle me into uncharacteristic tidiness. 'That'll have to do.'

I had been seen, I knew that. But why was my grandmother not angry? As I knocked on the door with its stained-glass window, I'm sure I bent my head so that I did not have to look my judge in the face.

'Here you are,' she said, in that gentle lilting tone. She carried a brown-paper bag, holding about a half a dozen apples. 'I haven't mentioned anything of this to your grandmother,' she said.

Although you were not supposed to cry, I seem to remember the threat of tears.

'Thank you, Mrs Barnes.'

'Would you tell her that ten o'clock tomorrow would be better for me?'

'Yes, Mrs Barnes.'

'You only need to ask,' she said, and smiled.

Chapter Twenty

Football was the best key to friendship. Andrew, for my tenth birthday, came good on one of his promises and bought me a real football, stiff leather with a leather lace to thread through the holes that stopped in the nozzle that fed the bladder that made the lump of leather into a football. The nozzle was always the problem. There would be a bike under the shed in the backyard or somebody around would park outside and I could borrow the pump to screw in the head and fit it into the wobbling little pink nozzle and pump away until the ball – which we called a Harriers, after the Wigton Harriers, our town team – was hard. Then came the tough bit. How to tighten the pre-prepared lace at the base of the nozzle so that when you licked your index finger and put a film of saliva over the tip of it there would be no indication of leakage, not even the smallest air bubble. The air would be intact inside the bladder.

Using a spoon, you levered open the stiff mouth of the new Harriers, thumb pushed and tucked the nozzle, now limp, from its string-tied root up, into the cavity. Then you tightened the lace, also already prepared in its holes, tugged as hard as possible, threaded it back through the neat stitching – a small screwdriver helped – and then, done! To be bounced, headed, tapped around and out into the world to meet the gang and others, eager to play with this dark brown leather grown-up ball. With the ball under my arm, I felt I was the bringer of all good things and anxious to get on with the game and break it in. Who did not want to play with such a ball?

At first, to protect the ball, I took it into the field where the Harriers played their home games, next to the West Cumberland Farmers' warehouses. But very soon, partly because Micky, Geoff and Eric's families had moved into new houses beyond the river, we settled for Barton Laws, across the Wiza, also known as the Show Fields, to be near them. Although there was what we thought of as a magnificent length of flat grass in the park, perfect for the game, football on the patch was forbidden. But the grass in Barton Laws, more laxly mown for rugby, was good enough.

There was a long wooden shed on one side of the pitch for changing rooms for two teams and a large unforgiving and deep cement bath. My uncle Wilson looked after this, including the painfully long filling of the bath with tepid water. All such work was voluntary; none of the officials or players was paid. This amateur aspect at that time held for the rugby union game up to international level. Though my father came from West Cumberland where, as in other mining communities in the north, professional paid rugby league was played, to which he retained a loyalty, he would always smile admiringly when talking about union and say, 'Those lads do it just for the love of it.'

The rugby goalposts were too wide so our jackets were planted inside them and mirrored down the pitch at the halfway line. The river faced the hut and the rule was if you booted the ball into the river it was your job to go and get it out, although with a sense of ownership I would always belt downriver to the bridge where it was shallow enough to wade in and save it.

For many weeks after, we played with the decreasingly new ball. The game could start after teatime and wind on into twilight, or occupy a full Saturday morning. We picked sides but were fluid about positions on the pitch. There was a lot of shouting – 'Pass!'; 'I am here!'; 'Get back!'; 'Hit it!' The treble chirps flew across the field scaring away the birds. Whatever the weather, I would wipe the ball down after the game, then take an old rag to it when I got back home. Dubbin was lavishly spread over every inch of the leather. The football guaranteed company. Also I was besotted by the game, its heroes, the teams, the league tables. For some time my supreme dream was to score Carlisle United's winning goal in the Cup Final at Wembley.

That football saw me through a year or two. Before the year was out it was introduced to the streets, where it took a lot of punishment from the walls and the roads and pavements, which also took their toll on our knees, trousers and shoes. There was just the touch of the battlefield about it.

The ball was further reduced to be hoofed around in our narrow backyard where every second kick knocked it against a wall and it became as saggy as the old punch-bag. The leather began to wear and flake; the gloss went altogether for lack of care.

It ended up being used to practise for penalties against the side wall of the house on which I chalked targets to be aimed at. It was scarred almost to bits.

Last of all, the bladder failed. The ball had a kind of honourable burial on the bottom shelf of my bookcase where it became a relic until, after a tidying-up operation when I was away, I found it was gone.

Its decline coincided with my going to the grammar school where rugby was the game. For two years I tried to keep a football team together. For home games we were loaned the Wigton Harriers ground, which is to say goal posts, on Saturday mornings. Away games on village-school pitches were not so easy. Getting at a respectable minimum half a dozen boys to stump up the bus fare for villages beyond a bike ride could be a full-time weekday job. We always had to ask the other team to find us a few players. Constant defeats did not help. We once lost 14–1. I was in goal.

My uncle Irwin, who played rugby for Wigton, took me to a few training sessions, which helped me overcome my antipathy for the grammar-school game. Soon I accepted it. But I never asked for, nor was I ever given, a rugby ball.

Chapter Twenty-one

The pub helped drive me out into the town and for the next few years, until I was fourteen and recovering from a crack-up, it was the town I turned to for my life.

I read but that did not interfere with daytime. Every night I read in bed, propped up against the pillow, listening out for any discordant notes in the sounds coming up from downstairs. Early on I raced through comics, *Dandy*, *Beano*, and a little later the *Wizard*, *Rover*, *Hotspur*, *Adventure* and *Champion* – small print, one illustration, five complete stories each week, featuring many characters who are still vivid in my memory. There was Wilson, who had slept for two hundred years deep in a cave in the Highlands to return in an ancient black running costume, barefooted, unbeatable as an athlete over any distance, and prepared to travel to Africa to take on Zulu champions at leaping across a pit of fire; Alf Tupper, a welder, the Tough of the Track, who broke the four-minute mile long before Roger Bannister. He did this between two road signs next to the garage in which he worked and slept; Limp Along Leslie with his club left foot and his deadly right foot that won game after game for Rangers; Sergeant Braddock, bomber pilot with superhuman reactions, and more, more, these boys' heroes effortlessly and week after week made memorable by writers in Scotland whose names are forgotten, whose skills were appreciated only by boys until Orwell and one or two others clocked their talent.

The books included *Biggles,* the 'Five' books, *Fifth Form at St Dominic's, Jennings and Darbishire*; above all others the *Just William* books, *Treasure Island, Robinson Crusoe, The Amateur Gentleman* and anything by P. G. Wodehouse after I had read his schoolboy book *Mike* . . . On they marched until they began to turn into, among others, *The Three Musketeers*, *Rogue Herries*, *Kidnapped*, *Oliver Twist*, *Jude the Obscure*, anything by Somerset Maugham and D. H. Lawrence, Graham Greene, shading into the Americans, Hemingway, Sinclair Lewis, Scott Fitzgerald, Mailer. Later there were the Italians, especially *Don Camillo*, the French, especially de Maupassant and Gide, poetry, the anthologies from the school library. I borrowed a weekly helping of literature from the library at school and from the town library, which had moved into the Quaker Meeting House. There was little television, save that over one span the BBC showed classics – Chekhov, Ibsen, George Bernard Shaw, Tennessee Williams – on Sunday nights and I saw them at my grandparents' after evensong. Radio was for comedy, like *The Goon Show*, which gave us all the characters and quips we needed to see us through the day, and for adapted novels, *The Mill on the Floss*, *Middlemarch*, Anthony Trollope, Dickens, Disraeli . . . It was more like feeding than reading. When Radio Luxembourg appeared, pop music joined the club.

Even so, I was out whenever possible. 'What do you want to be inside for on a day like this?' My mother would shoo me out when I was stuck into a book in daylight. Perhaps she wanted me to continue her patrolling the town. Certainly I could never go to a shop – we still shopped, save for breakfast, meal by meal – without being interrogated, that is the correct word, on who I had seen, where, at what time, coming into or going out of which shop, wearing a hat? With her daughter? I began to imitate some of the people I saw. Sometimes it made her laugh. Just as often she warned me off: 'Now then.'

So my invasion of the town for a few years became an essential element. And I too began to chart its characters and its features.

The fountain was the heart of it. Behind the fountain, to the south, was the King's Arms, the grandest pub in the town, more a hotel with a dance hall on the first floor. Peter, the landlord's son, had to sleep with an open window because of his TB. Next to the King's Arms was Dickie Thornton's garage. It was famous as much for being the depository for the mass of brambles, gooseberries, blueberries, in season, collected expertly by the poorer women, weighed and paid for by Dickie or his son, an alcoholic, and daily trucked off to Carlisle.

Dickie was also famous for his wife, who sat at the window of the flat above the garage daily, stately surveying the town. She was as still as a portrait. She wore old-fashioned clothes and seemed immovable and as modestly harmless as a picture in a frame.

In fact, in that window, which was situated like a town clock, she flaunted her condition as an abandoned wife. Dickie had given her up for his new love, whom he had moved into a bungalow in Highmoor Avenue.

Mr Ritson, a solicitor, was just on from the garage. His son, Glenn, would take over the practice. Glenn had been a prisoner of war in Germany for four years. He was a gentle, courteous man and when, at one time, it was suggested that I had a good chance of joining his firm as a junior, I could tell how proud my mother was.

To the west of the fountain was another hotel, the Royal Oak, which, like many buildings, had an arched entrance to the yard's stables. Then one of Wigton's more celebrated buildings, the Mechanics Institute, with its grand pillars and Victorian ambition. It was later to be pulled down by the council for no sane reason, an act of vandalism in the name of progress. Dr Goldsburgh's house was only two doors away from where William lived. His proximity to Dr Goldsburgh had made him uneasy about joining in the raid on the orchard but gang loyalty won, although he did say, once or twice, that if his mother knew that he was robbing her neighbour Dr Goldsburgh he would be in for 'the hiding of a lifetime'.

William's house was grand. A big Georgian place called Collingwood House, it had been requisitioned by various council departments until William's father rented a foothold, which became a ground floor, which became the whole lot, which he bought when big houses went for a song. There were several fine eighteenth- and nineteenth-century houses scattered in Wigton old town. A few yards from William's house was Howdy Williamson's farm, which opened onto West Street – the cows would be herded up and down the street twice daily for milking.

I was walked by my mother up King Street and the High Street when I was four to the infants' school built of clean red brick like a giant toy. I had been taken on that school route many times on Sunday walks. It was very simple. Top of Station Road – right; fountain – left; keep going. School on the right. After the first day, she among other mothers was waiting at the school gate to guide the chicks. She told me once or twice that when we got back home I asked her never to collect me again. Knowing that I would be within shouting distance of other mothers, she let me have my way. These wanderings back on my own in the mid-afternoon took me into a narrow lane into the Crofts, next to the school. At the bottom of the lane was an even narrower stream, ideal for dabbling. From there I went into George Street, which looked directly down to the Auction Market, so I knew where I was. Dad would sometimes walk me to the auction. By increasingly intricate ways as the months and years went by I would eventually land in Station House Yard. But the walk up High Street or, rather, the run, either because I feared to be late or could not get there soon enough, continued throughout my education. The High Street took me to the infants', to the national and finally to the Nelson Thomlinson School. For fourteen years it was my road to education.

It also took me to the church, St Mary's, and to the doctor's, Dr Dolan, whose surgery was opposite the Lion and Lamb. On the rare occasions I was taken there, my mother made sure I was scrubbed up so that there appeared nothing wrong with me. We sat in the waiting room as silent as headstones, afraid to cough. Even after the National Health Service came in, little changed the order of things in Dr Dolan's (son of Dr Dolan) waiting room. It was run by Peter, a slightly built, small and delicate man with a weak chest, always, whatever the weather, well wrapped up, a heavy pullover and muffler under his jacket. Peter was a Roman Catholic (like Dr Dolan), who had left school at fourteen with a passion for the work of St Thomas Aquinas, which he pursued for the rest of his life.

He was taught Latin by one of the priests and introduced to the work of that medieval master scholar. In time he was to contribute to scholarly journals, and go to rarefied conferences in his holidays. He lived with his mother until she died and then lived on alone in the bungalow whose interior was seen by no one but himself. He never lost his broad Wigton accent. He was busy and cheerful when he moved around the town doing the shopping, nodding to everyone. (The waiting room was one of the biggest communities in town. He remembered everyone's name and asked how they were with a professional air.) He would stop to chat, and always go into George Johnston at the shoe shop – George had been educated at St Ursula's, the small private school run by the nuns, and shared Peter's interest in detailed town talk. I joined them a couple of times. They were oral archivists. The town had no depths they could not plumb. Peter's face was as white as a clown's.

I went up King Street for some years from when I was about nine to be taught the piano by Miss Snaith, one of the three Misses Snaith, daughters of a father who had brought them up himself after the early death of their mother. He was a clockmaker, in a tradition that for more than a hundred years, through a number of families, had given Wigton some renown. They specialised in long case, commonly called grandfather clocks, the carpentry and mechanisms made locally, though often the face was bought in. Mr Snaith had set up a jewellery shop to subsidise his hobby and one of his daughters worked there from leaving school. The second looked after the flat above the shop. The third daughter, Fanny, taught the piano.

She was strict. If the scales were not played flawlessly, her pencil would rap you across the knuckles. Sometimes the minute blue bruises took a few days to disappear. In the well-off and heavily furnished sitting room above the shop, the piano became an instrument of fear. My mother's reasoning in sending me there was that I liked singing in the choir, along with the wireless and dancing at the socials, and there was that unused piano in the parlour. It would be handy for me and possibly for the pub. The whole misadventure lasted for about five years. During that time, like Miss Snaith's other pupils, I was trained to pass exams. Her sisters used to tell all who would listen that Fanny had the best pass rate in the north-west of England.

It was ground out of us. I wanted to play the piano. I wanted to play like Winifred Atwell or the men who played in bars in American films or the traditional jazz players who would turn up on the wireless, or even like Jack Atkinson who could handle a piano when pushed almost as well as the accordion. But I did not want to play Miss Snaith's piano. Between my mother's notional pleasure and Miss Snaith's iron will I was between a soft place and a rock. I stuck at it because I dared not back out and every autumn I passed another exam. Having been coached – with others – for weeks beforehand we would take the bus to Carlisle to the Gothic-gloomy Viaduct Hotel where we would be sat in a ballroom that seemed to be as big as a church and then, chilled to the bone, our names called to be led out and do our stuff. It was worse than any school exam because I felt that I was manacled and I didn't want to do it. There was no jury, only a judge. A week or two later, there was relief when the marks came through – but soon up reared the prospect of the next grade. Going for the lessons, I had lead in my shoes.

Finally I decided to break free. My campaign began by jumping up at one of the bars that held up the permanent awning above the street window of Toppin's butcher's shop. Barbed wire was wrapped around the bar. With a bit of luck I could draw blood without it hurting too much. That worked for a few weeks but eventually Miss Snaith guessed my game and told me that I was letting down my mother, myself, her, my future prospects. By that time she had marshalled me to stumble through a Beethoven sonata. After a pause I invented illnesses. That lasted no longer than Toppin's awning. I had begun to do homework more regularly and called that in as an excuse . . . Then I ducked a lesson. My mother was summoned.

She returned rather set-faced. 'You needn't go any more,' she said. 'So that was a waste of one and six a week.'

I went to King Street for fish and chips. The town had three fish-and-chip shops, but the jewel in the crown was Jose's or Manuel's, Jose's brother. They had landed in Wigton from Spain just after the war. Their fish-and-chip shop opposite the fountain was a barn of a room sporting one poster – of the three films on that week at the Palace Cinema. It was wholly unfurnished. There was a counter and behind it the frying paraphernalia. It thrived. The town's 'lads' took to Manuel, who bred greyhounds, raced them on the track at Workington nearby, and was deeply committed to his daily punt on the horses. Jose was Catholic, went to church twice on Sundays and confession on Saturday evening. Behind the counter she was like a will-of-the-wisp, thin, quick, and generous with scrams. Scrams were the chippings off the batter in the fish cauldron, which, scooped up every now and then, were heaped in a box and trowelled onto the chip helping of anyone who asked for them. They were delicious and could turn four pennyworth of chips into a main meal, which for many of the customers, especially the 'lads', it was.

Customers came almost exclusively from subdivisions of the working class. Men and boys cheaply dressed, who did the dirty essential work at the factory, the digging and ditching for the council, humped coal from lorry to coal house, low paid mechanics in garages, men and boys who fetched and carried in the bigger shops, and smaller businesses, worked in the auction, the slaughterhouse, the West Cumberland Farmers' distribution depot. They sometimes got a job on the buses or the railways, on the lorries that took up the weekly waste, or they worked for those who served the money-making sections of the town. If they were lucky, they were builders, plumbers and electricians. Descendants of centuries of labourers, they had been slotted into their role in life as the ones who held up the rest, like the foundation platform of a pyramid. I knew many of them through the national school and the pub.

The girls who came in for chips worked in shops, in Redmayne's factory, cleaned houses, went to Carlisle to the big factories there. It was a cheap meal and Jose's became a meeting house.

We were still in the days when every dance and film show ended with the national anthem, for which we all stood still, some at attention; some even sang along. In Jose's they were an unaggressive crowd, waiting to be fed, appetites tickled by the smell and frizzling of the boiling beef fat. I never saw a fight in the chip shop. Jose would not stand for bad language and Manuel's Spanish bark was obeyed. Four-pennyworth was the basic norm, with scrams; six-pennyworth was good; a piece of fish with the chips, ninepence or a shilling, was rich. Vinegar was diddled on until you said, 'Stop!' You shook on your own salt from a big plastic container.

I always felt safe in the chip shop. You could josh people without offence being taken, possibly because no drink was allowed.

Next door was Mr Donnelly's shop. Every morning, bare-chested despite the grey hairs there and the few hairs on his head, he set off on a three-mile fast walk, arms swinging. He went around the southern perimeter of the town, Syke Road. In winter he and his lady went to Switzerland to ski, where he was once caught in an avalanche, which he explained in detail to the AYPA with slides. In summer on Sundays they put on boots and caught the bus from Market Hill to Keswick to walk in the fells. He went regularly to the baths after he had shut the shop and ended his session by going to the top of the diving boards and launching himself into the six feet of water head first. He worked with and lived with a woman who was not his wife. Both had walked out of their previous relationships but they never married. Perhaps they had never divorced. That sort of detail did not come my way. Yet what I had picked up from the talk in the kitchen of the pub was not to be dismissed. It was (well, up to a point) their own business. She always smiled and said, 'Hello,' on the street, even if she didn't know you. But the gossip was that it was one thing for him as one of the school governors to appear on the platform on Prize Day but quite another for her to sit alongside him! They seemed not to have or need any close friends . . .

Across from his shop was Glaister's, famous for its bread, pies and cakes, straight to the counter from the bakery at the back of the shop in a lane that trickled into Church Street. Mrs Glaister had been in the same class as my mother. 'We sat next to each other right the way through school. She was always so happy,' my mother said. There was a tone of amazement. It was a friendship that was never to tarnish as far as I could tell. She married a large, boisterous man, a 'character' about the town. He had a few regular axioms, among them 'The meat in those pies was wandering about the fields a mile away on Monday, in the slaughterhouse on Tuesday, in the butcher's on Wednesday and in your pie on Saturday. Beat that for fresh!' Or 'Annie's pastry's so light it crumbles before you take a bite.' And 'She can make a birthday cake faster than you could smoke a cigarette.' They had a pony and trap, which Andrew drove on Saturdays, shifts allowing, making deliveries all over the town. He would take me along now and then and let me pretend to drive. I felt like somebody in a film, up there, reins in my hands, trying to click my tongue. 'Gee up!'

It was on the cart that I saw for the first time some of the old-established grand houses standing on Station Hill, looking over the town to the northern fells, the northern wall of the Lake District. And on a road running behind them, even bigger houses – inside their own woods as if they were in the countryside. I began to see the housing circles around Wigton, like the age rings you saw in the severed trunk of a tree, centred by the cramped, huddled old town with a few grand houses that stood apart within it. After that, built well into the twentieth century, a line of bungalows on the west side towards the River Wiza. Later, past the Show Fields, where land was cheap, even bigger houses for the doctor and the better-off businessmen. Some of the businessmen and professional men and women became fierce gardeners, as did their council-house contemporaries across the road on the Greenacres Estate.

Harry Glaister, widely liked, son of the family, a few years older than myself, became a professional jockey, to the delight of the betting men in the town and the horsy element on the farms. He was a prince, always smiling and so friendly to those of us who would hang around him when he came into town. He worked on a nearby farm, which boasted half a dozen horses, and early on he had made a reputation at the point-to-point meetings around the area. My father said they pushed him too fast. One year Dad got up a busload of Harry's fans. They went into Scotland to a racecourse near Dumfries where Harry was riding a much-fancied horse in a major steeplechase. 'And he was ahead,' my father said, 'he was well ahead. He looked very comfortable. He was on the way to being top class. You could have heard us cheering him back in Wigton.' The horse caught a foot on the top of the fence before the last one and Harry was thrown. His neck was broken, his head badly damaged. He died a few days later.

The funeral filled the streets. People lined the pavements, the men bare-headed, heads bowed. The shops drew down their blinds. Traffic was stopped. All Wigton mourned.

The Reverend John Mann, vicar of St Mary's for a few years before my teens, liked to use the nearby fells to illustrate the verse 'I will lift up mine eyes to the hills from whence cometh my help'. 'And we have our own hills,' he would say, many times, always beaming when he said it, as if this unique luck gave us a spiritual advantage. The Reverend John Mann was much liked. He lived in High Street in the commanding Georgian vicarage, with a huge garden at the front (cutting it off from the town), which easily swallowed garden fetes. He and his wife had adopted a son, a boy about my age: the novelty of this intrigued us, as did his determination to rope some of us in on a Saturday morning to play football on the vicarage lawn. He was referee and occasional enthusiastic participant. He was the first person to take us, the choir, beyond the hills and into the Lake District on a day trip. We went on a boat in Keswick and walked a little way up Catbells, where his arms swept out to show off the variety and size of the landscape, its enfolding hills, its distant peaks.

If you stood at the fountain and drew your gaze down in slow motion from Skiddaw, the overwhelming portion of the landscape was unhindered by human habitation: a few farms and cottages, the scrapings of a hamlet, a village hidden deep, little to disturb the ocean of turf, drystone walls and hedges all the way to the outskirts of Wigton and the buried ground of the Roman camp at Red Dial.

Arriving in Wigton, on course for the fountain, the first encounter of the gaze would be with Highmoor Tower, Wigton's unique feature: it signalled Home.

But more wonderful to me as a boy was the half-term week in autumn when there were the horse sales, boasted to be the biggest in the north-west. The town changed its character. From earliest morning, horses were led in from the surrounding countryside: great Shire horses that had pulled ploughs in peace and guns in war, Shetlands and ponies by the dozens and, more elegantly, a few hunters. The town's talk was all horse talk; buyers and sellers from far and wide over-brimming the side streets, but most of all occupying the full length of the High Street. For us, who ran excitedly about the auction and about the town centre, barely able to contain ourselves at this local vision of cowboy country, it was bliss. If we were lucky we would get a ride, or just to stand and hold the reins of a horse while the owner went into a pub.

The pubs had all-day extensions in and along the High Street, and the King's Arms, the Swan, the Lion and Lamb, the Half Moon, the Crown, the Kildare, the Crown and Mitre rocked with strong drink and hard deals. Salesmen turned up on the streets selling silk-looking scarves and embroidered handkerchiefs, ribbons and fancy goods. To be in the middle of it, as we, the gang, were, was to be wrapped inside another world, an ancient, warmer, richer world, which came and went in a few days, like a glorious accident.

When the pubs closed down and the lamps went on, when even Manuel and Jose's fish-and-chip shop was shut and the lights in the flats above the shops almost all extinguished, cat's time, the special silence that falls after the noise of a crowded street, the policeman on duty – might it be John Wallace, a calm and portly man? – was on his last beat. He would stroll up to the fountain, breathe in the peace of the town and see that all was as well as could be hoped for. Up to the auction, back through Water Street to cross to New Street and down into the police station to brew himself a cup of tea and smoke the last cigarette of the day.

Chapter Twenty-two

On winter nights we drifted up to the fountain, the 'we' being boys and girls, eight- to twelve-year-olds who lived in the town. A game had evolved that used the old town. It had the character of a labyrinth. Perfect terrain for what was a long-elaborated game somewhere between hide and seek and chasey.

When enough of us had turned up, usually at about six thirty when the streets were emptied of shoppers and the pubs still waiting for customers, when adults had gone home and no factory shift was starting or finishing, we would move up to the fountain, group around the black iron railings and dib for 'IT', 'You're IT' – the person who would kick it all off.

We stood in a line and we would stick out our fists for one of the older boys to dib us out. 'One potato, two potato, three potato, four,' he would count, as he went down the line and banged his own fist on another's with every 'potato', up to four. 'Five potatoes, six potatoes, seven potatoes, more, Eight potatoes, nine potatoes, ten potatoes – you're IT.' Or

> Inky pinky ponky
> Father bought a donkey
> Donkey died,
> Father cried, Inky pinky *ponky*
> You're IT.

IT had then to count – loudly – up to a hundred while the rest of us fled, like bats out of a cave, small shadows scattering into the dark nights, and disappeared into the town. IT gave chase and if he or she saw you, IT called out your name and shouted, 'Alan's on IT!' Alan then joined the original IT but he hunted alone. Somehow or other IT worked and without cheating. The game made a web, a net of its own, in the middle of the night town, somehow sticking to boundaries. These had just emerged. It was the perfect playground.

You could go up the extremely narrow alley beside Ellwood's the electrician and wind through the top yard into the Crofts but once in the Crofts lane you were not allowed to push further out of town: you had to double back down George Street to be safe, slipping away through William Street, a back street that had its own tributaries of minor back streets. We would be like rats infesting a crumbling old town. Or you could cut into Church Street and up towards but not beyond the church itself. The old and neglected church cemetery with its drunken, tilting head-stones and sinking tombs was still within bounds but spooky and all but impenetrable, with its wild shrubbery and uncontrolled trees. It was not a favoured place in which to wait and grow cold, and know that you would never be found. The best thing was to be caught, not too late, cease to be prey and become a hunter, or the game dwindled into eternity, boredom and collapse.

But once in Church Street you were in clover. The pig market took you through to Water Street and so did an alley behind the church, which led to Little Lane and Tenters and Birdcage Walk, which would lead to Market Hill, unless you doubled back and went up Vinegar Hill and then got into the complex around the Parish Rooms and the Temperance Hall . . . Hiding and hearing the fast footfalls scudding within a yard of you, running and just in time dodging the shadow at the end of the alley, turning, finding another secret spot; or waiting, the town seeming to be empty and the worry of not being found ratcheting up the anxiety so you broke cover because it was better to be part of the game than safe.

Now at least four people were IT, how did we know? We just did. We could make a dash for the fountain and touch the railings to be home, safe. But out of the four, two would be on guard, at the fountain, on patrol. All they had to do was touch you and you were caught. It could be a long wait for another game. Around the street we ghosted, ran, hid, ran again for a better refuge, listened to the names called out on the streets, how near they were, how far away. When should we make our move? 'Tom! You're IT. Noreen! IT! Robert, Joan, Maggie, Billy! You're IT!'

The game lit up the night town. We ignored the comings and goings of grown-ups. It was ours, which built up its own pressures of excitement and an occasional touch of fear.

It grew louder as more and more became hunters. A few would be left out by too good a hiding place, too much security, so they would make a reckless dash to a lesser hiding place only to be stung by the sound of their name and so back to the fountain.

'One potato, two potato,
Three potato, four . . .'

There was a time for conkers and a time for pasche eggs. Marbles and catapults came in all seasons, sledges in snow, and there was the drama of bonfire night.

Horse chestnuts, conkers, were tricky. First you had to get them. We – the gang – William, Eric, Geoff, Robert and Micky – would make for the Auction Fields behind the vicarage next to the Nelson Thomlinson School's playing fields. As the field belonged to the auction company it was only used on market days so there would be no cattle that we might have been accused of disturbing. We were secure on all sides. On one side was the large vegetable garden and orchard belonging to the vicarage; on the other, empty acres of auction pens ripe for games but not while we were collecting conkers; on another side the playing fields of the grammar school that would be deserted in the evenings, and on the fourth side the Auction Fields itself stretched away into further fields, which seemed unthreatening. We were covered. At the vicarage end of the field was a stupendous shielding chestnut tree. We could go to work in peace and safety.

You found a thick stick, stood back and hurled it at a nesting of chestnuts. With luck, after a few goes, you dislodged one or two. We had tried to climb the tree but couldn't find a way to get going and, besides, that would have exposed us to the vicar. So slowly, by way of the sticks, we gathered a modest but adequate harvest. When you took off the casing, the chestnuts were so deeply brown, so glossy, with that fawn cap on the top, so velvet to touch, objects to put on a mantelpiece rather than disfigure with a nail. But that was what we did. I was clumsy and impatient and would slam the hammer on the nail head as often as not splitting the chestnut. When finally I got it through and blew it clean and tied the knot in one end of a piece of string to make it fit for combat, I was already a bit frustrated with it. Perhaps it was a premonition: I was no good at conkers. Like everybody else I tried to harden my conkers (sometimes I had two or three) by putting them in the oven, or in vinegar.

At the time I just thought I was useless, but looking back, I think that taking off my specs before any sporting activity – football, conkers, marbles, rugby and cricket – meant that, however carefully I swung back my conker and aimed at the small dangled competing conker, my lash would miss more often than it hit. If you smashed your opponent's chestnut you took on his score: say his conker had twelve victories, you added them to your score. These add-on scores could be impressive. There were boys who were deadly and kept their conkers from year to year. One swore his was 104. The chestnuts became stones. I have no memory of any sniff of such glory accruing to myself or any of the gang. We played conkers because they were there.

Pasche eggs were for Easter, for religion and art, but even this we managed to turn into warfare. Pasche eggs were a commemorative way to celebrate the crucifixion, death and resurrection of Christ. Pasche, we had learned in church, came from the Latin word for Easter. The eggs were hard-boiled and then decorated. They could be painted. Some of the most striking were done in the factory by men who wrapped up the eggs in different-coloured layers of the filmy transparent paper produced there. By putting together different-coloured papers and placing the tightly wrapped eggs in boiling water for some time, they produced a swirl of abstract images, reminding you of the lurid sunsets across the Solway Firth, or a blinding irradiating sun, or they were just beautiful delicate patterns, glowing. There were men who could do miniature realistic paintings – say of St Mary's Church or a horse and cart. Friends of my father and mother would bring their eggs to the pub and we would line them up on the window-sills, displayed for all the passing town to see.

My mother boiled about three score of them in the pantry and used the Rayophone paper to give them their colour. She would sell them for sixpence each. Half the takings went into St Dunstan's blind box. The other half was for prize money. The dumping competition happened on Easter Sunday night.

You took the egg in your fist, exposed the sharp or the fat end to your opponent who 'dumped it'. He banged his tightly held, strangled egg against yours. Then you had a go at 'dumping' his. There was always somebody who would be the adjudicator. When one of the eggs was battered beyond dumping, the other was the winner of this celebration of the Resurrection. Then we would eat them.

There was a steep hill nearby, called Pasche Egg Hill, where, my mother said, in her time they 'all' used to go on Easter morning after church and roll their eggs down it. The custom faded but not the name. It became the best spot for sledging. It was steep and there was a big bump halfway down that iced over and, if you had enough speed, could make you gloriously airborne. We would trek there from all over the town, ignoring alternative hills. Some of us had sledges – all homemade – others brought tea trays, yet others flattened a cardboard box, and those without any equipment just launched themselves at the hill, skidded down and pretended they were skiing.

We played marbles in the town's gutters. There was little traffic at that time. There were, I had read, much more elaborate ways to play at marbles, involving rings and the flicking thumb and fingers. They were too fancy. We found the gutter served our purpose. This was to amass as many as we could of the small glass globes encircling little swirls of colour, blue, green, yellow, red . . . You rolled your marble along the gutter. Your opponent tried to tap it with his and if he did he could pocket it. And it would be his turn to go first. If you missed him he had a shot and so on. When you ran out of marbles you used ball-bearings. You could buy monstrous marbles but they were too big for the gutter and banned from play. It was a familiar sight while the craze lasted – it came in waves – short-trousered boys crouched in the gutters, studying the form as keenly as any grown-up bowler on the park green. Sometimes the marbles went down a drain and even if we managed to lever it up, it was impossible to fish them out. We virtually crawled our way up and down the streets, like pups smelling new scents.

Catapults were stupid, dangerous and irresistible. We would find the necessary two-fingered stem on a small branch, hack it out of the hedge and make it into a weapon. It needed two broad strips of rubber, which you could cadge from a garage or buy from Saunderson's ironmonger's – where Michael, his son, worked on Saturday mornings. You made a pouch for the stone out of a bit of leather, cadged again, or hacked out of wherever, or got in a swap, and then you had the deadly instrument. Good catapults could bring down a bird in flight. At first like others I played with it in school and when the teacher was turned to the blackboard or between lessons, I would load up with pellets – small buttons of paper soaked in ink from the inkwell on the desk or hard little peas – and let fly. When the girls' school amalgamated with ours and shared the classroom it was even more fun. We thought.

Soon catapults went out of doors to be used in the inevitable fights. They got more powerful. My uncle Irwin gave me a catapult he had made and rejected when he left school. It felt like a bow. Small pebbles were the regular ammunition at first. Their size grew and finally, when confrontations became more serious, staples and small ball-bearings took over. We would group behind a building or in a ditch and, to some extent, be protected from what had become an assault weapon. For one intoxicating period, a month or so, we could not wait to get outside for playtime and let loose at each other, until a boy's eye was badly damaged. All catapults were immediately confiscated. Possession of a catapult would, we were told, lead to instant expulsion. They were collected and burned. Letters were written to parents.

Bonfires involved no violence along the way but were aimed at a total destruction of the enemy's effort.

This was when we were just tiptoeing into our teens.

We knew that Guy Fawkes had tried to blow up Parliament on 5 November 1605 and been caught just in time. We had been taught to believe that Parliament was sacred. Effigies of Guy Fawkes were burned the length and breadth of the country – 'Remember, remember the fifth of November'.

We were out to build the biggest bonfire in the town and also to set alight, before 5 November, any bonfire rivalling ours.

There were several small bonfires in the town – Market Hill had a piddling little one. The two giants were on Highmoor, on some wasteland beside the Venetian-towered Great House, and Western Bank, where there were well-established housing settlements near the park and a perfect space, isolated from all buildings. We baggsed that.

My grandfather's house was nearby. I could claim to be part of the Western Bank gang. Indeed some of them, like Hector Stainton, had originally come from Station Road, which practically made us cousins. And if further authority were needed, my uncles, Irwin and Wilson, together with their generation, had built up the size and reputation of the Western Bank Bonfire some years before. And to put the seal on it, Tom Monkhouse, the boldest of the boys in the park, who would hang upside down on the structure supporting the American swing, grease the banana slide and play forbidden football until capture was imminent, was a friend. My passport was well stamped.

To build a real bonfire you had to start early. At least three weekends before 5 November – with luck the date coincided with the half-term week holiday – you went round garages to ask if they had old worn-out tyres; you haunted the back of the Co-op where goods were unloaded and begged for cardboard boxes; you went to the farms near Western Bank and asked the farmers what they could give us or what we could hack from their trees and bushes. Local door-to-door helped in the collecting of inflammable rubbish, which we piled into the middle of the combustible fortress we were building. Luck helped. One year we went to the sawmill on spec and came away with three barrow loads of rotten planks. Paper shops would give their remainders to us. Two or three of the boys had fathers in the factory and they brought gaudy rolls of vividly coloured Rayophone paper, which would give the flames even more colours, leaping out of the stockade, making fantastic shapes in the sky.

The only nag was that Highmoor's was said to be bigger. We knew the boys up there, from school, from games, from relatives. There were families of brothers, the Alisons, the Pearsons and the Hendersons, who were formidable. They had made a dirt track for bicycles imitating motorbikes in a tight cluster of hillocks, under the very nose of the Great House. They had legendary games of chasey around Highmoor and Brindlefield. They kept rabbits and ferrets, as well as budgies and canaries. We had to beat them.

We made sure it was dark when we set off. There was William, myself and Geoff. We had matches, dry paper, a torch but, more lethally, half a can of petrol, which Geoff had been press-ganged into filching from his dad's small and treasured garage at the bottom of their garden. We promised Geoff we would not use all of it, in fact use so little it would scarcely be noticed. Geoff said that if his father found out he, Geoff, would be killed. We said we were prepared to take that risk. We set off when it turned dark.

We went through the town along Low Moor Road and up Crozier's Field. Mr Crozier kept a lot of cattle in that field and they grew nosy and began to gather around the three of us. Their mooing and snorting in the deepening twilight was uncanny. We told each other not to panic because animals knew when you were frightened and it made them attack you first. So we walked, tightly together, at what we thought was a safe pace, with the big heavily breathing beasts closing in on us. William reminded us that cows could trample people to death. As usual, he said that in his quiet, certain way. Nothing to worry about.

When the gate was a few yards away we bolted. The cattle were just a few seconds slow off the mark and we were over the gate before they could crush us. They pushed against the gate in frustration. We decided to go back another way.

By now we felt shaky but we were near.

Their bonfire, silhouetted against a clear sky with a big bright moon and friendly stars, looked – and was – immense. Behind it the Tower reared up like a sentinel.

It seemed to be unguarded.

We tried making the last few score yards without benefit of the torch, but the ground was pitted and there was no path. We began to curse and then switched on the torch. The trouble was that when we got there we discovered that the cap on the petrol tin had been screwed so tightly that we couldn't open it. Our bits of paper and the Captain Webb box of matches seemed inadequate. Nevertheless William volunteered to burrow inside the bonfire, taking the matches with him. I was to follow with more paper. Geoff stood guard, holding the useless petrol can.

I don't know what William did and he could never work it out, but the part of the bonfire into which he had more or less buried himself began to collapse. Geoff and I pulled him out just before the crash imploded and the fine structure sagged. A window opened.

'Is that you, David? What's going on?'

We were going on. Going down the ill-lit but still lit Highmoor Avenue, past the houses of the Alisons and the Pearsons and the Hendersons onto the main road, and we did not stop until we reached the middle of the town.

We had not been followed. But you never knew with the Highmoor gang. We ignored the fish-and-chip shop and split for home.

From the next night, with three to go, we put extra guards on our own bonfire. On 4 November my father made one of those unexpected moves, the pin sharp memory of which still smarts the eyes almost seventy years on. An hour or so before my bedtime, he said we'd go out for a walk. We went to Station Road into the garage and up the ramp into the toy showroom above Henry Moore's garage.

He let me choose a box of fireworks and indicated the counter on which the bigger boxes were displayed.

I hadn't reckoned with fireworks.

The bonfire was the thing.

But the box I picked had rockets, bangers, Catherine wheels, sparklers, jumping jacks, volcanoes – and in quantity.

It was my mother who came down to see the bonfire, as it blazed away, throwing out hundreds of sparks. At the end we, the gang who had built it, squatted round the fire and threw on scrumped-up balls of the coloured Rayophone we had got from the factory men. The colours shot up high, streams of rainbow colours in the dark. We fed potatoes into the embers, stabbing them with twigs to get them out, biting into their black burned skins, watching the spitting and flickering remains of the tyres, tree branches and the planks shoring it up.

And finally, because I had been too busy keeping the fire going until now, I opened the box my father had bought me and we set off all the fireworks and watched them, every one.

The three rockets came at the end. Launched one after the other from a pint milk bottle. When the last one exploded in the starry night sky and scattered its own spray of stars, I guess I felt as happy as it is possible to be.

Chapter Twenty-three

Going to grammar school was not the end of the world I had feared. Partly because so many in my class at the national school also passed the scholarship to Nelson Thomlinson. Partly because it was all boys. Although I had been in mixed schools from four to eleven, the boys and girls had been strictly segregated. The only way we met publicly was when the boys raided the dens the girls made inside the big hawthorn bushes in spring. There were temporary crushes, but they had begun much earlier.

For instance I remember one when I was seven, which entailed me 'setting home' Kathleen Haile – walking a mile and a half after school through lanes previously unknown to me. There was a boy a year older than us who lived near her. They used to walk in together. I do not know how I displaced him. When we got near her house, she ran on – I turned back. Nothing happened, save that we walked through the lanes until I saw her house – one of three cottages in the middle of nowhere. She ran towards them and left me standing.

At the grammar school we were not driven into homework as some of the older boys had threatened. In the early forms, the homework was so light you could do it at school if you got there a quarter of an hour early. Or you could copy it from a friend. It did not eat into our after-school lives. We had uniforms – a brown blazer with a badge and the motto 'Fide et Operis' – By Faith and by Works. We had to learn Latin and we were divided into houses – like the boarding schools the school in some ways aped, as they in some ways had aped the older grammar schools. We had a morning assembly with prayers, readings from the Bible and 'notices'; and we had playing fields – two rugby pitches, one cricket square, room to mark out a running track in summer – and a gym. '*Mens sana in corpore sano*', we were told. A healthy mind in a healthy body. Latin always made a thing significant, a cut above – a mark of difference from the secondary modern into which those who failed the 11-plus exam moved. It was considered to be a step up the ladder, which many of us did not know was there.

All but three of the teachers were men. Some had served in the Second World War. In the teacher shortage during the war, several of the retired staff came back for duty. Two or three of them were still in place when I got there at the start of the fifties. A mellow, often absent-minded cluster, their sense of discipline had receded in their retirement and their age was given away by the copperplate handwriting in chalk on the blackboard. The war veterans – some in no more than their late twenties – were taking over but still there was much of the old-style eccentricity that seemed to be a necessary badge of honour, an insignia of the grammar school.

Mr Duff, the geography teacher, was rumoured to lift you up by the ears if you were annoying in class; Mr Nightingale, physics and maths, threw the blackboard duster at you with serious accuracy if you annoyed him – he played scrum half for Aspatria, then the best team in the district, and biked the nine miles to and from his home to school come what weather may; Mr Loveday spent more than twenty years taking two holidays a year in France, tracking down every nuance of the preposition *à*, which became his PhD. He was one of those who lodged in the town, as did Mr Burnett, a gentle man, another bachelor. He had a sadness in him that even we could sense. He was once temporary head-master for a week, and after the third assembly, gaining confidence from the first two, we broke him down completely by paying no attention at all to what he said. It was mass cruelty. He announced that the entire school was expelled. We left the hall and had to be hauled in from the playing fields later in the morning.

Mr Wood Senior taught Latin and lived with his mother, who was always ailing. She would not budge from her cottage twenty-three miles away, a journey he did twice a day without complaint in a tiny car. He tried his best to make us laugh, at the end of every term, with his Latin jokes. Mr Wood Junior, elegant, rather a dandy, almost film-star looks, also lived with his mother, forty-five miles away in the south of the Lake District. He travelled up on Monday mornings to lodge in Church Street, took no part in matters of the town, went back at 4 p.m. prompt on Friday afternoon to one of the rich villages in the pasturelands of the Lake District where he read the lessons in church. He said that his mother always warmed his slippers. He had been to Durham University and once told us that as there was a shortage of girls he 'had been reduced to taking out girls from Woolworths'. That didn't go down well.

Arthur Tillotson Blacka, who, we knew, had been in Czech-oslovakia during the war, bred donkeys, played cricket for Wigton until he was sixty-nine (slow left arm spinner) and taught English, largely by making us read it aloud. He was not interested in exams. This was not approved of, so we heard, by other teachers.

It was as if the teachers thought eccentricity essential in a grammar school, or we sniffed it out to make them appear extra special. Perhaps we associated it with the gentleman tradition of public schools. Between them they created a new and foreign world to us. It marked them out and, we were meant to think, up.

Borrowings from public schools – houses, formal assemblies – were easy to take on because I'd read about them in the Jennings and Darbishire books, in *Fifth Form at St Dominic's*, in *Mike* and *Tom Brown's Schooldays* and other school stories. These were always large, isolated, essentially fair and happy places where, instead of going home, the boys slept in dormitories and followed rules all day to fill the time. There were no girls and not a flicker of sexual abuse or torment (save in *Tom Brown's Schooldays* when Flashman paid the price for bullying). We were shielded from the confessional public-school books written by adults whose experiences had been unhappy. What we saw in the public schools was that they were being prepared to rule. They would hold together the empire. The empire's hold was being released, but very slowly. In my schooldays its style and manner and assumptions about Englishness held on strongly. For many in my childhood, Britain ruled not only the waves but much of the world.

Schools reinforced that belief with a confident and casual certainty. Until I was fourteen and began to try to think for myself, I, along with millions of others, believed that we were the greatest empire the world had ever known. An empire on which the sun never set. We had a credo that would not have disgraced a religion. We did not need to write it down, we just breathed it in. Our credo through the early grammar school years was:

The English (the British sometimes) were best.
We were the best fighters and never lost a war. (Or if we did, we went back and won it next time.)
We were the best sailors and never lost a battle at sea.
Our Spitfires had stopped the Germans occupying us and our bombers had knocked them for six.
We were the fairest of all. Our laws were ancient, true and unfailing.
We never ducked a challenge. We always rose to meet and overcome it, even if at the last moment, which made us even more special.
We had invented most of what mattered, from football to gravity.
We were not excitable like other peoples; nor were we lethargic like other peoples; we were in the middle, just right, like our climate.
The world was full of backward peoples, pagans and savages, whose lives had been improved by doing what we told them to do.
We did good. God was always on our side and white was right.
History lessons, then, were a triumphant procession of victories, which never involved cruelty to those we were fighting. All was fair in our wars.

It was not only in war and law. We had the best writers, the best painters, although that did not matter very much, except for Shakespeare who was the World's Number One.

We were cunning, brave, even heroic, merciful and courteous. We never cried.

The best thing to aim for was to be a gentleman. The worst was to show off.

It did not matter if other countries and even America seemed better or claimed to be better or seemed to beat us. We knew in our bones that we were the best and that was that.

British men had fought unceasingly for this. Women scarcely figured. If they did, they behaved like men.

Just look how small we were on that globe. Just look how much of that globe we owned.

What more proof could you want?

This was dripped into me and all of us at both the infants' school and the national school, but then came the full flooding of the mind in the grammar as in the public schools. This, however tactfully and factually disguised, was the agenda I subscribed to throughout what are sometimes called 'the formative years'. It was not so much an agenda, more a way of life. We could face down the world.

Those who objected were, at that time, few and not encouraged.

One powerful consequence was that this credo effortlessly endorsed the class system. Kings and queens were on top, aris-tocrats next, the public-school men and then down, down, down, down, a hundred cuts to labourers, paupers and women.

The Labour Party was the only place where, just knocking on the door of my teens, I found any constructive resistance to this sacred order. Not at the meetings. These, held in the Temperance Hall, were cheerful affairs mainly given over to reports of what had happened or announcements about what was going to happen. Here, I ganged up with Brian Henderson, whose mother also worked for the Party at the meetings. We would take off our shoes and skid over the floor in the empty two thirds of the hall. We stopped to listen when the announcements of outings came along. These were mostly trips to the industrialised west of Cumberland. The coastal towns of Maryport through Workington to Whitehaven (once the second port of England we were repeatedly told) churned with heavy industry. As our Labour-hired coach rolled through them for a rally or a carnival, we would pass pitheads, slag heaps, furnaces firing night and day, a coal and steel industry still powerfully charged after the war. It was where my grandfather and many of his brothers and their sons worked. Smoke, noise, the beat of mighty industry was thrilling. To me, from a market town, it was energy, force, the excitement of hard men and ceaseless machinery scooping into the earth, driving pit shafts for miles under the sea, engineering and fuelling the world.

The Labour Party rallies to which we were taken blew apart the gentle meetings in the Wigton Temperance Hall. Here were gaudy banners. Where we walked, they marched; where our band accompanied young maidens dancing elegantly, theirs led singing cohorts towards a new Jerusalem. The mines had been nationalised and there was a cocky atmosphere – you could feel it, even as a boy, and in case you did not feel it, throughout the day it would be broadcast on the Tannoy – that 'we are the masters now'. The mixture of dangerous, dirty work and a Brave New World was heady. And the serious weight of that mass of people in the west of the county was inspiring. Everybody seemed sharper than back in Wigton. The men were open, forever joshing each other, the women bolder than the Temperance Hall group, the girls so cheeky and confident: why would anyone not want to serve such a cause?

On our way back we sang, buoyed up by the certainty and cheerfulness of the Party in the west. The grown-ups talked about the mines and we children felt we had been dipped in the true faith. Soon we were singing 'Onward Christian Soldiers'. It was my first encounter with Labour in full spate and it began to give me a new idea of how to look at the way the world worked. It seemed neither strident nor disruptive. It was a better way to think about what was happening, and it carried a moral strength – it was the Right Way, as Christianity still claimed to be, but more relevant.

There were Labour Party children's sports, a Labour Party band, Labour politicians talking through a megaphone, and a Labour Party carnival led by the Labour Party Queen of the Day. The Party was not anti-monarchist. My mother found no difficulty in following the doings of the Royal Family unwaveringly and with detailed knowledge every bit as keenly as my father followed the horses, while she steadily affirmed her loyalty to the Labour Party. The word 'socialism' was rarely used in the town, save by some Tories who used it as an insult.

Mr Bell, husband of the chairman (as his wife was then called), insisted on talking about Big Subjects when he came to the meetings. People listened to him. He had a mild and light tenor voice, which, most people said, made his arguments all the more acceptable.

Ranting would have got him nowhere in the Temperance Hall in front of almost a score more women than men, all keen to get Labour elected again and extend the immeasurable achievements of Mr Attlee's post-war government. Mr Bell explained that the job was only half done, that trade unions should be part of those who controlled industry, that people should pay for privileges, that the rich should support the poor and there should be more hospitals . . . He was clever enough to keep it short. When he had done, the polite applause, though brief, was firm. If Mrs Godwin was there to play the piano, he would sing a few sentimental favourites. 'The Wings of a Dove' was always requested.

It was my mother's reporting of the accounts that was the highlight for me and I felt she had won a great battle when Mrs Bell said, 'Are we all agreed? Those not in agreement will raise their hands.' (No hand went up.) 'Treasurer's report passed.

Thank you, Mrs Bragg.' Finally we all thanked Mrs Phillips who boiled the water and Mrs Henderson who made the tea. The job of Brian and myself was to replace the chairs tidily against the walls.

Chapter Twenty-four

We were an unimpressive workforce, huddled together on a small flat cart towed by a tractor, breathing clouds of steam into the cold morning sky, too concerned to fight the cold to sing. The women came from the squad that collected rosehips, raspberries and blackberries in season, ruthlessly stripping clusters of bushes around the town. This was a chance to earn cash for otherwise kitchen-bound women to feed and clothe families, to swell meagre incomes. The women were wrapped up layers deep. Now and then a cigarette would be lighted up. They, too, were lit up to be out of the town for a day. Children, theirs and others, sat next to the rickety rail around the cart and put their faces into the wind to enjoy the sting of it. I was eight, with my aunt Margaret, my father's youngest sister, at thirteen trusted to keep an eye on me.

It was half-term, which coincided with picking the potato crop – 'tattie pickun week'. We provided the cheap labour. The farmers' wives would provide the tea or hot chocolate from an urn at dinner time, our midday break. We took sandwiches.

For me that first morning of my first week as a worker was another playtime. The countryside flattened as we drove towards the sea. Villages, busy already, a few of us raised a little cheer at the farmers, the sky became enormous the flatter the land, and beneath it the beckoning stretch of the sea. We were driven through the farmyard to our working field. A few women and children, local, were already there, impatient to begin. Held up by these townspeople. Stitches, according to our bossy farmer, could only be allocated when we were all present.

The stitches, lengths of land, variable, averaged about thirty yards. Mr Edmondson, the farmer, encouraged us to make something approaching a line as at a hiring fair and walked up and down, picking first the women who had done the job before. They got the longest, most profitable stitches. Culling continued, until he reached 'kids', us. I was the smallest, which would count against me. Margaret, tall for her age, ginger-haired, which signalled feisty, was scornful at being so dependent on the judgement of the farmer, who seemed to enjoy this selection process. When she produced me as her second, the farmer noticeably shrugged. We were given the shortest stitch, which meant less money, but the farmer couldn't risk having a stitch that was not cleared, one that would hold him up.

The tractor and side plough went up and down at a steady pace, stopping at the top of the field while we picked the potatoes and put them into a wire basket. We tipped the wire baskets' harvest into a small cart behind the plough when it came round next time. At the top of the field the baskets would be tipped out onto a heap and the farmer would then rattle down the field to start again.

He had a sharp eye. If he saw potatoes still lying there from a previous stitch he would jab his finger and yell, 'What about them? Get them for next time.' Very soon we were – Margaret and myself at any rate – beginning to be frightened by this remorseless man on his big machine, churning up potatoes from under the crust of the earth, letting nothing get in the way of his progress. And telling us off.

Margaret worked it out. I was deputed to pick up the missed potatoes in furrows that had not been fully cleared: she tackled the new stitch on her own. It worked. She was a strong young woman.

Margaret endured a deal of teasing from her brothers, who enjoyed tormenting her. They did it, as they thought, in a light-hearted way but the effect on Margaret was to disturb her. She was an innocent, kind, an easy target. She was high-spirited and, as the saying went, 'highly strung'. The brothers played on that. The problem was that she loved them. She was made aware that she was not as clever at school as they were, that is at the things at which they were clever, although in many ways she was more skilled. So she took their ragging to heart. She believed that she was a lesser member of the family and often walked around that warm Park House in some anxiety.

Margaret was already essential to her mother in the kitchen and loved being asked to help her father on the allotment, just the two of them working together. She had friends in the area who came to play and she went to their houses but, save on exceptional occasions, her father forbade her to go into the park alone. He had seen disturbing things happen to girls.

It was a cruel rule. It is true that the park was more the habitat of boys, and that when girls went in they tended to go in small groups. It was a hunting ground for some predatory male adolescents, but little more than other open spaces, although with its pavilion and woods, its shelter and screening privet hedges it had more potential for sexual encounters of varying kinds. And there had been a rumoured incident when several 'lads' (two of them from the grammar school) had persuaded a girl to follow them to the deserted putting green and taken her clothes off. Then their nerve had failed them. But Harry saw enough to bar his daughter. She could come in with one or two friends – one had to be Ann Monkhouse, older than her – but even then she was not to stay long and never to go on the swings, which swished up the girls' skirts.

So, Margaret found her worlds outside the house in school and in church. She joined the AYPA but soon left it. She did not enjoy the constant competition in the games they played and she said, 'I was made to feel ignorant.'

I was something of a much younger brother to her. To be dumped on the draining board in the kitchen and scrubbed clean, behind the ears, the neck, hair fiercely combed. Just for her to enjoy the power of it? And we played games, some of which we

thought were naughty. She had a crackling energy, and her tender
heart was always on her sleeve; all she disliked about me was
when I called her 'Aunty'. I trusted her absolutely.

Much more lightly worked, I soon treated 'tatie pickun' as a
game. I scurried to and from the basket with a jersey front turned
into a bucket for the fresh earth-caked spuds, tipping them in
and haring off again while Margaret, bent back rarely straightened, went through the new arrivals.

Flocks of gulls came in and circled the field with loud
squawking and steep dives. As they swirled in the sky in mass,
not in ranks but somehow joined together, I became mesmerised
by them, glancing up at every opportunity, keeping my eye on
my aunt Margaret so that she did not catch me dodging work.
I think we enjoyed the grandeur of the long line of pickers up
the slight slope of the vast field. It was like being part of an
army.

The farmer noticed that the older furrows had been tidied up
and shouted out, 'Well done, you two!' as he dug into the rich
Solway soil to make another stitch. Margaret didn't look at him.
She had taken against him, she said, from the moment she saw
him. After he had moved on, she would stretch her back and rub
it hard with both hands. She never teased me. Apart from an
occasional 'Well done, lad' she was too bitten into her own
thoughts, and walked slowly down her patch to be ready for the
next stint.

She had brought two teacakes with a thin slice of ham in each,
two rock buns, two slices of gingerbread and an apple sliced in
two. Plenty enough for both of us, Margaret said, ignoring the
egg sandwiches and drop scones my mother had provided.
Margaret liked to share but she never ate food that had not been
made by her mother and herself. The urn was filled and then
filled again with thin but hot chocolate. It tingled my throat and
the unexpected bonus of a second cup was like a medal. When
we walked past the farmer on the way back to the field, he said,

'You're the best two in the field.' I believed him and swelled up. Margaret looked away.

The farmer began to tease her in the afternoon. She didn't like it. Her skin flared scarlet with blushes and when he said, 'Give us a smile, then', she shook her head and bent further down to pick up the potatoes.

We finished the field earlier than expected and there was half an hour or so to wait while the farmer stowed away the booty of the day. One of the boys had brought a football and that settled the boys. Margaret made a point of sitting alongside some of the older women, who noticed that Mr Edmondson would flash her a wink or a special nod of the head when he walked past and came to pay them. 'He fancies you,' they said, and laughed as she blushed. She tried to screw herself into an invisible ball.

Heavy low clouds came at us from the sea. A cold drizzle set in. Attempts to start a sing-song on the way homeward failed. Tiredness drove it out. Mr Edmondson went too quickly and we bounced and swayed on the flat cart. When Highmoor Tower came into view there were a few cheers.

Margaret took me back to Station Road. Yes, he'd done all right. Two shillings for him. Five for me, she said, holding out two shiny half-crowns. She wouldn't stay, wanted to get back home before rain set in.

She stood at the door and had to force herself to say, 'I'm not going tomorrow, Ethel.' My mother's expression asked the question. 'I didn't like the man lookin' at me,' she said. 'He gave me the creeps. Sorry.'

Then she was gone. She must have done something wrong to be given such unwelcome attention. She must have done something bad.

Chapter Twenty-five

For a time, at the beginning of my teens, Wigton swimming baths were the be-all and end-all of the day. The pool was twenty yards long, which meant five lengths for the usual racing distance of a hundred yards, and eighty-eight lengths if you wanted to swim a mile. There were slipper baths to which those without a bath at home could come for a soak, diving platforms and narrow galleries running the length of either side of the pool. On a narrow space alongside it were small cubicles – boys to the left, girls to the right. The Saturday night galas packed out the place with tarpaulins over the knees of those who sat on the benches in front of the cubicles. There was a fine view from the galleries.

We went to 'learn swimming' once a week from the national school; we went from the grammar school; we went to watch the galas – races and water polo – with other, all bigger, towns, Carlisle, Workington, Whitehaven. But most of all I went alone. It was cheap. And you could stay in for as long as you wanted. In the summer holidays you could get a card, which, as a schoolboy, gave you free access throughout the five-week holiday. I'd 'spent' the face value of the card in the first week. I was there every morning save Sundays and usually for about two hours and left the pool shivering with cold, heading for the machine that delivered hot cocoa.

Swimming was the only sport at which I was any good. But it was not the swimming that took me there. Nor was it the games, though they became addictive. Mr Cook, who was the supervisor, preferred to sit in the office or to go down to the boiler room where a pal would drop in for a chat or a cigarette. We were largely unattended. That was the pull.

We were – especially between nine thirty and twelve – about half a dozen. Boys. None of the gang, none of whom was interested in swimming. At the baths were boys who wanted to be at the baths as much as possible. The pool seduced us. There was something about diving into the water, swimming under water, swimming a full length under water, heroic, holding your breath, basking, floating, stroking lazily from one side to another, just pushing yourself against one wall to take you on a motionless glide to the opposite wall, feeling so protected in and under the water, so safe, letting the water become more important than anything, as if you were meant for the water, were being baptised into an older time (although this was not conscious, not even considered until later, but it was *there*). I loved to be deep in it, free and weightless. I wanted to stay in it for as long as I possibly could. I felt so content there: why should I ever come out?

There were our games. There were always games. The structure in the roof of the pool was like a barn, with rafters. We would walk along the narrow galleries, stand on the ledge of the railings that secured the spectators, jump out onto a rafter and grapple across it until we were above the centre of the pool, far higher than the highest diving board, then bomb down, clutching our knees, trying to make the biggest splash possible. That was the best one.

Games of chasey, of course. Why was it that of all the games in every context chasing each other in order to tag someone was by far the most popular? We made it as difficult as we could. You could only dive in to avoid pursuit if you were in the deep end and made for the other side: no lingering or dodging in the pool itself. You could go up the diving steps but only to the top – why? You were not allowed to run alongside the pool. But however skilfully and intentionally we constructed and reconstructed the game, it remained chasey. Half a dozen slender boys, glistening with water, darting in some sort of organised way around the pool as if obeying a ritual.

Then there were races, but they were not as much fun. At the galas the races were handicapped by Mr Cook. There was a period when I was quite quick at the two lengths. Unusually both my father and my mother came to one gala. In the boys' sprint I was the back marker at twenty seconds. There were six of us. Four of them dived in on their handicaps number at not unreasonable intervals but Blob, known as such because he was stupendously fat, had already turned at the other end when, from Mr Cook, I heard my trigger – twenty seconds. Partly I am sure because I wanted to show off in front of my father and mother I had never swum as quickly. When I turned at the far end, Blob was bobbing in the distance about to enter the shallow zone. I scarcely took a breath and, anyway, just managed to touch the bar before him. There was cheering. I looked up to see my parents smiling and clapping.

Later, Dad said, 'Mr Cook said it proved his handicapping system worked. I would have put good money on you. I knew you'd do it.' That was the peak of my swimming career. My prize was a pen and pencil set.

One way in which the grammar school tugged us away from the town was the Boy Scouts. There had been a First Wigton Troop of Boy Scouts before the war, led by a remarkable man whose childhood polio had crippled one of his legs, which he dragged like a ball and chain. He was one of the Robinson family. His bigger and stronger cousins had protected him early on but soon he needed no protection. His tongue could be very sharp. He spoke a polite version of the Wigton accent, rather effeminately. He bred Pekinese, which won best of class at Crufts. He conjured what became a distinguished First Wigton Troop of Boy Scouts out of lads who would never, save for him, have crossed the line into that rather skilled and upper-working, lower-middle artisan class, which characterised the Boy Scouts.

He found ways to relax the code of dress, carved woggles out of thick twigs from the branches of a tree, got his sisters to make the green neckerchiefs and, through a dog friend, who was the chief salesman at Redmayne's, found a stock of black berets, which did the job of the traditional khaki Scout Stetson. 'We can't have looked that bad,' he would say. 'We won every competition we entered.'

He had become a legend. He taught the boys to snare a rabbit, skin it, boil it; how to keep a fire going through the night; how to catch, roast and eat hedgehogs. He tramped them up to the unexcavated Roman settlement of Old Carlisle – a good mile and a half from the East End. There he pointed out humps and hollows in the ground – once barracks, once kitchens, the biggest hollow an amphitheatre, all laced together with overgrown pathways perfect for tracking, signs in twigs on the ground every few score yards. They built a bridge across the river. They caught fish, made fires. A friendly farmer might give them sausages.

He went to London soon after the war where he became a gentlemen's gentleman to wealthy twins who lived in Kensington and required at least three changes of clothes a day. 'When those boys went out,' he said, in his unchanging rather camp Wigton accent, 'they were immaculate.' He emphasised every syllable heavily. 'Nobody could fault them.'

Our troop – the Second Wigton Scout Troop – was set up by the chemistry teacher. We called him 'sir' in school, 'Skip' in the Scouts. We had a room above the library for our kit and our den. The school hall was where we assembled. The playing fields were ours whenever we needed them.

Skip, Mr Beaumont, rather stout, bespectacled, was hairy – the head, the ears and, when he put on his shorts for meetings, we were confronted with very hairy legs. He was a bachelor. He had come to the town from the south. He bought a large Victorian terraced house, going cheap, one of six, in Victoria Place, overlooking the fields to the River Wiza. At the top he installed a big train set, which he let you control from a panel in the middle of the room. In a parlour there was a small organ, which he played with vigour as we sang songs of Woad and the Ancient Britons. A year after he came to the school, in one of those weeding exercises with the timetable that small schools had to do, I dropped chemistry and so I have little memory of him as a teacher, save that he appears to have had no eccentricities. He was a most self-contained and self-sufficient person. Now and then, at Scout meetings, you might catch him humming to himself.

All of us had the correct uniform. Grey shirt, grey short pants, grey long socks. We went in for badges – bird spotting, tree spotting, knots. We were in four patrols of six, mine was called the Eagles. William was in it, so were Eric and Michael. We wore the bush/cowboy/proper Baden-Powell Scout hat.

The Second Wigton Troop was for grammar school boys only.

We marched with the army, the air force, the navy, the churches and councillors from the fountain to St Mary's on Remembrance Sundays.

We were ordered about and learned to order ourselves about and order others 'to do my duty by God and the King'. Rules were all about us.

It was a long way from the baths.

Skip liked to fix trips. He had a large van. In the back was a bunk bed and a bench. Four of us sat there. William sat next to him in the front. We set off for Oxford promptly at 7 a.m. There, we were to board a houseboat, which would take us down the Thames and back up again for eight days. We were not required to wear our uniforms.

He was not a good driver. The van jerked along in spurts and brakings. We found a roadside petrol station and small café, which kept us going. Just in case, Skip had loaded a few basics. It was a relief to get out of the van.

Oxford was a cluster of boats, and by the time we cast off and moved down the river we were tired. It was the first week of the Easter holiday.

The boat was a treat. A small kitchen, half a dozen bunks, a lavatory and shower, a room for drying off and storing things – and the open deck, a travelling terrace.

The best thing was to help manage the locks. To go in at the bottom of the small enclosure. To feel the boat rise or fall as the gates opened and the boat was raised or lowered to another level. Soon we could not wait to jump off our boat and help the lock keeper. We would make a thing of tying the thick wet rope around the capstan, becoming instant experts.

The weather held fine all that week.

We had never seen such rich countryside. It was the opposite of Wigton. That there was such a place in the same country!

We went very slowly. Woods coming into full leaf, fields unploughed, pastureland decorated with docile cattle, now a slow curve in the river that revealed yet more of a green and pleasant land unspoiled, without hovels, unclustered, open to the sky. Where were the poor people?

But it was the houses that captured me. From my mother I had caught and never lost the bug of noticing and admiring houses. Her dream to have a 'real house' not only rubbed off on me, it sank into me, like the deep unspoken longings with which parents can infect their children. I had never seen houses such as these! Built back from the riverbank, serene, appearing to float in their gardens as we floated on the waters of the Thames. So grand and so many. Who could live in them? Which film stars? Which millionaires? People who'd won the pools? Only they could buy such palaces. What would it be like to live there and just walk out every morning, pass a swimming-pool or a tennis court – a private tennis court! – and come to the water's edge where there would be a landing stage or a little pier with a handsome boat cosily moored. A house and a houseboat both! Two houses.

Other boats on the river, some splendid but most about our size, a fleet of contented people none of them with anything better to do than muck about in brightly painted boats, some with a table on the deck. Some would wave and we would wave back. On a long straight stretch as far as you could see there were these boats, little floating homes, with white-painted names, no logic to these. *Annabelle, Drake, The Crescent, Dolly, The*

Trout, Mexico, Irish Eyes, Jane, The Admiral: they made it seem fun, all this luxury plus making fun of it!

Yet in the end we assured each other loyally it was not a patch on Wigton. The places where we stopped to wander around seemed a world away, too posh to be real. I had been on a few day trips into the Lakes and been swallowed in that landscape. But here, and in villages and towns our size along the banks of the Thames, it was different. It was so much richer. And with that came calm. Unhurried shopping, hardly any stopping in the street for gossip. There was a gentleness in these places, as if nothing hard or terrible had ever happened there or ever would happen. The people always well dressed, the quaint shops, the many antique shops! No spitting. No real poverty. No lounging against pub walls. No lurching unemployed. An invitation to be happy as the Thames flowed on.

On the fourth day, just before we were to turn around to go back, we navigated a tight bend and heard a violent noise. The lock was ahead of us, controlled, unexceptional, but beside it were figures, screams, the sight of a turbulent vortex of spinning water.

We pulled in, got off the boat and made for the shore nearest to the tumult. Two boys, it seemed, from the fractured messages shouted out by other jangled and indecisive bystanders, had tried to swim across and got into trouble. They would be caught in a whirlpool effect. They would not be strong enough to swim out of it. We watched and I knew . . .

I could swim. I should swim out to help them. I should do it straight away. The cries were desperate. The noise of the thrashing killing water seemed to grow by the moment. I had to go in. I had to go in.

But I stood on the shore, bending like a sapling in a high wind but not moving. I was scooped of feeling.

The two boys drowned.

That was when I knew that at heart I was a coward. My father would have dived in.

Chapter Twenty-six

I can't remember when it began to happen. I was about thirteen. There was no severe illness to start it off, no injury to my head, no violence on any front. For some time I was able to keep it at bay. Then it became aggressive. In the early days it showed itself when I was alone, in bed, and it would appear. In the top right-hand corner of that narrow bedroom there would be a light. Distinctive. A reflection of nothing. The light was a thing in itself.

It was my mind. From whatever cause, the core that makes you know that you are you and what you are had slipped out of me. It had become the light in the corner of the room when I was in bed in the dark. My body felt without life. I felt that it would be dangerous to do anything because I had not the slightest idea of what might be happening, save that I had to concentrate everything I had on that small light and try to get it back in my head. All I can truthfully report is that there had to be a connection between the light and what had been me, otherwise . . . It was terrifying.

This was when the pub had closed. My parents had gone to bed. Or, much, much worse, had decided to go for a stroll if the evening was still warm. The front door banged shut, and until Andrew came in from a night shift – which sometimes would be just after six o'clock in the morning, once every three weeks – I was pinioned to my bed and transfixed by that light in the corner.

I could not and never did cry out.

There was the sense of a most powerful spell about the terror I felt that must not be broken, not broken under any circumstances. Least of all by my voice.

It got worse. On my way to school, when I passed the double stretch of windows of Johnson's, or Redmayne's shop, and glanced in, my mind would eject itself from my head and I would see the image of me as the real me and have to wrench myself away. Worse if I caught my face in the mirror when I was cleaning my teeth or washing. Worst of all when, over many months, this disassociation from myself began to creep into the classroom when I was trapped. How could I hide what I was feeling? It sucked out my energy. I had to devote myself to containing the fear.

It had to be hidden. How could it be explained? And to whom could I explain it? I could not even explain it to myself. My father and mother? Unthinkable. I could find no words. Friends? Teachers? The church, the AYPA, the Scouts? No, no, no. Incomprehensible that I should take even the first step to explain the incomprehensible, which, most certainly, would appear trivial, to be made a joke of, and you made a fool of.

It would go away. Sometimes for a night, very occasionally for both day and night, for days and nights. Then without fear I would get on with things. But it was soon back. Soon threatening me with that helpless blankness.

It must have begun to sap me. I began to behave badly; irritable at school. Swore. Said crap, bloody, even bugger. Was sent out several times and ended up in the headmaster's study. Mr Swale's den.

He was long overdue for retirement but he had held the school together through the war and that, perhaps, was the reason he was allowed to stay on. His was a room spilling books from every wall. Armchairs. School photographs. I remember his messy desk and him looking at the report when I was sitting in front of him.

'It would probably be best to expel you now and get it done,' he said. 'You're holding everybody back. I could arrange a transfer to the secondary modern.' He let the suggestion linger in the air.

I can reassemble his words with, I'm sure, a degree of accuracy. My reaction has long disappeared into welcome mists.

The secondary modern school?

I think he had expected a reaction.

Perhaps that crossed his mind.

'I'm sending you to Three L for the rest of this term and then we'll see. Report to Mr Southam,' he said. He scribbled on a piece of paper. 'Give him this.'

3L was not in the main building. Together with the Music Room and the Art Room – each staffed by women teachers – 3L had taken over one of the rooms of the vast house built for the headmaster and his family. I had been cast out. If I could have formulated it at the time, I would have said that those in 3L also felt cast out. It was the pariah form. Mr Southam, the form master, had been given the class. He was thought to be very poor at keeping discipline. What logic was at work there I do not know. 3L was created to be badly disciplined, save when one of the tough teachers came in to give their particular lesson. Mr Southam taught geography.

I went in after the dinner break. Word had got around. I was too upset to join in any of the usual games with the usual gang. I went to a corner of the big field and looked over at the chestnut tree in the Auction Field where we had gathered so many conkers. I must have been distraught. When I went into the 3L classroom it was worse. There was jeering. Mr Southam tried to ingratiate himself with the class by too often saying 'Oh, Bragg will know the answer to this. You've probably done this already in 3A?' My mind shrank to a pinhead of shame – at being in 3L, at knowing the answer to the question, at being afraid to give it, all the time worrying about what would happen to me when the first break came.

Four of the bigger lads from 3L guarded the toilets. They stood in a clump a few yards from the entrance, not making much of an attempt to conceal that they were smoking. They surveyed everyone who went in, assessing whom they would scrag and whose head they could duck down the lavatory. At least two of them had been 'held back' a form and were older than I was. All four were enduring a process they knew cared nothing for them and taking revenge. Their only ambition was to leave school. They participated in nothing, save the occasional fight, which they provoked. I was putty.

Three of the teachers could handle them and there was some respite but not much. Soon that teacher and the protection and the interest in the subject that had provided at least some distraction would go after the forty-five-minute class and I would collapse back into a misery I dared not reveal because that would be certain to bring out mockery.

There were just over four weeks to go before the summer holidays. At an early stage I made the mistake of trying to attach myself to the Guardians of the Toilets; to my shame I flattered them. It was not a good move. They knew it came from fear, as bullies always do, and so whenever they could they turned the screw. Just one wrong move and . . . I was too sick at heart to play with my previous friends and, besides, what would they want to do with someone so disgraced? School became hell.

There was a gap between school and bed. I still went to the AYPA and the Scouts and to choir practice. But I never lost the feeling that I was being tormented and felt somehow hollow. I made extra efforts, frantic at times, to show that I was all right. But I wasn't: I knew it, they knew it. Friends, William particularly, did their best to act as if it didn't matter, but it did. And the threat of being sent to the secondary modern had got out.

There was something in me, a spunkier side, which, at times, asserted that the secondary modern was Great. It was a new, white, streamlined building – most of us had played there in the evenings when the workmen had clocked off and the watchman was dozing. The scaffolding was a gift: the mounds of sand were perfect to jump into, and when the watchman chased us, that was a bonus.

At the secondary modern you could get two days a week off to go to Workington Technical College and learn a trade; you did not have to wear uniform; you were not accused in the streets of being posh or a snob; you could play football and there were girls there. And you could go up the back way to get to it, past Tenters and the gasometer and up Stony Banks, totally avoiding the town and the grammar school.

It didn't work. I had failed and soon everybody would know it.

In the last week of what I knew was the last term at the Nelson Thomlinson, I began to feel sick. I had not dared to tell my parents. To describe and discuss the sliding out of my mind into the light at nighttime, to confide it to them was impossible.

Thursday, late afternoon, one day to go before I was banished, I was shivering badly and was suddenly sick at my desk. It was disgusting. The smell, the sight, the shame. Mr Southam took me out into the corridor, went to the door that connected the headmaster's house with the school and knocked firmly.

The headmaster's wife opened the door. Mr Southam explained. Mrs Swale took me into the kitchen, swabbed me down and warmed some milk. As I was drinking it, Betty, the headmaster's daughter, came in, flowed in, smiling. Her mother explained. Mr Southam was not up to answering any questions.

Betty was a friend and contemporary of Dad's youngest brother Irwin – they had gone out together. She was also in the choir, and made a fuss of me, which made things worse. She asked me what was wrong, which was unbearable, I cried although I tried to disguise it as sniffing, holding out my mug of warm milk with two hands like a begging bowl. Betty, who was doing part-time work in her college vacation in Mr Ritson the solicitor's office, took Mr Southam aside to a corner of the kitchen and asked him questions. She then came across to me and explained to her mother that I was in the choir and how good the trebles were and tried to cheer me up.

Mr Southam took me back to an empty classroom. School was up. I collected my satchel and, feeling more like a thing than alive, I walked across the front of the now empty old school, out of the back gate into Low Moor Road and passed by the gleaming white secondary modern.

I walked down towards the baths. There was a path just along from it, which led by a stream to Speet Gill where we had swung on creepers and yodelled like Tarzan.

I walked along the narrow path still feeling the sick in my stomach and a weakness in my legs. I was looking for a lair. The path seemed deserted. I picked a few large dock leaves, went behind a tree and shat. The cold water in the stream cleaned my hands and, I hoped, wiped away any suggestion of tears from my face.

I sat nearby on the stump of an ash tree.

I was finished.

Instead of going back the shorter and my usual way, I walked past the front of the baths towards the town. That way I could keep houses in sight.

My mother had left food on the table. She came up to make me tea, and when she asked if anything was the matter, I said no.

In my bedroom, I listened to the wireless and waited for the dark to come so that I could get it over with.

In the last class on the last day, Mr Southam asked me to stay behind. He wished the class a happy summer holiday and winced when his message of goodwill was met by the violent banging of desk tops.

Soon we were the only two in the room. I had stayed at my desk.

'I have a note from Mr Swale,' he said, and showed me the envelope. He made a fuss of opening the envelope and reading the note to himself. He gave me a not unkind smile. 'Mr Swale says you can come back next term and go into 4A.'

Chapter Twenty-seven

I can scarcely believe how I managed to stay stable during those twelve months or more. It is difficult to conjure up lengths of time. It seemed never ending. The out-of-mind experiences were visceral. They came at night, malign visitations from another world. How did they exist with the other parts of my life? How did my silence hold fast? Fear? More fear? Ever present fear. It began to seem to go but it never has. It has been suppressed, overlaid, blocked out by life anew, but never eradicated. Still I can feel it in an uncontrollable rush of nerves, just talking to someone, especially just talking to someone as if I were afraid I would be found out, covering my tracks in incoherence. It happened on several further occasions as I met more and more strangers whose mind-language I did not know. I would either be dogmatic or bluster or want to be somewhere else. A sudden burst of temper, of rudeness, of lies, of aggression, or uncontrol could give me space.

There were periods, an increasing number of them and of increasing lengths as time went on, when it was OK, and then I had a sense of what resources I had. Even now, sixty-seven years on from that adolescent experience, I can go into what can accurately be described as a spasm, a wipeout of memory, a 'blind panic' before making a speech, before doing a programme, or just, worst of all, stall for no reason at all and have to find a solitary small physical space, stay there for five or ten minutes until what is trying to resurface and wreck things somehow passes on or is pushed away. In the early days I began to try to get the panic over with before I did something I thought would unnerve me. I would have to play a part – myself – even when, as happened often, I did not know what the part was. I was imprisoned inside myself. I was not me.

I know I went to ground in that summer holiday. The baths were still a regular destination but something had gone. We still played but I would look at the clock and want it to go faster. I would get on my bike and take a long way back, go out of the town, follow minor roads, without purpose.

At some time over the next year the mind-slipping events became less frequent. It took longer for the force of that fear to become a reliable absence. As time has passed and life filled up, the light in the corner dimmed but did not die. It can still come back to destabilise me, as if to say, 'I won't let you go.' There can be no complaints. Many people have had so much worse and come through. On the graphs of pain and misery it scarcely registers. But for me – you speak as you find.

If I did anything in those summer-holiday weeks, it was to drift. I began to walk out of the town in any direction. It was partly a tentative act of defiance. I could always turn back and make for the town, for home. But I wanted to walk on my own, for no reason I could think of then, none now. Perhaps as simple as to challenge and outface the fear. I could walk for two or three miles, beyond Old Carlisle, into narrow roads that netted the lower fells, like the drystone walls higher up, and all would be well until I caught the sound of my breath. I felt that I did not know how breathing worked or whether it would keep working; it was just a sound and yet I had to keep doing this breathing. It became too difficult – as if I had forgotten how to do it and had to learn again. To breathe. The panic was there and I was solitary in the country without a house in sight.

Sometimes I ran to shake off the fear but it pursued me. It just made it harder. But eventually it would dissolve. And, for whatever reason, I would go out again the next day of that school holiday. Otherwise? After the baths and dinner – stay in? That was impossible and, besides, I felt that my mother and father were alert to something odd in me from a look, a concern that threatened to dig out the truth I could not speak. So I walked again.

Sometimes William and I went for bike rides. I'd met William when we were both about five. We became best friends and remained so until his death. There's no accounting for it save, luck. Those four letters will have to do for a complex of emotions, backgrounds, tastes, on you could go. We just clicked. We were quite different – did that help? He was easygoing, a natural athlete, often overworked, I thought, by his father on the milk round on which I would go along with him when I could. He was quiet, but he could be inflexible and I knew that and did not want to provoke it. We just 'got on' with each other from the start and never tired of each other's company.

The bike rides usually had a purpose – to go to Silloth and swim in the sea or the docks. Or sweep up Brocklebank and then fly down the steep drop into Caldbeck. It was a little later on that we pushed into the Lake District and even later when we would look in village churches, curiously at a time when I was losing faith. We biked for a few hours after the middle of the day. William had to be back to help with the bottling of the milk: I would help, to be with him. The bottling plant was intense, noisy and busy with a lot of clatter. It could be enjoyed.

But, I think, though this is where memories can be unreliable, I remember my father giving me more to do in the pub. In the mornings helping to set it up, in the early evenings to offer the minimal help needed in the bar, and sometimes taking me along to the hound trails. I suppose I am saying I sensed that he was keeping an eye on me.

I was changing – the on-creeping of hormones, shifting gear, uneasy in my own skin. There could have been some of that: such change is common enough. I think I was one of those who had been badly shaken and forced to change, self-pressured to become different. What had been was no longer safe or service-able. Safe was the key. But something happened. I was no longer who I had been. And I had to make something else of myself.

I think I can recall a moment now, in that upstairs room, which was not yet transformed by G Plan and was airless and lifeless. That summer I would sit there and be unable to read. It was the only time in my life when that happened and I can bring back the extreme lassitude, the picking up a book and not reading it, not being able to read it despite knowing I wanted to. But I couldn't. I sat there looking at the closed piano. Whatever was happening, it was something that shifted the arrangement of myself. I went out alone to let it ride through me.

I went to school for the autumn term in my first pair of long trousers. Following the splicing of the two schools, the upper school was now across the road, in the Thomlinson Girls School, which was built around a substantial old townhouse. Everything old was new to me. I was back with those I'd shared classrooms with for most of three years. I felt like a new boy. In 4A. I was nervous but able just to get on with it. If I knew anything, it was that I had to make a new life. Wherever I could find it. I dared not give in.

Chapter Twenty-eight

Over the next two years the school gradually became the town to me and I began to find a way out of the fear. 4A, 5A, O-level exams, and then the idea was you went out into the 'real' world where you made a living. What made those two years so distinctive was the influence of two teachers. They gave me a purpose. They sparked an interest and then a passion for learning, which began to block out fear. I pulled myself together through work.

Mr James had been brought up in Madagascar, one of the seven children of a Congregationalist missionary. Like his brothers, he was sent to an English Congregational boarding school when he was twelve: he did not see his parents again until he was in his early twenties. He won a place at Wadham College, Oxford, volunteered for the RAF after his first year, became a Spitfire pilot specialising in reconnoitring behind enemy lines, returned to Oxford to continue his degree and a few years later landed up in Wigton as head of history, married. He was dedicated to converting to high scholarship what he saw as largely working-class and under-privileged children. This became his mission.

He sought no favours. We were not told of his service in the RAF – information that would have transformed him into an untouchable hero. He saw his job as familiarising us with the composition of British/European history from 1066 to the First World War. For Mr James every event had three causes. There were three causes for victory, three for defeat, three causes for economic success, three for failure, three causes for great leadership, three for failure. In between the spokes of this grid were detailed points of discussion, which often contained questions he left to us to answer His method was to begin with a short lecture from which we were expected to take down key notes. For the last lap he asked us to answer questions on what he had said at the beginning of the lesson. Finally he would set us homework.

He had been brought up in boys' schools, been to a men's college and into a man's war, and first taught in boys' schools. Girls distracted him. We spotted that but his authority was so tight that we had no leeway to tease him. Boys were easy. They were surnames. They were bluntly called on. But girls? Clearly he had difficulty rattling out the surnames. Even more – in the early days – on calling on a girl by her Christian name. He would use both. Sometimes he would stumble and the slight hesitation would flood his face scarlet.

Over-emphatically he would plough on. We thought we had found a weak point but he out-manoeuvred us. He would just look at the girls' side of the room and direct an accurate nod to Valerie, or Barbara, or Catherine, and she would respond. If balked he would say – to the girls' block – 'Anyone have an answer to that?' Someone dutifully obliged. As time went on he would use a Christian name, but rarely.

It was the vigour of the man. He marched into every lesson primed for takeoff. A civil 'Good morning', 'Good afternoon', and then he was off. It took some time for him to be liked but none at all for him to be respected. His energy swept across the thirty bent heads, like a stiff breeze over a cornfield. Somehow you felt compelled to 'keep up'. Now and then at the end of a lesson he would say, 'Thank you,' before he marched out.

His energy helped to recharge the school. He set up a debating society and a history society; he came to watch the rugby matches, be timekeeper at school sports. As those two pre-O-level years went on, he took a few of us on educational trips, deliberately opening up Wigton to a wider world. He was given the job of reconstructing the timetable, which, with almost five hundred pupils in two sets of buildings divided by the High Street, had to include lessons in laboratories, gyms, the Music Room, the

Art Room, rooms used for a variety of purposes. He made it a labour of love. It was the toil of an Easter holiday for which he received no payment. Some of us began to catch his true value. When you looked at his first draft of the timetable, it was like seeing the back taken off a bust radio. When he had finished, it was a fine example of technical expertise. He was to stay at the school for more than fifty years.

Most important of all, though, was his ability to inspire and to plant the study of history deep into my mind. He was in no way eccentric. He just wanted you to know your stuff and made it exciting. It was energy, energy that went through the school like a fuse, which was powered by a conviction that when you learned to learn you would come to the faith of scholarship.

The school was lucky. As well as Mr James, there was Mr Stowe, who arrived as headmaster just before Mr James and, in his way, had an impact almost as profound. He was born in Aspatria, one of the three towns, almost an equilateral triangle, that fed the grammar school. A mining town shovelled up over an ancient Romano-Celtic settlement.

Mr Stowe marched – crunch, crunch on the gravel, left, right – from the school house to the main school building with an almost show-off briskness. He was short, always neatly suited, fit, constantly pecking the air for the birds he so meticulously 'spotted', brighter than any bright morning. He was a Methodist, son of a Methodist preacher. He had gone to the Wigton grammar school when he was eleven to emerge seven years later with a rare scholarship to Oxford, into the army, became a major in intelligence, back to university to serve out his degree and fulfil the requirement of his scholarship to get a degree, get a second degree in teaching and be fed into the grammar-school machine.

Within a few years he was married, hired as headmaster at the Nelson, and every morning, as he crunched the gravel and pecked the air, he breathed a deep contentment. This was his estate. For this least worldly of men, it was exhilarating. When the school amalgamated with the girls' equivalent, his estate doubled and that braced him up even more.

There was a sumptuous school house. It had a lawn tennis court (his only sport and exercise), kept trim by the school's groundsman. The ancient late-medieval school had been supplanted by a neat classical Victorian sandstone building, built to a reliable public-school formula. Nearby was a bright red twentieth-century addition – the New Building – six more class-rooms, and then the neat green cricket pavilion. Further beyond acres of fields, the Venetian Tower could make his neat moustache twitch at its absurdity.

Across the playing fields – rugby, cricket, a running track – there was a gym, and two prefabricated buildings that served as the canteen for four of the schools crowded around them. Further fields. A small copse. An educational estate! And he was going to make it hum with the best of them. It was his to perfect. Already, in his first term, he was feared by the pupils and at a standoff with his less like-minded staff. His habit of nipping unannounced into classrooms with 'Please ignore me. I'll sit at the back' was not endearing.

At the end of the first term his detailed trawling of the marking system was hard to bear, partly because he had a tendency to seize on a loose phrase or a weak run of marks, which demanded an explanation, a skill the older teachers had long grown out of. At the end of his second term, two of the older teachers left voluntarily. At the end of the third, two more were asked to move on. Things were smartened up. We felt a seismic tremor go through the school: the James-Stowe effect.

Yet he was not 'brutal'. He had a merry smile. He knew how to handle men. Knew praise as well as censure. He was hard to fault. And the exam results improved. He was constantly giving advice or encouragement – a pat here, a helpful suggestion there.

He decided that the school needed a choir – local competitions were a feature of the area. That was acceptable because he read music, could play the piano and had an unabashed loud tenor voice. But he also lent his weight to – or interfered with – the debating society and the Scouts. He reinforced the 'house' system – Skiddaw, Catbells, Blencathra, Gable – named after the local fells, gave them colours, encouraged them to compete against each other at the end of term, awarded certificates on Speech Day.

In their first two years, with Mr Stowe at the helm and Mr James in the engine room, the lazy, sleepy school felt the force of two talented and driven men prepared to work themselves to the bone. It suffered a transformation. It was a time when the great grammar schools of England challenged the public schools for merit, especially in the harder sciences, while the girls' equivalent high schools soared in scholarships. Mr Stowe wanted his mixed school to take on the best of them. He had a gift for organisation, a taste for urging on effort, and a determination to 'get the best' out of the pupils, some of whose fathers and mothers he had been at school with. He had seen in the army that talent could be found in people from the most unlikely backgrounds. Like Mr James, he made it his job to find it and encourage it.

He staked out his ground. He went to the sparkling white new secondary modern to talk matters through with the headmaster, Mr Postlethwaite, who was impressed by the visit. Mr Postlethwaite had joined the local regiment and spent two years in Burma.

The men talked about the future of the generation they were teaching. Mr Stowe was keen to learn all he could about the technical work and strategy of the secondary modern. Mr Postlethwaite told him of sending the boys two days a week to technical school in Workington and into engineering works on the west coast.

'That is exactly what we most need,' Mr Stowe asserted. 'It's those skills we have to build up and develop – far more important than the humanities if we are to serve. Would I be able to send some of our boys along to you? We could offer – what could we offer in return?'

Mr Postlethwaite smiled. 'We're pretty self-sufficient,' he said.

'We could work on it!'

'I don't know. All they need is to be taught to want to learn.'

'Exactly! Exactly. We must keep meeting. Let's see what comes of it.'

'The shame is,' said Mr Postlethwaite, 'that the boys, especially the more working-class boys, with the exam system at eleven, are cut off from the lads they've knocked about with all their lives.'

'I can't see what can be done about that.'

Mr Postlethwaite hesitated. He could see no solution. But he said, 'Let's think about it. It's such a pity for them and for Wigton.'

'Oh,' Mr Stowe beamed, 'I like Wigton. A lot can be done with Wigton!'

This was the gem that Mr Postlethwaite took from that first conversation. He would relish it and mutter to himself and tell others, 'A lot can be done with Wigton'. And smile.

Chapter Twenty-nine

My father came up to the sitting room one summer night near the end of what I thought was my last year at the school. I was reading *East of Eden*, which my father was to read as soon as I had finished it. We would discuss it, clumsily, not having any of the tools of a literary conversation but full of enthusiasm and (usually) applause. I was lounging in an armchair, surprised at this visit, my father if anything more disconcerted than I was.

'You don't have to,' he said abruptly, 'if you don't want to. Your mother and me were talking it over.'

I felt as if I were reluctantly pulling my head out of the fast hold of the novel.

'We would be able to manage without your wage,' he said. 'We've managed so far.' He was now sitting on the edge of the other armchair, cigarette in his left hand, his right propping up his chin.

'It's entirely your choice,' he said into the silence. 'Your decision.'

I distinctly remember the thaw of numbness.

'So,' he said. 'Up to you.'

I folded the top corner of the page and put down the book, all done in slow motion to concentrate my mind, which scattered in agitation. What was it about?

'Would you like to? Stay on?' He paused. 'At school.'

'Stay on?' It began to click.

'Yes. They say your marks were good enough.'

'I'm going for that interview for a job with Mr Ritson on Thursday.'

'We could cancel it.' My father was almost nonchalant.

'What would he say?'

'It's what you say that counts.'

'I thought you both wanted me to leave.'

My father drew deeply on the cigarette.

'That's true,' he said, 'but we've had a talk . . . It's up to you
. . . that's the point.'

I think I remember thinking nothing.

'You don't have to decide now. Just let us know by breakfast.'
He smiled. 'Either way, it's OK.'

He stood up, and tapped the book. 'My turn next.'

'Yes.'

'Any good?'

'So far.'

My father gave a little wave as if he were seeing his son off at
a station. At the door, he paused: a pause premeditated. He
looked at the floor, a little shyly. 'Your friends will be working
for their fathers or they'll get jobs. They'll be earning. I worked
out that if you could build up a bit on what you're doing for me
now, I could manage about fifteen bob a week. It'll be a job.'

'Thanks.'

One final pause, a last pull on the cigarette. And another smile.
'They likely think you're up for it.'

I didn't know who to tell. Whoever I told could accuse me of
boasting. Not one of my close friends was staying on. I picked
up *East of Eden* but what had just happened unsettled the pages.

Staying on.

I went down the stairs, into the backyard, and seized my bike.
It seemed to move itself, down to the East End, along Kirkland
Road, past Mrs Cavaghan's house and on, turning further away
from the town, switching from one village to another, pushing
hard on the pedals, wanting to shout out but afraid – of what?
Only biking faster helped. Finally I ended up on the Caldbeck
road, a flat stretch on the way to the village, until abruptly the
hills swept up and pulled at your legs if you insisted on going as
fast as you could up Brocklebank. The only sounds on that
summer evening were of the birds getting ready for sleep, the
occasional tractor in the distance and my own gasping breath.

Staying on!

I swung my bike down the steep incline deep into the bowl that held the village of Caldbeck. Just as fast as I could. As fast as anybody could . . .

I biked back slowly, along the valley and over to Castle Inn where I switched pace again and made hell for leather for Bothel where I could survey the plain stretching to the sea and pick out Wigton in the distance, look back on the fells, sunset swept, and then, with my last energy of the day, let loose for the town and arrive at the pub sweating happily.

Bike in, straight out, AYPA, one of the last meetings before breaking up for summer – so, records, waltzes, the quickstep, the Boston two-step, the Three Drops of Brandy, not allowing myself to tell a soul . . .

Even after we came out of the Parish Rooms and wandered down into King Street, the energy was not used up. Too young to drink, and with no coffee bars in the town, there was zilch to do. With Eric and William I walked back to West Street – but William's equivocal mood suggested there would be no-go inside that household that evening. Mr Ismay liked to watch television in peace between eight and ten o'clock. With Eric I walked down towards Western Bank, across the Wiza, and along to Greenacres, the site of Eric's new council house. Mrs Hetherington wanted no dithering around. 'You're late,' she said to Eric, not particularly unkindly. And to me, 'They'll be expecting you back home by now.' The door closed.

There was relief. It was such a calm evening. I strolled back into town past the new houses in their own grounds where over the years I had harvested a reasonable Christmas income by carol singing. Dr Dolan's was one of those. He had just built himself a big house in wide grounds, overlooking the Show Fields. When Eric and William and myself had landed on his doorstep, we had been invited in after the first verse.

Dr Dolan was a breezy man, who carried a distinctive Edinburgh accent after his four years' study in Scotland's capital. He smoked a pipe throughout surgery. He played tennis for the town despite having a wooden leg, which made him hop around the court.

We had not seen the inside of a house in Wigton so plush. Flowery wallpaper, big sofas (two), and easy chairs in the same pattern (four), photographs and paintings on the walls, an extravagant fireplace piled high with logs. We sang 'Silent Night' to finish off with. It usually worked.

Dr Dolan was particularly enthusiastic. 'Sometimes we used to sing that in Latin,' I said. 'In our church.'

'I must hear it!' Dr Dolan tapped his pipe vigorously, waiting for the treat.

William didn't know it and, anyway, never much liked carol singing. Eric would get twisty sometimes – this was one of them. So I began:

> Nox silens, sancta nox,
> In tranquilla, omnia . . .

Two half-crowns! Two!

We had made no more calls that night. For ever afterwards Mrs Dolan, who had never recognised me and was noted for her Sunday climbing expeditions to the Lake District, would now give me a cheerful nod whenever we passed on the street:

> Alpha es et o-o
> Alpha es et o.

I crossed the River Wiza over the bridge that always seemed like the true gateway to the old town and got home for supper just after closing time. A meat and potato pie and a bottle of dandelion and burdock. In bed just in time to catch Radio Luxembourg's pop hits and fill my room with rock 'n' roll, hoping for some blues.

I was first at breakfast.

Andrew had left just before six for the morning shift.

My mother was by the cooker, avoiding my gaze. 'When you're ready,' Dad said.

We sat down together. Porridge and milk and a teaspoonful of sugar. Egg, in this case boiled. Toast. Tea. Clickety-click, every school morning.

The silence seemed to stretch to splitting point.

Dad fished inside his jacket pocket and held out an unsealed envelope. Addressed to Mr Stowe, Headmaster, Nelson Thomlinson Grammar School. 'Hand this in,' he said. 'I believe this is the last day for it.'

A nod, which all but swallowed the egg whole. The letter accepted the offer to stay on. Back to silence.

'You can still leave whenever you want,' said my mother.

'But he won't, will you?' said Stan, speaking to Ethel, looking at me. 'He'll stick it out.'

'You'd better hurry,' she said. 'You'll be late.'

'Thank you.'

'Well now.' Stan waved his egg spoon and nodded, happy.

I still remember that look. Happy. Happy for me. Yet as time went by I realised that he was saying goodbye to what had been his chance: the scholarships not taken up. Never mentioned. His sister Elsie always said, 'Stan was very clever as a lad, you know. It was a shame they couldn't afford to let him take up that scholarship.'

This must have bitten into my memory. Years later I understood. I had understood as a child; as a man what I saw was his deep relief that I had taken a course denied to him. He had held down that disappointment for years and he still did but now he could express it in that encouragement to me. His early life had been harsher than he would ever admit. This was my beginning of an end he had only dreamed of.

I can pull it out from that morning. So ordinary. No great fuss but the moment was marked – for both, for all three of us. And that look of his, happy. At the time I did not realise that I had noticed it. Later, when the idea of leaving the town began to come to mind, it was this scene – the breakfast table, waving the egg spoon, above all the warmth in his eyes, the gladness there, for me – it was that which never left me. It said, 'You go, go on, you try, I will be with you.' I can't remember an occasion when I felt closer to him.

Sixty-one years later I had a conversation with Mr James. He had retired to a bungalow in a small hillside village neighbouring the town. He was in his nineties, widowed, both children well away from home. He had stayed on at the school one way and another for more than fifty years, and still then, as we sat in his neat parlour, photographs from the war – Spitfires revealed at last – from his old college and of his family, in an otherwise austere living room with one wall a picture window looking out across the sea to Scotland.

We would meet and talk now and then. Generally Jimmy homed in on politics – present and past – with undiminished accuracy. But he looked uncomfortable that day. Fidgety. And he was beginning to look his great age.

'I've thought a lot about this,' he began shyly, looking out towards the sea. 'But on the whole I think you ought to know.' He took a breath. 'Are you sure you're OK for tea?'

'Yes, thank you.'

'It would be no trouble.'

'I'm fine.'

'You see, Stan and Ethel didn't particularly want you to stay on at school. They didn't want you to stay on into the sixth form.' (So long ago, so very long ago.) 'So I went to see them. Three times.' I said nothing. 'I think Stan was worried that you wouldn't be comfortable in the company you might find if you went on to university, which I must admit I told him I thought you could do. But that was not the point. Rather,' Mr James shifted uneasily in his well-cushioned chair, 'I presumed to think that it was not the point. Not in the sense that you or I would understand it. What,' he cleared his throat and looked towards the ceiling, as if he wished he had never embarked on this awkward confession, 'I gathered, perhaps wrongly, was that perhaps your mother had somehow put a spoke in the wheels.' Having concluded he looked quite distressed.

'My mother never wanted me to stay on at school,' I said. 'She was really pleased that I might get a job at Ritson's and stay in the town.'

'I guessed that.'

'She just didn't want me to leave Wigton.'

'I could sense that.' Mr James all but grimaced. 'I may have put my foot in it, then, because when I suggested that if you stayed on for two more years, you could still get a job, possibly a better job at Ritson's or . . . where was it? Yes, in the accounts department at the factory. A lot of this was guesswork on my part. And it was very awkward. You see, something of a family disagreement.'

'So what did you do?'

'I went to see Stan on his own. In the afternoon, when it would be closing time. We sat in the Darts Room and I explained the possible advantages to you of staying on and compared those advantages with the much greater loss of a once-in-a-lifetime opportunity passed up. You see . . .' Mr James reasserted himself '. . . when I came to Wigton I saw and I see now boys and girls of great ability who would never go beyond Wigton, Silloth and Aspatria, beyond where they were born. And they needed someone to give them a push. Now. "He's your son," I said to Stan. "You know him much better than I do but I can see some potential there with him and one or two of the others."

'I remember that your father nodded and smiled. He said, "So you have his best interests at heart."

'"I do," I said.

'Then he stood up. '"Well, Mr James, you've helped me make up my mind. But now it's clear. He needs his choice. Thank you." That decided it.

'Then we shook hands,' said Mr James, 'rather as if we'd concluded a treaty.' Neither my father nor my mother nor Mr James had mentioned any of this to me more than sixty years earlier.

*

The sixth form was a different world. Inside the town but apart from it, almost sealed off.

I felt as if I were walking the streets with a brimful bucket of water on my head, forbidden to lose a drop. The acute and threatening self-consciousness that had wrapped me in such anxiety and which would forever come back to test me was transformed into a different consciousness of myself. I was somewhere I had never dreamed of being. Nor had I especially wanted to be there. I was someone on paths untrodden by those who had gone before me.

I was staying on!

I was in the lower sixth form (arts). From now on, I sensed, nothing would ever be the same. I was the only one of the gang who had stayed on. I was the object of amiable teasing on the streets – 'When are you going to get a job?', 'What's it like to do nowt?', 'Jammy bugger . . .' There were continuities. The dances, which were just heaving into view, would refill and recharge the bran tub of the old town and all would be well. But a difference had been chalked up, perhaps a line drawn.

I was now embarked on a unifying experience that would exile the fear and feeling of disintegration. I had a new story that would hold me together.

Chapter Thirty

For some weeks the sixth form seemed too foreign. The classrooms were very small. Lower-sixth (arts) accommodated seven of us. It was part of an old townhouse, probably a parlour at one time. Next to our classroom was the library, a handsome Georgian room, wall-to-ceiling books, to which access was allowed in leisure periods to sixth formers – lower and upper – who needed somewhere to work. Largely unsupervised, too chattery to be much use for concentrated effort. There was a table-tennis room down the corridor – reserved for sixth formers – and a newspaper room, where they could read national magazines and newspapers, which the school got at cut price. A grand staircase swerved up from the front door – next to the library – to the headmaster's study and a fresh cluster of rooms.

The atmosphere and gentility of a fine townhouse rubbed off. The gentry had departed. We were the occupants now. It had been modified with the least possible disturbance to the old layout. There was a poshness in it that was unlike its utilitarian partner, the Nelson School, across the road. The library end made you feel that you were fortunate to be allowed on premises not made for the job of being a school but on loan from a privileged past. You strolled around.

In those first weeks I found it difficult to know what the point was. You only studied three subjects – in my case, history, English and Latin – with one French class and one religious-instruction lesson thrown in. This, I later realised, was for the benefit of Mr Stowe, who wanted to keep up his teaching. In the fifth form there had been eight or nine subjects and therefore three times as many homework demands.

The teachers drove us less hard. After all, there would be no exams of any consequence for two years. The whole sixth-form set up was relaxed, even collegiate; we were no longer schoolboys. You could rattle about in the Nelson School. Here you felt you had to respect the history and manners of the place.

It could not have been more tailor-made to give us a sense of the entitlement that surrounded the idea of the centuries-old boys' grammar school and the girls' high school. By the time we came to the sixth form, all of my good friends and most of those vaguely like me from the other towns had melted into the work force, the farms, the factory, their fathers' small businesses, local government . . . This was in the mid-century. Many still felt obliged to leave school, though changed circumstances would have given them a chance to stay. The rift would grow over the years despite my effort to prevent it happening. In the beginning those who had left often felt better off. As they were, financially.

At the school we were encouraged to think of ourselves as students not as schoolchildren, and it went to my head. Then in the snap test some way through the first term, I did poorly. When Mr James returned my papers he said nothing, but shook his head. Five of us took Latin. I was bottom. Five of us took English. I was fourth. History, bottom again. Val Little top in both history and English.

I could console myself that the tests were not pre-announced: no time was given to prepare. But it was the same for everyone and I was bottom of the class. There wasn't even any bravado to be found in it. Mr James, who was form master as well as history teacher, dwelled on the matter very lightly, calling it a 'wake-up call'.

For me it was a death knell. Did it mean I would get chucked out at the end of my first term? How had I suddenly slumped, and so badly in history and English? Latin I could always excuse. The Latin teacher had disliked me on sight – fair enough. She came from a refined Carlisle family and had 'taken' a first in classics at Manchester, and I was a Wigton scruff. Or perhaps I just couldn't get the hang of it. But her antagonism, spiced by sarcasm, rocked my confidence in Latin. I had tried to swap it for maths, but Mr James objected. He had an endgame he did not yet reveal. Latin would be essential.

I was a sixth former now and the answer and the action were in my own hands.

They came accidentally a few days later by way of Catherine Duckett. She was from Silloth, rather refined, I thought, but very pleasant with it. I think her father was a doctor. We had always been friendly. I was alone riffling through the magazines one afternoon in the small reading room when Catherine came in, asked if I minded, said the library was too full and got down to her homework. That was a revelation. I thought homework was just that. School was for being taught by others or, if you had achieved the heights of the sixth form, for strolling around between lessons looking for somewhere to do nothing.

Catherine, a quiet girl, hair cut short, school uniform immaculate, non-NHS specs, got to work on the week's essay. She had a new exercise book. The old one had only one or two pages to go and she put it aside. She had a neat stack of notes from the class and other notes, which I was to learn came from her independent reading of books in the school library.

But what impressed me most was that she had filled an entire exercise book with only three essays. Mine was less than half full.

She wrote calmly, in a stately hand, checking a fact or an argument now and then, head down, concentrated. There was no lesson. She had forty minutes and just got on with her work. I shuffled through the weekly magazines we never saw at home but my eyes were on that notebook of hers. Three essays only in the narrow-lined exercise book! What had she found to write so much?

I wanted to read her essays. If I read her essays I would know what was expected and what I lacked. If only she had left the room for a few minutes. She barely looked up. She could have been consumed by elaborate embroidery. There was an old-fashioned station clock, too big for the room. It clunk-ticked every minute.

'Your brother was here, at this school, wasn't he?'

Catherine neatly completed the word or sentence and looked up.

'Yes. He's gone to Durham. He wants to read oceanography.'

Read?

'Did he give you any tips? About – about what you did in the sixth form?'

She put down her pen, took off her spectacles and considered the question.

'He said to be careful. It looked easy but it wasn't. They left more up to you than in the earlier classes. It seemed you had all the time in the world but you needed it.'

'Was that it?'

'I pushed him,' Catherine said, smiling. 'There's Sheila next in our family and she wants to get into the sixth form as well, so there's no wasting time. Everybody can come now, free. It's once-in-a-lifetime. It's all up to you.'

Her head went back to the essay.

'One thing,' I said. 'This essay business. It seems to be different from—'.

'It is.' She pushed her completed exercise book over to me. 'You can read it if you like.'

Her essays were so long! Where I would write two or at most three-page answers as I had done in the fourth and fifth forms, hers were fourteen, sixteen and one stupendous twenty-two pages, the last one, which Mr James had marked 'Excellent!' and given it the highest of the Greek marks – alpha plus.

It was easy to read. Her script was beautifully even, clear, unsmudged. Every full stop was as neat as a pinhead. There was a stack of material that had not been in Mr James's talks.

'Is the extra stuff from the library?'

'Yes. There's a very good section over at the Nelson School. I don't know why they haven't brought it here. But you can sign

233

it out just the same.' She smiled. 'Now,' she said, meaning, 'I've got work to do.' She put on her spectacles and bent her head.

So that was it. Length. New stuff. But, above all, work a lot harder.

I carried that to extremes. I could think of no other way to reach the goals demanded by the sixth form. The vision of going to university appeared and then disappeared in a blink. This was to do with making myself sane. The only thing I could do was work myself to exhaustion. Then I might have a chance to justify this blind commitment. I had no idea or example of what would be enough. So I settled for exhaustion.

What began to happen was that the goal of university disappeared and the work itself became something between a drug and a pleasure. This was the way to a different self. Slowly it healed the fracture that had threatened to splinter my mind. It kept the fear at bay.

Knowing more for the sake of knowing more was what came to matter. I overworked.

Chapter Thirty-one

I started with a timetable. Sunday to Friday – nothing on Saturday. I made a graph – days to the left, subjects next to the days, hours aimed for in the next column, hours achieved in the final column. The days were added up and signed off on the Friday. It would somehow be humiliating and a burden on Mr James to ask him about this. And something else held me back: the sixth form was where you worked things out for yourself. There were regular lessons and regular demands but the core of it would be what you did on your own. Those few minutes with Catherine had delivered that message: it was down to me.

To realise that fully took some time. I grasped that the essential point of being as free as you were in the sixth form was that you ought not to rely on being supervised or prodded. You had been given the opportunity to be self-scheduling outside the school hours. I took it. My father had stepped up the pocket money. The extra work I did in the pub was a fair exchange. It was a job.

That realisation clarified everything.

There were two parts to this. One was working at school, but with the temptations of drifting and sport, I found it difficult to set up a productive routine there. Home was the factory. I would get back from school at about four thirty, have tea and be ready to go at five. My father and mother would go downstairs to open up the pub.

I commanded the new kitchen, sat at the table looking out over Market Hill to Highmoor. From that time it became a study. For my O-level exams the previous summer I had stuck in my bedroom, using a small table at the foot of the bed. Why on earth it should be so I don't understand, but to have full possession of the smart new dining table gave me a boost: it was a promotion.

In that first term, I would average up to three hours' homework a night and four on Sundays. I offloaded. The AYPA went – it totally wrecked an evening. Choir practice had ended due to the cracks in my treble voice while the honking replacement of a gravelly tenor tone had as yet no place in the choir stalls. The Scouts was a tough decision but after six months that too went. For inexplicable reasons I enjoyed much more sitting on my own at the table working at what I chose to do. I would make a cup of tea, take a biscuit, put on the wireless for a ten-minute break, look out of the window and think I was not wasting time but thinking. Only thinking could produce what I wanted, but thinking needed material to work on. Then the more the better.

I became addicted to sitting there for hours, working on an essay, memorising a poem. Just digging out this learning, happy to hope it lodged and grew and set up interactions with other gobbets of knowledge, made patterns. As time went by the passion for this solitary confinement grew. What I had feared and avoided about solitude began to dissolve in those early months as the intensity of learning levered itself into my mind. Not because I was being instructed to but because I was being led into learning by myself. It was like entering and conquering a foreign territory – small, insignificant, but something I myself had found. The more I read the more familiar this strange life became and the easier to deal with. It was the only way I could be.

I'm sure many people experience this – the sensation that your brain, or part of it inside the skull, is being taken over. The phrase I would use, as would others, was that I lost myself. Once, that had been into darkness. Now it was a light into a foreign place, another space. And this time I knew that I would come back.

As time went on, I grew more intrigued about where thought went and therefore how it arrived. Questions that were outside my range but that did not stop them absorbing a sort of dream time. It nagged away. Where does the 'lost' self go? Why? And when does it decide to come back? And why? And what is it? Questions best answered by adult specialised minds. Yet somehow it seemed important to a teenager grappling with facts that could be both fascinating and elusive. It set me off on a pursuit that took me there and back. But where and back? I could be writing about a character in the *Canterbury Tales* or Henry VII and then I would be, if not living it, at least inside the story, the poem, the character as if I were that character, story, poem. It must have been a fine line from the near screaming I had experienced a year or two ago when my body disappeared. But whereas the one was Bad and destructive, the losing myself in this work was Good and exciting.

What tumbled out at first and for months were long loose essays. Nevertheless, Mr James began to mark up my efforts.

It was not all a magic roundabout. Latin was a grind. I could not understand why Mr James had insisted I take it. He knew that Miss Anderson and myself were chalk and cheese. And I had no chance against her. But I had to convince her that I was at least competent.

That was difficult. I had no love for Latin, no ease in that language, little ability to unlock those Roman sentences. Just slog, slog and slog again, for hours, learning chunks by heart, desperate stuff, and then the reward: 'average'. It was the best I could hope for. It made my head ache. This was not improved by the fact that the three others in the Latin class – all girls – sailed through.

Latin homework I did on Monday to get the taste out of my head.

This intensified as the two years in the sixth form went on. The overworking and over-reading for many hours a night grew. I could not see how else I was going to pass those exams dangled before us by Mr James. I was lucky that there was sport at school. I kept up swimming but not that much. What took me out of the ever-tightening cell was Saturdays – rugby, bike rides into the Lake District. Dances in the evening.

It started with three hours a night, hard to fill. Eighteen months later it was twice that and sometimes all but impossible to stop, dizzy with it.

But that first year was a first slope getting steeper when the first year's exams came around.

By then I was beginning to feel confident that I could drive my way through an increasingly self-demanding timetable at home and also be the sixth-former who enjoyed strolling through the graceful corridors of the school as if owning them. Meanwhile new limpets locked on – the school play, debates just arguing for contradiction's sake on topics often set up by Mr Stowe: 'Should we have dropped the atom bomb?'; 'Are we at the end of the British Empire?'; 'Is democracy the best system of government?'

But most of all this increasing lashing of myself over homework and especially the extra books suggested by Mr James – Collingwood's *Idea of History*, hard but just about possible to grasp, or Bertrand Russell's *History of Western Philosophy*, which was a rush to the head of the greatest ideas served in digestible portions. It made my mind either seize up or clang like a belfry.

Out There, especially in philosophy, was Infinite Knowledge. You had to try to find it and hold it. Wherever you looked there were these thoughts on offer, no permit needed, an unboundaried library. I was often defeated. But all you needed to do for the rest of your life was pick up the right book.

There was not only a breaking away but a breaking through. The very act of not having to do paid work – a real job – began to cut me off the main flow of those who had surrounded me all my life. It was deeper than losing contacts in my own generation. It signalled a fork in the road. I inched further and further away from the town life in which I had been so closely wrapped. If my senses had been sufficiently sensitive, perhaps I would have heard the many small fractures and the tearing, as I was very gradually ripped away by myself from a previous self in a deeply cohesive community.

Sometimes I felt like a traitor.

Chapter Thirty-two

Just as I had taken off on a furious bike ride when I realised I would be allowed to stay on at school, so it was the bike I turned to again for respite, the half-slung handlebars, the racing frame handed on to me by Irwin, my father's youngest brother. And just like my new decision to concentrate on homework, wholly unlike the way in which I had skimped work until then, this urge to get as far into the Lake District as a day's biking would take me was another aspect of trying to change who I was and find out who I was becoming.

Sometimes I went with William, but as time went on in that first year in the sixth form I went alone. It seemed I wanted to challenge the panic again, freeze fears I had once had of being alone, change the fear of being alone into the richness of solitude. Being alone on a bike on an empty road, with hills to strain up and then to swoop down face first into the weather, feeling air, sun, rain on the skin, cold knuckles, hot forehead. Or simply sit still letting the cells rove wherever they would. But most of all I was wide open to the landscape as I went deeper into the area I had only skimmed – through those trips from school, church, AYPA. Now I felt in the emptiness of it, in those bare fells, such a rush of life, such an exaltation that I laughed aloud at times, and swerved around hairpin bends recklessly, yet felt protected. Just to be alive was enough.

I would find a lonely tarn, pull up and sit there, taking a careful portion of the sandwiches I'd brought, and just look. I knew what I was looking for but couldn't name it. In front of me were a tarn, a minor fell, a straggling copse, sheep all but painted onto the fields, a sky that never settled. But that was not what I felt I was looking for. I wanted to understand what it was that had taken me over, and led me to look in this way so demandingly. This time not lost in solitude, but somehow found in it, turned another way, a different path through the woods.

Or I would stop by a waterfall – all this at a time when the district was only modestly visited – and again hugging the drama of the sight and sound of the cataract, I would be mesmerised by the detail in the fall of water, by the splits and splinters in direction as it hit the rocks, by the quiet water sound further up the mountain that then surged and gurgled with a reassuring steadiness further down until it went several ways, dwindling, making its own pattern behind rocks long tumbled down from the fellside. Everywhere I had a feeling that I was part of everything.

That race out of the town into the country was another separation of myself from the town. There were to be other moments deep in the western fells, in the valleys of Borrowdale, or on the perilous Striding Edge in a high wind, ready to be blown across land and sea, other places of untroubled calm along the shores of a lake like Esthwaite. Or beside one of the arch-backed dry-stone bridges that controlled the teeming waters from the fells, at times there would be only a silent trickle. Or a taste of wildness, which still survived high in the fells when the weather had broken or the mist had come down so thickly that the best you could do was sit tight and try to catch reassuring sounds inside its deep draperies.

Over the next few years, alone and with others and eventually with one other, I made for the Lakes.

Those first days when the solitary bike became part of the newness of things, it seemed both an escape from the town and the discovery of new territory, which could be just as absorbing.

I had taken a long way round, to push myself, to feel the challenge of the place, and biked out of Wigton uphill to the village of Bothel. There, almost proudly out of breath, I swung down south and headed for Bassenthwaite Lake. Downhill.

Pushing the old bike as hard as I could, racing into the northern Lakes. At Castle Inn I swung off and made for Binsey Fell. This was a small fell, the most northerly of the fells.

By then it was afternoon and I was hungry but I wanted to go up the fell beyond anything else. The air was dry. There was still enough sun. As I rode towards it, the old massif of Skiddaw kept me company. There was a copse at the foot of Binsey and I lifted the bike over the wall, pocketed the tomato sandwiches and the lemonade and set off.

It was an easy slope with a slightly steep tug halfway up. I tried not to look back because I knew the view was the reward. As I reached the top the sun was just beginning to set in the west across the sea to Scotland. The clouds were thin, racing, showing off their paces.

At the top of Binsey there is a broken-down sheepfold and what was thought to be the remains of a small Celtic fort. To the north was the Solway plain; to the east, just perceptible, the backbone of the north, the Pennines. After tossing a pebble onto the cairn, I chose a flat stone as my chair, took out the sandwiches, the tomato now squashed into the bread. I looked straight ahead.

The exhilarating sensation of being there, commanding that view, provoked the beginning of thoughts that were to strengthen and become set over the next two or three years. But I believe I can claim that the intensity of excitement at that particular time, together with the intoxication in my mind, the fierce reading of poetry, sparked the memory of what happened on that evening.

The sunset brought bronze to the hillsides. Strong bronze, almost warrior bronze, its deepening colour like a shield breasting the northern fells, defending their integrity. Skiddaw was slatted with differing streams of light and shaded grey, forever shifting as the light began to fail. The sunset over the Solway and the Scottish hills held on and shot through the thin clouds with peach and faint shades of yellow, red and white. Across the fields on Bassenthwaite Lake, a sombre shadow shrugged its way over the barely wrinkled water and beyond that, more fells, across to the

Newlands valley and even beyond that. The place seemed deserted but also full of its own life that had been, was now and would ever be, forever changing, forever the same – lulled by the calling of birds already at their nests for the night and, it seemed, not a soul save me. Animals, birds, but of humans, none.

I doubt if I had ever felt more complete. I would come and seek out similar moments for the rest of my life. This was life itself. I felt both helpless and in some way invulnerable. This was life, all of it, and it would go on way, way beyond me. Finally I looked into the dazzle of the sunset over the Solway. The sun's slowly dipping golden rim was almost too metallic to be true. Gathered around it were streams of crimson and blue, escorts into the underworld as the sun dragged the day down. And this would be here for as long as I wanted to see it.

I biked home slowly, unable to form thoughts, let alone describe sensations, but later I knew that on Binsey Fell, that evening, I understood something that was valuable and barely expressible. And I was part of it.

Chapter Thirty-three

'Which of you thinks we should have an atom bomb?'

Almost all the hands were raised in this mixed lower and upper sixth arts group, gathered together every first lesson on Wednesday for religious instruction supervised by the headmaster, Mr Stowe. We sat in three rows of four. All dressed in the green blazer trimmed with navy blue and white braiding. Smart, the head thought, tidy, alert.

'Why? McDowell.' He must take care not to favour McDowell. 'How else would we defend ourselves?'

'How is it a defence?'

'I should have said deterrent.'

'So, because countries know that we possess an atom bomb they will not attack us?'

'Yes.' McDowell was firm. 'That's it.'

'Do we have any evidence for that?'

'Well, they haven't so far.'

'Johnston?'

'If we don't have our own bomb, we'd have to rely on others.'

'And?'

'Maybe it would not be in their interests to be our ally.'

'Valerie?' She came from Aspatria, once a mining town; she could always be relied on to have an opinion.

'There's no point. They blow us up, we blow them up, there's nothing left. Look at Japan.'

'So?' Mr Stowe prowled along the first row of desks, like a fisherman casting and recasting, waiting for a bite.

'There's no winner.' Valerie blushed as she threatened to be the centre of attention.

'So why should that stop us having the bomb? Isn't it better to be safe rather than sorry?'

'What's safe about blowing other countries to smithereens?' I asked.

Mr Stowe smiled. And waited for me to go on.

'Best to stop it in its track before it takes hold,' I said.

'Takes hold?' he asked.

'Before everybody's making atom bombs.'

'Wouldn't that neutralise the matter? Wouldn't it cancel things out?'

'Somebody will always think they have the advantage. Wars start up all the time. Once atom bombs are available – why not use them?'

'McDowell?'

'That's the point. You wouldn't because the other side would and so nobody would.'

'How do we know? If you're losing you'd try anything. They're a menace and always will be,' I said.

'So what is your solution?'

'Do away with them,' I said, suddenly confident. The argument had been going on in the pub for months.

'How would you do that?'

'Force people. We won the war. We should say to the Americans and anybody else, it's done enough damage to show what it can do. Let's put them in concrete and throw them to the bottom of the sea while we can.'

A single handclap from the back. Later tracked down to Catherine Duckett.

'We should make it part of a peace treaty.'

'What if everybody else refused?' said McDowell.

'They should be forced to accept,' I said.

Mr Stowe smiled. He enjoyed it when we became vehement.

'But what if they refuse and start another war?' he suggested.

McDowell laughed. 'We would bomb them!'

'Just because something's there doesn't mean it always has to be there! If we had never changed anything we would still be in the Stone Age,' I said.

Mr Stowe took a couple of paces back. The discussion was gathering its own steam. Just as it should. They were often too diffident to take on such arguments in the classroom or, he suspected, in the interview room when later they tried to get into university. There was almost a mob feeling developing but he would let that build up. He could defuse it in a moment.

'We'll never give up a bomb like that.' Val came back in.

'I agree. What's to stop us?' McDowell.

'God!' The word escaped from me. 'Or Jesus Christ. The Sermon on the Mount. "Blessed are the peacemakers,"' I said.

Mr Stowe rocked on his heels with pleasure. For a few moments the class stalled. How could you argue with that? The statement had left me hot and nervous.

No one wanted to pick up the baton. McDowell, from a Labour family in Mr Stowe's old town of Aspatria, was reluctant to be silenced. Even though God had been an almost unfair intervention and the Sermon on the Mount – which all of us would have heard time and again at school assemblies – was a hard one to argue against.

It threatened to become an argument between the two of us.

'You can't count on God.' McDowell was tentative but he got the words out.

'I do.' That was Valerie. 'We all do, don't we? We all count on God.'

Unease in the room.

'How do you know?'

'You pray,' said Valerie. 'And He tells you.'

That was a big one. McDowell girded himself.

'There was an experiment somewhere where a thousand people prayed for whatever it was, I forget, as an experiment. They prayed night and day and nothing happened.'

'Perhaps God had better things to do that day,' said Valerie, rather brusquely. 'He can't always be sat up there just listening to the likes of us.'

McDowell retreated.

'It's the peacemakers that are more important than God!' I said. 'Sorry, sir. But if we don't have peace when we have these weapons, sooner or later we'll wipe each other out and that will be that!' I could feel myself getting over-exposed and out of my depth. Yet I had the attention of the room, of Mr Stowe himself, and that was exciting. 'We have to make peace!' Didn't they understand? 'We have to! It didn't matter as much when there weren't so many of us, but even then we managed to kill millions, but now with this thing – we can kill everybody!' I saw mountains of the dead. 'That's what we have to understand.' My voice rose and my conviction took hold of my words. I lashed on. 'We just HAVE to do it. Don't you see? If we don't make peace then all of us, all of us here, everywhere, will be buggered!'

Oh, no! I flung my head between my arms on the desk. There was the sound of sharply intaken breath.

'Sorry, sir. Very sorry, sir.'

'I'll see you outside my study.'

'Yes, sir.'

By the time the headmaster arrived, I had managed to stem the welling up and make a lightning visit to the lavatory.

I followed Mr Stowe into his study.

'Over there.' He pointed to a chair and took down a cane. Six swift strokes. They hurt.

'Sit down.

'Swearing is not allowed in this school.' As he said it, he remembered that a week or so ago his wife had said, when I turned up particularly hair-oiled and yet scruffy, 'You can take the boy out of the pub but you'll never take the pub out of the boy.' She was a draconian teetotaller.

'Sit.'

I could have been a dog. It stung but I sat.

'Why did you use that word? Apart from everything else it betrays an impoverished vocabulary.' He leaned forward. 'Now then. Why did you say, "Blessed are the peacemakers"?'

A gulp of breath and a whisper.

'Speak up.'

'Because that's the only way to solve it, sir. And Jesus Christ said so.'

'Is everything he said to be believed and acted on?'

'Yes, sir.'

'It hasn't been so far.' 'We'll have to . . .'

'Speak up.'

'We'll have to try harder then, sir, won't we?'

Mr Stowe leaned back and played with the cane.

'I don't want you to give up on those arguments,' he said. 'But swear once more in class and the wrath of God will descend on you!'

'Yes, sir.'

'You are in detention for the next two nights until five thirty. You will write an essay explaining in some detail why we should bless the peacemakers and how we can make it work. Out you go.'

Alone, Mr Stowe took a moment. His normal control was disturbed The boy was so passionate! But how he had phrased what he thought was not to be tolerated if he was to go far. That was one of the problems the school had.

Chapter Thirty-four

It was the first school dance and the last. It came about as a Boy Scouts fundraiser. The Scouts agreed on condition they did not have to wear their uniforms. The upper sixth seized on the opportunity and the teaching staff went along with it, pleased to extend the reach of the conjoined grammar and high schools. It would be a Good Thing. Perhaps it would mark the different character that had been grafted on to the old paying schools by the new Education Act, which had let in for free children from the working class.

It seemed an organised and adult thing to do, even clubby. The music to be supplied by gramophone records. The special feature was the Memphis Five.

This was Tich Parker on bass (packing case, broomstick, baler twine), Eric, washboard and a kick drum on loan from one of the two Wigton trios who did most of the dances, Robert on the acoustic guitar his older brother had got for Christmas two years ago and abandoned, Paul Alleston (ukulele) and me: singer, organiser and provider of rehearsal room, the Singing Room at the pub. Lonnie Donegan was the chief inspiration. Elvis Presley was in the wings but too good to copy.

We'd had two engagements. One was at a dance at the Drill Hall, a Thursday-night, more a middle-aged affair where there was some sporting applause and one or two compliments. The other, at the County Ballroom in Carlisle, a big venue with a twelve-piece band on a Saturday night, generally packed and with a space for a 'new act' in the interval. We gave them 'Rock Island Line', 'Cumberland Gap', 'Fifteen Tons', and, mistakenly, I sang a Little Richard screamer. Way before 'Fifteen Tons' the large ballroom was deserted, save for one or two fugitive fumbling couples in the darkest corners, taking advantage. When the band returned, there were two reactions 'Just a bit more practice, lads,' one said, and the other, 'I've heard worse.' We went to the snack bar for our free lemonade and crisps in a thoughtful mood. We talked about changing our repertoire. To what?

There was a lot hanging on Wigton.

William and I stacked up the records in order on one side of the platform. I was MC. The deal was that when I wanted a dance, William would take the mike and announce it. 'Please take your partners for a quickstep, a Canadian three step, a modern waltz, the Three Drops of Brandy.' It was not a task he took to and his method was to mumble as fast as possible and then take little care to drop the needle on the record without scratching it too deeply. But the job got done.

On the other side of the platform was our performance area. The instruments looked rather forlorn on the deep stage, which every morning accommodated about twenty teachers and was otherwise used for debates or prize-givings. The hall itself had a balcony floor, which jutted a third of the way across the space. We closed it off for the dance. Mr James, who was in attendance, considered it too dangerous, although he did not specify why; Miss Rogers, who was his female counterpart, would have cut everything off. She was a monument of disapproval. She taught domestic science. She had taught in the girls' school for many years and deplored the arrival of boys, non-paying girls and those she called – in the staffroom – the scruffs. There was no attempt to disguise her snobbery and most people got numb to it.

Miss Rogers, who was near retirement age, lived with her mother in a large bungalow near the cemetery. It looked down on the town, which, I later thought, was just what she wanted. The view was due south to the fells. The bungalow was christened 'Mountain View'. In the holidays when I could persuade my father to let me finish the work in the pub by 7 a.m., I would deliver papers for Mr Easton on Friday and Saturday mornings. These were the heavy loading days when paper bags, including the comprehensive *Cumberland News*, threatened to drag you off the bike. Miss Rogers took the *Daily Telegraph* and the *Daily Mail*: one, we all agreed in the shop where we sorted the papers, to read, the other for show. She was the last call on my round, and watched out of the window as I parked my bike at the gate and brought the papers into her porch. Before I had reached her gate, the door would have opened, the papers swallowed in her arms. She never gave a tip. It was not worth carol singing outside her door.

The paper round introduced me to Rachel. She lived with her aunt at the bottom of Meeting House Lane, where Jack Rook and the Muirhead twins lived. She was, we told each other, stacked like a film star – Jane Russell was the model – and much lusted after, not least by the Muirhead twins, Jack Rook and myself. I came across her when I went down to the Muirheads for a cup of tea after the paper round. She was bonny, easygoing and happy to join in our pontoon games in Mrs Muirhead's kitchen.

Within a few days of the midwinter half-term holidays the sole question was – which one of us would she go out with? She liked all of us, she said, rather casually, and that made a difficult matter all but impossible.

Jack's solution was simple: the five of us should go for a bike ride into the woods beyond Old Carlisle. There we would each spend some time with her – ten minutes was agreed – and it would be up to her to choose the winner.

We set out after dinner on a Saturday afternoon. It had snowed, then the frost came in and the ground was icy and not entirely reliable under the bicycle wheels. Our breath puffed out, like the smoke from a train. By the time we left the road and freewheeled down to the woods the cold had begun to cut through the clothes. The veins on the back of my hands were swelling.

We'd had the sense to bring our coats. These were not substantial but we laid them down on a patch of snow-free frozen turf. Alan Muirhead went first, followed by his brother. While we waited we stamped our feet and swung our arms and wondered what the hell . . . Jack went last.

My turn was, I suspect, typical. She was serious and let you lie on top of her, fully clothed, of course. She was warmer than the rest of us because she kept her coat on. There was little conversation in case the others, not far enough away, would pick it up. Minimum fumbling around her breasts was permitted but only through four layers of clothing and full stop at the bra. Neither of us had any plan of access below the waist, as far as this love feast was concerned. All that, it went without saying, was forbidden. After a few kisses, which were pleasant enough, the whole thing petered out before it had begun and ten minutes seemed a long time. 'I like you very much,' could only go so far. 'I've always liked you' again met with the faint smile of minimal response. One or two attempts at French kissing failed. She was strong. It was hard not to look at my watch, but that felt humiliating and bad manners so we lolled around in a state of arrested passion just getting colder.

Little was said on the way back. We shivered on our bicycles as what there was of the sun sank away.

Despite all that, I hoped I had won. Yet I was relieved when it turned out to be Jack. He was by far the biggest. And it would have been hard work.

Jack brought her to the school dance. The Muirhead twins passed on it: they said one and six wasn't worth it when there was no real band.

Rachel turned up, looking like a film star, especially compared with the girls from school. A few dozen town girls were there but none had her confidence or the pleasant manner that made everyone friendly to her. Most of them, like Rachel, worked in Redmayne's factory.

The girls from school – not only from Wigton but by bus from Aspatria and Silloth – were dressed in their best and several were lovely, but Rachel was already a woman. She had put aside girlish ways.

Jack was a sport. He let me have a dance with her and even hold her quite close. She loved dancing. So did I. Jack, thankfully, had two left feet. He knew I was a good loser, and though he kept an eye on us he didn't make a thing of it.

It was nine o'clock and the dance floor was full – young couples gliding around almost in formation like their elders. We were little elders. The boys wore suits, a clean, usually a white, shirt, a tie, shoes that, more often than not, had tasted polish. They were polite – they went across the room to ask a girl when the dance was announced and escorted her back to her place afterwards. When Three Drops of Brandy or the Dashing White Sergeant was called there were those unfamiliar with them, but that was useful, teaching broke any ice, group dances that occupied a lot of space.

I wanted to turn down the full glare of the lights. Miss Rogers shook her head. She was seated about halfway up the room talking to three of the older girls who had known the school when it was all girls and, Miss Rogers was reminding them, 'So much more of a family . . . so much more . . . Is "distinguished" the word?' None of the girls replied, not wishing to extend this conversation, which had so far taken them away from two dances.

At a quarter to nine, the Memphis Five, as pre-planned, went to the ping-pong room for a final rehearsal. No one took their instruments but we could hum and sing along a bit. Nerves were not holding up. There were too many people we knew, and previous experience did nothing to reassure us. We practised our opener 'The Rock Island Line', banging the ping-pong table to give us some rhythm, making a strong sound with our American twang in that rather confined space. Tich suggested we should jump around a bit more. The rest vetoed it. We had rehearsed as much as we could. This was merely to settle our nerves. We were in full voice when Mr James came in. He was not wearing his gown. For Mr James he was reasonably relaxed in a blazer and flannels.

We stopped instantly.

'Just a last practice, sir.'

He nodded but clearly he wanted more.

'What is it you were singing?' It was said not unkindly.

'"Rock Island Line", sir. Lonnie Donegan sings it.'

To do him justice he tried his best to minimise the embarrassed pause.

'I'm afraid I couldn't quite make out the words from the corridor.'

'It's in American,' said Eric, honestly trying to be helpful.

'It's a folk song,' said Robert, saving the day.

Mr James's puzzled expression broke into a smile of relief. 'I see. A folk song.'

'Yes, sir. It's about this railway.'

'Ah.' All tension ebbed away. 'I suppose we sound just as odd to them.'

We let this pass.

'We were doing a run-through, sir.'

'Ah. A run-through. Of course. I must not disturb you.' His smile was irresistibly encouraging. 'I look forward to the real version.' He left.

He had knocked the stuffing out of us.

'Should we rehearse the end one?'

'We rehearsed it for nearly an hour this afternoon. We know it backwards.'

'It'll be a riot,' said Eric, as dry as it was possible to be. He was good at that.

'We can jump about a bit on that one.'

Tich was ignored.

'It'll soon be over,' said Paul.

That helped.

The room was jostling. Some of the local lads – young men – who had not initially fancied a school dance at one and sixpence, deviated from a pub crawl to take a look in just after nine. There was no one on the door. They were in free and up for it. One of them went out to the Crown and brought back half a dozen bottles with a lead opener. They kept them hidden from the authorities whom they had spotted immediately.

I was standing near to Miss Rogers, who was beginning to look flustered. William had turned up the sound to full. Annie – I knew her brothers – sought me out. She was one of those still lodged in Water Street, defying the drift to the outer town.

She came across and ignored Miss Rogers, who looked at her as if a bad smell had entered the hall.

'It's startin' to liven up a bit,' she said. 'There's a few here just after me mint, Melvyn, but they're not gitten' it. Come on then, gadji!' She spoke in a broad accent, which she at times enjoyed making as coarse as possible. Miss Rogers looked as if she'd been stunned.

Annie held out her arms. I left William to put on another record as Annie and I glided around the floor. She was a wonderful dancer, like most of the town girls, and managed to keep up conversations with any pal along the way. Both of us had learned with our mothers at the Congregational socials in Water Street.

'Posh, isn't it?' The big orchestras on the records kept not only the sound but the feeling warm and lively.

'Not that posh,' I said.

'No, not that posh.' She glanced at the conventionally clad schoolgirls. 'And some of them can be nice.' She grinned. 'Me brothers and a few of them have just come in. They'll liven it up.' She laughed and glided on, slicing through the crowd, apprenticed on film musicals.

When the music stopped she gave me a light slap on the face. 'You're a good lad,' she said. 'I was in the morris dancers, you know. Can you not get them to lower these lights?'

Annie's brothers and three others – making up a clique of half a dozen – were clumped at the far end of the room. They were undoubtedly a new element in the stately hall, older, looser, laughing a lot. They had been in the pub but were not much the worse for wear. They wore rather battered suits, shirts open at the neck, and shoes that could do with a brush up. They smoked.

Miss Rogers looked out on a dangerous species. She was transfixed by them. They inspected the premises carefully as if they had turned up at an auction.

Laurie, who lived down the road from the Blackie, waved at me and when I got over to him his grin was irresistible. The record was Glenn Miller's 'String of Pearls'. Laurie spoke as broadly as he could. 'Some baary morts here t'neet.' He nodded to the dance floor. 'We're runnin' outa drink.'

'There's lemonade.' I told him. 'Homemade.'

'Dear God. Is that it?' He nodded to our rather isolated clutter of instruments on the platform. 'Where's everybody frae?'

'Here, Silloth, round about, Aspatria.'

'Spaytree?' Laurie looked around as if scenting fresh meat. Aspatria was the Enemy. For tribal reasons, no less fierce for being absurd, when a man from Aspatria strayed into Wigton, or vice versa, it seemed a matter of duty to start a fight. Knowing that . . .

'They're at school here,' was the best I could manage.

'Ah'll mix in.' Laurie slapped my shoulder. 'Thou dissent loss thisel.'

'Now then,' said William, growing in confidence at the mike, 'we have – I don't know what to call it – some sort of – is it a performance? Anyway, they call themselves the Memphis Five. You'll know them all.' He said that very slowly for some reason.

We went onstage.

Some people moved towards us.

As we set up I think that all of us felt how stupid this was. Many of those watching were our friends. They knew us too well to think we could transform ourselves into performers. They were rather hazy about why we were doing it at all. The balance between being thought of as good for having a go and being mere show-offs was a fine one. Mr James stood well back beside Miss Rogers. Perhaps he thought she might need a little managing, especially as the Wigton lads had given a particularly loud ironic cheer when William had announced the name of the group.

We were ready, dry-throated, scarcely able to look our audience – our friends and critics – in the eye. Paul strummed an opening phrase, Eric got down to the washboard, Tich had a run on the baler twine attached to the broomstick stuck in the packing box. I picked up the mike and all but dropped it instantly. William had left the sound system turned full up so we were not the little group tinkling in the distance – as we all joined in – but a huge sound battering the walls of the Nelson Thomlinson School hall and, for all I knew, whacking out over Wigton. It was a wonderful accident. I belted it out.

'"The rock island line is the road to ride!"'

Miss Rogers clapped her hands over her ears.

'American folk song!' Mr James bellowed cheerfully, enjoying it. People joined in. A few started to dance.

'Cumberland Gap' was next and we hammered it, on the crest of our wave. Las Vegas beckoned. 'Very relevant,' said Mr James. As if having teeth pulled, Miss Rogers's head moved up and down.

'Sixteen Tons' brought together the lads, the school lads and the town lads. Unconsciously we slowed it down a bit and all of us joined in. Feet were stomped as at a Red Indian war dance.

Then, full pitch I all but yodelled, '"I owe my soul to the company store!"' By now Tich was hyperactive, Robert and Paul moved about the stage, Eric had closed his eyes as if playing a multiple drum set. There was some applause, even one or two yells.

To end. Our surprise number. The song that had disrupted cinemas and dance halls across the western world. 'Rock Around The Clock' with Bill Haley and His Comets.

'"One two three o'clock, four o'clock rock; five six seven o'clock, eight o'clock rock!"'

The room went wild. Some of them could jive. Billy Nelson, who was apprenticed in Redmayne's shop, one of Annie's brothers, had recently won a competition and gave a performance deeply to be envied and with difficulty copied. Those who couldn't tried. The Wigton clump spun out like satellites, took any available arm and followed Billy's lead. A good number of those from the school were well up for it, to the alarm of Miss Rogers, who kept muttering, 'It's not "gonna rock tonight", it's "*going* to rock tonight", *going*, please!' The floor appeared to bounce. Mr James, fearing a loss of control, came nearer to the band and rehearsed his thank-you speech, but it was pointless. As soon as we finished we started again to even wilder scenes. We were unquestionably on the road to the London Palladium! 'Hooligans,' Miss Rogers said, to the girls around her. 'Hooligans!'

Mr James went up the side steps onto the platform and looked with almost pleasure at the pounding, jumping, twisting, twirling, singing figures on the old school floor.

There was only one thing for it.

Before we could launch into a third go, he came to me, took the mike, smiled, genuinely, and announced, 'I'm sure we'd all like to thank the band for the effort and work that must have gone into these American folk songs. Could we have a round of applause?'

'More! More! We want more!'

'And to remind you that the last bus back to Aspatria leaves at ten twenty and to Silloth at ten fifteen, each one calling at all intermediary villages. Thank you.' He ushered us off.

We took the hint.

'Thank you, sir.'

The next dance was an 'Excuse Me'.

Rachel, as the evening went on, increasingly the most popular girl in the room, but always aware of Jack, was dancing with a boy from Aspatria. Jeremy, in the upper sixth, was the son of a teacher in a nearby village, a big smooth young man, a good athlete.

Vince, one of Laurie's friends, strolled across the floor to make his bid. Both Laurie and Mr James were nearby, Laurie in an immediate state of preparedness. Vince had form. He nodded to Jeremy. Rachel smiled and disengaged. Jeremy was disgruntled. Within a minute, a smirk plastered across his face, he tapped Vince on the shoulder and said, 'Excuse me.'

Vince looked at him unthreateningly. 'Thou's just hed a go.' He stayed clinched to Rachel and danced on. Laurie went nearer. Mr James, to his credit, also clocked that something was going to happen which ought not to happen. Jeremy tapped Vince's shoulder once again, once again beaming a smirk. Vince didn't bother to turn but clearly said, 'Fuck off.'

Enough heard it round about for Jeremy to take this as a challenge. He went up to Vince again. Before he could tap him Laurie was there, grabbed him, hauled him away. 'None of that here.'

Not wanting to let anyone take on his fight, Vince spun away from Rachel only to face Mr James. 'Now then,' Mr James said, 'Jeremy – you were in the wrong. Apologise! You were certainly in the wrong.'

Vince was temporarily halted and unclear as to why this school-teacher was interfering. A widening pool of excited spectators. Laurie pushed his face into Jeremy's. 'Say sorry,' he said intensely, 'or he'll murder you.' All in an instant Rachel reached out to touch Vince's shoulder, Mr James was steady, Jeremy looked directly at Vince, paused, muttered, 'Sorry.'

'Well done,' said Mr James. And to Vince, 'Well done you too.' His nods eased Vince back to Rachel. The dance went on.

A few minutes later, Laurie and his gang left for the Crown where there would just be time to get a drink at last orders. On the way out Vince said, 'My mother's friends with her auntie,' which he thought explained everything about his dance with Rachel.

Eric went back to Greenacres through the Crofts, Paul caught the bus to Silloth, Robert biked back to Old Carlisle, Tich insisted on humping his double bass through the town to the East End. I helped William clear up the stage.

I was the last to leave. Mr James was at the door with Miss Rogers. He would give her a lift home. As soon as she saw me, despite Mr James's calming arm work, she boiled over.

'I hope you're satisfied,' she said.

I was. I thought it had gone well.

'Thank you, miss.'

'That was a disgrace to the school. This school was founded to educate girls into gentlewomen and yours to educate boys to become gentlemen.' Mr James shook his head but she would not be stopped. 'All these new reforms have ruined that! Ruined it! But never as much as tonight. You and your hooligan friends.' She looked at me with undisguised disgust. 'You will never be a gentleman.'

Before I could reply, Miss Rogers walked around Mr James's car and took her seat in the front.

Mr James smiled. 'On the whole I think we can count it a success. Well done.'

'Thank you, sir.'

By the time I was outside the church, the town was quiet. A few walking up towards Brindlefield, no shouting, modest street lighting.

I went from the church to the Black-A-Moor where we had met in the afternoon in the empty Singing Room to practise. Where we'd decided on 'Rock Around The Clock'. You could shout! You could jump about! My treble voice was gone but some sort of in-tune sound had replaced it and 'Rock Around The Clock' fitted it well enough!

I strolled through the town. I liked to swan around the place at this time of night. So many dark alleys somehow setting off good memories, so calm with the poor lighting adding to the cosy sense of the town as a thing in itself preparing for sleep.

The fish-and-chip shop was open until eleven and I just caught it. Chips and scrams. I hadn't realised I was so hungry. I walked down King Street slowly, not wanting to arrive home with a bag of chips. I imagined that the feelings of those who lived in the houses and over the shops seeped into me as the town breathed in and out together in the dark. It was enchanted, as far as I was concerned. This plain, ordinary, some would say even mean place seemed at this hour like something I was seeing in the cinema, a place flitting with images, memories, adventures . . .

Just beyond the Blackie, I saw Laurie coming up from his house with his dog, a Border terrier, on its last walk of the day. I waited for him. Laurie stopped.

'It wasn't sek a bad do,' he said. 'I liked that teacher.'

'Vince would have?'

'Mullied him. Vince can't stop once he's started. I've seen Vince clear a bar.'

Laurie moved towards Tenters. 'Comin'?'

We fell in step.

Past the old jail, across the bridge along to Tenters, the Gashouse and Stony Banks where Laurie sat on the seat provided at the crossroads with Little Lane.

'Want one?'

'No thanks.'

'Wise man.'

He lit up and pulled deeply.

'I like it when it's so quiet,' Laurie said, 'and these laal lanes tricklin' off yaa way an' t'other. And thou can't even hear the factory. Non-stop. Twenty-four hours.'

'My dad worked there.'

'So did mine,' Laurie said, 'before his accident. I went down for a job after national service but it didn't suit. So you've stopped on at your school?'

'Yes.' Feeling overprivileged.

'I nivver took to school,' said Laurie. 'They would go on about this and that. I just wanted to be rid of it. I should have gone in for farm work.'

'Why didn't you?'

Laurie took his time.

'I tried it for a year but – thou's on thee own ower much. I missed being with pals. We've mostly ended up on council work – digging holes and filling them in again! Or the dustcart – you might not believe it but I like our dustcart. There's a clique of us. It's friendly. You won't stay in Wigton.'

'I want to.'

'You won't. Wigton's changing – these estates. Anyway, they

wouldn't have let you stay on if they didn't think they could mek something of you so you'd git out. Mebbe a teacher?'

'I wouldn't like to leave Wigton.'

'We'll see.' He threw away the stump of the cigarette. 'It does me,' he said. 'I just fit in. Whenever I go anywhere else for a day or two, I always want to come back and when I see that Tower,' he pointed to its location in the dark, just across from where we were sitting, 'I feel, you know, it's a good feeling. Thou'll miss it.'

'I'm not leaving.'

'We'll see.'

He stood up, and we walked back.

'Thou gave "Rock Around The Clock" a good seeing to!'

'Thanks.' Pride rushed in like a gulp of fresh air.

'You've a strong voice and all that else.' He laughed. 'We started a band once.'

'You were in the choir when I joined. You sang solos.'

'I did. I liked the singing. I liked the choir practices. It was all the rest.'

As we walked past St Ursula's, the Roman Catholic school staffed by nuns, 'I just can't fathom them,' Laurie said. 'You couldn't meet pleasanter women on the street and yit all that mumbo-jumbo.'

We walked down to Laurie's house, which was the last in a row of six cottages built alongside Scott's funeral business where the horses were stabled and two grand hearses stood under a corrugated-iron roof.

'Fancy a cup of tea?'

'Yes. Thanks.'

You went straight in off the street.

'My mother would love this!' I said, looking around. 'She'd say it was lovely.' Inside the well-furnished cottage I took more notice of Laurie, his slim muscular neatness, a certain 'way' with him, his blond hair always well brushed, a tidy man.

Laurie smiled appreciatively at the genuine enthusiasm. 'My mother and our Beth have sorted it out. Beth's great at sales. And the old man and myself put another room onto t'back so we could look out at yon garden – we have a big garden. That tent at the end is where Father has to sleep when he's bad. While we were about it we put another bedroom on top of the kitchen. It surprises people, the size of it.'

The tea was served in dainty cups. Laurie placed a biscuit in each saucer. He poked a little life out of the embers in the fire. We drank in silence for a while. There were paintings on the walls – landscapes. When Laurie caught my eye he said, 'Next to nowt. In the sales. Cheap as chips. Them as well.' He pointed to a fine-looking table and chairs. 'Not many like old stuff,' he said. 'We do.'

He saw me to the door.

'Do you know that Jeremy?' I nodded. 'Tell him – now this is serious – tell him to keep out of Vince's way. Vince sometimes gets through to Aspatery. He won't forgit.'

We stepped outside. Laurie pointed up into the sky at the moon above the bus garages. 'You would know how it gits to be crescent-shaped.'

'No.'

Laurie grinned and slapped me on the shoulder. 'Much use school then.'

Chapter Thirty-five

For all the efforts and energy directed at the school by Mr Stowe and Mr James to raise confidence and exam results, it was a small dumpy man, quietly spoken and with little to say, melancholy, brought up in a Wigton pub, who put the shine on its reputation. Mr Morton, 'Jimmie', was one of three Nelson School boys who, many years earlier, had played for English Schools at rugby. Their photographs were outside the library, tassels carefully draped halfway along their caps. Mr Morton had studied sport at teacher-training college and landed up back in Wigton.

He was competent enough at teaching gym. Bored out of his mind with cricket but happily a couple of members of the Wigton cricket team, which got free use of the school pitch and pavilion, would coach the more capable boys on summer evenings. Rugby took all his energy.

As a rugby coach Jimmie Morton was outstanding, by far the best coach of boys' rugby in Cumberland and Westmorland. This was a man who from one school in over three years would turn out almost a third of the English Schools national team. And it was one of the smallest grammar schools in the country. He was lucky in inheriting some fine athletes. But where he shone was in moulding not only them but the rest of the plodders like me into a team. People shook their heads in admiration. Wigton men – players for the town's team – came to watch school games on Saturday mornings.

When the autumn term began and the rugby season got under way, everything was to do with rugby. The pickings in the lower and upper sixth were not rich and he would sometimes reach back into the fifth form but he managed to get a caucus of his potential first team together for practice twice a week after school. The physical education classes – once the regulation exercises were out of the way – were about line-out tactics, or touch rugby at high speed, or packing against the parallel bars that lined the gym's walls. Making the pack tighter and lower, not a sloppy slip allowed. Ready to obey every instruction instantly: 'Ball in', 'Hold!', 'Hold!', 'Push!', 'Out!' This was an era in which such severely enforced tactics were outside the ambition of most teams, a more gentlemanly time, a time to get your breath back. Not with Jimmie!

He had a selection from the three towns. The Aspatria lads who lived on the border of the professional rugby league game, which several of them would end up playing. They were always sharper. Geoff Edgar was from Aspatria, as was his younger brother; both played for England. I played in the same team as Geoff, and David Atkinson, again from Aspatria, who sprinted in the English athletics finals. Silloth provided three greats (for those days), Walton, Edmondson and Johnston. Wigton had the captain, Brian Robson, and Robert Wilson, who was to win the hundred-yards hurdles in the English championships, and a full back of genius (a word we used), Keith Warwick, England again. Not all of them were in the team at the same time, but often four coincided. It was a joy to watch them and now and then to remind yourself that you too were on the field.

Perhaps Jimmie's greatest strengths were his willingness to teach by example and his tetchiness, even bad temper, if we got it wrong, especially in training. For such a mild, diffident man, the rap of a reprimand when we were training was quite a shock, and always pointed. Or he would suddenly come as near to losing his temper as he was able, especially when one of the big forwards was barging through the defence and Jimmie's cry, 'Tackle|! Tackle him!' was ignored. He would race across, launch himself like a missile and grapple the much larger body around the thighs and bring him down. He would immediately jump up. 'He can't run without his legs!'

His passion for the game and excitement when even the most average among us showed some talent at it were infectious. We loved the game but for Jimmie we loved it even more. Sometimes it was more like dancing. It was exhilarating to win and so often. The school and eventually the whole town were taken up with pride at this wonder team. Mr Morton would never be drawn to comment in public. In a four-year run he became the key man in boys' rugby in the north-west and when we were not playing he would take the bus to other school games and stand on the halfway line apparently absorbed in his notebook.

In those four years we were never defeated. There was one hiccup in year three. We drew when we should have won but had two tries disallowed by a Catholic priest, a teacher and the referee that day. We were at the mighty St Joseph's Roman Catholic boarding school – 1500 boys – at Dumfries in south-west Scotland. The ref's indefensibly biased judgement provoked Mr Stowe to fury. The headmaster, like Mr James, occasionally went to away games and he wanted to visit this famous Scottish boarding school. But in his Monday morning assembly address after the St Joseph's match he went as near reviving the Wars of Religion as he legally could. Those tries were clearly valid! It was prejudice at work! It was typical!

In one season the entire team, including those who, like myself, were makeweights, got their colours. Mr Stowe devoted a morning assembly to the virtues and qualities to be found in sport. He was cock-a-hoop when we won. It must have seemed to him that his golden touch spread throughout the school.

After home games, Mr Morton would come into the dressing room and showers and it was there that he found the place to pay individual compliments. He would move from boy to boy as we towelled ourselves down and find at least a sentence or two of accurate comment and encouragement. With the better players, the stars, he would often wander around and start a discussion about a move, which could go on rather longer than the boys wanted, although they would be flattered. After the game we would go to the school canteen with the opposing team for a school dinner. Mr Morton stayed until the final boy left and then he would tidy up the changing room.

I did not realise how close he had been to the old Wigton until the day I broke my collarbone. We were playing at Workington, known to be a hard team. A bigger school on the thriving industrial coastline of the county, they were determined to break our record and re-establish their superiority in the league.

I had been half hidden away playing blind side loose forward when a high punt flew up from their half: I was perfectly placed. I took it, leaned back and hoofed it downfield into their half. I was off balance. I heard a snap. I fell back, my collarbone was broken. Luckily it was my left shoulder. It was an illegal tackle – what we called a 'dirty tackle' – but their home ref let him get away with it. We were well ahead.

Jimmie took me to the Workington hospital: their sports teacher gave us a lift. He waited until they had set the bone and strapped it up. They gave me a couple of pills and both of us a cup of tea.

He took me back to Wigton on the regular bus – the school bus long gone. The furnaces and heavy lighting rigs at the side of the coast road made it a dramatic journey. The bus was all but empty. Mr Morton sat on the seat behind me as if ready to steady me should I fade a little. The bone felt a little odd but there was no pain.

We walked across Market Hill to the pub, already quite busy early Saturday night. My mother led us upstairs. 'It's nothing serious, Ethel,' Jimmie said. 'It'll just be a matter of a few weeks.'

The news had been brought by one of the rugby team, whose bus had reached Wigton hours before ours. The table was laid. Jimmie was hesitant, almost shy.

'You'll both need something.' My mother nodded both of us to the table.

'It doesn't hurt.'

'As long as he takes two of the pills four times a day, he'll be fine.'

'Sit down, Jimmie. There's ham and a salad. And I thought some scrambled eggs would warm you both up.'

She poured cups of tea and indicated the thinly buttered slices of bread. 'You must be starving.'

It was difficult to place the tone between Jimmie and my mother. Picking up on my sense of puzzlement, she said, 'Jimmie and I were at school together. At the national, before he went to the Nelson School. He was a class down from me. Everybody liked Jimmie.'

He blushed and looked at Ethel gratefully.

'She was always very good to me, your mother.'

'He needed looking after.' She whisked the eggs and talked with her back to us.

What did that mean?

As if she heard me, my mother continued, 'He was small. But very game. And then there was . . .' she should not have started but now she could not stop '. . . Audrey, his mother, had a terrible accident when you were?'

'Seven.'

'She was such a good woman. A lovely woman.' Ethel wanted to make it up to Jimmie for being so crass as to mention it. 'There was nobody like her.'

'There wasn't, was there, Ethel?' he almost pleaded.

'Nobody.'

He nodded and looked away, unguarded. 'You know, Ethel, I still miss her. Does that sound funny?'

'No, Jimmie, it doesn't. She thought the world of you.'

By now I was watching the two of them very closely. A new world! Jimmie's lip may have quivered.

'Here we are.'

She shared out the scrambled eggs, laid them neatly on the slices of ham.

'This is very good of you, Ethel.' Jimmie's tone was humble.

'Would you like a drink?'

'Well,' he plunged in, 'a bottle of pale ale would be welcome.'
She went downstairs. Jimmie tucked in.

Once she was well out of the room, Jimmie said, 'You have a good mother.' There was the slightest break in his voice. 'Ethel's been nothing but very nice to me. I had a bad time after my mother died. The way she died. Father found it hard to cope. The Old Vic was not an easy pub to run.'

It was Dad who came back with the pale ale and a bottle of lemonade for me.

'Thanks for looking after him, Jimmie.'

Dad lit a cigarette and said no more for a while to let Jimmie finish his meal.

'You've made a great job of those boys,' my father said. 'If I can fit it in before opening time on a Saturday I try not to miss them.'

Jimmie nodded, now suddenly sure about himself. 'I've been lucky. Some of those lads, they don't come along very often.'

'When they get going,' my father said, 'you'll not see better rugby anywhere.'

'Yes. When it works.' He tried to suppress the surge of pleasure he always found in talking about his team.

'You must be very proud of them, Jimmie. Wigton's very proud of you.'

'Ah, well.' He took a last pull of the pale ale and stood up. 'I have to go now, Stan.' He looked across the room. 'You've got it very nice.'

'That's Ethel.'

'I didn't think it would be you, Stan.'

'Good night, Mr Morton. Thank you again.'

'It was a late tackle.' Jimmie was grim. 'You have to watch those Workington lads.'

Downstairs, Ethel came out of the bar and onto the steps.

'Back to Thursby?'

He nodded.

'Is Edna well these days?' There was a note of apprehension

in her question. Again he nodded. His manner was now brisk. He looked across the hill where the Carlisle bus, which would call at his village of Thursby, was ready to leave.

'That was a lovely supper. Thank you.'

He walked quickly across to the bus.

He bought a ticket to Carlisle. He hadn't been there for three weeks, too long. An incident on that evening led to his dismissal from the school.

At a literary festival in Cheltenham about fifteen years on, I was signing books when I caught sight of him. He hovered against the wall, his three-piece suit, like his face, much the worse for wear. 'I'll just be a minute,' I said, to keep him there.

Despite what had happened in Carlisle I felt happy to meet him. When I went across we shook hands and he attempted a smile, which brought on a rim of tears.

'We should have a drink,' I said. 'There's a bar somewhere.'

He shook his head. After a pause, he said, 'I just wanted to say hello. I'm pleased you wanted to as well. You've done well. That's all I came for.'

He nodded, turned away and went down the busy hall, past strangers. He looked unbearably lonely but also determined to be alone. Soon his small figure disappeared in the crowd.

Chapter Thirty-six

Before we knew it, Mr Blacka was in the classroom. His gown slung over his right shoulder was like a hump. He was short, accentuated by a slight stoop. In his dark sports jacket and black gown he was rather like a snail. He made no fuss when he came in, no calls for order, no greeting. He seemed to enjoy playing the dour Yorkshireman. He went to his desk, put a few books on it, looked around and waited. We were a small group.

We were keen to get going. The way he taught English was both relaxed and rigorous. Aside from the family of donkeys in his garden and his passion for cricket, watching, and playing it for Wigton until he was in his late sixties, he seemed to have made an early and deliberate decision to eschew show. He would wear an enigmatic smile, which helped convince some of us that he had been a spy in Czechoslovakia, as was rumoured in leaks from the staff room. He had a very strong jaw.

His method was based on reading aloud. Poetry, drama, essays, whatever came up on the syllabus and beyond it (he soon got through all the set books) was to be read aloud. All of us had to take part and however much we stuttered, stumbled, choked and blushed, he said nothing, just waited until we'd finished and moved on. At the end of the set piece he would murmur, 'So: what did you make of that?' and pick us off one by one, bestowing neither much praise nor censure, just a little corrective nudge now and then. He encouraged us to learn passages by heart.

Our set Shakespeare play for the A-level exams, many months away, was *King Lear*. A book of Hazlitt's essays provided the prose. The obligatory book of poetry was a selection of the Romantics, dominated by Wordsworth, Coleridge, Shelley and Keats.

'Wordsworth,' he announced, 'national poet, national treasure, nature poet on our doorstep, set out to change the language of poetry to find a place for the words and experiences of ordinary people. What did you make of his cottage?'

He had taken us to the cottage in Grasmere where Wordsworth and his sister had lived for some years.

'I thought it was poky, to be honest,' I said. 'I thought it would be a bit grander.'

'Why?'

'Well, he was poet laureate. He was famous. People came from London just to see him. I expected a big house.'

'When he came to Grasmere he had very little money. He wasn't poor. But he struggled.'

'I just loved it.' Catherine had made sketches of the cottage, the garden, the view from the top of the garden over to the lake. 'I loved the panelling, those tiny rooms, the creaky staircase – all of it. You could see him writing there.'

'Is there a particular place a poet should find to do his writing?' Mr Blacka almost smiled.

'Yes.' Catherine was firm. 'A poetic place. And that's what the cottage is.'

Val asked, 'What do you yourself think of the cottage, Mr Blacka?'

He paused but decided to stick to blunt.

'I think it might have been a pleasant enough place to live in, at the time, but the way it's preserved and pampered doesn't do him justice. It makes him too cosy. He was a radical young man in his heyday. He'd had an illegitimate child in France before he landed up in Grasmere. At one time he was suspected of being a revolutionary. The cottage is now the first thing most people think of and it's too tame. When he went to Keswick to see Coleridge, he would walk over Helvellyn to get there, sometimes by moonlight. That's more like him.'

'It has an atmosphere.'

'How would you describe it?'

'Happy?'

Mr Blacka was not impressed.

'Maybe I should have said "content" or "calm",' said Val, 'just right for thinking.'

Mr Blacka smiled ungrudgingly. He looked at the clock. 'Now. We just have time to look at the Four Short Lines that some people think contain his radical philosophy.' He spoke the words slowly:

> 'One impulse from a Vernal Wood
> May teach you more of man
> Of moral evil and of good
> Than all the sages can.'

'"Expostulation and Reply",' said Catherine.

'Correct. What does it mean?'

Catherine was ready. 'It means that if we really listen to nature, and really make ourselves part of it then it will enable us to know more about ourselves and about good and bad than all the religious books and books of wisdom put together.'

'Everybody agree?'

Everybody did.

'What is an impulse?' Mr Blacka asked.

'A feeling,' said Catherine. More assent.

'What sort of a feeling?'

'You can just feel it inside you.'

'How do you know the impulse comes from the wood?'

'Because that's where you are when you feel it.'

'Do you feel you want to sing? Or to dance?'

'No! It's what he says. It makes you think that if you are part of nature then that's the best way to understand life.'

'Does it have to be a vernal wood? Could it be winter?'

'That's not fair, Mr Blacka.' Catherine needed support. 'It doesn't matter.'

'It gets worse! What if there are wolves in the wood as there were round here not so long ago. Does all that also not matter?'

Catherine looked around. Surely she had done her bit. 'He takes it for granted you're up for it,' I said.

'How?'

'That you're looking for something like this because the wood is so beautiful and suddenly you feel that you belong to it. You don't know why, you just do, and that's the point.'

'Good and evil?'

'Yes. Both. Just seeing the trees and nature bring them on.'

'And what are you taught?'

'I don't know.'

'Valerie?'

'To be a better person.'

'How would you know that?'

'We all know,' said Val, rather spikily, 'when we're good or bad. Nature brings out what's good.'

'More than the Bible? As he claims. Or all the teaching of ancient philosophers?'

'It could do.' Val passed to me.

'He's saying thinking is not all there is. There's feeling, which might be stronger and better than thinking.'

Mr Blacka nodded. The bell went.

'No need to be so pugnacious,' he said. 'Good points made. Learn that whole poem – there are two of them as it happens – "Expostulation and Reply" by next lesson. There's more to talk about.'

The smile faded only slowly as he went back to the desk. 'They're starting to think!' he said, as if to himself, but just loud enough for us to hear. 'Well, well!'

By this time the lower sixth had found that they could talk informally to their teacher, now and then. A few days after that lesson, I caught Mr Blacka in the corridor.

'Sir. What do you think of Wordsworth?'

The teacher paused.

'He's undoubtedly a great poet,' he said. 'Mostly because he's so quotable and his radicalism caught and still catches a strong contemporary feeling. He's memorable and that's no small thing. But for me he doesn't always stand up to cross-examination. Sorry. And you?'

'He's written things I keep thinking about.'

'No better tribute,' said Mr Blacka.

Chapter Thirty-seven

The Market Hall was smack in the middle of the town. Its ambitious Victorian structure had destroyed several old streets. At the front it was all square with the High Street. At the back it opened onto the ancient marketplace that had been outside the church for several centuries. The great hall itself was teeming on Tuesday, market day, with salesmen and their stalls from across the north. When we were on holiday it was a rich addition to our play area, wriggling in and out of the stalls, skidding on the polished floor, slipping through to the cold fish market at the church end, just to smell the full force of fresh fish.

The salesmen were onstage. The patter – 'I have here a box of handkerchiefs, ladies, the finest linen! Two and six. And to this I add not one but two boxes, three boxes, ladies and gentlemen, and still for two and six! Where else could you get value like this? Three boxes! That's tenpence a box! I'm giving them away, ladies. Is anybody bidding? Over there! And there!

'This gold bangle – pass it round. Feel it, ladies! Weigh it! Anywhere else – ten shillings. Here – for you – it's my birthday – not ten, not nine, not eight – seven shillings! A present for all occasions. Just feel it in your hand. Right. See this little necklace with the silver crucifix – I'll throw that in. Seven shillings the lot. I tell you, go to the bazaars of Constantinople and you will not get a better bargain – over there! We have a lady who appreciates quality and class. And over there?'

I could never understand why everybody did not buy or bid. 'Six pairs of black socks not six shillings, not five, not four – two shillings!' If only I'd had money I would have bought the lot. Surely they would have lasted for a lifetime. 'This silk scarf, add this shawl, and this priceless – take it, feel it – bracelet – ten bob the lot. The day is closing in, I'm feeling generous . . .' What a wad of presents that could be for my mother.

It was as near Wigton, at that time, came to stand-up comedy. The salesmen loved teasing the women, who enjoyed being part of the performance, which never varied but never palled. For me it was Aladdin's Cave – goods tumbling from stalls, words streaming into the air, laughter and the banging of mallets.

Then there were the hall's multiple uses. For old-age pensioners' Christmas teas, for short-mat bowling for the over-sixties, for old-time dancing. It became a theatre not only for the schools and their plays but for the Wigton Amateur Dramatic Society, much admired with a loyal following of its cast – possibly the most class-blind of any organisation in the town – a doctor, banker, estate agent, working men, builders, a carpenter, women who served in the shops.

Winter was badminton for the tennis crowd, the occasional public meeting, dances for self-selecting groups – the Police Ball, the Young Farmers' Ball, both open to the public but ticket prices were stiff.

The glory of the place, as far as we were concerned as we broke through the obstacles of adolescence, were the Saturday-night dances. The band would, sometimes, be big and accomplished. There was a Wigton band when it was a small or local do, and then the numbers melted away. But Saturday night at the Market Hall after the war could draw in a crowd and pack the place. There was excitement, good dancers from a couple of generations turned up, as did those who, like my mother's uncousins, biked in from the villages. They stood in regiments of hopefuls around the hall. They came from Kirkbride, they came from Oulton, from Bromfield and Micklethwaite and even Thursby. Wiggonby would be represented and Waverton and Waverbridge, Fletchertown and Mealsgate, Rosley, Caldbeck, Ireby, Red Dial and Dundraw. They came at eight o'clock to get the most out of it, the best of it. Rain and drizzle did not stop them and even snow would not weaken their determination to come to the Wigton Saturday dance.

It was well organised. Cloakrooms, bouncers, refreshments – no alcohol – and the police putting in an appearance as the night went on.

Now and then there could be a flare-up, but in the early fifties it had not got a reputation for being regularly rough. To go to the Market Hall on a Saturday night was, within a large circle of the community, the thing to do. For people my age it had a glamour that was not matched anywhere else in the town.

William had been summoned to go with his father to collect the cans of milk a few miles away. Usually I would have gone with him but this night, having decided to be suited and booted for Saturday, I was more ready for the dance than a ride to a farm-yard some miles away where we'd all have to roll out and hoist the large cans of milk onto the cart and hang around until the chat between the men was over.

No café was open. I'd seen the film on at the Palace. Pubs were forbidden – I was under age. The baths were closed. The dance or other friends' houses were the only options. It was almost routine on Saturdays that I would go round a few houses and ask if William or Eric or Geoff wanted to come out, but that felt rather depressing on this Saturday, compared with the lure of the dance. Or I could go back to the pub, up into my room, block out the downstairs sound with the wireless and read. I wandered around the twilit town, noting the few movements from pub to pub, the men walking their dogs. I tried to imagine what was going on behind the drawn curtains of the flats above the shops. I began to enjoy the feeling of being on my own. I could be an American private eye casing the joint.

Rumours had been flitting around the town all afternoon that a gang from Aspatria planned to come to the dance. I'd just caught a whiff of it. There seemed no danger. I thought I might go home after all. Not much fun to go to a dance on my own, even though I would know people when I got there and it would be no embarrassment to ask someone for a dance.

At the fountain I turned right to go back to the Blackie. As I walked down the street I saw, about forty yards ahead of me, a strange even alien figure, all arms and legs, fully occupying the pavement, slowly using two sticks to help drag his near-powerless legs up the slope towards me. I walked down to meet it, and in the dismal streetlight, for a few moments, imagined it might indeed be a foreign creature. It stopped when I drew near.

'Brave man!' it – Ronnie the barber – said. 'Brave man out on the street tonight.'

He leaned against McMechans, breathing hard, taking the chance for a rest.

'Ronnie! What's up?'

'Saturdays,' he said, with a gasp of breath. After taking his time to settle, 'I always walk to the shop and back on Saturdays, stay open later, tidy up, here we are.' He paused, and then, out of the semi-darkness, he said, 'They can be a bugger, legs, eh? You?'

'I was going to go to the dance.'

'Don't. Good man. Keep away tonight.'

Ronnie propped his crutches against the wall and took out a Woodbine. 'You? No. Sensible.' He lit up. 'Can't smoke in the shop and the mother doesn't like it in the house.' He drew in deeply. 'You don't know about tonight?' He smiled. 'You've stayed on at that school too long. The Aspatria gang's coming through.'

No penny dropped.

'Dennis,' he began, referring to the biggest and the fiercest of that core of Wigton lads who played ducks and drakes with the law. They concentrated on fishing, poaching and pubs. 'Dennis,' he repeated, 'and a few of them went to Aspatria two or three weeks back, where he meets this lass, Jackie – you'll have seen her! Nearly as tall as him, hair jet black to his blond – what a pair they look! Anyway – she was engaged, it was all set up, but Dennis just sails in and there was a heck of a battle and next

278

thing we know she's on the bus with him and the lads and brought to Wigton.' Ronnie almost gargled the next sentence. 'They can't keep apart! That's what they say. They just can't keep off each other.' He got his breath back and took another deep puff on the cigarette.

'She was told to go back to Aspatria by her family and by the fella she was set to marry but no chance. Her sister brought her a suitcase of her stuff. There was a spare room at Dennis's mother's. You must have seen her! She's better than a film star. About seventeen. And very nice with it, they tell me.'

He took a last pull of the small cigarette, so carefully calculated that another millimetre would have burned his lips. Then he threw it away and took up his crutches. 'So the word is that her Aspatria fella and a gang of them are coming through to get her back. It'll be at the dance. I'd love to be a fly on the wall! Give us your shoulder for a second.'

Together we hobbled up the rest of the street. There was no traffic. I set him back to his home, which, because life wasn't difficult enough, was a first-floor flat up a steep flight of stairs. Ronnie put the crutches under one arm, grabbed the banister rails and heaved himself home.

I had to go. Not to go now that I knew would be cowardly and, besides, I had seen one or two skirmishes at dances. This promised to be on a different scale.

The entrance to the Market Hall, off King Street, was in effect a tunnel, where two shops had stood. It was poorly lit and glistened at this time of night with an uninviting air more like the entrance to somewhere rather seedy, even a little dangerous, than to a hall of music and dance. Its function, the music, was signalled through the closed doors behind the trestle table that served as the box office.

It was staffed by Arnold Nixon, who issued the tickets, and Harry Elliot, the bouncer. Vince, his younger brother, was hanging around. They were as pleased to see me as I was them; rather relieved, in a way, for something of the danger of the evening seemed to have seeped out of the hall despite the cheerful dance music.

Vince laughed when he saw me. 'School dance!' he said. 'My God! "Rock Around The Clock"! It'll be Elvis next!' His laughter was transforming. Vince was tough, wary and hard. He was handsome, and when he grinned there was a warmth, even a sweetness, that made me feel good. His older brother Harry was also warm in his welcome. I felt relieved that I had allies. Both of them had well-stacked quiffs.

We had a rather unusual friendship but it was close. Their family lived at the bottom of Union Street, one of the poorer streets that sloped down steeply to the River Wiza, where the cottages were always damp. Cheap as a consequence, freighted with those who could pay least and, like similar areas in Water Street, for example, the occupants were often dismissed as trouble-makers, feared for the possible effects of their crammed poverty on their behaviour. Condemned as their houses were condemned.

It was there, in a yard at the bottom of the street, that my father had found the only house available after his marriage. The rent was cheap. Like so many houses in the town it was two-up-one-down; four houses shared a washhouse and an outside lavatory. To Ethel it had been a shock. After the ample Station Road house, it was tiny. She felt suffocated. The walls were damp and not much better after Stan and a couple of friends had stripped and repapered them. The kitchen, knocked into a wall, was crudely equipped, the furniture poor, carpets worn out: the low rent was no compensation. Not a place people liked to visit. She went out with me in the pram whenever she could. Stan was at the factory and on shifts. This was just before he joined up for the war.

My mother's private upset and fears were not what she talked about. To put up with things was what you did. But it must have been hard. There were occasional visits from a friend in the town when they could find the time. 'I wouldn't have got through it if it hadn't been for Sally,' she would say.

Sally Elliot, mother of Vince, Harry and Kathleen, who had left home to go and stay with better-off relatives in Whitehaven. Sally was originally brought over from Ireland to the west coast of Cumberland when her father and his brothers came across to make a living in the coal and iron-ore mines. She changed her Irish name for the English Elliot when she was eighteen, soon after she had met Sam Elliot at a dance. They were a good-looking couple; she slim, a heap of auburn hair, which when unbound swept down to her waist, always neat, a fine pale skin, dark eyes, intense; he 'The Big Man', as she called her husband, easygoing, wound round her little finger, hard on the boys. At one stage he kept a fox as a pet and had a hutch for his ferrets in the yard. I think his family had been Travellers.

Wigton was something of a magnet for some of those Travellers, who finally decided to put down roots there. The McNeils, descended, they declared, from the family of kings of Ireland, had settled higher up in Union Street and established a trade in antiques – old stone urns, fireplaces, or statuettes, which could be sold for the gardens of the new middle-class houses around the town: quaint ornaments, horse and pony trading, dog breeding, above all anything connected with the history of Wigton, which they adopted as their own. With this and trade around farms and big houses near the town, they kept above water.

There were others like them around the town. Diddler and his family, who had settled in condemned cottages opposite the Salvation Army in Meeting House Lane; the Slaters, the funfair family who stored their rides and stalls in the town and eventually wintered alongside them in the area between Wigton football pitch and the road to the factory.

Sally and her husband were rather ostracised. Sally because she was Irish, Catholic, attractive, kept to herself, spirited, 'The Big Man' because you never knew what to make of him, and the two boys growing up to be troublemakers. Even when Harry got the job as a bouncer that didn't calm the unease of the neighbours. For some it made it worse. The boys had a reputation.

'I felt like I was in a warren,' Ethel said, 'underground some-where.'

'The same when I landed here.' Sally poured another cup of tea. 'It was bad in Whitehaven but not as bad as this. It made you feel you had to be on the lookout all the time.'

Ethel shuddered. She would never entirely cast off the memory of those early days. The cottage forever damp that autumn, so cold when the winter was creeping in, no comfort to be found. 'We had a fire on day and night.'

Sally nodded. 'It hit you hard,' she said. 'That's the way with some of us. And you had the child. Your milk dried up. You'd have thought sleep was that child's enemy. He could scream. You stuck it, though. I never heard you complain.'

Ethel smiled. 'That's because I didn't dare let it out.' The smile turned into a laugh. 'I say it again, Sally, without you I wouldn't have got through.'

'You would, you know. But I appreciate what you say.'

Often the women were chatting on in Sally's house while I was a child – pinpoint tidy, no dust dare settle, no stain go unnoticed. 'The Big Man' had raked in furniture from his finds and bargains around the sales at the farms. These were above the ordinary and gave the place distinction. There were photographs of their wedding on the mantelpiece and a shining silver crucifix with a rosary draped around, photographs of their children on the surface of a chest that housed cutlery and crockery. Constant fires and plastering had driven out the damp.

'It's such a nice house you have,' Ethel said.

'It took a bit of time.'

'I feel so good when I'm here with you.' She did not say 'safe' but it had almost escaped. For Ethel that was a rare confession of trust and friendship.

The women met regularly after Ethel had moved out of the house to Station Road. Ethel made a point of going down to Sally's most Friday afternoons for the talk, an hour or so before Sally's communion when they would walk back through the streets together. There would be tea and the biscuits brought by Ethel. I went with her, especially in the early days when Sally's boys would take over and we would play in the yard and in the street. They all but adopted me.

It was good to be in their company. They laughed a lot and never ran out of things to do or to say to each other. The attachment between the two women never slackened. The boys liked to call out Ethel's name across the street and have her wave to them. When Ethel and Sally went up the street together, they linked arms. When the boys reached the right age they went to the Blackie, but only at midday when it was quiet.

Dad found out why. They had a deserved reputation for being involved in fights. Sally had told them they would never cause trouble in Ethel's pub or they would have her to answer to. They were rather proud of that and passed it on.

It was a message given only once but they clocked it and stuck to middays for the Blackie. Fights were for nights.

Just before I went in to the dance, Vince took my shoulder. 'It's going to get rough,' he said. 'Dennis is mad on her. He won't let her back, and they won't go back to Aspatria without her.' He looked around. The tunnel entrance was filling up. His voice became urgent. 'There's a side door down next to the fish market. Stand near that. It's always open.' He smiled. I felt drawn to smile in return. The protection suddenly moved me. He took the lapels of my suit in a mock threat. 'Don't try to be a hero.' He went back to stand beside Harry, and I went into the hall where, as the doors opened, the whoosh of the band transformed my mood from apprehension into excitement. I walked in step to the beat.

The floor surged with couples doing the quickstep. Most of the men suited; the women in their good dresses. The mass moved as one. They were used to obeying orders and here they were, wholly obedient to the rules of the dance. Couples in dance halls holding a thousand or more would move in this placid uniform pattern, drilled as soldiers on a parade ground. The majority of the men would have been in the war, the younger men recently released from their two years of national service. The women were led by the men, who guided them through the tight spaces as if they were steering a dodgem car. There was a deep contentment about the scene. It was somehow hypnotic, the regular movements, the well-known faces, the songs often hummed or murmured by the dancers. They were like a swarm of starlings, twisting and turning in their pattern. When the music stopped the swarm broke up and a brief round of clapping took the dancers back to the seats that ringed the hall.

The Wigton gang had established a position against one of the two long walls. Dennis and Jackie were in the centre, prominent as tribal chiefs. She, tall, dressed up to the nines in a red clinging dress, bare arms, red high heels and her hair fit for a wedding. Jackie was a real beauty and had been a beauty all her life. She was neither coy nor vain about it, which was why so many of the girls liked her. Her smile was constant. When Dennis came near her it was radiant.

When he was close to her it was clear he had to struggle to keep his hands off her. They exchanged rather goofy expressions of love, unable to repress them even in public. Dennis was a head taller than she was. Blond to her black, lean where she was sensuous, edgy where she was calm, holding his hand, locked together. Two of her girlfriends and one of her sisters stood by, rather nervously.

Dennis worked a day job at the factory, humping heavy boxes of goods from the factory floor to be lifted into a waiting lorry. He liked the physical strain of it. His father had been exceptionally hard on his sons, even by the standards of the town. He believed in body building and had some weights. He was proud of his own comparatively well-paid job as a painter. In the yard he had a shed turned into a gym. He taught his sons how to box and to wrestle. He was not afraid to dole out punishment. When he died, of a heart attack, Dennis did not admit it but he was not sad.

Round about him, against the wall, were half a dozen of his friends. Some of these had nicknames in the common currency: Nasher, Boot, United, Lol, Dog – names that had come out of a moment's joke and stuck. These were the men who did the heavy lifting in the town. None of them had dreamed of staying on at school and those who did – like me – were regarded with pity or derision. They were as devoted to their town as any Highlander to his clan.

They formed a rather ragged force around Dennis and Jackie. Their girlfriends were on the fringe. Some of them danced, but never too far from base. The more nervously perceptive who danced past them decided they might pick up their coats rather early from the cloakroom.

When the Aspatria gang came in, in about the same numbers as the Wigton men, there was a dent in the mass on the dance floor, a moving away from this new disturbing force, which took up its place on the wall opposite to Dennis and Jackie. A few of the more faint-hearted immediately drifted away to collect their coats.

The boyfriend, Leslie, who had been deserted so abruptly or, as he thought, stripped of his fiancée, was clearly in charge. He was broadly built, worked out west in the steel plant, played professional rugby and was known for his temper. He, like Dennis, had gathered a posse who had crammed themselves into the butcher's van to come through to Wigton: the butcher's son, Jake, was part of the gang. One of Jackie's sisters was with them.

A strategy had been worked out, refined in the Red Lion in Aspatria before they set out, and polished in Wigton in the Swan opposite the Market Hall.

When the dancing stopped and the dancers resumed their seats or places near the walls to wait for the MC to announce the next dance, Leslie took his men across the floor. The men around Dennis and Jackie self-organised themselves more solidly.

Leslie began.

'I want to talk to Jackie. So does her sister.'

'Nobody's stopping you.' Dennis was nonchalant.

'I need to talk to her on her own.'

That line had been rehearsed but even so it was delivered with difficulty.

'You'll have to take what you can get.'

'You're a disgrace!' Jackie's sister Eunice would not be contained. 'What do you think all of us think? Mam's out of her mind. Dad wanted to come through and kill you but Leslie here stopped that. He's just carried you off! It's terrible!'

Leslie was still sufficiently controlled to let there be a pause. Then he resumed. The MC decided to give the band a break until this was cleared up. Harry, in his capacity as bouncer, came into view. Vince was a few yards behind him. The police would be outside.

'Jackie! Why did you do this?'

She hesitated, but not for long.

'Because he asked me.'

'What about me?' It was almost a cry from the wounded and bewildered jilted man.

'That's how it is,' said Dennis. 'So why don't you just bugger off?'

'I'm warning you!'

'You're what?' Dennis held on more tightly to Jackie's hand and looked directly at her. 'Do you want to go with him or stay with me?'

'Stay with you.'

'That's it, then,' said Dennis.

'You're a disgrace!' Eunice repeated. Jackie, to Eunice's fury, smiled.

'You don't know what you're saying.' Leslie came closer to Jackie. 'He's got you trapped! He won't let you go in case you bolt. He's just a filthy rotten bastard!'

Dennis let Jackie's hand drop and went for Leslie, who was ready for him. From my vantage point – standing on a chair in the corner next to the fish-market door – one minute nothing was happening, the next was a turmoil of fights, fists, not knives. 'Please,' said the MC, and turned up the sound system. 'Please, lads.' Dancers drained from the floor, some making for the exit, others, like me, transfixed against the walls.

The fight took over the centre of the floor.

It soon became one on one until one or the other was downed. Vince was having a hard time of it. Harry abandoned his role as a neutral bouncer and tore a man's jacket in two as he hauled him away from his brother. Sometimes it was art. One Aspatria lad specialised in letting someone rush him, stepping back, putting out his foot to trip the man and then with his right hand chopping the back of his neck to floor him. Two of them gathered around Nasher, wrestled him to the ground and punched him sickeningly before help came; Vince and Harry had combined and stood almost back to back, feet kicking out like swords, arms swinging fists to land the heavy blows; everyone mad to land a kick or a punch; bodies sprawled and rolling on the floor, blood-splattered white shirts. The MC disappeared to seek out the police and then there was a space in the centre where Dennis and Leslie were still battling it out. Leslie was quicker and Dennis seemed to be tiring until Leslie darted across and grabbed Jackie and carried her towards the door, his friends coming to shield around him.

When Dennis saw that he let out a shout that put the fear of God into people. He made for Leslie, wrenched Jackie out of his grip and then, memorably, despite the Aspatria man being heavier, grabbed him from behind by the shoulders of his suit, pulled him off balance so that he was just a body stretching in Dennis's grip, then swung him around and around, scything his way through any bystanders and finally let him loose so that his bulk skidded across the floor, followed by Dennis who kicked him in the stomach, pulled up his face and hit it, and was only restrained by one of the policemen who had arrived. Dennis's own face streamed blood from a cut above his left eye.

'The music will recommence in five minutes,' said the MC. 'Five minutes, ladies and gentlemen.' The band, who had enjoyed a grandstand view, took their seats rather gingerly, not entirely convinced that the fire had been thoroughly damped down. Enough people had stayed in the hall to make it worth their while. The police were having difficulty herding the combatants into a biddable group. When Vince saw a gap he indicated to Dennis and Jackie and they slipped through it to the small door that led into the fish market He waved me in. By this time a bloodied Harry had resumed his role as a bouncer.

In the fish market, Jackie went into the Ladies and came out with a towel soaked in cold water, which Dennis pressed to his eye. They opened the doors at the back. Vince went his way, taking me with him. Vince's jacket was ripped to bits. His shirt was red. What looked like a broken nose. 'Just a bump,' he said. 'I'll make me own way.' He smiled, rather crookedly. 'We kept her, anyway.'

The police were heard but not seen. Dennis and Jackie went their way, across and into the graveyard and tick-tacked a path through the tombstones across to Proctor's Row, down into a yard, across the silent street, one more alleyway and home.

Dennis's mother was not happy with the sight of them. Jackie had been smeared with some of Dennis's blood, her lovely dress was torn, her hair had collapsed into wild straggles.

When Dennis's mother talked about it on the street over the next few days, she described a loving young couple, cleaned up, sitting on the sofa, snuggling up, drinking tea.

'I told them,' she said, 'the sooner you two get married the better for all concerned.'

Chapter Thirty-eight

I've taken long enough to try to remember when I first saw her and I can't. This goes against the pattern and the rule. The pattern is that you spot her, or she you, at a village dance, on the playing fields, at a party – somewhere easy to remember – and from then on you never forget her or she you. Then the rule kicks in and you meet and fall in love and after a quarrel or two you live happily ever after. That was the message from the romantic novels and stories in women's magazines and the films. They were persuasive messages. They dominated the songs on the wireless, which for most of the time about which I am writing told us that love and marriage went together like a horse and carriage so consistently it became a commandment. Confirmed in the Bible. See her, meet her, marry her, have children, die happy.

In a small community you could see outward evidence all around you. 'They'll have been married, let's see, thirty-five, nearer forty years . . .' Uttered with satisfaction. That proved it *was* a small community, everybody knowing everybody. The few separations were silently observed in the fifties as if they were fatal illnesses. Love and marriage was the thing and all the better if the two of them were virgins; second best was that she had to be a virgin; next best (only if the couple were popular) was 'That's the way of the world.' The pattern could change, the rule could be challenged, promiscuity had its secret webs of connection, as did couples who, after a few years, never talked to each other again. But on the whole, the pattern and the rule daily drummed home by films and the wireless, as well as the Church, held steady. And once you had sex you had to marry. There was no getting out of it.

It's most likely that I first saw her at a dance. In the holidays and on a Saturday night, William and I would bike off to anywhere within five or six miles. Most of the villages had halls and in most of the halls there were dances. There would be a three-piece band, non-alcoholic refreshments and, when you were lucky and older, a nearby pub. The hall would be brightly lit. The girls would often be dancing with each other until the boys and men trundled in. It was still a time when the middle-aged and even the elderly would turn up for the village dance that had not yet been taken over by The Young. There was a steadiness, order, good-heartedness about the occasion.

We would put our bikes around the back of the hall – as everyone else did: I'm sure we had no locks – and in our case, soberly pay at the door for the indelible stamp on the back of the hand, which would readmit us without charge. Oulton, about two miles from Wigton, was her village and we went there many times.

There would be a raffle – prizes could include a sack of potatoes or a glass bowl – the usual group dances, the Dashing White Sergeant, Three Drops of Brandy, the Hooligans whooping and clapping, urging on the band. But if it was not there, then, romantically, she came from out of the blue.

Yet that is nowhere near the full story. Her father and mother had been brought up in or near Wigton. She went to the grammar school as I did. At a certain peak teenage time both of us, who had had brief, previous, tentative, virginal 'dates', were clearly ready. The bee looking for the pollen, the mating game in the air. Like most Wigton courtships and marriages, it was a very local and formalised affair as it had been for centuries: it was always going to happen.

At first it was hide and seek. Not, I think, that she consciously hid in those early days but her paths around the school and the playing fields with her friends could easily shake me off. Without meaning to? That, for the first few weeks, was the question. She certainly threw me a smile every now and then, but did she throw others a smile? And was it the same smile or was mine a little less or a little more encouraging? The smiles had it for some time. It became part of the web that there were two other boys interested or, as we said then, 'after her', one of them a serious contender. Alan, a year older than me, one of the all-stars in the rugby team, had had a trial for English Schools. His father was headmaster of a village school. He was the odds-on favourite. Her friends seemed to me to hustle her away whenever I came within sight: they would just slide off – deliberately? Sometimes I could have sworn I heard unencouraging giggling.

This was towards the end of my second term in the lower sixth and Sarah's in 4A. She was headed in a year or so for the first grammar school high jump, the O levels, I for the second, the A levels. Both sufficiently far from the tests to make time for each other. Our months were now counted out in exams. There was no rush, I thought. But that strategy began to look fatally misguided. Word went round the library table that Alan was not dallying, he was moving in, and that Sarah was showing worryingly little sign of disinclination.

I can still summon up that sudden feeling of panic. Sarah was now occupying a substantial part of my emotional life. I couldn't stop thinking about her. Every time she avoided me I felt more eager but I did not know how to analyse it. If it was a manoeuvre or a tease, so be it. If it wasn't, now what? And shouldn't Alan, who had been held back a year, be made to realise that he should just quit? How? And didn't Sarah realise how much she meant to me? Clearly not. What about the smiles? The weekend approached.

Word in the library was that Alan was intending to invite her to Silloth pictures on the Saturday. Do I still feel that lurch of alarm? If not, I can imagine it.

The next time I saw her alongside her friends, I suddenly found myself walking straight at her. As if pre-rehearsed, the friends stepped back. Sarah looked at me, half smiling, confident.

She was of average height, hair black, long, and the word I would have used then 'shiny'. Figure – well, how could I spell it out? Great! And, in more detail, smashing! Slim without being skinny, curviness without troubling the word 'plump'. Sexy? You couldn't fake that. Face? Eyes dark brown, skin fresh as a dairy-maid's, face rather oval-shaped, the nose – the index of the character – strong. But it was the smile that hooked me. Mischievous, slyly bold, the smile telling me what she was really like, as smiles can.

I braved myself.

'Your dad,' I said, 'used to play dominoes with my dad in the Lion and Lamb.' She looked at me gravely.

Then she laughed aloud. Her face was transformed by the laughter while I smiled tightly, wondering what I'd done wrong. She put a hand over her mouth.

'Did he?' she said. 'Thank you.' And then her laughter overcame her once again.

'What is it?'

'It's just . . .' she took a deep breath and smothered it '. . . just that you're supposed to be this Mr Romantic brain-box and everything and the first thing you say is to tell me about your dad and mine playing dominoes in a pub! The very first thing you say!' Once again she laughed, and I, thank the Lord, joined in. Then I asked her to come to the pictures on Saturday.

It was a shock seeing her out of school uniform on that first Saturday night. Where was the white shirt with the school tie, the green cardigan or pullover, the below-the-knee skirt in matching green, and the bulky school blazer ribboned around the edges, the badge? All gone. She looked so much less like a schoolgirl.

Her navy blue coat was open. Her skirt was blue. She wore a roll-neck pullover again in blue, but a lighter shade. And not the made-to-last school shoes but almost red ones, almost high heels. And lipstick. I had not the words to say how transformed and wonderful she looked. 'Hello, I'm glad you could make it' had to do.

I'd booked seats on the balcony on the second to back row at the end next to the wall. The coveted back row was booked out. We went up the once-plush stairs of the Picture Palace, through the doors and up again to our seats, both blushing, both convinced that 'everyone' was looking at us, neither of us 'caring' but both of us suffering from the possibility of unwanted attention. The lights could not go out soon enough.

The trailer, the comedy item – I hope it was the Three Stooges, but I can't remember – and then the Errol Flynn. Unfortunately he was not in his swashbuckling character. He wore a suit, the plot was too obvious and the kissing made me squirm. On the plus side I put my arm around Sarah's shoulders and drew her a little closer, and one of her breasts pressed itself against me.

We biked back slowly to her village. Her father's farm was about two miles out of the middle of the town. On fine days Sarah would skip the school bus and bike in. It was a calm evening, only slowly darkening. Our bike lights were feeble in the bigness of the dark acres of farming lands. I was trying to work out what to say when we reached the farm.

It was neat and compact, on the edge of the village. Her father had put down a deposit on the freehold out of winnings on the football coupons. Before that, with his two brothers, he had worked a larger farm tenanted by his father.

The winnings changed his life. Before that, by all accounts, he'd been a bit wild. He drank at weekends and went to dances. There were fights – he was particularly strong. He made his money through the week and spent it over the weekend. Now he scrimped, he saved on everything possible. He took down his stake in his father's farm – at a loss, he always said. He was a clever man and knew his farming and within a few years he had rented a couple of substantial fields to add to his holdings. He worked all the hours God sent seven days a week, and only very rarely, and then reluctantly for a family occasion, went into a pub where he sipped at one pint.

Now for the kiss. I was not a novice here and there was still the memory of the magnificent kiss from the girl in Silloth two years previously. But then it was she who had taken the initiative. It had been my call since then. My track record was not great. Mostly snatched at either AYPA or school parties during 'knock knock' games. Now and then I had just got going only to be pushed away when I got too close. Once or twice it had been comfortable but that was out of Wigton with Aspatria girls from school. I went there on Saturday for a date at the café in their picture house, which had a jukebox and direct access to the queue for the double seats at the back. And there was one extended courtship with a girl from Carlisle. We met at Burton's Corner on a Saturday night and went to a docile local dance.

The problem was sex. I was old enough to be aware that some sexual encounters in Wigton were varied and active. But the in-action among my generation was a plague. The heart of it was – what did you do and when, and would she let you, and if so, where did you go to buy a contraceptive, and were you sure you would be able to put it on? Overhanging all that was the obstacle of the mystery of sex, which steamed you up and slowed you down and made you think too much, and there was always the command-ment of no sex without marriage.

There had been coarse, obvious and desperate sex jokes for some years, well-thumbed pages from Hank Janson, lingering looks at *National Geographic* in the newsagent's and lurid boasts of the older and racier lads already way down the track, or so they claimed. They were envied. Their girlfriends, if known, were regarded with awe. That she *let* him! That she let *him*! That *she* let him!

But that didn't really matter. What did matter was how you – I – kept love pure while satisfying lust and clinching a sense of possession. And would she mind? Of course she would!

We were taught sex from scraps of smutty unreliable experi-ences. There was no education. We knew nothing of foreplay. We were innocent of all forms of stimulation. Like other boys

I knew I was frightened of despoiling someone I loved. Love was, surely, sacred. And sin was not out of the equation, a constant brake. We did know that consenting sex between two men and two women was not unknown, even in Wigton. Later I learned that there was a small swapping of pornography. And even later than that, that sex could be embraced as liberating, joyous, exhaustingly consuming.

We were stuck in a limited place and time that appeared to prefer no sex to anything but marital sex. Before that you could take risks and be anxious or be celibate and suffer. The fifties were not extravagant in options. Those were the options. Add to that the practicalities, finding of an appropriate quiet space, suitably erotic, or most difficult a perfect time of the month. Although the increasing lust was becoming need, and then almost a sickness, you still knew that you had to get it right from the beginning. As told in the films and in the songs, you only had the one chance.

With Sarah it would be different. I did not know how I knew that but I did. Even so I believed that the first serious kiss could be make or break.

Some yards away from the farm gate but well clear of one of the few streetlights in the village, we found a little nook where hedge did not meet hedge and, after laying our bikes on the grassy bank, Sarah allowed herself to be steered into the gap. I had not the nerve to hang about. As I kissed her she, as it were, kissed me back and as I pressed her to me she did not resist. It could have gone on for ever.

As it was we must have stood there in the dark for a good ten minutes as still as statues. Only two cars passed by, their lights causing us to pull apart: one of them beeped. So the word would be all round the village tomorrow, Sarah thought, but said nothing at the time and returned to the by now easy lingering kissing, eyes closed, bodies, even through the coats, felt by hugging, with the occasional pause for a quick breath.

The arm she had thrown across my shoulders revealed her watch. She pulled back. 'I've got to go. I said before half past nine. I told him I was with my girlfriends from school, but I bet he didn't believe me.' The car beeps made her grimace. 'He'll kill me when he finds out about this.' She pulled further away. 'Never mind. I know how to stand up to him. But I have to go.'

'When could we?'

'We have a phone,' she said, with a certain pride. 'I'll give you the number. Have you a pen? Of course you have a pen!'

I copied down her number while she held in her fret.

'That was lovely,' she said, and the smile wiped away all anxiety. 'Best to phone in the late afternoon when he's milking.'

Mid-teens, mid-century. Trapped in shyness. Dumb when it came to admitting or declaring 'love'.

Was it because the word was too dangerous? Too life-binding? Or too soft, unmanly? Too common, or too like a silly love song? 'Love' the word failed us. Ignorance and embarrassment and anxiety blocked it.

But didn't being unsaid make it more powerful? Weren't words flimsy compared to feelings? Somehow I stumbled to that conclusion.

As time went on, we became more intense and found a new world of sensations, self-renewing, as necessary as breath. Not to see her meant a much lesser day. The love songs and the high-end poetry made new sense. It was as if I had a twin. Nothing was like it, and when it developed more fully I wondered how I ever had lived or ever could live without it. It took me over, mind and body. It was a new world. It promised a new life.

And it seemed, in a way I could not describe, that Sarah and I were bound together in a way not unlike the way I was bound to my work.

Sarah's holidays, like mine, had largely been confined to short visits to nearby relatives and school trips to Silloth and Keswick. I wanted to take her into the Lake District and stay at youth hostels. Sarah was keen. She suggested it would have a better chance of success if when asking for permission we said we were going in a group.

When we met on the following Saturday, I thought I could sense defeat but she concealed her feelings well and it was not until we had biked back to Oulton that she said, 'I talked to him. He won't have it. We sat opposite each other at the table. I felt I was in court.'

'I knew something was wrong as soon as we met.'

'I told them about youth hostels. All he did was to wait for me to finish so he could say no again.'

'What about your mother?'

'She's on my side but she could tell he was ready to hit one of his moods and she got on with cooking the supper.'

'Did he give any reasons?'

'I asked him. He said he didn't have to give reasons.'

'"All the others can go," I said.

'"Let them," he said.

'"You don't trust me, do you?" I'd wanted to say that to him for some time.

'"As long as you're under my roof you're my responsibility."

'"Until I'm sixteen! And get a job."

'"That's as maybe."

'"No, it isn't. I'm sixteen in less than a month and after my exams I'll have a job and move out."

'"We'll see."

'"You will!"

'"I'll have none of your cheek. And I know all about those Saturday nights!"

'His temper was getting up. I could feel his anger. I'd seen it before. It would possess him. He'd never hit me but I knew once or twice it had been a near thing. If he lost it . . .' She shrugged. 'I backed off,' she said, 'and left him with the table to himself.'

'Did your mother say anything at all?'

'I heard a shouting match. It didn't last long. When I came

down later she looked upset and said nothing. He'd gone out so there was time for her to say something but . . . I think she was always scared of him. That wasn't all of it but it was part of it. I told her I was going to have another go. She asked me not to.'

'No,' I said. '*I* will.'

'Why?'

'It was my idea.'

'He won't like it.'

'When's a good time on Saturday? Morning?'

'No . . .' Sarah paused for a while, as if weighing up my chances. 'Are you sure?'

'Best time?'

'About two o'clock. Mother and I will have cleared up after dinner and he'll be looking at the *Cumberland News*.'

I had spoken with a bravado I did not quite feel at the time after Sarah's account of the grim exchange with her father. Curiously, the bravado did not melt away. If anything, it changed into something more steadily resolute as the days went by. I had seen my father deal with difficult men. I was sure of my ground. And however hasty my promise to Sarah had been, there was no way it could be broken.

Sarah's mother answered the door and seemed to know about it. Her husband was in his armchair beside an unlit fire in a kitchen dark with cumbersome second-hand oak furniture. He looked up, stared for a moment or two, and then carefully wrapped up the large newspaper.

'What's this?'

'I've come to talk about Sarah.'

The words came reluctantly, like pebbles struggling to get out of my throat. 'What about her?'

There was a false-faced patience about him.

'We want to go away for a few days with four of our friends to the Lake District and stay in youth hostels.'

'Do you now?'

'Yes. They're very safe. Male and female are housed in separate dormitories. We all have to muck in and help with the cooking and cleaning, laying the table, that sort of thing. And it isn't just young people. Teachers go. You can't arrive there by car or bus. You have to bike or walk. It's very cheap. Thousands of young people use them.'

'Thousands of young people do many stupid things.'

'This isn't stupid! It's the way for us to have a cheap holiday in a great place. Nothing wrong would happen. They don't allow it.'

'Why did you come here?'

'I came to get your permission and to tell you there's nothing to worry about.'

My voice was rising. There was a tremor of fear threatening to break loose.

'Get out! Or I'll throw you out.' This was very near full volume. He stood up and revealed the barrel-chested stockiness of the man, only just held in check by broad braces, the massive arms and shoulders, the bullock nature and the menace in him.

'Who do you think you are, just barging in? Who are you anyway?'

I told him.

He looked puzzled as if he had been deliberately outfoxed. He stared at me closely and the tension in his body began to relax.

'Ethel and Stan's boy?'

'Yes.'

There was a significant pause. All I could do was stand my ground and say nothing.

'I used to play dominoes with your dad in the Lion and Lamb,' he said. 'We used to go to dances with them when we were younger.'

Most unexpectedly, he smiled.

'They were good times.' Again he stared. 'I can see something of Ethel in you,' he said. 'She was a bonny lass.'

He sat down and again seemed to be silenced by a recollection of past times.

'Well, I'll be buggered,' he said.

I laughed and the laughter seemed to lift a ton of fear.

'Sit down.' He pointed to the armchair across from his own. 'How many?'

'Four plus us.' I listed their names; he nodded in recognition at every one. His smile was enigmatic.

'I'll think over what you've said.'

'Thank you.'

He smiled. 'What is it you do?'

'I'm staying on at school.'

'I see.' He paused. 'Putting off the evil day.'

'That's it.'

He left the room and took with him the tension, as if it had been a presence that he controlled. I realised how nervous I had been. Sarah came downstairs as soon as she heard the door shut.

'I'd better go,' I said.

Sarah went out into the yard with me.

We stood beside my bike.

'There was a moment I thought he might kill you! You were getting under his skin.'

'Could we walk for a few minutes?'

'I have to help clean the house.'

'Do you know what he'll decide?'

'I think I do.' Sarah took her time. 'He'll have been impressed that you didn't seem frightened of him and then there was your ace card.'

'Stan and Ethel.'

'Yes, Ethel and Stan.'

'Later . . .'

She went back into the house. When I got on the road I felt possessed of supernatural energy and flew back to Wigton, singing and now and then ringing my bell on an empty road.

Chapter Thirty-nine

I was proprietorial. Sarah had been to the Lakes once, to Keswick on a school trip, and inevitably it had rained. Still, she was game for the six-day adventure, mostly, I thought, because it was six days away from the farm and she would be with her closest girl-friends, Jean and Alice, and William and Michael, whom she knew well enough.

I don't know why I wanted her to like it as much as I did. From the boat on Ullswater I pointed out Aira Force, a waterfall with an adventurous path alongside it leading to the top. We could climb that. And there was the spot along the lake where one evening the boy Wordsworth had stolen a boat and been terrified by the mountains, which seemed to rear up before him as he rowed. It gave him lasting nightmares. After the first day she said, 'I want to like it because I like it not because you say I should like it! You're putting me off!'

She took to the youth-hostel life. There was a bounce about it, a cheerful equality, people from other places milling together for a night at a time and making the thing work. Something Spartan about it, still a tang of wartime make-the-best-of-what-there-is.

Boys in their dormitory to the right, girls to the left. Between the two the dining area, the ping-pong area, the drying room and the offices. The boys laid the table, cleared up and swept up; the girls helped with the cooking and made sure the boys did their jobs properly. Nostalgia easily gives in to exaggeration but, in the Lakes anyway at that time, the early fifties, there was inno-cence. We as a nation had been oppressed throughout the war and we spent the next decade piecing together a present. At that time, in those hostels and fells, there was a sense of setting out anew, unburdened, among the young crowd that we were.

After a drenching first day when my scheme to arrive at the first youth hostel by travelling the sixteen miles of Ullswater on a pleasure boat was nearly sunk by the deluge, we were lucky with the weather. And that first day gave us all a laughing coherence. So that's why there are Lakes! The drying room became a common room of misfortunes – to be sloughed off. The group of us there, in that hostel, discovered that we might meet up with other groups once or twice over the week. Instant friendships came from minor discomfort.

The storm had rolled away by the morning and most of us set off to walk over Kirkstone Pass to Ambleside. A group from Kent hooked up with us, led by a tall blond lad, Nigel, who had just got into Cambridge University and was their chieftain. And there were half a dozen from Manchester and others who formed what became the post-drenched pack.

The next day we swung around the southern Lakes, into the Langdales, out to Esthwaite Water, following the hostels, like hounds following a scent. The weather was perfect, now sunny, blue sky unblemished, now cloud burdened, then the big clouds breaking up and a disorderly scattering of infant clouds chasing each other in a growing wind. The next day we walked alongside Buttermere and over the Scarth Gap pass into Ennerdale. By then I was so immersed in the place that I couldn't talk about it. More than the drug of swimming. More than work. More even than the feelings I had for Sarah, although that must have played some part in it. I felt that the place had wrapped itself around me and barred all intruders. The feelings I had from the sight of the rocks and stones and trees, the sounds of water and wind. The sensations inside my head were governed by the huge space outside it. Perhaps the infusing of nature with its exhilarating comfort and richness of feeling was a reward for enduring the out-of-body experience.

As we stood on the land between Buttermere and Ennerdale lakes I felt isolated but thrilled, and secured by the sense of dramatic emptiness. Sarah and I moved away from the others. Ennerdale was a long valley over-planted with firs. I had learned to edit my enthusiasm, but I could not resist pointing to Pillar Rock, where so many of the English mountain climbers who had spawned the sport had earned their spurs. 'They climbed in clunky great boots. Two of them even hauled up clumsy camera equipment. They must have been fearless.' Sarah seemed to brood on the bare steeple of rock, and nodded. She looked at me intently: permission to go on. 'If you look over that way you can see Scafell and Scafell Pike, the highest mountains in England.'

'Are they?' She swung her gaze away from Pillar Rock, then looked again at the bare steep rock. 'People climbed up that?'

'Yes.'

'Could we?'

'Yes. If we wore sensible shoes and on a dry day.'

She fixed again on the heights. 'I'd love to climb over there as well. To be on the highest spot in England! I'd love that,' she said passionately.

'Another time.'

'Promise.'

'Promise.' She turned and, following an impulse unusually in front of our friends, she hugged me. 'That would be great!'

Eventually we headed for the Black Sail youth hostel.

As days passed more and more quickly, Sarah seemed to become increasingly absorbed in the strangers who joined us. I had anticipated times alone, just the two of us, our friends easy to disentangle, but she seemed far happier with the crowd. 'I can see you all the time at home,' she said, 'but I like talking to people I don't know, from other places. I talked to two Norwegians the other day and three girls who had come up from Nottingham.'

We linked up with Nigel and his friends in Keswick. After supper we walked down to the boating station and along the shore under Watendlath. The path was narrow for the most part and the dozen of us soon straggled into Indian file. There was a makeshift bridge over an estuary and it took an age for some of the party to negotiate its insecure handrails. I had been bringing up the rear, and by the time I had crossed, the leading group was far ahead. It was the best part of a good day. A mild evening, calm and free, the lake to the right, scarcely rippling, Catbells across the water etched out clearly, the sound of voices playing along the shore.

Through a gate and into a broad pasture. In the distance, Nigel and Sarah were apparently engrossed in each other, walking closely, he leaning over to her, she looking up to him. I walked faster and then, as they suddenly disappeared – the lakeside path went into a wood – I stopped abruptly, struck still and with a pain I had never before experienced. Why wasn't Sarah with me? The pain stabbed my chest. I wanted air and yet I began to run, following them into the wood, passing others who waved until I came to a clearing jutting out into a small promontory and there, on the edge of the lake, framed by mighty oaks, Nigel and Sarah stood just as naturally as on their walk, Sarah attentive, Nigel spouting like a waterfall.

I slowed down and caught my breath. Sarah saw me and waved me across to them. She was smiling. Nigel was not pleased to see me. 'Nigel's been telling me about his parents. They have a farm in Kenya. He's going there after the trip and staying until he goes to university.'

'Cambridge,' he said.

'Yes.' Sarah smiled at me. 'That's good, isn't it?'

Nigel shrugged, rather elaborately. The gesture was, I thought, a clever way of showing off.

'He was talking about the animals: zebras, lions, hippopota-muses – -uses?'

'Hippopotami.' Nigel's correction was smilingly offered.

'Thank you. And rhinoceroses or -*i* or whatever. He'd just got on to wildbeasts.'

'Wild*e*beests.'

'That's it and the thousands of them that trek across the country. He said it makes the Lake District seem a bit tame.'

I gritted out a smile.

'It depends what you're looking for.'

'That's what I said.' Sarah moved towards me.

'I agree,' said Nigel. 'The Lake District's got everything.'

'But not zebras!' She was now by my side. 'He said I was welcome to go and stay there any time he was there.'

Nigel's smile was untroubled. 'Just a thought . . .'

By that time I could have choked with what I had now identified as jealousy. Better still, choked *him*.

'I thought of going on round to the hotel at the Lodore, having a drink or two, and catching the boat back down the lake to Keswick.'

This was addressed, as an invitation, to Sarah.

'I think we'll just go back and join our friends,' she said.

With an understanding, perhaps even a pitying, look he waved us goodbye and went on his way.

'I thought you were going to explode,' she said. She smiled as she said it, and for a moment I wanted to wreck anything that was and ever had been between us.

'You were jealous,' she said, and linked arms tightly.

'No, I wasn't.'

'You were! You should have seen your face!' She grimaced. 'I didn't want to make you jealous. I'm sorry. And . . .' she paused, stopped and looked straight at me '. . . I was trying to get away from him! He wouldn't stop going on about his farm. I felt like telling him about ours! Hundreds of Kenyans working on it, "Such good chaps!", the farm bigger than Wigton by the sound of it. What a SNOB! I couldn't believe it. And one of his posh friends has a castle in Kent! They'd been skiing. Why it was so useful – his mother had told him to see "something of the other side". That was the youth hostelling! Us! We're "the other side"!' Her laughter pealed across the meadow. 'He was hilarious!'

It was as if I'd sloughed off a skin.

We walked back to Friar's Crag in contented silence. As we approached the steps up to the crag, Sarah looked at me. 'After you'd faced up to Dad, I never said anything. I should have done.'

Compliments came with difficulty. 'It took a bit of doing. He doesn't like not getting his own way.'

She looked at me closely, then glanced around at the scattering of walkers along the lakeside. She tended to avoid public demonstrations of affection – no holding hands, staying in an embrace at the end of a dance, or slinging arms around each other, certainly up to now kissing within sight of others. Now, after a hesitant glance around, she put her arms around me and kissed me forcefully on the lips.

'That's what I think about you,' she said.

That was our first summer.

Sarah put in some time on extra homework for the exams. She had taken a shrewd view, based on her mock-O-level results, which had been uniformly sound, and pitched her working schedule accordingly. I tried more than once to persuade her to stay on at school but she shook her head.

I pursued my schedule, encouraged by Mr James, who made it clear that the next year would be the Year of the Big Push. The nights were lighter longer. I would go through to Oulton on Saturday and Sunday afternoons. We walked down a track onto the marshland, near to a place called Black Dippo, just outside the village, where a few Travellers quartered in winter. A small man-made lake – made for fishing but not heavily patronised – gave the place a focus. You could lash together a raft and pole or paddle across to one of the several tufts of islands or, better, the small concealing copses. It was there that we went through the apprenticeship of lovemaking, as we thought unseen. It took us over. The power of it was as strong as the fear but transformed into indescribable pleasure that wiped you out. We would come up for air as if we had been deep-sea diving.

We would stroll back into the village – had we gone too far? Had we not gone far enough? Dreams of racing across the Scottish border to marry in the forge at Gretna Green, expelled, rejected by society – but wouldn't that be good? We could do what we wanted – we could lie in the long warm grass every day . . .

On the way home from a ride to Lake Bassenthwaite we saw a poster on a gate in Bothel advertising hound trails that evening.

I asked one of the men where the slip was to be and where the finish. We looked at the dozen or so betting boards fronted by the bookies. It was a clear but chilly evening. In a corner of the field I saw Andrew.

I had seen him in Wigton since Dad had kicked him out, but much less often than I used to. His route to the factory from his new digs on Howrigg Bank took him along the Shade Walk past the West Cumberland Farmers and bypassed the Black-A-Moor.

He looked smart. That was certainly a new overcoat. He sported a neat brown trilby and when he smiled we saw his teeth, which I couldn't remember ever having seen before. They almost flashed in the evening light.

I waved and as we walked towards him I remembered. He had struck it lucky with a dog he'd bought 'out of Ireland' and which he called Whiplash. It had proved to be a champion. My father and others had mentioned it in the bar. For a third season it was leading the table and word was that if he wanted to sell it he would get 'a fortune'.

I introduced Sarah. He scrutinised her.

'She has a look of Ethel as a lass,' he said. 'A definite look. You can just catch it.'

Then his attention was distracted by the loudspeaker's call for the dogs to go to the slip. Whiplash was led to Andrew in a rather ceremonial way, accompanied by comments and glances that made him smile even more and nod around to the dog's admirers. He bent down and nuzzled his face against that of the dog.

'Should I bet on it?'

'He's odds on,' Andrew said. 'It's hardly worth your while.' He looked again at Sarah and nodded. 'Still. Here.' He produced a pound note from a new-looking black crocodile-skin wallet.

'Put that on to win. You'll get five or ten bob winnings on the back of it.'

He nodded and was gone into the crowd.

'Who was that?'

I gave her an edited version.

'What are you going to do with that pound?'

'Put it on.'

'I've never put a bet on.'

'Here we go, then.'

The bookie 'Walter of Frizington' put my note in a big leather pouch rather like the pouch on a kangaroo. I was given a ticket.

The noise from the waiting hounds rose higher into howls as we walked over to the slip where about thirty owners, mostly men, were crouched over their hounds, which had just picked up the scent. The leads were off. They held them – often with diffi-culty – by the collar and then the trailer appeared about fifty yards away. He was dragging the bundle of rags and aniseed, which were as potent as the smell of a fox. The hounds went mad. The trailer reached the marker who waved the flag, releasing the hounds, which howled as if in pain and bounded over to the track of the trail and were gone into the hills, the sound soon dwindling away.

'What do we do now?'

'Wait. About half an hour.'

'Can we see them?'

'Better if we had binoculars but we might catch a glimpse of them among the fells over there.'

'So what's to watch?'

'It isn't for watching. It's for the hounds.'

This time she laughed more loudly. 'It's crackers!'

'That's right. Would you like a bowl of soup while we wait?' I pointed to the refreshment coach, which had one side down, as a counter.

It was thick tomato soup in a cardboard mug. The bread was brown and warm. We followed the drift of men beginning already to go to the hillock from which they would have a grandstand view of the 'finish' down about half a mile of open fell side.

Soon enough they came in sight and the whistles and the calling went across the hills. The hounds swerved direction to be in line to meet their caller. Andrew had taken off his hat and was waving it up and down as he blasted out the homing song of Whiplash on a dominating whistle.

When Whiplash crossed the line well ahead of its rivals, he put on his hat, pocketed his whistle and slipped on the dog's collar as soon as it reached him. Ignoring the congratulations and ignoring his new coat, he knelt down beside it and caressed its head with one hand while the other unclipped the bait tin that held the meat and potatoes and bread, more than the common quantity of reward for a hound at the end of a race.

We did not know whether or not to interrupt him. I wanted to thank him for my winnings. Sarah wanted to look more closely at the black and white sinewy hound that had just run over fells, jumped walls, forded streams flat out for thirty minutes. But both of us felt excluded from the intense companionship between Andrew and his hound.

'Cheerio, Andrew,' I said, from some yards away, 'and thanks.'

He did not look up but took one hand from the collar for a moment and waved it without turning to face us. By the time we got to our bicycles, Andrew, who had put the hound's coat on, was on his feet, Whiplash gently trotting beside him, both headed for a small tent on which was the notice 'Winners and Runners-up' to get their prize money and the red rosette.

As we got onto our bikes, Sarah said, 'Andrew thought I looked a bit like your mother.'

I set off slowly and she soon caught up. We had the west wind at our backs and the early mellow glow of what promised to be a glorious sunset shining way beyond us to the sea and the hills of Strathclyde. From here it was downhill all the way back to Wigton. The roads were empty; the sky, a steady darkening blue, hosting tranquil groups of small white clouds, the landscape before us scarcely populated, the wind pushing us on to pedal faster and harder and then freewheel until I thought we might be gliding.

This should be our life until the end, I thought. Never to leave each other, never to leave the place, always to glide through the days and years, not wanting much, no ambitions that would obstacle the way, just the two of us swooping down to the plain, nothing to change, always other moments like this, gliding, effort-less, gliding together, the warm wind at our backs. Free.

Chapter Forty

It was the last Saturday before I returned to school and she began her job at the Midland Bank. We went to a dance in Carlisle at the County Ballroom just outside the railway station. I had been there with the Memphis Five and memories of the occasion had deterred further visits. A few people from Wigton had made it their regular Saturday destination. We joined them on the train, which got in at 7 p.m., just before the dancing began. The big band was the Carlisle version of Joe Loss or even Glenn Miller; the ballroom was already full of keen dancers, about two hundred of them, the turning ball in the ceiling casting a kaleidoscope of colour to spice up the semi-darkness. It was a quickstep.

Sarah found it much easier to dance here than in any of the village halls. Unobserved, she relaxed and let herself go. She no longer made it clear that she regarded it as a struggle for supremacy between us as she had done at the village dances. Now, in this unthreatening, anonymous crowd, she relaxed. She went with the music and discovered that she enjoyed it and could be good. Dancing could be happiness. When the number stopped and the dancers applauded, she let me continue to hold her and was quick off the mark for the next. In one of the darker corners, I spun her around, her pink and white frock whirling. In the darkest corner of all, we swayed closely together, scarcely moving, clinging to each other.

We danced only with each other. At the village dances there were frequent partner swaps and some of the more traditional dances themselves entailed groups. We noticed a few couples from Wigton across the room but a nod was enough. The crowd of young people moved as a mass in time to the music, almost mechanical in their discipline as their elders were. The majority were local; the elite were the apprentices or the younger workers from Cowans Sheldon, the engineering works that served the railways.

There was something of an overture about this dance. It marked the start of a new life for the two of us. We stayed in the ball-room for the interval to watch the new talent, as the Memphis Five had once been. Two girl singers, Scottish, hard but sweet voices with that folk drone-twang, a guitar, a real double bass and a drum kit. They were good. They were better than we had been. Much better. They had a following, too, modest in size but enthusiastic. Sarah and I applauded along with their fans.

We were a quarter of an hour early for the train back to Wigton – three coaches that went along the industrial coast to Whitehaven. The doors were open, the lights were off. We were daring, safe from being disturbed.

At the bank Sarah settled in quickly. She took to the job. She liked the others who worked there. Adding and subtracting other people's money, cashing cheques, banking the takings for this and that shop held no boredom.

She was virtually a stranger to the town. The school, the house where she left her bike, the cinema and that had been it. She took advantage of the midday dinner break to wander around the place.

From her work in the bank she recognised some of the name plaques of solicitors and dentists. After a few weeks she was aware of the affluence that sustained certain shops. It surprised her how much money some of them had. Then there were the farmers who would stride in on Tuesdays: she tried to duck them – the last thing she wanted was to be known as 'that farmer's lass in the bank'. Some of them were very well heeled. On her walks she was aware of an unhurried material contentment in parts of the town. It seemed securely self-sufficient, though not rich. Ration books had just gone out: we felt liberated.

She noted the number of churches and the number of butchers, bakeries, sweet shops and pubs. And, to a lesser extent, jewellery shops, clothes shops and hairdressers. She enjoyed totting these places up. The village in which she had been born and brought up was a collection of farms and cottages that served the farmers. One shop, one meeting house, one telephone box.

As she grew bolder she pushed out towards the edges of the old town. In every direction new estates were continuing to be built, roads dug up to service them. Some day, she saw, they would overcome the old town. No bad thing either! she thought. The tight lanes and interlocking squares and yards in the town centre could only be called slums. Not a word she'd use publicly to anyone about Wigton. If she came to live there, she would much prefer a house on a new estate. But she had learned that people were prickly with pride in Wigton, sometimes especially about those twisting and tormented alleyways and cramped little houses.

Not too small like Oulton, not too big like Carlisle – Wigton was just right, she thought. She could settle here, hard to find anywhere better.

I went back to school after the holidays with a plan, more intensive than before. Now it was not 'like work', it was work. The chafing 'When are you getting a job?', 'Still living off your mam and dad?' went on, and though it was without spite, it was a reminder. It was a time when few working-class children stayed on at school for this long. When – later on – I began to suspect that I was being guided towards trying for a university place, it was quite difficult to absorb. Only five per cent of people my age went to university in those days; the majority came from public schools. It wasn't part of the thinking. Staying on at school for two years extra was bad enough; pushing on further was off the radar.

I still felt embarrassed to be a burden – the jobs my father gave me and for which he had upped the payment to fifteen shillings a week were clearly a sort of charity. I calculated the sum of it and would pay it back The money was enough to stay with my pals in the herd. It came out of the past, my father's thwarted past. His past made my present seem unfairly privileged. To say this was part of my guilty thinking is to tell the truth. I couldn't just stroll, fool around, waste the chance. I owed him more than that, more even than cash repayment.

The timetable was the key. Lessons were enjoyable, the more time we spent in those small classes the easier it got to bounce back at the teachers. Save for Latin it was teaching by enthusiasm, Mr James, Mr Blacka, Mr Stowe – theirs and ours. Latin was killed by the teacher's sarcasm.

But it was at home, alone, that I felt I was really learning.

As before, I enjoyed the routine of it, once again comforted by the repetition. I would get the upstairs kitchen table to myself before five, by which time I'd had tea and my parents went downstairs to open up. A cheerful space, the G Plan still shining, a sink where I could make tea, a cooker, a coal fire for winter, still the view across Market Hill to the country, and The Timetable in front of me. It had developed a lot since the first year.

I took pleasure simply in looking at that timetable. Divided into five one-hour sections with a half-hour break for a potato pie or crisps from downstairs. The last hour was general reading: 9.30 to 10.30. The advantage of that placing was that I could continue in bed without breaking any of the rules of The Timetable.

Saturday was free. I could read a book for pleasure but no work. The evenings were taken care of at the County Ballroom, the days increasingly blocked out by rugby. I was at best average. But I had grown to be very keen on the game and Mr Morton encouraged keenness. I got a place in that stellar team. A lowly place. Blind side loose forward. About as invisible a position as it was possible to imagine. But I got a game! Home and away most Saturdays from September to April. When we travelled we would sometimes not get back until early evening, which meant that the dance had to be sacrificed for the pictures. Playing at home meant it would all be over after the morning game and a meal for both teams in the canteen.

Having a place in that team mattered. On Friday afternoons I would contrive to get to the notice board in the hall without being observed and see if, in Jimmie's neat print, I had been picked for Saturday's game. Yes, and it set off the weekend to a happy start. No, and I felt like hiding in a cupboard. Selection for the second team, even as vice-captain, was no consolation.

Sunday-morning church was dropped. Seven hours, much of it general reading time, which could take up the whole day if nothing had been arranged with Sarah until the evening. Evensong now and then partly to appease my aunt Margaret, who was a soprano in the choir. On cold dark Sunday evenings there were few options save church. But we would still meet up on Sunday evenings, and put in the time. Sarah was not too keen on church, but she suffered it occasionally.

The week's homeworking hours added up to forty-two, which was a proper week of factory shifts. As I had no idea what I needed to know to pass the ever stiffer exams, I just worked till I was tired.

As before it became not only addictive but a guaranteed pleasure. Even Latin when I worked out a way to get through it without being tripped up or put down by Miss Anderson. As for history and English, it became like going downhill in top gear, faster and faster without any effort beyond concentrating on what was in front of your face. There was time for all that. In English we, as a class, had read the three set books in the first term of the first year. Now Mr Blacka unleashed us on more Shakespeare, more Romantic poetry, and liked to quiz us on our private reading. I couldn't go on a bus without a book. Non-timetabled waking hours were filled with fiction and drama.

Knowledge had bitten in deeply. Acquiring knowledge was living life as it should be lived. That made staying on worth it. It was not so much to pass exams, it was to know more and to learn how to know more and discover that knowing more was the meaning of life.

Sarah and I were publicly together. It looked as if it would last. We seemed a Good Match and all was right with the world. And it was, as far as we were concerned. The closeness between us, coupled with the approval of our seriousness, despite our ages, gave our life an unexpected glamour, freedom as well as sexual exhilaration.

I did not realise my luck with her at the time. So many disturbing feelings and uneasy sensations were resolved. Sarah somehow complemented the work. And, as embarrassing to write now as to say then, I loved her. I could not see her without feeling happiness like a secret smile unknown to that degree anywhere else with anyone else. And, as far as I could tell, for Sarah was a reluctant romantic, she experienced something of the same. What she withheld in words she showed in actions. We had clicked. I wanted it to be without end.

Chapter Forty-one

My mother had always enjoyed Christmas. She laughed about the fact that as a child her presents had been an orange and a sixpence. What she liked most were the decorations. The town stirred itself to bunting, especially around the fountain from which streamers swooped in all directions. In High Street and King Street Christmas paper models of various characters – fairies, reindeer, Father Christmas – criss-crossed the streets. The shop windows were in competition with each other for 'best display' and behind these modest panes scenes of fantasy appeared overnight and were solemnly judged by people in the town, who would 'do' the shop windows in the late evening or at weekends and mark the efforts on forms provided by the council. The three Snaith sisters won something every year with their elaborate displays, drawing on their father's treasured clocks as well as decorations carefully preserved from the Victorian age. Harry Moore's toyshop had a Father Christmas (Jimmy Hodgson in tremendous form) on Saturday afternoons in December. Everyone, it seemed to my mother, made an effort and everything, she thought, was wonderful.

The church choirs would be out on some of the nights, singing their four-part carols by the light of lanterns and torches. Boys, such as myself, saw it as a godsend – no better time to make money than by touring the town, singing at the door, then 'Knock, knock, rapper, ring, ring the bell, please give us something for singing so well.' Laurie was the highest earner: he always ended with 'I Believe', which some thought was cheating because it was not a carol, but as he pointed out, it always 'got them' and it was about God.

*

It was Jimmy Hodgson's finest time. Jimmy lived in one of the small terraced cottages opposite the Catholic church and was a favourite with the nuns even though, as he said many times, 'I am a devoted Anglican.' He was an only child. His mother had dominated his timid father, who worked in the accounts office at the back of the Co-op and hid from life by collecting stamps from the British Empire He had inherited money and his thrift was notorious, which was to leave him with some income. In the evenings Jimmy would spend a few hours in charge of the pumps at Mason's across the road. That paid in cash. And there was the unemployment benefit. He was well set up. Being Father Christmas was a bonus.

Jimmy had been a churchgoer for years, walking at the head of the choir in his early days, carrying the cross, part of the procession from vestry to choir stalls. Part of the pageantry that embellished the prayers. He helped to clean the church. He fussed over the vicar. He spoke in a broad Wigton accent, which could easily be mistaken for the voice of a middle-aged woman. He was given to dramatic gestures on the altar steps.

He was a bulky man, often padded out further with an accumulation of clothes. He liked to talk about sweets: his favourites, he would tell you, were Japanese Desserts, Dolly Mixtures and Creamy Whirls. He bought himself a box of chocolate liqueurs every Christmas and a single one could make him feel happily 'dopey', as he was fond of telling people. His face was large, always red, given focus by a pair of National Health spectacles, which seemed too small for his untended eyebrows and bristling nose and ears. Constant grimacing kept them in place. He had little idea of the space and time he could take up in the lives of those he buttonholed. Christmas week was one of the busiest of the year in the pub, yet Jimmy would lean comfortably against a wall in the rather narrow corridor, blocking it, and cheerfully carry on a conversation with my mother, who was pulling pints, pouring bottles and totting up prices.

Part of Jimmy's fame came from his spectacular behaviour on the great feasts and holy days in the church. He would take care to be the last to receive Communion. After he had drunk the wine he would step away from the altar rails and all but throw himself down the chancel steps, face down, spread-eagled in submission, whispering more prayers. The service had to slow down, even stop. The choirboys tried not to laugh, some of the congregation were embarrassed, others moved at this passionate evidence of his faith. In his own time he would get up, bow deeply three times to the altar cross and then turn to face the body of the church. Unfortunately, by then his white surplice was halfway down his body, the black cassock had rucked up, showing very short black socks and very white legs, and, with his dreamy smile, he looked like a circus clown, one who made you grin although you felt he was a sad man. The vicar was seen to look away and clench his fists.

His other mark of distinction was that he had left his first job after one day. He got a start in Stoddart's the ironmonger when he was fourteen, came home after work and announced he didn't like it and wasn't going to work again. Nor did he, save for helping out at the petrol pumps. He took to photography and became part of Mr Scott's Friday evening group.

At Christmas he appointed himself cleaner-in-chief in the church, overriding the ladies who arranged the flowers. He went into the countryside and found holly and ivy to wreathe along the pew ends. Again he greatly annoyed the vicar, but what could the vicar do?

The Black-A-Moor was on his way back home – the house in which he had lived all his life and changed not a bit since the death of his parents. Jimmy didn't drink but he liked to stand inside the door next to the hatch to the bar, unperturbed by the rush and bustle around him. He would order a packet of crisps and pick through them slowly, payment for his stay. The fourpence would be extracted from his purse with reluctance.

*

Just before Christmas, when I was seventeen, my mother and father had a conversation.

When the pub closed, with the night's accounting and cleaning done, the helpers entertained in the kitchen and they too gone, Ethel, tired to the bone, at last plucked up the courage to say what was on her mind.

'I think we should give this up.' She spoke very quietly.

'Yes?' He looked up from his paper.

'I think we've done enough. Well, I have.'

'In the pub?'

'Yes. I'm tired out with it, Stan. You've made a good go of it, but I've had enough.'

'You look as if you enjoy it.'

'I have to.'

He put his paper to one side. 'We all feel like that sometimes.'

'Yes. But this time I know I mean it.'

'Why now?'

'It's been building up for some time. I have no life, Stan, outside the pub. We don't have a house to go to after our day's work is done. I can't remember the last time we went to a dance or to church. The three of us have never once been to a café or a restaurant together. When I go to the pictures it's with an old girlfriend if she's free or if not I go on my own, which is not terrible but it's not what other couples do. I lost hope that we'll ever have holidays together – one of us has to be here to look after the pub.' She looked away from him. 'Others manage it. Jack and Margaret at the Lion, Alistair and Gladys at the King's Arms. There's plenty in the same situation but they still manage.'

He did not interrupt, hoping that she would talk herself out of it.

'But it isn't any of that. It isn't even getting started at eight o'clock, getting him to school and you your breakfast and then the floors, the fires, the polishing, the pub opened with a space in the afternoon when nobody I know is around. That's all the time I have to do something. So I go to Carlisle and look in shops, then we're open and it's all go until now – what is it? Twenty past eleven, seven days a week.'

She paused. It was not easy for her to say this. 'It's not the work. I like some of that, and the talk. It's . . .' she paused '. . . it's not a life I ever wanted. I just want an ordinary house, both of us out to work – we could get jobs – back together for tea, weekends to ourselves, people like us in houses like ours, nothing special but our own house. That's what I've always wanted. We could have it now. He's almost off our hands – he'll leave Wigton for one thing or another, I can tell that. And us just getting more and more tired with the same people – nice people – never mind that.'

Still he kept his peace.

'It's all right for you. You've got your hound trails. There's the football at Carlisle on Saturdays when you want it. You like men's talk about sport and what's in the papers and you have all that on a plate. You like organising things like the darts teams and the hound trails and the domino league, and talking to the better-off men who come in now and then. You like all that. The pub is your world on tap. Admit it.'

'It seemed to suit you as well.'

'It did for a time. But not any more. I want us to leave.'

'You've said that before.'

'Yes. And you've taken no notice. And we've had terrible shouting rows, which I'm sure he heard upstairs, when I threatened to walk out and you said you could easily find something else. Admit it. Then it calmed down. We calmed it down. And I went along with it. But not any more. Not any more, Stan. After this Christmas, count me gone.'

'Where will you get work?'

'Is that all you have to say? Don't you realise? You've given up as well. Just look at you. Gone to fat. Worn out most of the time. Pushing yourself – no time for anything but what's to do with the pub.'

'It's our life.'

'Yours – yes. Mine – not any more, Stan, and I want you to believe me.'

'What would we do?'

'I've thought of that. We have some savings now. We could get jobs or put down payment on a shop . . . get a mortgage . . .'

'Go on.'

'A sweets and tobacco shop. There's plenty in the town. Eight thirty to five thirty. I'm sure if we made an offer one would come up sooner or later. And if we're short of money, I could always go back to cleaning or part-time work here or somewhere in Carlisle.'

'A sweet shop.'

'When you look around they have nice houses or flats attached and some of them – Miss Peters's, Miss Turner's, maybe even Noel's, he's been there since I can remember – maybe one of those, or we could look in another town. You're always saying that real Cumbrians live in the west. What about Maryport? That's full of little shops.'

'Leave Wigton?'

'Yes.'

'*You?*'

'Yes. If it was the only way out. You see you still don't believe me, do you?'

'A sweet shop!'

'They seem to make a living.'

'But . . . Ethel, look at what we've got.'

'I do. And I enjoyed helping to build it up and I can see how much it means to you with all its connections – dogs, darts, sport, being The Landlord – don't deny it. There's a bit of a swagger. But, how many more times do I have to say it?'

'You've had it.'

'I have.' Her voice was low, weary but, he knew, her mind was set. 'I'm sorry, Stan.'

Before he could reply, she stood up and looked directly at him, through the faintest film of tears. 'I'm sorry, Stan,' she repeated. 'I really am. But I can't and I won't go on here.'

As she left she turned to him, looking for a way out, bit her lip. He returned her gaze and her lips trembled. He saw that she looked ill with tiredness. After she left he lit a cigarette.

It took time for me to stitch together that encounter. My father gave me the gist of it quite soon afterwards but the tone was transmitted in small asides, unexpected confidences, the slow patchwork way the three of us would work things through.

Chapter Forty-two

The next morning she felt embarrassed about her confession. Her life had been characterised by enduring, not complaining and, above all, not drawing attention to herself. All that had been put on a bonfire of feeling. She slept badly and worked out sentences of apology, but in the morning she did not find the right moment and her resolution drifted away with the day. She had said it. It was up to him now. That had to be that or the whole outburst would have been no more than self-indulgence. She was well used to carrying her own hurt without revealing it, to consuming her own anxieties and laying layers of forced cheerfulness over them. Cheerfulness had been her armour for years.

Stan, too, appeared to have nothing to say on the matter.

Christmas came and was as boisterous as ever. On Christmas Eve Kenneth gave them 'Silent Night' in the Singing Room. The darts men surrendered the board to let more drinkers into their room. Even more shorts were ordered in the kitchen. 'O Come All Ye Faithful', sung in all four rooms, brought a warm and spirited end to it. Some trickled up to Midnight Mass, others just strayed home. The dance would close at eleven thirty and the pubs had been given an extension to eleven, and better a bird in the hand. Harry, now openly supported by Vince, had a quiet night on the door of the Market Hall. Dennis and Jackie danced quietly near the band and never left the floor between numbers. Now and then he stroked her slightly swelling belly and smiled.

The men, the 'uncles' from Kirkbride, who used to come to the Station Road house now left their bikes at the Black-A-Moor, tasted a pint or two and walked up to the dance.

Andrew would be at the factory on the lucrative holiday ten-till-six shift, double pay. He would come off it and walk through the town and up the hill to be with Whiplash and take him for a morning walk.

Jimmy, on his knees beside his bed, was muttering his prayers, preparing for his spectacular prostration in front of the altar.

Peter, Dr Dolan's assistant, had come home early from the surgery and seen his mother through a lightly poached egg. He had sent her to her bed, which had been well warmed with a rubber ribbed hot-water bottle. Now he sat down with St Thomas Aquinas' *Summa Theologica*, which he re-read every Christmas.

Curiously, Ethel thought, she felt less tired than on the previous days. It was as if sharing her unhappiness had taken off pressure. She enjoyed this Christmas as much as any, and when she thought it might be her last in the pub, she even felt sadness, but the resolution had not weakened.

On Boxing Day, I took Sarah home for tea. It was in part excruciating; in part it just about scraped through as OK. My mother took the initiative and talked about Sarah's parents and when they were young at the dances and about the town. Stan was interested in her work at the bank and that went well. Once the initial clumsiness searching for a subject was over, it rolled along. To my surprise it was Sarah who, when warmed up, took on the brunt of the conversation: Ethel could have been waiting all her life for a daughter to chat to. At one stage they broke away into their own conversation and Dad and I dug deep into the fortunes of Carlisle United.

We left for a party being given in the large flat above the Midland Bank by Alex, whose father had been transferred from Lancaster to manage the Wigton branch. Alex, parachuted into a new school, saw the party as a quick way of entrenching her position. There would be beer and wine, canapés and music from a two-speaker gramophone. Both Sarah and I felt we were being moved on, awkwardly, into a posher world.

'I'll take the leftover cake and sandwiches down to the bar,' Ethel said to Stan, as she tidied up after we had gone.

'I'll help you.' He took a slice of chocolate cake. 'There's enough here for a regiment.'

'She was very nice. A strong look of her father. He was a handsome lad.'

'She was more comfortable than him.'

'He was bound to be nervous. In his own house.'

Outside, Sarah said, 'Your mam's great.'

'Yes.'

'Your dad was good at making us laugh. But it's her you're like.'

Up the near empty streets we dawdled, taking our time, not wanting to be early. We linked arms. When I thought no one was looking I stopped, turned to her and kissed her.

'Thanks for getting that over with,' I said.

'I liked them. Your mother asked me if I'd go shopping with her in Carlisle some Saturday afternoon.'

'Window shopping?'

'That'll be it.'

We went up two flights of newly carpeted stairs and into the flat above the bank. It was a room rich in Christmas decorations. There were bookcases along one wall, two large Lakeland landscape paintings on the opposite wall, comfortable leather furniture, a marble mantelpiece crowded with family photographs in silver-looking frames. Ella Fitzgerald was singing softly. Alex opened her arms to us. 'How good of you to come,' she said. 'Merry Christmas! Come in! Come in!'

Stanley believed in charity without show. It is therefore embarrassing and, my mother would say, 'will seem like boasting', to refer to a Boxing Day ritual, which had been going on since the year after he got the Black-A-Moor. He loaded up his overcoat with about half a dozen miniatures, one or two whisky, mainly port, a few bottles of stout and some packets of cigarettes, and went around Market Hill and into two of the yards leading off it, to visit some of the old people who lived alone. Just as he never passed by a tramp without putting a coin in his hand. 'There but for the grace of God,' he once said, more to himself than to me, but I have not forgotten it.

My father was not the only one to help out in small ways. There were children who cared for their parents, wives who devoted themselves to husbands or brothers grievously injured in wars or worn down by age's attrition, sisters looking after younger sisters, shopkeepers who added an extra portion free, neighbours who regularly visited. I have a sure belief that this town, like so many others, was held together by small acts of kindness. Understated, unextravagant, reliable. I saw it most openly among the working class, but I'm sure it stretched across the classes: one solicitor, an alcoholic, was nursed into reasonable efficiency by his wife, another wife, stricken by a stroke, lived on and with something like happiness because of the devotion of her husband, an accountant. So it went.

I guess that rationing had made the town more equitable and fair in the decade after the war. Everybody had the same number of coupons for food and clothes and sweets and such, and although there were dodges, on the whole there was acquiescence and that must have encouraged some sense of fairness, which, especially after the war, saw fair play and helping out as the way to behave. The National Health Service emphasised that new sense of fairness.

And we were run by our own. We could challenge the elected councillors who made the decisions. They were not a separate cadre, not a superior generously paid clique. They were just people you had been at school with, people you could beard on the street and to whom you could write a personal letter, knowing it would be read, considered and answered.

Boxing Day had its own atmosphere. It was a day for visiting relations, or friends, for playing interminable Monopoly or tiddly-winks with the children, eating cold cuts from the Christmas dinner and being thankful that Boxing Day was a holiday. The streets were as empty as Sundays; the pubs would not open until seven and there would be a few customers in the bar and the Darts Room, the other two rooms empty. Stan could handle it by himself, comfortably. Ethel would go to the upstairs sitting room and, with me out of the way, have it to herself, put on a coal fire, read *Woman's Illustrated*, find some music on the wireless, doze.

Seen from the air, save for the blaze of the factory, the town centre would have appeared as a modest cluster of low-energy streetlights and pinpoints from the flats and houses. Further out, the inner ring of new estates was poorly lit, and beyond them, darkness, a few farms and the big houses, scarcely visible.

On Boxing Day the centre would be bereft of the urchins scurrying and hiding, chasing games and shouts of 'You're in!' and 'You're IT!' The churches would be dark. Now and then a man walking a dog. At set times men going to or coming from the factory. A skeletal bus service, mostly passengerless.

Peace seemingly everywhere. That was what Stanley most savoured as he went on his rounds. Something of the promise of Christmas still in the air but without the commercial clutter that he thought undermined the miraculously ending story of the birth of the Saviour of the World in a stable.

The Catholic church was deep in a candle-lit swoon of prayer. The Irish nuns had excelled themselves, as they always did, celebrating the birth of their Lord and treating the orphans with a programme on the television, rarely present in the rest of the disciplined year.

On Boxing Day evening, Barbara Wilson would be relaxing with her first gin and tonic in Kirkland House, her splendid Georgian manor outside the town, after a successful day's hunting. Boxing Day was one of the blue riband days for the hunt. It had met outside the Royal Oak for the stirrup cup accompanied by a gathering of enthusiasts who were there to follow the hunt in cars, on their bikes or motorbikes. They had set off towards Caldbeck. Applause and pride sent them on their way, a cavalry of scarlet and black, high mounted in impeccable uniform on gleaming horses, the pack of hounds before them sniffing the air, keeping the discipline, a spectacle created largely by landed money and inheritance and replicated in villages all over the country, Old England mounted in splendour. The real England, its participants thought.

Barbara's horse had been groomed to within an inch of its life by Kenneth Wallace, who had started on such work at ten years old. He and his family, Ethel's near neighbours when she was a girl, crowded into a house in Station Road opposite a yard of stables, whose owner specialised in buying and selling horses. They were walked up from the railway station, washed and sent to their new homes. Kenneth had been seen by the owner, Mr Ivinson, as a willing boy, and needed little persuasion to devote any spare hour from school and then, at a beggar's wage, every hour there was as what Mr Ivinson called 'an apprentice' to work with his passion. Horses. After Ivinson's death Kenneth went to the factory where the wage seemed otherworldly after Mr Ivinson's pittance. But he kept on with the horses for the rest of his life.

Finally in this God's eye view, there was Greenwood House, where my mother had worked for Mrs Cavaghan. Her children, Annette and George, who had long ago left the state school to go to their private-school destinations, were home in force with friends from school and the county and a few from their old days in the town. Mrs Cavaghan had seen that an invitation to me 'and a guest' had arrived for their big party a couple of days before New Year. We biked there and were met with exuberant hospitality. There were a few Wigton faces but I was aware that my accent could be thought rough. Annette, even more stunning than when younger, took us under her wing. One young gent to whom we talked tried on an imitation of my heavy Cumbrian accent. Annette was furious. 'This was the first boy I kissed,' she said loudly. She looked at Sarah. 'I missed my chance there.' Not too pleased to be picked out and then defended, I did a fair exaggeration of his posh voice.

'Very good,' said Annette. Waving an apology he blushed and faded away.

The party was like those Mrs Cavaghan had given when Annette and George were children. We had the run of the place unbridled, just as we had played together as kids. The new element was dancing to the gramophone. There was still the grand buffet and the serene sailing presence of Mrs Cavaghan herself, glass in hand, blonde hair slightly tumbling, face rather over-flushed with goodwill.

We biked back slowly, cutting through the darkness, enjoying raking over the past few hours.

At night, on Boxing Day, Greenwood lay at rest, a small outpost of a town grown over centuries, like a natural thing, now lost in the dark. As God's eye view pulled back, even that grand mansion was just part of the landscape. And there were stars, not just in the east, but everywhere.

Chapter Forty-three

It was not difficult to get back into the routine. I was pushing it now. Not more hours but working more intensely, enjoying it more, testing myself at the end of every session. My answer to the chronic Latin problem was to learn the set book practically by heart. Cicero's *Pro Milone* would count for a substantial number of marks. With a crib I looked at the Latin until it was branded on my eyes. I was still nervous about 'unseens' – a page or two of Latin hitherto unknown, which I had to translate into English prose from the Latin with little confidence. I had decided that to blame the teacher was feeble. I worked harder. My marks inched up.

I read more around the English set books and, without trying, found that chunks of Hazlitt's essays, *King Lear* and the Romantic poets had stuck and, under Mr Blacka's guidance, I moved out into further reading. Mr James was delighted that I had 'taken to history', as he put it, and piled on more reading. In those hours above the pub, with Sarah always in prospect, I was as content as it was possible to be. The exams were still far enough away to cause no tremors.

In February we did a run-through – the mock exams. The marks in English and Latin were much in line with what had been given for the essays over the year; the history results were below.

'It is the organisation of the material,' Mr James said. 'You have plenty to say – possibly too much – but it's thrown down like some sort of challenge to the examiner to sort it out. He or she doesn't want to know all that you know. A well-worked essay is the way forward. The trouble is that you try to cram the huge essays you do for your homework into four forty-five minute answers. You lose the argument.' He handed me a book of essays.

'Read these. You'll see they have a structure – beginning, middle, conclusion, all three stages connected, all giving as much information as is needed for the space and time available.'

He was kind but severe, and he looked disappointed. That was the worst of it.

'Practise doing answers in forty-five minutes,' he said. 'Not part of your homework. Just practice – practice makes perfect. I'll give you some old exam questions and go over them with you.'

Both Val and Catherine's marks were higher than mine, which was galling.

I did as he suggested.

There would be scholarship papers as well as the A levels. Both Mr Blacka and Mr James had entered me, Catherine and Val for these. Both Mr James and Mr Blacka said the same. Don't do a repeat of the A-level papers. Write something more reflective, less fact bound, more original. 'It's asking rather a lot,' said Mr Blacka, 'but that's what they're looking for. Somebody who can think for themselves. The scholarship papers make the difference.' He was trying not to mention university at this stage and I was determined not to bring it up, but once or twice he said, 'If you want to go further, it's the scholarship papers that do it for you.'

Mr Blacka did the same for all our year. I felt even more now on the racecourse, being shuffled into the starting box. The race would soon be on. 'And,' said Mr James, finally, 'it is a competition. You will be against other schools. Some very good schools.'

When I told Sarah about it, she said, 'Sooner you than me.' I was up for it. The biggest worry was that I would get an attack of 'nerves' – 'panic' would have been a better word. But that had been long ago and, despite a few brief recurrences, I thought I was through it. Sarah had helped settle that.

'We have something to tell you.'

My father's voice was serious, although he buttered it over with a smile. My mother sat alongside him on one of the fitted leatherette wall couches in the kitchen. She, too, smiled. It was a Monday, a quiet night, no need for any of the helpers. Jack Waters was looking after the bar. I sat at the old kitchen table and waited.

'We'll be moving from here just after Easter.'

That had impact. I waited.

'To Workington.'

'What for?'

'I've been offered a job by the brewery. Not another pub. A job in their offices. I've been for two interviews over the last month and just got word that I've got it.'

Again I waited. It was hard to work out the consequences. I think I felt shock.

'They're reorganising the business. They need somebody who knows pub life and can help manage the development they have in mind. They've bought another brewery – smaller – but they want to make it one business.'

'Why do you want to go?'

'Your mother and me need a change. It'll be an eight–to–six job. Five and half days. Better money than here. And nothing like the work. Your mother and me can have a bit of a life together. Weekends, nights, holidays.'

I felt strange but as yet I could not focus.

'What do you think?' I asked.

My mother took her time. 'It's a good offer for your dad,' she said, rather strained. 'They seem to be nice people.'

'In a month?'

'About that.'

'I'll have to change schools.'

'Yes. Workington Grammar School's very good. I asked that at the second interview. And they have the same curriculum as yours. I checked. So there won't be any problem there.'

'Where will we live?'

'Your dad's got his eye on a rented property in the middle of the town. I'm going through tomorrow to see it. Then we're looking to buy our own house.'

It was even now too difficult to absorb.

'I don't know anybody in Workington.'

'Good people,' said my father, promptly. 'I've always said that real Cumbrians live on the west coast. And there's plenty going on. More than here. A theatre, pictures, there's the rugby league team and the football team – it's a thriving place, a big industrial centre is Workington. It's the future. You'll soon fit in.'

I picked up on my mother's nerves. 'What do you think?'

'As your dad says, it'll be a change. I think your dad already likes the idea of the job.'

'But what do you think?' I pressed her. 'What will you do?'

'I've thought of that. We've talked about that. When we've got the house sorted out, I'll find a job.'

'There's hotels in Workington,' my father said. 'Proper hotels.'

'Maybe I could get a part-time job in the bar in one of them – in the middle of the day – and as your dad says, there are some lovely shops. Maybe I could find work there.'

I paused. Consequences began to emerge. 'What's wrong with here?'

'This is the chance of a lifetime.' He spoke rather solemnly.

'Do you think that?' I asked my mother.

'It would be a lot easier for me. And I'm sure your dad would make a good go of it.'

'Why can't you make it easier here?'

'We've thought about that,' he said, 'but whatever way you look at it, here there's work to do from when you get up until bedtime and there's no changing that. Your mother agrees.'

'What do you think?' She looked directly at me. 'It must be a bit of a shock.'

'It's not Australia,' Dad said cheerfully. 'We backed off Australia . . .'

'New Zealand.'

'Was it New Zealand? Just after the war. Your mother wouldn't go.' He smiled at her affectionately.

'I was worried about how we'd get back.'

I knew they were waiting. Without thought, it seemed, my response came out, fiercely. 'I'm not going.'

There was no response.

'I'm not going,' I repeated.

'It's bound to sound a bit strange at first. You'll get used to it.'

'I won't. I'm not going.'

I made as if to leave the kitchen but found that the energy had gone. My legs were weak. I held onto the edge of the table.

'There's nothing to be scared of.'

'I'm not scared,' I said.

I was.

'You'll get used to the idea.'

'I won't.'

'What is it most bothers you?'

Everything!

'Is it the school? We know how hard you go at it. They'll have good teachers there.'

But not Mr James. Not Mr Blacka. Not Mr Stowe. I was relying on them. What would those strangers be like? It didn't bear thinking about. There was a tightness in my chest, a choking sensation. But I controlled myself. And my friends in the town, the town itself, which fitted me as if bespoke and which I would happily live in for ever. And Sarah! What about Sarah? I braced myself. My world had just been scooped away.

'I could go and stay with Grandad through the week,' I said.

'There's not enough room.' Dad said this in as gentle a way as he could. 'Irwin's doing his higher nationals and works there at night. Where would you find the space to work? And Irwin and Wilson already share a bedroom.'

'I could sleep head to toe with Wilson.'

A silence began to set in. I found that I was breathing unnaturally deeply.

'Skip!' The Scout master. 'He has spare rooms in his house. Sometimes he lets them out.'

My mother shook her head.

'If he stayed in Park House he could always come back to Workington at weekends.' My father saw a compromise, looked at my mother for support.

'We would never see him,' she said.

Weekends were for Sarah.

'I'd be best finding a place to stay in Wigton full-time.'

'It'll only be for two or three months!' Stan appealed to Ethel.

'Not necessarily.' Another deep breath. 'Mr James has talked to three of us about putting us up for university. If we got the results. It could mean to stay on until Christmas to take exams for that.'

'If you got the results.'

'I'm going to bed now,' I said.

'Good. Think it over.'

'I have.'

It is often impossible any way accurately to remember what I felt sixty-five years ago. Defining incidents stick.

We're told that memory changes and adapts with age and mood and experience, which makes it unreliable. But I am sure I felt calm.

There was no question of going to sleep. I drew the curtains and put out the light. I thought it through. At one stage I found that I was using Mr James's fundamental method. Three reasons. Were there three reasons to go along with my father and mother and, if so, what were they? And what were the three reasons against? I remember clearly that, though I was badly shaken, I had a sense of certainty and calm.

On my parents' side the basis of their case was to recognise and be grateful for how much they had already done for me. They had given me both security and liberty. My mother had steered me through the early war years, which could easily have been damaging. My father, when he came back in 1945, had sorted out order for all three of us that found its perfection, as he thought, in the pub.

My mother had seen to it that, again within the limitations of the period and the purse, I lacked nothing. I was rich in everything that mattered. There was nothing humble about us. If challenged as to what class they were, both would have said working class. For them that was not an issue. We were secure in what we were.

FOR.

First. They had every right to change the lives they had. Second, they were not jumping on a ship to the other side of the world. Workington was a Cumbrian town, bigger and richer and more industrial than Wigton, but really 'just about down the road', seventeen miles away. And, as my father had said, there was a good grammar school, cinema, theatre, sport, heavy industry, a port – all on a bigger level than found in Wigton and therefore providing greater opportunities. Third, it seemed selfish to stand in their way.

AGAINST.

First, I was certain it would disrupt preparation for the exams. I was dug into routines and relationships connected with work that could not be replicated. Who could guess what the teachers would be like, and how could they be expected fully to take on board a newcomer and help prepare him for exams just a few weeks ahead? Besides, there was the school: it was my place now. It had become my town. What was, where was, Workington Grammar School on my map?

Second, I would lose Sarah. How could I see her often enough? I had to see her frequently and talk to her daily. We had worked it all out.

Third, there was Wigton. It would be like transplanting a tree. I could already hear the roots screaming.

It was as if I were on Skiddaw and a violent wind threatened to blow me away. I remembered once being up there in a furious storm. There was a hawk nearby, wings extended, still as a stone as the wind buffeted it, waiting. Then there was a gap and it let itself be swooped away, scarcely visible within seconds. This would take me away. I did not want to go. And I would not go.

Breakfast was quiet.

I set off for school at the usual time.

*

'He'll come round.'

She nodded, but waited for more. They were in the downstairs kitchen, about four o'clock in the afternoon of the next day, all cleared up from a desultory midday opening, all ready for the night. Both had unsipped cups of tea.

'You could see it was a bit of a shock.' Stan seemed to be persuading both of them. 'Maybe we should have eased him into it. We could have told him what a good place Workington is. Ships, the car factory, its own MP. It's the place of the future. Wigton's dying by comparison with Workington. If he plays his cards right, he'll do well there.'

'I think he's worried about the school more than anything else. And the teachers.' Ethel spoke very quietly.

'They'll be just as good at Workington. Maybe better. It's altogether a more go-ahead place.'

'But he always says how much he owes to his teachers in Wigton,' she said.

'He'll change when he has to.'

'He's banking a lot on those exams, Stan. And he's worked very hard.'

'But what's to stop him working?' He lit a cigarette. 'Don't say you're arguing on his side. You do want to move, don't you? You do see the benefits, don't you?'

'Yes.' Her voice was firm. 'Yes. And I can see how much you want it.'

'Lots of lads about his age have to make a change. They have no choice. He'll be up for his national service in no time – then he'll be off to Germany or Malaya or somewhere and what then? Thousands of young lads leave home about his age and look for work and opportunities somewhere else. I'd changed jobs twice by the time I was his age. We can't featherbed him.'

'He's very set on these exams.'

He stubbed out his cigarette with some force. 'We've never spoiled him.'

'No.'

'I'll talk to him one to one. Tonight. That job won't wait for ever. Jobs like this don't turn up very often.'

'I know that. I think you're right. And I want to go, Stan. I do.'

'I'll talk to him tonight.'

It was not until Saturday afternoon that we met. The rugby match had been in the morning and Stan had turned up, as had other parents and old boys and men from the town's rugby team. As usual I was embarrassed when I saw him on the touchline but at least he did not shout out like some of the fathers.

'You played well,' Stan said. They were in the bar, a coal fire just refreshed.

'I don't have to do much.'

'Everybody's part of the team. You're all equal.'

'But some animals are more equal than others.'

'*Animal Farm.*'

'Yes. He pulls it off, doesn't he?'

'I'll say.' I was excited. Stan couldn't work out this switch of mood.

Inevitably, Stan took out a cigarette. Tapped it on the box. Cupped his hands around the lighter, drew in deeply, sat back. He gave me a detailed outline of what he and my mother had said the night before. He wanted everything to be clear. Then he said, very firmly, 'So where are you?'

'I've found a way out.'

'Have you, then?'

'Yes.' I took my time. It was like being forced to answer one of Mr Stowe's questions.

'Do you know Mr Loveday?' Dad shook his head. 'He teaches French. We give him a hard time because, well, I used to think because he was soft, now I think it's because his mind's on something else and all he wants with us is to get the class over and go back to his lodgings and work on his book. He has lodgings in Highmoor Avenue, just along from Mr James. He must have two rooms, don't you think? Well, I could take lodgings. A lot of people in Wigton are in lodgings.'

339

'Go on.'

'I could stay there through the week and come to Workington say late Friday, stay some of Saturday depending on the rugby and then come back here for the dance.'

'So you'd spend one night a week with us?' 'Yes. Maybe a bit more at half-term.'

'And who would pay for these lodgings?'

'I've worked it out. You've said you're getting a mortgage for a house. You could get a mortgage on me for the rent and for pocket money. I would pay you back as soon as I started earning.'

'I don't think I could take out a mortgage on you.'

'You could find out. And if not you could just add it to what you're taking out for the house in Workington.'

'It would be expensive. Lodgings like Mr Loveday's won't be cheap.'

'We could look around.'

'Hold on.' He smiled. 'You've decided not to come to Workington, haven't you?'

'Yes. Not to live there.'

'It wouldn't be cheap to pay for good lodgings.'

'I'd pay it off. You know I would.'

Looking back, I can now see this from his point of view. I can see his thinking. He looked at me closely. Just about grown to man size now. Fresh-faced, eager, confident. Despite putting the pressure on himself, I still did all the jobs around the pub as before – the firewood, sweeping the front, sluicing the Gents, bringing up bottles from the cellar . . . And I'd become much easier behind the bar when needed. Look at him now. Brimming with life. Certain that his idea would solve everything. Just like that!

'It's money I'll myself need now, not in a year or two's time. But that's not the main point,' said my father.

'What is?'

'We're a family. We should stick together as a family.'

'You didn't.'

'I had no choice in the matter,' he said.

'Nor do I!'

'Don't be so daft.'

'It's not daft.'

'There's nothing forcing you. You want your own way, that's all, and you're frightened that new teachers might not be as good as the old. They could be better. You're behaving like a cissy that can't leave his mam.'

'It's her that's leaving me! So are you. It's the other way round to what usually happens. That's all. And I don't mind.'

'I did what my father told me. To help the family.'

'You and Mam will be just as well off without me. Better.'

'Do you really believe that?'

'Well. Do you believe I haven't thought about this? It's not just a whim.'

'I think you're a bit frightened.'

'No, I'm not. It'll be harder without you and Mam. It'll be harder without the pub and the people. But I'm not frightened.'

Stan took his time. 'It'll be quite a dent in my income to pay for your lodgings.'

'I'm sorry. But surely you can borrow the money for that short time. It'll be over for me in about three months. Then I'll get a job and look after myself.'

'Haven't you been hinting at university?'

'That'll have to go. It was Mr James's idea, anyway, not mine.'

'But if you leave school doesn't most of your case against moving fall down?'

'I don't know. But I guess I'm most likely to get a job in Carlisle.'

'Is this all a bit stupid? Just bite the bullet and come with us.'

'I can't, Dad. I'm sorry. I won't.'

'It's Sarah,' she said.

'They're only kids.'

'It's Sarah.'

'They'll get over it.'

'And the teachers. But mainly Sarah.' She smiled. 'It's romantic, when you think about it.'

'It could be over in a month or two.'

'He doesn't think so.'

'Can't she get a transfer to Workington?'

'That wouldn't work for her.'

'Have you asked her?'

'I don't need to.'

'You talk to him. I have to tell the brewery one way or the other by the end of the week.'

'It would be a climb-down for your dad. He's very keen on it. He sees it as changing our lives.'

'I don't want my life changed.'

'People move all the time.'

'Some don't.'

We were awkward, talking across the table in the upstairs sitting room. My books occupied most of it. My mother had come up immediately after closing time without staying to help clear up.

'I want to leave here,' She said this in a tone empty of any pleading. 'This place has tired me out. And I want a different life and so does your dad. You'll soon be away. The odds are that your dad will never get a better job offer at his age. We could settle down in our own house. We could go out together more. Your dad always says that people in the west are nicer. And I'm sure you'll find friends.'

'I've got all the friends I want.'

'Is it Sarah keeping you here?'

'Partly. Yes, partly. Maybe a lot. And the town. But Sarah. Yes. I'm sorry.' I looked straight at my mother. 'I would marry her if I could.'

'Does she feel the same?'

'I think so. I've not asked her. But I think she does.'

*

'Let me tell you something straight out,' my father began. "You're being selfish.' I flinched. 'It's time somebody told you. Selfish. Your mother needs, *needs*, relief from the work she's been doing for the last ten years. She wants a quieter life, a more normal life, and we can get it if I take this offer. It's the best offer I've ever received and at my age the best I'll ever get. It would suit me down to the ground to run that part of the office. In every way. But no. You have to put a spoke in it.'

'It isn't a spoke. I could call you selfish for just upping and offing without taking me into account. What would you lose? I can stay here.'

'You know very well that's not the case. You're deciding to cut yourself off from us.'

'You're the ones doing the cutting off.'

'You keep repeating that.'

'Because it's true.'

'Because it suits you.'

'You can have both.'

'Not here. Your mother will be upset by this. God knows how long it's taken her to own up to this tiredness of hers. How can you expect her to enjoy it when you've turned your back on it? And it's no good saying we've turned our backs on you. Families follow parents and what we want to do is better for your mother, better for me and it could be better for you, if you had any feelings for us. But no. It's you. It's all you!'

'That's not fair. It seems fair but it isn't. How are you going to suffer? So I come with you. I still work at nights. I'm still at school all day. I still come back to Wigton whenever I can – how does that make me an integral member of the family? Once, yes. But not now. School's a job now and nobody moves a job for a worse job.'

'I admire obstinacy in a good cause. But this is just pig-headed. Pig-headed and selfish, and with no regard for your mother. For of course she'll fret and of course it won't be for just a few weeks. When you take these exams of yours you'll be even less inclined to come and live with us. She'll have lost you. You're her family. You can't seem to understand what that means to her.'

'So I follow you. Am miserable. Fail the exams. Lose all my friends in Wigton. And my girlfriend. Then what?'

'At least it would give us a chance. Together.'

'No, it wouldn't. I wouldn't be "together". How could I be?'

'There's nothing more to be said.'

'He looks terrible,' she said. 'Every time I look at him I think he's going to burst into tears.'

'The letter has to go off today.' He had his pen out.

'I'll follow you, Stan . . .' It was an effort to make that sound positive.

He smiled at her.

'You're an exception,' he said. 'You really are. I've not told you that often enough.' And 'with difficulty': 'I'm as much in love with you now as when we went out with the cycling club.'

'On that terrible tandem.'

'They were a good gang.'

'They still are.'

'Yes. Well. What I'm going to do is this – if you approve – I'm going to book us a week, maybe two, on a cruise. They set off from Newcastle. I'm sure with Harry and Jack and the others the pub'll be in safe hands. When we come back I want you to promise you'll finish work by twelve o'clock and not start again until seven at the earliest. And we could take one or even two weekday nights off together. We can afford it. Would that be OK? That'll give you the time you need, I hope, and I'll make sure we go out together to things. I've been selfish. I should have done this ages ago. Is that OK for you?'

'But what about you, Stan?' She struggled to hold back her tears. 'I want what you want.'

He did not need to reply. It had become clear to him that, above all, he wanted what was best for her. He wrote the letter.

Chapter Forty-four

We'd played away from Wigton in the morning. By the time we'd eaten and made the journey back to Wigton it was mid-afternoon. The pub was closed. When I went in, I saw Dad sitting alone in the bar, smoking, of course, the *News Chronicle* beside him on the settle, the fire recently built up. He waved me in.

'Score?'

'Twenty-four–eighteen. Last-minute try. They're a tough lot.'

He indicated that I should sit down on the settle beside him. 'That's Whitehaven for you.'

He smiled very gently. I was still nervous.

'Don't worry about things. What's done's done. And,' he drew deeply on the cigarette and looked across the room and out of the window, 'you've been dodging me over these last couple of weeks. You needn't. I've been thinking it all over. It might not have worked out. It could have been a pipe dream.'

'I feel . . .'

'You feel guilty about it. But I said that if I worked as their coordinator it would seem to have been eight till six and back home, but it wouldn't have been. Their pubs are all over the area. You'd have to stop for a chat and a drink here and there. Your mother would have been on her own a lot of the time and in a place where she knows nobody whereas here she knows everybody. And there's you. You put up a good fight!'

'Maybe . . .'

'No. You needn't regret it. And the way things are already beginning to work out is better for your mother. You never know. Then there's the cruise.' He laughed aloud. 'The CRUISE! When she found out that all the trips now were headed for the North

Pole, it was no. She hates the cold. So I've booked a time in late July, the Mediterranean. I could get used to it.'

'Sarah said I had a cheek.'

'Did she? But it didn't make any difference, did it?'

He turned in his seat to face me squarely.

'It's over. It might have worked. Or not. But you're happy – though you look anything but – and your mother's perking up already.'

'And . . .'

'I'll be all right. I've been through worse.' He leaned across and, most unusually, patted me on the shoulder. 'Just do your best. You can't do more than that. And I'd put money on you.'

'Your dad said you had a talk.'

'Yes.'

'I'm glad it's sorted out. You look very smart. Carlisle?'

'Yes.'

'Your dad and I are going to a dance in Silloth on Wednesday. They say they've spent a fortune on the ballroom. We haven't been there for years. There's a few of us going. He's a good dancer, your dad.'

For the next ten weeks I locked myself in a capsule. By then the homework was drilled in deeply. I could improvise on top of it. I did essays from old exam papers, essays timed to forty-five minutes. Four essays a paper. Two history. Two English. Two Latin. One general paper, plus one scholarship paper each for history and English. On some nights I hovered between exhilaration and exhaustion. I lashed myself on. I set the alarm for seven so that I could read, starting with *David Copperfield*, for an hour before breakfast. I tested my memory of lines from the set books. Revised. Swotted. Re-revised.

The exams and Sarah. The County on Saturday nights. Still the walks late on Friday down to the Moss, especially as the lighter nights were on us. Still the risks and the monthly relief and the risks again. On Saturdays when the rugby finished I would go to the school grounds and run around the playing fields until I'd got a good sweat on. I'd stopped saying my night-time prayers some time ago but I was still on whispering acquaintance with God when necessary.

As exam day drew nearer, the whole world was in that capsule. It became more and more tightly sealed. The town fell away. I knew what was meant by living in a world of your own. I enjoyed it. Only Sarah could break through and she recharged it.

The exams would begin on the Monday. The rugby season was well over so on Saturday I went to the baths, which had dropped out of my schedule. It was early morning and the place was near-empty. I swam with no urgency but, as the lengths went by, I drifted on to half a mile. Swimming seemed the best way to live – life held up by water, water so easy to go through, best to be a fish. So I trawled up and down the small pool, happy on a planet years in the past. Then I floated and let the time pass. The small eddies of water were cradling movements.

I had decided that this should be, like every other Saturday, a day off. But the hours to come, between the baths and the dance at Carlisle, seemed wasted if I did not steal four or five of them and do more revision. But that would mean breaking the schedule I'd followed for months now.

I broke the schedule. Seeing Sarah in the afternoon, walking together, finding our special place, it could all wait for another week.

I was beginning to feel the first signals of a recurrence of the former panic.

On Sunday, before I went to see Sarah, I was with my parents for tea. It was late afternoon, the pub was closed, and I said, would they please not wish me luck the next morning before I went to school, would they not ask how it went, would they not bring it up in any way with anybody in the pub. So stupid. So self-centred. At the time it seemed essential. I needed all the voodoo going.

There was no reply from my mother and father. But the atmosphere was not hostile and I shot off.

It became even more ridiculous.

Hands shaking the next morning, I was convinced I would not be able to hold a pen. It was excessive. It was embarrassing. I could do nothing about it.

I went to school a long way round.

There were seven of us in a small room next to the library. On the door was a sign: SILENCE. EXAMS IN PROGRESS. Our desks were well separated. There was a substantial wall clock imported for the occasion. We had all been at morning assembly.

Two hymns, a lesson, words from Mr Stowe, a short opening and closing prayer. After that I had disappeared into the lavatory, my watch set five minutes ahead.

Mr James was the invigilator for the three-hour stint. He marked essays as he sat at the old-fashioned high desk. The question paper was face down on our table, as was a sort of exercise book specially adapted. Our names, date of birth, form number, school and the date were printed on the front. If we wanted more paper we were told to put up our hands and a nod from Mr James would release us to the ready pile of fresh sheets.

He checked his watch against the clock.

There was a tight choking feeling.

'You may begin. You have three hours.'

I turned over the exam paper. English history.

Four parts. Stick to one part at a time. Scan all the questions. Pick the one you most want to answer. Make a few notes. Begin. Stick to the forty-five minutes.

Why was there a need for the Magna Carta?

It was if my pen found its own way to the page, my mind engaged itself without prompting. Structure emerged out of the thin air, the answer full, rooted in a vault of facts, seasoned with well-taught insights, even stretching to fresh evidence I had picked up from my own reading. My ink glided across the pages, excited into life by a stream of knowledge demanding to be used.

The silence in the room had a buoyancy. Later, I thought it must have been like this in the scriptoria of the monasteries. Silent monks in silent praise intent on translating manuscripts or copying them out, hunting for the right word and colour for the lavishly decorated letters. 'Better far than praise of men is to sit with book and pen'. Now and then I paused, just to hear the silence, to feel part of this community in the room, which, for me, was to become an ideal. Concentration keyed to its pitch to reap in knowledge. What could be better? And this feeling of soaring, of looking down on an earth of order and argument, arguments for and against, giving them a shape. Perhaps I even smiled as my pen filled the pages, eating them up, soon time for more sheets, a feeling of power over these matters. Just the pleasure in being able to deliver.

Why did Henry VIII discard Cardinal Wolsey?
Mr James's Law of Three kicked in.
Discuss the significance of the Gordon Riots.
Had the 1745 uprising any chance of success?
The Jacobites had marched through Carlisle!
'Ten minutes,' said Mr James.
If only they had not stopped at Derby!
The Stuarts were hopeless.
'Five minutes.'
And the Duke of Cumberland! What savagery was that?
Just in time.
'Time up. Pens down, please.'

I was weak, I was happy, I was confident. I was all that was positive for fully ten minutes. And then the anxieties bit in as the second paper – on European history – heaved into view for a two o'clock start. But the anxieties were slighter and now I wanted to be back in that room.

*

When it was all over days later, at midday, what to do? Float over Wigton in a hot-air balloon? Bike out into the country and on and on until I was drained and Sarah would have finished work? Go down to the Spotted Cow with the others, drink coffee and plunder the jukebox? We talked briefly, those of us who had seen out the week, and carefully downplayed our expectations, exaggerated our mistakes. I wanted to hold what I'd done to myself: it would even be difficult to talk to Sarah about it. She was not one for cross- examination, but a few answers would be needed. 'I thought I did OK. I was lucky in the Latin – I'd memorised some of it. In the general paper I wrote about Old Carlisle. I made some of it up but I felt like writing it. We'll just have to wait now.' And bury it. There were bold suggestions of which pub they would go to that night. I said that Sarah and I would join them if they were going out of Wigton. Bromfield, they said, there's a German woman has the pub. It's a cracker, olde worlde, and she doesn't ask your age. We'll be there from seven.

It was only fair to tell my parents that it was all over.

'And what do you think?'

I wanted to give my father an answer. But . . .

'There's no way of telling.' The innocent question had the effect of making me embarrassed and, unfairly, a little annoyed. I covered it, I thought, and later felt ashamed of the feeling.

'As long as you did your best,' he said. 'Your mother's in Carlisle with Frances.'

'I'll be back later,' I said.

'Did Mr James have any comments?'

'No . . .' That seemed rude. 'He won't know until the papers come back. They're sealed up and sent to the examiners.'

He saw and understood that I was impatient to go. 'This is for you.' He handed me an envelope. 'Whatever comes of it. You did your best.'

'Thank you. Thank you very much.'

The rush of gratitude almost made me tearful.

'I'll see you later.'

He lit up and understandingly nodded me away. I felt guilty that I was going to celebrate at another pub in the village of Bromfield.

I stuffed the wad into my back pocket.

We rode to Bromfield along the back lanes. The gang of them filled the snug. Sarah had a Britvic orange. I managed two bottles of Guinness, drank one and a half and that was enough. We made a lot of good-humoured noise. Crisps were ordered to give the occasion a flourish. Two of the lads smoked. The seats and the lower half of the walls were covered in tapestry, which gave the place distinction. The others had come in a couple of cars. I had deliberately missed the offer of a lift by slipping out of school back home. Our bikes gave us an excuse to leave early.

It was still quite light. A soft west wind coming in from the sea, the Solway just a few miles away. I looked around the small village centre of Bromfield. The pub must have been the one my grandfather was bribed – by sixpence – to go to of an evening so that the too many children in the farm cottage could have space to play, even to dance. Those massive Clydesdales in the fields could be the descendants of the horses he had groomed and walked so proudly to the shows. Over there was the small school at which my father had won a scholarship but been unable to take it up because his parents couldn't afford it. I told Sarah this and both of us looked at the school carefully when we left the pub.

'Does he regret it?'

'He never says. It was my mother who told me. I'm beginning to think he does.'

She looked at the school again. 'A nice little place. Like ours in Oulton. Just think what he'd have done.'

'I do. Think that.' We were wheeling our bikes. 'Did you enjoy that pub?' I asked her. 'Did it make you wish you were staying on at school with them?'

'They're a good crowd. I like them. But I don't miss school.' She spoke firmly. 'We can still meet up with them.' We got on our bikes.

We took it slowly. The tracks were sometimes very narrow, blind corners, single file. She stopped, pointed to a lane even narrower than the others. Overgrown.

'If you go down there,' she said, 'it takes you to Black Dippo. To one of the spots we go to. We should celebrate. Don't you think?' She smiled broadly, sparkling. 'Come on,' she said. 'Before it gets too dark!'

Chapter Forty-five

It was thirty pounds!

I caught my father at breakfast.

'This is very good of you.' I held the notes in my hand, or rather my fist. 'I don't know what to say. Thank you.'

'You've said what matters.' He raised his teacup as a toast before taking a drink.

'It's very generous.' I had finished my breakfast. 'I'd better get on.'

I went down to the cellar and began to bring up the crates: the usual – pale ale, Mackeson, Guinness. Each bottle to be wiped, put on the shelves, label to the front, as if ready for drill on their parade ground. Then sluicing out the Gents, sweeping the front before the school buses from the surrounding area came onto Market Hill to unload the paying customers. No chopping firewood needed: it had been a warm week. It was a calm fulfilling routine. I got out my bike.

Where was I going?

It was a Saturday. The town was opening but sleepy still. I went to see William. They could always use another hand for deliveries on a Saturday morning. That was the reason William had been effectively barred from playing rugby for the school despite being such a good athlete. I resented his father for doing that. William never seemed to mind.

We set out in the milk float for the new estates just beyond the old borders on the Carlisle road. A steady routine. Draw up. Reggie, who drove the float, knew all the orders. William and myself went up the paths with the bottles in a small crate, took back the empties, and any note stuck in the neck of a bottle, moved on. Reggie enjoyed trying to outstrip us so that he could pretend to tell us off.

We started at Kirkland Avenue. The men had come in from the night shift. Workers were setting off for their jobs in the town in garages, shops, houses. Some waited at the bus stop to catch the last lap of the earliest bus from Carlisle into Wigton. Boys played football in the car-free avenue. A bald tennis ball. One or two men already in their front gardens. Others going over to the allotments and pigeon sheds, just across the road beside the tip.

The float clattered through the middle of the town to Greenacres and from there to Brindlefield. Once or twice inside the estates, Reggie let us have a go at the wheel. That was worth the morning. When we came back we washed the returned bottles on a clanking, rackety old machine in the dairy.

For two years now, since I went into the sixth form, my mother had made it easier for herself on Saturday by farming me out for dinner. Either I got money for fish and chips, which I brought back and arranged on a plate, which made it a legitimate dinner, or now and then she gave me two shillings chiefly to support the recently opened café upstairs from the bread and cake shop of her old schoolfriend Jean McGuffie.

There were eleven tables. I liked the small table furthest from the window. Joan, who brought the food, was not much older than I was, which made it more acceptable. I had Spam and chips with peas and bread and butter, pudding with custard or cake of the day and tea. I read, ate and didn't linger.

William didn't have to work that afternoon so we decided to bike past Red Dial to Caldbeck. It was six miles away over a gruelling little fell, Brocklesbank, but promising a unique satisfaction once we had got to the top and looked deep down into the bowl in which Caldbeck nested. There was a breathtakingly steep descent, which you could make even hairier by putting the bike into top gear and pedalling hard. It increased the speed to what felt like a dangerous rate, which was what we wanted. No braking allowed until we went over the bridge and past the CALDBECK sign and slowed down.

We parked our bikes next to the pub in the centre of the little town and walked across to the Howk. It was a spectacular waterfall hidden in the woods. As we scrambled up the side of it, I remembered Sarah's smile the night before, and her invitation, such a light 'come on'. The Howk would be a good spot. The trees in full leaf made it like a tunnel. The best thing was to find stepping stones and dart across the intermittent torrent. It was sunny enough when it opened out at the top for William and myself to lie and look at the sky and say very little. The sound of the torrent inside the wood was enough. We drowsed.

The test coming back was to see if we could bike up the steep hill without getting off. We swung sideways across the road, to find a level moment before standing on the pedals and heaving the chain into service. I gave up and got off. William made it. My legs were watery; we took a moment and now it was downhill all the way back to Wigton. It was like swooping down to a nest . . .

I was with Sarah in the alcohol-free snack bar at the County. The interval was over, the band had started up but we were in no rush.

'I'm looking for a job. For the holidays. Or until I get the results and have a better idea of what happens next.'

'You could always offer to help Dad with the hay except he won't pay you and he can be very bad-tempered.'

'I'll think that one over.'

'Let's see. I bet there's vacancies on the dustcart.'

'They've already turned me down.'

'On the dole before you've even started out?'

'Let's go back in!'

I was lucky. Len Arnison had set up a lemonade factory on the Sands just down from the pig market, beside Little Lane. He kept a couple of hounds. He was teetotal, a Methodist. He made use of Dad's buses to the hound trails. As soon as he knew I was looking for a summer job, Len told Dad they were always on the lookout for cheap help in summer. Why didn't I go and talk to his son, Bill, who had taken over the day-to-day running of the business?

I started two days later.

It was no more than a five-minute walk from home. The hours, eight thirty to five thirty, were good and so was the money. I could stay until the end of August if I wanted to, but if trade cooled down at any time I wouldn't be needed. If I planned to leave, a week's notice would be acceptable.

Sarah thought it was funny that I went from a pub to a lemonade factory. I gave up lemonade after two days.

The building, which had been used for storage, was vast, deteriorating and very cold. This was a good summer. On day two I wore a pullover and took a jacket just in case. Wellingtons were essential. The floor was constantly sluiced with running cold water. The bottling machinery had been bought second hand many years ago. Everybody came from Wigton. It was a terrific place to work.

Best of all was going out on the delivery lorry with Wally. The lorry was open-topped. The many crates of lemonade shook to fizzing point as it rolled around twisting lanes and neglected roads. When it rained, there was a tarpaulin.

Summer meant bigger orders and Wally needed a second pair of hands to help him unload the new stock and load up the empties. It was easy work. Real pleasure lay in the variety of places that took in lemonade. All the pubs, all the sweet shops. From big orders, like the Arcade on the Green in Silloth, to the hut in the dunes at West Silloth, to the splendour of Armathwaite Hall overlooking Bassenthwaite Lake, with its ha-ha and grounds, to the back doors of houses – like my grandmother's: she always kept a crate in the porch for those who came across from the park.

The quaint shops left over from previous generations were often run by ageing daughters of the original owner, like Mrs Smith's in West Street. It was a narrow flagstone-paved shop backed by a kitchen-cum-sitting room, two bedrooms upstairs.

You would have thought no one even noticed it, but Wally would take in two mixed crates every week in summer and stay for a chat. Its slender profit was probably made from being open on a Sunday, contrary to rules but nobody bothered. You could get groceries and lemonade, sweets and balls of wool when everywhere else was closed. Charlie Smith, probably her son, lived with her when he was not in Garlands, then brutally called the local lunatic asylum. He worked in the factory when let out and he sang in the choir. On one choir outing to Morecambe, I must have been six or seven, my mother had bought me new shoes. My feet started to blister and bleed after less than an hour walking along the front. Charlie put me on his shoulders and carried me for the rest of the day.

Wally was full of talk. 'We'll have to be quick here. If she gets you talking you'll never know where you are before she's making you a cup of tea and cutting a slice of her cake and you can't refuse. You could lose half an hour'; 'This one always wants help on something or other. She says her husband's useless so would we move a wardrobe from one bedroom to another or nail a chair leg back in.' And 'I have no idea why she sells lemonade. She's rich enough to buy half of Wigton. But how did she get her money in the first place?'

And 'This couple's very queer. The house stands on its own. She and her husband come to the gate with the empties and the exact money for the new crate. Sometimes you see the boy in the doorway or sometimes he'll get out and stand in the porch. Poor lad. He'll be about twelve now but they won't let him out. They've let him get very fat. His mother was their daughter and she took her own life so they got him. But they won't let him go to school or go out to play or go down street shopping with them. I don't know how they get away with it.'

When I got home I had more to tell my parents than before and learned more in return. 'Wally had a bad time at school,' my mother said. 'He was teased. That awful lip. It started as a hare lip. The doctor did an operation on it when he was not much more than a baby and made it ten times worse, his mother said. She would never let him near a doctor again. He used to cover up his mouth with his hand when he talked, poor lad. You couldn't meet a nicer boy.'

I never mentioned Wally's hare lip. I tried my best not to look at it, or be seen or thought to look at it in a way that implied there was something awful about it. Wally never made any reference to it. His stoic attitude must have come from his intense lack of self-consciousness carved out of years of the opposite. His genuine lack of self-pity swept him on, made you like him more.

At the end of the first week I gave half my pay packet to my mother and refused to take money from my father for the morning jobs. They expressed no surprise I was still left with more than I'd had before. And those thirty pounds were beginning to burn a hole in my pocket. I couldn't just let them float away. But I couldn't think of anything I wanted that even approached thirty pounds.

I got a note from Mr James saying that the results were in. Would I like them posted or, which he would prefer, would I like to pick them up? He would be available in the school library the following Wednesday from two to seven.

I was the last to turn up. I waited in the room in which we had taken the exams. My mouth was as dry as on that first exam morning. Valerie opened the door, smiling broadly. 'You next,' she said. She closed the door quietly.

Mr James indicated that I sit opposite him at the large library table.

'Hello. Your results are in the envelope on the table. It's not sealed. You can read them here and we might have a brief discussion. Or you can take them away with you.'

I had not expected to be asked to make a choice. Simple as it was, it seemed difficult. But better here than in front of my parents.

I drew the envelope towards me, took a steadying breath and opened it, clumsily, aware in some part of my mind of the hours I had spent working for these results.

I looked, looked up at Mr James, looked down again.

'Thank you,' I said. I folded the single piece of paper carefully and manoeuvred it back into the envelope. There was a silence.

'Well!' said Mr James. 'I have only one word for it – congratulations!'

A warmth came over me, a return to life, the beginnings of a smile.

'Thank you,' I repeated.

Mr James took control. First he retrieved the envelope and popped a note into it. 'For later,' he said. He leaned forward and dropped his voice as if in fear of being overheard. 'I can't remember seeing results like these before.' He gritted his teeth, not wanting, I was later to think, to let out too much praise, which might do me no good.

For the third time all I could do was nod and say, 'Thank you.'

'You can be proud of yourself.' He managed that with a flourish.

All I felt was shaky. 'You won't tell anybody, will you?'

Mr James barked with laughter. 'Why ever not?'

'I don't know. Not yet, anyway.'

'You feel vulnerable, is that it?'

I looked at Mr James intently.

'How do you know that?'

'Don't worry. But there's a scholarship for the best awards in the region, in any subject. I'll eat my hat if you don't pick that up. Then there'll be a state scholarship. You'll get that.' He laughed. 'Then it'll be out!'

I nodded, blank.

'What do you think you'll do?'

'Think about it.'

'I'll be blunt. I think you ought to try for university, for Oxford. I think you'd get in. Would you mind if I talked to Stan and Ethel about that?'

'I don't know. I don't know what to think.'

'I understand.' He took his time. 'But I would like, at the outset, to clarify one issue with them. The financial side of things.

From what I know of them I think they would find what I have to say helpful.'

'Maybe. But university? And there's national service to get in. It'll be years before I'm earning.'

And Sarah. What about Sarah?

'You won't need to earn. Those scholarships will give you enough to live on. The army . . .'

'Air force.'

'. . . will pay a fair wage. That's what I want to tell your parents. But only if you agree.'

'Well.' I looked at the envelope. 'I haven't got used to this yet.'

'I understand. I'm rushing my fences. Apologies.' He stood up. 'There will be plenty of time to talk these things through. But meanwhile . . .' he held out his hand. We shook very firmly.

Nothing was said, save, when I left the room, there was a last expression of my inarticulate feelings as I turned at the door.

'Thank you, sir. I mean *thank you*.'

When I went in, my father was in the bar with two customers. 'Any news?'

'Yes.'

'I'll come upstairs. Your mother's there already.' To the customers: 'I'll just be a minute or two.'

My mother sat upright and tense at the dining table. Then, firmly, she said, 'I want to get my say in first. Whatever the results are you did your best and that's all you can do.'

My father sat opposite her. Between them was the window looking across Market Hill to the Tower. I sat down feeling odd.

They waited. Suddenly I was fed up with feeling so muzzled.

'Mr James said he can't remember seeing results like these before. He talked about me trying to get into Oxford University.' My father's eyes glazed over.

I handed over the letter. My father scanned it in moments, my mother glanced at it, put it down and smiled broadly.

'Well,' she said, 'that's a relief.'

'"Can't remember results like these."' My father spoke the words as if blowing out a perfect smoke ring. He repeated, 'Mr James said that, did he? Well.' Then murmured, 'He must know about these things.'

'Yes. I owe him a lot. And the others. English was – OK as well. Mr Blacka.'

'But in the end it was you who did it,' my father said, adding, awkward at the word, 'congratulations.'

'A good job we didn't go to Workington then,' my mother was to say, later.

'There's this,' my father said. He held up the note Mr James had tucked into the results envelope.

'I haven't read it.'

It was short, handwritten, on school notepaper in an envelope from the headmaster's office. *Congratulations. The school is very proud of you. Well done! Best wishes for the future. Ivan Stowe.*

My father had still not recovered from Mr James's comment. 'Oxford University.' He might as well have been talking about the rings of Saturn. 'That's where the toffs go, Ethel.'

'It won't happen,' I said, 'but—'

'Very good of him to say so!' My mother was shy with pleasure. 'I've always liked Mr James. Whenever you meet him on the street he stops to talk.'

'I'll go and have a word with him,' my father said. 'I'll go tomorrow morning, catch him in just after breakfast and find out more about this university idea'.

'Off to see Sarah?'

'Yes.'

'I thought so. I have a good view of the phone box from behind the bar.'

'You should have been a spy!'

'What do you mean "should have been"? She is.' Dad smiled at her. 'Nothing that happens here goes by her.' We laughed, gently, fondly, together. It was a good moment.

*

We sat on the low stone wall just past Paisley's farm. It was as near to a bench as Oulton got to public seating.

Sarah studied the letter before handing it back.

'It's marvellous . . . good for you.' Her tone was rather tentative: part of her was already sensing difficult consequences. She pulled herself together. 'As long as it doesn't make you big-headed!' Then she kissed me, warmly, on the mouth.

'It's a pity there isn't a dance on tonight.' She looked around. 'I don't feel like a walk. We can't go into the pub here, even for a Britvic – Dad would kill us.' She hunted around. 'We could have a cigarette.'

'We have to move on.'

We went further down towards the tarns.

I was just a learner and not keen. Sarah already smoked like a grown-up.

'Don't worry,' she said. 'I've some mints.'

The cigarettes were enough to keep us occupied for a while.

'Do you think we could have a week off together in summer?'

'Not in August. I told Arnison's I would definitely stay until the end of August unless they didn't need me.'

'Early September then. The bank's asking when I want to take time off for summer holidays.'

'I could buy a tent.'

'I'm not going on holiday in a tent!'

'Why not? We could pitch it wherever we liked. We could go to a café for something to eat or make our own, like I used to do in the Scouts.'

'Tents can stay with the Scouts! No thank you.'

'We could go to Morecambe.'

'Old folk go there. And, anyway, we couldn't stay anywhere, could we?'

'That leaves youth hostelling.'

'I enjoyed that,' she said. 'We met lots of new people.'

'We could go along the Roman Wall, Hadrian's Wall, this time, from Bowness to Wallsend. It's supposed to be a good walk.'

'Let's see if I can get that week off first.' She paused. 'Or why don't we go to Oxford?' She laughed. 'Or is that jumping the gun? I'd like to have a look at it.'

As we walked back, she said, 'You've worked for it.'

As we passed by the Paisley farm Sarah dropped her voice. 'There are three brothers there. Two of them about my age. We all went to school together. We always got on but nothing more. Word is that they've seen us down in Black Dippo. One of them follows the hounds and has a pair of those German binoculars. The little buggers! We'll find a different spot.' It was not difficult to sense her anger.

She brooded on it and it began to fester. Although she had apparently lightly dismissed it, it had embarrassed her and made her angry. Who did they think they were, those Paisley boys, boys she had known since early childhood, with whom she had shared a classroom in the village school, played together, boys on a farm bigger than her father's and generational, passed down, as it would be again. And they had spread their spying around the village, she could see that in the mocking eyes, the twitch into a giggle, the over-hearty remarks – 'Still keen on him?' The speck of irritation grew into an inflammation. She would deal with it.

'It was a bold thing to do,' I said. 'I wish I'd been there.'

'I couldn't have done it if you had been there.'

We had walked way down the road towards the Solway. The sunset was delivering one of its gaudier displays – the sky laced with peach and milky light greys, behind that the crimson beginning to gather around the sinking sun sliding into Scotland, broken clouds chasing through the sky.

We stopped at a gate and sat on the top to look across the miles to the sword-shaped Solway Firth from which the faintest salt smell drifted inland.

'It was because of you, really,' she said, as if a testament were finally being tortured out of her. 'It just made me mad the way they wanted to have a go at us, but mostly at you, I thought.

And,' she took a quick breath, 'you're different from that lot. I mean, not better – but you have your own ways. You're much – you're much gentler than they are.' She blushed. 'And you want to hear what I have to say.' She looked at me boldly, directly. 'I'm not having them spoiling anything.'

She slid off the gate rather awkwardly but not so awkwardly that we did not hold each other close, and for some time.

Chapter Forty-six

I got to Oxford just before twilight when a thin October fog was drifting aimlessly along the streets. I had read about Oxford and the fog wreathing its way through magnificent buildings. I was glad I hadn't missed it. I checked in at the college and dumped my suitcase in my allocated room. I went out immediately to rove around. In a circular sent to all the boys applying for entrance, I had been told that dinner would be served in the Hall at 7 p.m.

I turned right outside the college, looked up and down the curving High Street. Another college, I assumed, was opposite Queen's: further down on the left there was a bridge and the nudge of an ancient tower. Even though the university was 'down', on holiday, the street to me seemed characterised by studious-looking young men and one or two young women. They seemed to drift like the fog. They were on another plane. Or so I thought then. Everything fitted snugly into the cliché I had rapidly compiled before coming to the place. But the sight of it was fresh, like an old painting come to life, become a film.

I turned right and went up to a high-spired church, right again, and came across the domed Radcliffe Camera, the dominating library flanked by yet another college: All Souls with its spires and the high gates to keep in the Distinguished Scholars.

I floated with the fog. Small pubs that looked as old as some of the colleges, shops devoted to college scarves, opulent book-shops, more colleges, a museum, all melding into a vision of learning, which was to be pursued in architectural masterpieces and even now, when most of the students – called undergraduates

– were on holiday, the place and the few who remained emanated learning and, I thought, the quiet, confident magnificence of study. It was intoxicating. I had never dreamed that a whole city could be anything like this. I felt lifted into a different sphere in those two hours. In those meagre two hours of ignorant awe, a fantasy of centuries of Scholarship and Thought was crystallised. I was smitten. It was a place for the privileged and for those who had and would rule over us.

Where did I fit in?

Dinner in the Hall at long tables. A few boys were from the north. Queen's College had a regional connection to the north; its initial funding had come from there. Glad to be through that and back to my room – as big as our sitting room, a cubicle bathroom, crammed bookcases, photos and paintings on the walls, battered furniture, an open fire, a sort of luxury I had never seen or imagined. Before I went to sleep I thought through the possible questions in store.

As soon as my father and Mr James had decided I would try for Oxford, I'd started to spend two or three hours after work back at the Timetable. After the first week in September, youth hostelling on our skim across the Roman Wall, dipping into Hexham, even managing to get to Lindisfarne – lorries in particular were generous to young hitchhikers – I went back to school.

It got me out of the house in the day.

I was allotted a very small room next to the headmaster's lavatory. I still went to morning assembly and the school choir practice. I had dinner in the canteen, then took most of the afternoon off – walking for two or more hours out towards Rosley or along the minor road to Thursby, and then got back home at the usual time.

It was not difficult to get into the routine. It was a relief. I was back at work. Near the end of September, a fortnight before I was due to go to Oxford for the entrance exams, Mr Stowe called me into his study.

'Sit down.' Kindly said. He pointed to a chair the other side of the large desk. He was not a man to waste time. 'One of the features of these exams is that you will be interviewed after you have taken them by those who will be marking your papers. They'll have your A level results in front of them. I disapprove of this procedure. In Oxford and Cambridge the interview is of disproportionate significance.' He enunciated the last nine syllables with slow distaste. He was formal, but once you were in the sixth form he tried to be more of an equal than a teacher to a pupil. I relaxed more. And, retrospectively, I was flattered. He continued, 'It allows privileged boys with mediocre marks from certain boarding schools to go there as if it were a finishing school. But that's Establishment England.' The dissenting Methodist in him had spoken. 'Now. Business.

'There will be two or three of them. Tutors, dons they like to call themselves. They will be very polite and clever. What they want is to hear your opinions. Sometimes this will be on the subjects you have chosen to answer in the exam papers – they'll have glanced at those. You'll be able to deal with that. Then they'll rove around. "Do you think that Eden was right to go into Suez?" You spoke well on that in the school debate, and I have a hunch they'll want to know what someone like you thinks. They'll already have a cardboard cut-out caricature of Northern Working-class Scholarship Boy – quite an original beast for them. So I wouldn't be surprised. "Should we abandon the atom bomb?" Again, when we debated against Carlisle Grammar you were very emphatic about that. Don't try to soften it down. If you feel emphatic, *be* emphatic.' He afforded himself a smile. 'But watch your language!

'They might go right off your spectrum – "What was Einstein's contribution to physics?" If you can give it a shot, do so, but tell them it's just a shot. If you have nothing to say, tell them that. They might want to talk about your background. Don't be embarrassed. They will be talking in what you would call "posh" voices, but I believe that they will be kindly disposed to you. Stick up for your background – as I know you do. I've heard you say, "It is rich in everything that matters." A good phrase to have up your sleeve. Towards the end they'll ask if you have anything to ask them. That's up to you, the mood of the moment. Don't be afraid to say no.'

The hall was full. I had a place near the back. After the A levels it was familiar. As were one or two of the questions. Just history. Two papers – one in the morning, one in the afternoon. The interview – the viva – the next morning. They asked history questions and then the one about the atom bomb; a question asking me if I thought that 'the cinema would eventually replace the novel', which I found I could tackle, and then a couple about my background, something of an anthropological investigation. I spent another evening browsing around the city. I could understand how it seduced people and made them feel special just by being there.

An early-morning train took me back to Planet Ordinary.

The nerves had saved themselves up for when I received the letter from Queen's a week later. My mother had brought it up and put it on my plate. Clearly marked 'Queen's College, Oxford'. Dad was still in bed. I opened it. The paper was thick, cream-coloured, grand. My mother refused to look. She had her back to me, watching the poached egg. It was easier without Dad.

'I'm in. And they've given me a scholarship.'

Mr Stowe announced it after assembly in the morning.

It's difficult to write this but the Oxford scholarship had a worrying effect on my father. We had scarcely seen each other the first six years of my life. After the war and the year in intense cohabitation we had been together in the Station Road house but part of a strained group. He worked hard, never less than two jobs. When I walk around nearby London parks nowadays and see and hear younger dads skilfully shepherding their children, I am taken with the difference of times. Being a father today in middle-class England is a devoted hands-on business. Not back then. Now and then I'd go to see Carlisle United with my dad but soon I was going on my own or with William. We were closest together in the pub and that was the best of it, when I was working for him or guarding the bar during the dead hour of the evening.

He never – not once – chivvied me to do homework. He was reluctant for me to stay on into the sixth form. He was pleased about the A-level results. But the scholarship to Oxford University discombobulated him for a while. It was in the *Cumberland News*: 'Wigton Boy Gets Scholarship to Oxford'. A small photograph and a smaller paragraph but enough to make him famous on his walk up street and to regulars in the pub. Something had been triggered. Perhaps a deeply buried dream of his own had surfaced and that the scholarship was for me and not him was neither here nor there. It was a shock, a wholly unanticipated new reality for both of us.

The man I knew became added to by someone else. He began to regard me as an excruciating cross between the *Encyclopaedia Britannica* and the Delphic Oracle and, in some even more mysterious way, a person to be deferred to. I would be called downstairs to be introduced to a customer who had seen the *Cumberland News* and stand in severe embarrassment for ten minutes, like a three-year-old colt being shown off at Doncaster sales. He would tell me that this shopkeeper or that bowling chum had asked after me and would appreciate a word. It was a well-meant torture. I had to stick it out. There was a customer from Carlisle who brought his twelve-year-old son with him sometimes. My father would say that I would 'help' him (he was slow at school) and he was sent upstairs to be 'helped out'.

Many years later I got to the root of it. Just as it took more than fifty years for Mr James to tell me he had been to see my parents to urge them to let me stay on at school for O levels, so it took much the same time for my father to tell me what Mr James had said to him after the news of the Oxford scholarship. It had somehow knocked him off centre so much that he was uncomfortable to live with for a while.

Once again the two men met. And yet again they kept to themselves this exchange for decades.

It was later, when my father had his first intimation of the serious nature of his lung cancer. He liked me to sit by the bed and talk when I came to Cumbria, which I did even more frequently because of his condition. He liked to ask me questions impossible to answer – 'Why can't you get the BBC to do this?', 'Why can't you tell John Major to do that?' I could usually divert it but not without effort. And I felt ungenerous. What's a question?

One time he said, 'Mr James.' He shook his head admiringly. 'After those exam results and then Oxford he came down and told me they were "outstanding", that you had a "rare" – that was his word – "capacity for hard work". And that your marks were "nearly flawless".'

So that was it. Mr James's determination to firm up my father's will to support me had led him to use language which had bowled my father over. It had worked in its way, but it had also driven my father unbalanced – for a while.

Most of all, my father wanted us to talk about Important Matters. I felt churlish and ungrateful but most of all I was tongue-tied. What did I know compared with him? His experience was vast, mine a thimbleful. His views had been developed over years in the war and the factory and the pub, with some of the men who came in and talked good sense from a close knowledge of whatever subject it was. He was like the editor of an oral newspaper and those men *knew*. Whenever I talked to them I had the sense to listen most of the time.

My mother protested – 'Leave him alone, Stan!' I began a quiet rebellion. It died down but it never altogether vanished and remained an uncomfortable strand in my life. I suppose you could say that for a while he 'lost himself': the worst thing you could do in our town. But then, gradually, thankfully, he became his old self again. What deeply buried lost hopes and pride and pain had been stirred up to transform him? God alone knows. But eventually it ebbed away.

*

A month after the result from Oxford I got a letter from the government telling me that, alongside thousands of others, my birth date excluded me from national service. The universal call-up would cease. Those born after May 1939 would be exempt. I wrote to Queen's asking if I could come up in 1958 and not, as previously agreed, 1960 after national service. They wrote back politely, saying that all the places were taken for 1958 and I would have to stick to 1960. It was a sickener.

I didn't say anything to my parents. After all, the scholarship still stood.

I called Sarah and asked if we could meet after her work. If we got to Bromfield at six thirty, soon after opening time, my guess was that very few, if any, would be in the snug bar. We could eat. I'd noticed they advertised Scotch eggs and 'freshly made sandwiches'. She could easily make up a reason for being a couple of hours late back home.

I told her about the letter. 'Is it so bad?'

'It means I won't be going to Oxford for about three years.'

'You could get a job.'

'After three years I'll have forgotten everything I've learned.'

'National service would have been the same. Even worse. We wouldn't have seen each other for months on end.'

I did not take comfort in that, which perhaps Sarah thought I might.

'What job?' I sounded, to myself and therefore certainly to Sarah, quite tetchy.

'You're the brain-box,' she said. 'Something or other.'

Fields of opportunity failed to appear in my mind's eye.

'What sort of job could you get that you would have to tell them that the most you could give it was about two and half years?'

'Why not in a pub? You know how to do it.'

'For two and a half years!'

'There are worse jobs.'

'I suppose I, or we, could take off around the world, work in bars and hotels along the way. One or two people do that. Writers.'

'Bang goes my job, then.'

She had finished the Britvic.

'Another?'

'Please.'

'And a Scotch egg?'

'No, thanks.'

'What are you really thinking about?'

The bar was still empty but Sarah looked around.

'What about us?'

I waited. I too had made the calculations but hoped that she had not gone there. 'About three years before you go to university. Three years at university. Six years?'

'I've thought about that,' I said.

'It's a long time.'

'It is but we could get engaged. We could even get married before I go to Oxford. Mr James was married when he went to Oxford after the war.'

'Maybe we could.'

'You don't sound too enthusiastic.'

'I'm not sure it would work.'

'I could just jack the whole thing in and get a job here, now. Eric went into local government at Carlisle after his O levels. He seems happy enough. I think I could get in. Why not?'

'After all that work you did?'

'I liked doing it. I didn't do it because I wanted to go to university. I did it because I wanted to do it. I've started to have doubts about Oxford now that I've seen it. It isn't my world, Sarah, and it certainly isn't the be-all and end-all. We could get married in a year or so and stay here.'

'You have to propose first.'

'That wouldn't be hard. You'd have to accept – that could be the hard bit!'

She laughed and shook her head.

'What would Mr James think? And your dad, especially your dad?'

'Well. I proved it to him, maybe I proved it for him. I could go to night school. Irwin went to night school and got what he wanted out of it. I like it in Wigton. With you and everybody else.'

'Are you serious?'

'Yes. I am.'

'I think you're mad.' She sipped at the new glass of Britvic.

'I don't know. As soon as I said that, just then, about us staying here, I felt relief. I felt free. I was making my own decisions.'

Sarah did not respond.

'There's plenty to do here,' I said.

'I hope you're not doing this for me. I'm not going to be the one who held you back.'

'You're the one who's brought me to my senses.'

'You say that now.' She shook her head once again. It seemed that mime was winning against words.

Neither of us spoke for a while.

'What do you say?'

'I don't know,' she said.

'How can I convince you?'

'I'm sorry. I don't know.'

It was drizzling when we got outside. The continuous drops of light rain soon soaked us as we biked back to Oulton. Sarah was shivering when we got to the farm.

'You'd better go right in. I'll belt back home.'

We kissed each other.

'We'll think of something,' she said. She didn't sound altogether convinced.

But when I swept back to Wigton in the pelting rain, my bike knowing the road home like a horse headed for its stable, I was full of the new plans. I was soaked. Rain was streaming down my face, like convulsive tears. My trousers clung clammily and coldly to my legs, my small headlamp was all but rendered useless by the density of the drizzle, but I felt that a great burden had been lifted off me. I had done what had been put in front of me.

Just like I ate the breakfast I was given. A burden of expectation had grown out of a simple desire to learn as much as I could and to be tested on it and that burden was gone. I didn't have to go to university or prove anything.

When, soaked to the skin, I came into Wigton, I decided to pedal around its empty streets, down alleys that connected with other alleys in the central spider's web.

Back home I ignored the comments on my sodden state, parked the bike, ran up the stairs leaving a trail of water and locked myself in the bathroom.

I wrung out in the bath what clothes I could and hung the others on the pulley. I cleared the bath and filled it with hot water in which I soaked myself, ducking my head to make sure that nothing was left cold.

I stood on the stairs in my dressing-gown until my mother came out of the kitchen. She brought me a hot pie.

Safe and warm in bed, I picked up *Tonio Kroger*, bit into the pie and felt clearer-headed about who I was and what I would do than I had for many months. I would stay. The place, the people, parents, friends, I was clamped to it and happy to be.

There was a comforting rumble of sounds from downstairs.

'It's a bit of a shaker,' said Mr James, 'but it needn't be a setback. What do your parents think?' We were in a corner of the hall, just below the stage, the only quiet space Mr James could find.

'They don't know. Nobody knows,' I lied. 'I'd rather nobody did until it's sorted out.'

'They sent me a personal letter too! They think very highly of you. They want you there, that's for sure. And they were impressed by the viva. I passed that on to the head.'

He smiled. I could see that he was trying to help me over what he saw as a disappointment.

He waited. It was my turn.

'It's a long time to wait.'

'It'll go by like a flash. You'll see.'

'I am a bit . . .'

'Down? I can see it. Any ideas on what you might do in the interval?'

'One or two.'

'It'll come to you.'

'Won't I forget all I've learned with such a long time off?'

'You must make sure you don't. You're always welcome to come back here and use the library.'

'Thank you. Did you enjoy being at Oxford?'

'The first year, before the war, was great fun. When I went back I was married and it was after the war – a whole different experience. A lot of us were married by then.'

'Was it harder?'

'Harder?'

'Being married.'

'I felt much more secure.' He hesitated. 'There could be another way out of all this.'

Mr James was playing every inch the magician. And now the Rabbit out of the Hat.

'Are you fed up with taking exams?'

'Yes.'

'I don't blame you.' Mr James laughed aloud, the almost honking laugh he employed sometimes. Not a real laugh, a signal – in this case of a gear change. 'Why don't you go round the world? Work your way round. You'll never get a better chance.'

'I'm thinking about it.'

'Good. There are cheap tickets across Europe for students. You could hitchhike. You've done that before. I believe you could get casual work as you went along . . . It's just the experience you need.' Mr James enthused himself. 'The rich used to send their sons on a Grand Tour after they had finished school. This could be yours.'

To some extent I was caught up in Mr James's enthusiasm but I knew I was only trying to please him.

'Of course it would be better if you could find a pal to go with but my wager would be that you would find one along the way.'

The memory of the conversation with Sarah kicked in hard. 'It's a good idea. Maybe. I need time to think about it.'

I felt that Mr James was realising that I was in danger of moving away from his influence.

'There is one other option,' he said, dropping his voice although we were the only two in the school hall. 'The Oxford colleges organise their entrance exams in three groups. Roughly about ten colleges in each. Queen's was in the first group. The second comes up at the beginning of March. One of the colleges in that group is my old college, Wadham. I rang up the bursar. He confirmed what I had thought, which is that those who obtain a place in March would be accepted for the following October – that is to say, you'll have to wait for no more than a few months. If, that is, you get a place.'

That changed things. Didn't it? Or was I still in the same mind as I had been up to five minutes ago – to abandon all exams, to be liberated?

'We would accommodate you in the school if necessary over the next few months – that would only be fair, I think, under the circumstances.'

'When do I have to make my mind up?'

Mr James paused. So his hunch had been right! He gave as much loose rein as he could.

'The bursar said that if we put you down, your name, in the first half of January, that would be perfectly acceptable. I told him about the situation at Queen's and he pointed out that such circumstances are not uncommon.'

I think my reply surprised, even shocked him.

'Do you mind if I think it over?'

'Of course! But of course!'

'Thank you. Thank you very much.' I left. I felt he felt I had let him down.

*

'So what do you think?' I began.

'It's what you think that matters.'

It was a bright, imminently frosty afternoon. To pass the time we had decided to bike to Silloth and walk along the shore of the West Beach. The tide was well out, the sand only a little wrinkled. It felt comfortably ours. A few clouds seemed stuck against the sky, heading for a clearly etched Scotland. There were two men with dogs and two solitary walkers. Otherwise we had the beach to ourselves. The salty air nipped sharply at our faces.

'I don't think that's true,' I said.

'I think it is.'

She squeezed my linked arm but would not commit herself further.

'I was all set until he brought up this other college.'

'And now you're not?'

'It changes things,' I said, 'or it could. If I got in, then I'd be off to university in a few months, not in three years.'

'But the other day you said you didn't want to go.'

'I don't. I didn't!'

'But "it changes things". What things?'

'The length of time we'd have to wait. Unless you'd agree to get married when I was at university. Say, in the second year.'

'You've worked it out!' She smiled. 'You are a cunning beggar.'

'But I still think what we decided the other day was better. We both like it here. Why should we leave? We could have holidays abroad – but why leave for university and then who knows where?'

Sarah took her time. She looked away. She delivered her words resolutely. 'I'm not sure what I should do if you go to university.'

'There you are.'

'There I am *what*?'

'Being honest.'

'You're in a fix, aren't you?'

'I'll get through it. It was the surprise. Mr James, out of nowhere, turning up with this new proposition. It's brought back all the hornets in my head I was rid of after our last talk. Now

I'm asked to be back inside some sort of system that doesn't fit me or you or us.'

'Let's just walk for a bit.'

I took her hand. We strolled into the beginning of sunset in the west, beyond the fishing villages. The industrial coastline was a few miles away past a range of sand dunes. On some Sundays my mother would have brought me here, sometimes with William. The best sport was to find the highest dunes and jump off the top of them into the deep sand the sea washed up.

'We could walk on to Allonby,' I said. 'We used to have donkey rides there.'

'What is it, when the tide comes in up the Solway?'

'It can outpace a galloping horse.'

'That's it.' She stopped and looked at the distant flatness of the sea. 'It doesn't look dangerous.'

'It could be a killer,' I said. 'English and Scottish armies tried to cross it when it was like this. When the tide came in, they drowned.'

'I wish I'd taken history more seriously.' She laughed. 'I think I'm just saying that!' She stopped. 'Time we went back. You don't have to make up your mind today. Mr James said after Christmas. Why not wait till then? See how you feel.'

'*We* feel.'

'If you like. Come on. There's a dance to go to. Come on!'

The problem was to get a job to carry me through to Christmas. Arnison's was out. Nothing else came up. I still did the morning round for the pub and there was enough left from the thirty pounds and what I had saved from Arnison's to keep me going. Back to school was not an option. The Oxford scholarship had done for my time there. I could not endure the idea of being in the house for most of the day. I took up daily swimming again. I did not tell my parents about Mr James's suggestion.

It was the post office that came to my rescue. It began to hire casual workers as the Christmas rush built up. Students were the perfect fit. My mother told me who to see. I was in work from the last week in November. Until then I fretted, read more and more, unsuccessfully tried to take up the piano and failed to come to a solution about university. Sarah was fed up with talking about it.

I sorted the post, delivered it in the old town, and bought a pair of boots at Johnston's for when the rain would come. Sarah got me a brown duffel coat for Christmas. Big pockets, fake bone toggles, a warm hood. I felt I had been initiated into a new order. I bought her what looked like a gold bracelet from Snaith's. I wanted no more than we were lucky enough to have. Neither did Sarah, I believed. But her reservations would not subside.

Chapter Forty-seven

Overnight rain had washed it, a bright sun gave it polish. Wigton had cleaned itself up on the last day of the year. I went out after we had heavily stocked up in the pub for the night ahead, always the busiest. Nothing to do until I met Sarah after her half-day at the bank. It was an uncommon sensation, having nothing to do, no objective, no plan. It made the town seem new, even a little foreign.

As I walked up King Street on that fine New Year's Eve morning, I would have been aware of the separations, even divisions, but also a cohesion. Shopkeepers were sweeping the pavements in front of their premises as I had just done and it was rare that anyone of any background passed by without 'How do?' or 'Aa reet?'

The dialect was the most common tongue in the town. Not among the better folk. A few, like young Mr Ritson, stopped me to talk about Oxford. He had been to a local public school and his accent was Queen's English BBC perfect. My mother admired that in him but would have been embarrassed if I had imitated it.

So far I have only rarely used the dialect here although it was the basic language of the town. It was a mixture of Old English, Norse, and many words picked up after 1066 from French. But what distinguished our town's dialect and its deeply absorbed local twang, was the element of Romany from the gypsies who camped behind the cemetery in winter and words from India where many of the men had been with the army.

Wigton prided itself on the impenetrability of its 'tongue'. Only when circumstances allowed it without embarrassment could I recover it. 'Deke's yon gadji ower yonder wid t' baary mort.' 'Wigton speaks a language that the strangers do not know' was much-valued evidence of the town's unique quality.

After Mr Ritson had wished me luck, I went down Union Street, drawn there yet again to see if I could divine just by staring in which house my mother had been born. I went to the bottom of the street into the yard in which my parents had had their first house.

Vince was mending his bike, which was upside down outside his house. 'Wat's te 'ere for?'

'Just nosing about.'

'Thou can hod this while aa tek off t'tyre.'

I did. A spoon did the job. Vince looked up and smiled.

'Did aa heer say thou was gan to some posh spot? For a mare skjeul?'

'We'll see.'

'Beats me. So what's on toneet?'

'Some do in Wigton.'

'Fancy a pint?'

'I don't like going into pubs in Wigton.'

'Ethel git mad?'

'No, but . . .'

'It's ganna be a quiet neet.'

'No dance?'

Vince stretched his back and shook his head. He had tempered his dialect. Most of the dialect speakers were much broader.

'Not efter last yeer's riot.'

Already then, caught between two tongues, I flinched at my local dialect, not through shame but because to use it seemed patronising. Yet BBC English felt affected even before it reached my tongue.

I went to Park House.

When I said I was going to McGuffie's café for dinner because my mother was too busy, my grandmother said, 'I've never heard of such a thing. You'll have your dinner here.'

Afterwards I walked through the three Show Fields, surprised to find them empty on a New Year's Eve, and out past Arnison Mink Farm. To spin out the time, I went into the grounds of the Nelson School. The building was exactly the same as it had been when I arrived in my brown blazer just over seven years earlier. I stood way back, and just looked at it. What a chunk of my time had been passed in that place! I tried to summon up life-changing recollections to make this moment significant, but I failed.

By now Sarah would be near the end of her shortened afternoon stint. She came out of the back door of the bank, a little flushed. She noticed I noticed.

'A New Year's glass of sherry,' she said. 'It's strong, isn't it?'

'Let's go down to the Spotted Cow for a cup of tea. William might be in.'

I wheeled her bike down the street, beginning to crowd as businesses closed early, last-minute shoppers made a dash for last-minute provisions and the men from the factory, released from the shift, piled into the pubs. The New Year's Eve spirit was spreading.

Only two of the tables were free. We sat in the corner. William wasn't there.

'You'd better have some water. You're flushed.'

She pulled out her powder compact to camouflage the effect of the sherry. I collected two teas, one glass of water and one thick slice of home-made gingerbread. For some reason I thought it would help with the flush.

'Is it better now?'

'Yes. Don't worry.'

'I thought only little old ladies drank sherry because it was harmless,' she said.

'Some little old ladies could teach you a thing or two. Some of them come to the side of the bar on Mondays and other quiet afternoons to stock up. Think you can make it back to Oulton?'

'Don't be daft.' She took a draught of water. Then another. 'That's better.'

'Tea with no milk's supposed to be best.'

She took my advice.

'Better. Ready to go.'

'I thought I'd go in and have a word with your dad about tonight.' There was no response. 'You're going to be very late back. I don't want him sending out a search party.'

'How late?'

'Three, four o'clock, might even be later by the time we've got round.'

'I can talk to him.'

'I can tell him about first-footing.'

'He'll know about that.'

'I could tell him about the parties. The Hadwins in the bank, the Ismays, the Johnstons for a start.'

'I'll do that. Best if you want to come back now and then go right back to Wigton.'

'Not come and pick you up?'

'No. That's too much. And I'd rather tell him in my own time.'

As soon as I walked in my father said, 'Jack's going to be late. Could you take care of the Darts Room?'

It was the easiest room until they closed the board at eight o'clock and put in more tables.

I enjoyed it. The place was just warming up. I knew most of those who came in. The Pearson brothers came to snatch a last game or two before the board was closed down. Maurice and Dickie, who knocked about everywhere together, made it their first stop from the East End. Their occupation of the room's centre made it trickier to carry a tray of drinks. Wives were out in numbers. Jack Atkinson was beginning to squeeze backing chords out of the accordion in the Singing Room. Kenneth had not yet turned up but this would be a big night and he would not miss it.

The pub felt like a bit of Wigton built on its deepest foundations – the workday faces, the accent, the talk of football, dogs and gossip, the *Cumberland News*. Tom Mix was there in the corner of the bar, allowing himself an extra pint and a deeper drawl. Mr Johnston, next door but one, had brought in his dog unusually early for a longer evening walk and treated himself to the first of two gin and peppermints. Harry was helping out behind the bar, crisp white shirt sleeves neatly folded up above the elbow. Lily, his wife, as always looking spectacularly glamorous, was in the kitchen with her mother. Frances and Cathy were in their place, local humanity was in harmony and all was right with the world. I wished Sarah could see this. We could have stayed there until after midnight with no doubt of certain happiness and a much better farewell to the old year.

Jack Waters arrived. I went upstairs and put my best suit on. White shirt. Tie. Doctored quiff. The duffel coat.

Sarah was in her usual parking place, at the house of her parents' friends. We walked around to the bank. The streets were just beginning to crackle. The Hadwins' party was, as before, in their large sitting room above the bank. They had laid on a splendid and expensive buffet – cold meats, salads, small sausages, cold fillets of trout, desserts galore . . . Candles were perched everywhere. The Christmas decorations, heavy, ornate, old-fashioned, were still on display. There was a pile of logs beside the open fire.

'Ah! Our scholar,' said Mr Hadwin, over-welcoming, shooting out his hand to me and ignoring Sarah, 'welcome to our humble abode.' He wore a navy-blue three-piece suit, the waistcoat buttons under some strain.

'Where do we leave our coats?' Sarah said, extra politely.

'Oh! Janice will take them.' He waved.

Janice, who worked in Mr Hadwin's bank at much the same level as Sarah worked in hers, collected our coats rather frozen-faced.

'You know each other?' Mr Hadwin seemed surprised. Janice nodded.

'Very well,' said Sarah, untrue, but some mischief had crept in.

'Everybody knows everybody in Wigton, don't they?' said Mr Hadwin. 'That's what we found since we came here. It's a true community.'

Although I would have agreed with that, something about the way Mr Hadwin said it made me want to object. But it was early and I was a guest and uncomfortable in the rather formal atmosphere. And, besides, he was being generous. I held my tongue.

'Here you are,' he said. A drinks tray turned up borne by another junior employee from his bank. Had they volunteered? Sarah smiled warmly as she took an orange juice.

'Try the fizzy wine. Not champagne. But not bad.'

Sarah raised her glass of orange. I took a glass of light ale.

'You ought to consider banking when you've done Oxford,' he said. 'We need people like you.' He waved his free hand around the room. 'It isn't such a bad life.'

Alex, his daughter, came across. She had settled well into the school but it was here that we saw her at her most confident.

'You're not to hog him.' She smiled particularly widely at Sarah, who was happy to accept it as a warm welcome and returned the greeting. 'Lots of people here you know.' Alex talked to me and then led me away. 'There's somebody you should meet.' Sarah hesitated for a moment and then, briskly, she went to talk to a group from school.

There were those whom both of us knew from school, and in my case also from the town. It was a double generational. Mrs Hadwin played Victor Sylvester and then Glenn Miller on the gramophone. As time went on, one, two, three of the older couples, on the suggestion of Mr Hadwin, shuffled around the central cleared carpet in time to the music. By then the younger set were deep in the detail of their friends' lives.

'*Au buffet!*' summoned Mr Hadwin.

The older set, who felt they had been made to wait rather too long, immediately fell into an orderly queue.

After everyone had eaten, Alex tried to introduce charades; it became obvious there were no takers. Soon we were all dancing again and Alex introduced 'Excuse Me' waltzes and, as time went on, rock 'n' roll.

'Would you mind if we went up to the church for "Auld Lang Syne"?' I asked.

'I was looking forward to your views on our economic outlook,' said Mr Hadwin.

'I always go,' I said. 'The whole town goes.'

'Is it a community event?'

'Yes.'

'Well. Of course. Maybe I'll go myself.'

'Thank you very much. It was a good party.'

'I'm coming with you!' Alex was dragging on her coat. Others followed. We made for St Mary's.

The pubs were decanting in droves. They came out of the Swan, the Lion and Lamb, the Crown, the Half Moon, the Crown and Mitre, the Kildare. They flowed out of the King's Arms in King Street, from houses in the old town, Water Street, Church Street, Union Street, and the new Brindlefield, Kirkland, Greenacres estates.

The crowd seemed to be all of Wigton. They knew what to do. A large circle was formed, which could be said to have begun at the church door. It ballooned out, across the High Street, up towards the auction, pressed against the churchyard wall, growing by the minute. Half a dozen members of the town silver band played tunes you could sing to. Jack McGee of the Salvation Mission had brought his big drum and kept time. Jimmy Hodgson stood on a box and waved. The crowd was 360 degrees friendly. It seemed it would never stop growing. Little circles developing round the big circle.

Then big booms from Jack McGee, gathering strength all the way, and the trumpet blew a note, which announced the countdown.

Ten! Nine! Eight! Seven! Six! Five! Four! Three! Two! One!

The church bells pealed.

'A Happy New Year!' from hundreds of throats. The band began to play 'Auld Lang Syne'.

We joined hands at various points in the song, and traditionally moved in and out of the rings we had created as the words of Burns sang another year away.

Should auld acquaintance be forgot
And never brought to mind?
Should auld acquaintance be forgot
For the sake of auld lang syne . . .

At one stage – singing it for the second time round – the entire vast crowd was moving in unison and singing in unison at the top of their voices as the band played on, the bells pealed and the drum never faltered. We repeated the chorus one last time. We turned to those around us.

'Happy New Year!'

'Happy New Year!'

Ringing with hopeful certainty.

'Happy New Year!'

As if, indeed, we could wipe away the old and start anew. As if this new day could bring us a new life. Indiscriminate shaking of hands, of everyone, everywhere, 'A Happy New Year', a wonderful hope in the words, magic words, said to people you had not met for years, might never meet again, peaceful, happy, never-ending hands held out to be shaken, smiles to be exchanged. The new year so innocently welcomed in.

Sarah and I hugged each other as if we had been saved and born again.

'Let's go down to the fountain.'

The two of us, arms slung around each other's shoulders. Many men and women with arms around each other's shoulders. We walked down High Street, busy with the overflow from the pubs. The Christmas lights were still on. As we turned down King Street, there were the flashes and bangs of the fireworks.

'I thought that dress you were wearing tonight was really good,' I said. 'It fits your shape just right. And that colour – is it brown? – suits you.'

'Auburn. You should set up as a fashion writer,' she said. 'It's a such a relief that you think it fits my shape.'

'You know what I mean.'

'I know it's the best you can do. Do you think this is a good idea? This tour.'

'Yes.'

First-footing had begun. People left their doors ajar and their friends and acquaintances trawling the streets would pop in for a New Year's drink, chat, and then move on to the next blind destination. It would go on until four or five a.m. We went to the Blackie.

The pub was emptying. Many of the customers would be off to do first-footing. I had a key. Mam was giving a brisk sweep to the corridor. Cathy and Frances had just finished cleaning their rooms. Harry was well on with the stack of glasses; Dad was doing a rough first count of the takings.

'Happy New Year!'

'And to you.' My mother hugged Sarah. 'I'm glad you came to see us.' She smiled at me. 'You as well.'

'Wishing you all you wish yourselves,' said my father, solemnly, as he came out of the door holding a wad of as yet uncounted notes. 'Be with you in a minute. They're in the kitchen.'

'I'll go in with you.' My mother propped the brush against a door and escorted us in. 'This is Sarah.' It was just past New Year's celebration, a loud chorus of 'Happy New Year', 'Good to see you both' and a quieter 'She's lovely', 'They look good together', which Sarah picked up and blushed. My mother sat next to her. I went over to Jack Atkinson, a rather fragile figure without his accordion, and Jack Waters, well down his first pint of the celebratory evening.

It had been a well-behaved night. 'Did Kenneth sing?'

'He gave us "I Believe",' said Jack. 'I'd never heard him give that before.'

'He brought the pub to a standstill.'

'And when he did that last verse a second time and went up half an octave,' said Jack, 'he caught me by surprise but I kept up. I've never heard it sung better.'

'He gave me goose bumps.'

'It's a shame, really.'

'Laurie – Laurie from down the road – came up to me after-wards,' my mother said, laughing. 'He said, "I was just winding up to sing that. 'I Believe's my song."'

My mother looked at me directly. 'You were a good singer.'

'Nothing like Kenneth.'

'You don't have to be like Kenneth to be a good singer. There was that solo you sang in church with the school choir behind you. What was it?'

'"Three Kings from Persian Lands Afar".'

'And the choir sang a different song alongside you. It can't have been easy.'

'You'll be showing baby photos next!'

'I'd like to see those,' said Sarah. 'Has he changed much?'

'When he was very small I put him in a sort of frock. I always wanted a girl.'

'I've heard that before. Sorry I let you down.'

'Who would like another?' Jack held up his glass.

Frances said, 'Sit where you are, Stan. I'll get them.'

'Was there a good crowd at the church?'

I described it.

'I'm glad these things keep up,' my mother said.

'You always wanted Wigton pickled,' Stan said. 'And you've passed it on to him.'

'It's changing, though,' said Jack. He turned to Ethel. 'And not before time.'

My mother began a one-to-one conversation with Sarah. Jack Atkinson, a Labour Party man, took advantage of the closing-hours talk to lambast what he called the 'slum centre' of the town. Jack Waters and I talked about the hunt. Frances kept saying she ought to get off home but made no move. My father sat quietly, smoking, drinking very little, content in the company.

*

When everyone had gone and Ethel had done a little more tidying up, they sat in front of the embers, almost too tired to go to bed.

'I think she'll be good for him.'

Stan nodded.

'A big night,' he said and, after a pause, 'a big year one way and another. The Workington business was touch-and-go. I only stayed here because of you, you know.' Ethel was silent. He told me this a few days on. He wanted me to know they had made peace.

'You saw how much he needed to stay. I thought he would take it in his stride. You knew better,' he said. 'I could sense that. It was like seeing a tide going out in your eyes when you changed your mind! He'd never have done all he has if we'd gone and left him here. And he wasn't going to budge, was he? You're looking tired.'

'I'm a lot less tired than I was. The next time you get an offer that suits you, I'll go along with it. Whatever it is.' She was as usual when they were just the two of them, on the little stool close up to the fire. She had spoken quietly and with her back to him. Now she turned and smiled. The circle was closed.

The Johnstons had one of the biggest houses in the town. A double-fronted mid-Victorian sandstone masterpiece, it had ample grounds, and a settlement of kennels for the Basset hounds, which had brought the family two best of breed at Crufts and elevated the current George Johnston to become an international judge. The money came from the big shoe and boot shop smack in the middle of the town, founded by a George Johnston a century earlier and in the hands of George Johnstons ever since. There had also been a skilful acquisition of houses, which they rented out. On the way to the Johnstons' we had made two uncharacteristically short stops, pleading tiredness.

Sarah enjoyed the Johnstons' best of all. She liked dogs. George was flattered to be asked such intent questions by 'this attractive young lady', as he later described her. He even got out his industrial torch and took her across the lawn to see the kennels and look in on the cuddled heap of Bassets. She talked about their two sheepdogs on the farm, pretty old, which had been petted but were now (she felt ashamed even to think this in front of George) rather neglected, certainly taken for granted. He listed the qualities of the Border collie.

The company at the party was some townspeople, dog breeders, a few farmers who lived close to, almost in, the town and two reclusive sisters, who lived around the corner, and kept Jack Russells, which George thought were too much for them.

Having been flattered by her attention and her questions, George, who was sparing with compliments, told me later that she was also 'an intelligent young woman'.

William's, another grand house just at the edge of the old town, was one of the favourites for first-footers. Over the years the Ismays went out of their way to welcome folk. This elasticated the old first-footing custom way beyond its original intention, but it had stuck and William's house was now a prime target. It was big, it was convenient, and everybody knew the milkman. It was an open invitation to gatecrashers. Mr Ismay, a cautious businessman, cast off his careful nature on New Year's Night. Crates of beer, a few half-hidden bottles of spirits for selected guests. Cakes and biscuits were brought up from the shop. When we arrived it was as rowdy as any pub had been. The Holiday sisters and their husbands who ran the AYPA and had been brought up in Union Street, friends of the Ismays for years, turned out without fail. Quite a few professional people: the Ismays had been in Wigton for at least two centuries and always managed to retain the smack of class and a gift for making money. On a night like this they mixed easily with the lads who were drinking their way to the new Greenacres estate, seizing the chance for a last one to see them along the road. Then there were the locals from Union Street and round about who traditionally saw it as their personal last port of call.

Mr Ismay went to bed early. Mrs Ismay, helped by the two women who worked in the café, supervised the drinks and fed the hungry. William, as serene as always, coasted around, a glass of beer in his hand, smiling, talking to everybody, making sure there was no trouble.

'We won't stay long,' Sarah murmured. 'I've a home to go to!' But it was said with good humour as we edged and shouldered our way to the drinks table, another Britvic for her, pale ale for me.

William waved but didn't rush over. He was talking to his cousins from Dundraw. We teamed up with Eric and his girlfriend Betty. Just in time.

'We're on our way,' said Eric. 'It's worse than the Crown.'

'I don't know how people can face giving over their house to just anybody who comes in from the streets.' Betty glanced around in horror.

'A good night?'

'You?'

'Usual.' Eric smiled. 'See pals. Get drunk. Go to church – sing "Auld Lang Syne"! First foot. Pals. Go home. All over.'

'You shouldn't have had whisky.'

'One for the road?'

'I'm taking you home.' Betty linked his arm and guided him to the coats.

There was a minor surge towards the door, shouts of 'Thanks!' and 'Happy New Year!'

'A lot of them leave about this time,' said William. 'Manuel lays on free chips at half past one.'

'Bye, pal.' Held up by Betty, Eric, even less sober than he looked, was steered towards the door.

'More space now,' said William. 'This lot,' he swept his arm towards the group around the fireplace, 'like a bit of a singsong before they go. There's Robert. He likes to sing – yes – here he goes . . .'

Robert, a builder, in his deep, slow voice, not always certain of the tune, sang a moving version of 'Sixteen Tons', the story of a man driven to an early grave by being exploited in the mines. There was enough applause to lead him into 'Water', the tale of a man driven to insanity by thirst as he crossed a desert. Less applause but enough to set him off on the one about a man who killed his wife, mistakenly.

'Can we go now?' Sarah's whisper was picked up by two women nearby. They nodded.

'Barbara has to sing,' said William.

Barbara Toppin had won a scholarship to a music academy in Manchester where she developed a passion for playing the cello but kept up the singing. She came back to Wigton less and less frequently but always for Christmas and the New Year. Her family and William's were friends.

She was tall, a handsome young woman with the very dark hair and the fine skin of the Toppins. She stepped forward, paused for an almost silence and smiling, wholly unselfconscious, sang 'Jesu, Joy of Man's Desiring'.

'More! More!' They applauded – but she shook her head.

Jean Holiday had been waiting for her moment. She leaped from her seat. 'And now from the sublime to the gorblimey! Come on, you!'

She pointed at me. It happened every year.

'We'll go after this, I promise,' I said to Sarah.

'Why didn't they let her sing an encore?'

'She never does. Oh dear!'

Jean put her arm around my shoulders, then broke off to take another deep drink from her whisky and ginger. The Holiday family had lived in Union Street for many years. All three daughters sang in the choir. Their father, also in the choir, worked at the factory, could sing the first verse of 'Abide With Me', without taking a second breath.

'Right,' said Jean. 'We're on! Wigton's very own anthem. Here we go!' Sung with feeling and mime. She tightened her grip around my shoulders, whether for friendship or dear life was not clear.

Now we are the Two Wigton Mashers
We often go out on the mash
We wear our tall hats
We've no shirts on our backs
And it's seldom we have any cash
We always bring in the new fashions
It's seldom we stick to the old. ('Join in!' They did.)
Singing tra-la-la-la-la
As we walk down the street
For style and perfections we ne'er can be beat
The ladies declare that we are a treat
We're the two Wigton Mashers from down Union Street.

'More!'

This time Jean's sisters joined the line, Robert jumped up as did Harry, who had popped in for a nightcap on his way home from a serious pub-crawl.

They sang it again, adding another verse and concluding,

So we dance. And we sing
And we don't give a jot
We're a very fine lot
And we're jolly good com-pa-ny.

'Where did you learn that Mashers song?'

We were cycling back rather slowly. There was a half-moon that gave us enough light.

'We sang it on choir trips.'

'Barbara has a lovely voice.'

'She does. Everybody round here wants her to be the next Kathleen Ferrier.'

When we reached the farm she went straight into the yard to park her bike. There were no lights on. She leaned against me, more for support than out of affection. I pressed myself against her.

'I'm too tired,' she said. 'That was a great night. We don't go that far in Oulton.'

'I'll phone tomorrow morning.'

'Good.' We kissed each other chastely. At the corner of the house she looked back and said, 'We have good times, don't we?'

I let the bike do the work down the hill and over the bridge until I was forced to pedal up the next hill. This part of the road took me past a dense afforestation of trees unpenetrated by the light from the moon.

My legs were heavy. The forest was a gloomy presence. The day had stirred me to increasing confusion about what Sarah and I should do.

I felt it first at the nape of my neck. Then the sensation swept over and into my skull. Now it took me over. It had come back a few times over the last years, the old feeling that I was outside myself. I had pushed it away. Now on the empty road halfway through the night, it seemed to take the opportunity to control me. I pedalled harder. It made no difference. The person I was on this bike was not me, it was a thing. Outside, somewhere in that forest, was light, the soul, the reality of me. I heard my breath, panting. It seemed to give strength to a pursuer. I pedalled even harder until I passed the forest, was on an open road, just a small incline taking me up to Standing Stone when I would see Wigton. There it was, in a shallow bowl, illuminated only by the ever-pulsating factory. And I saw, across to the even deeper, larger darkness of the fields, around the mass darkness that would be the fells.

I sped down to the railway bridge and swerved under it. There was relief in hearing the churn and seeing close up the lights of the factory. Alongside the river, walking alone, I saw a figure I recognised. I made a U-turn and stopped. So did Andrew, reluctantly.

'Andrew! Happy New Year!' The sounds coming from my mouth helped me.

'I see who it is now.'

Andrew was hunched. There was no new coat. He was dressed in his worst for work.

It was awkward.

'I never got to say well done about Whiplash. Second season top of the league?'

'Third.'

I had got off the bike and stood beside him. The lights from the factory played on his face. It was a mask of unhappiness.

'They took him away from me,' he said, his voice almost breaking. 'They took him away from me, Melvyn, the rotten buggers. They've sent him into Ireland – to breed.' He stopped and looked at me as if pleading for help.

'What was it?'

'Bookies. They took the money and when I couldn't pay up they took the hound.'

Andrew's evident misery was unbearable. We were the only two human beings in sight. The factory churned on.

'That's terrible.'

'It is.' He all but shouted now: 'It is! It is!'

He wiped his coat sleeve across his eyes.

'There was never a hound like him,' he said.

'Never will be again.'

'I'm sorry.'

'So am I! So am I!'

His voice reached out and up to the sky.

He settled himself.

'But I'll buy him back. I'm going in now for a half-shift. They're short-handed at this time of year. Then I'll stay for a double-shift at double pay tonight and tomorrow. I'll never bet again. I'll save up. I'll get him back. Just wait and see. I'll get him back. He's my dog.' He shouted out again to no one and to everyone, trying to relieve his pain. And on that sentence he walked on, along to the factory gate, to punch in his ticket and work himself to death.

I watched him until he reached the gate, as if I were making sure he was safe.

Chapter Forty-eight

'There are three terms, eight weeks each term. That's twenty-four weeks at university, twenty-six weeks back here. I could come back at least once in term time. You could come to Oxford at least once. That would break it up. We could give it a year and if it doesn't work, pack it in or we get married and live there while I finish the course. That's if I get in.'

'I knew you'd want to do it,' she said. 'I think you should have a go. You'd never forgive yourself if you didn't. It seems a bit unfair,' she added. 'Catherine and Valerie will just sail off to Durham. Never mind.'

We were upstairs in the sitting room, sat across the table from each other, on our best behaviour in the G Plan.

'I think if you have to wait for three years just to get there it could be difficult,' she said.

'Why?'

'I don't know. It would be a long wait, I suppose. But then again, we'd be all right. Wouldn't we?'

'Yes. And even if I get in I don't *have* to go.'

Sarah shook her head. 'Let's wait and see. But you should do it.'

I looked around the room. 'At this rate we'll be late for the pictures.'

'Never!' she said.

I chose to talk to Dad in the bar, when it was empty in the late afternoon. Dad and I sat at each end of the oak settle. This was mid-January.

'I can't seem to get a part-time job.'

'It's the time of year.'

'There's what I do for you, of course. That's helping.'

'I've been thinking about that.' He crossed his legs, right over left, and, as always before 'a talk', tapped out a Capstan Full Strength from an already depleted packet. 'I think you can give that up now.'

'Why?'

'Well,' he struggled, 'it was all right when you were going to school but now it seems a bit . . . Do you mind doing it?'

'I always have! But it's fair enough.' Both of us laughed. 'And the money was very helpful.' I paused. 'And who would do it if I didn't? You and Mam work hard enough. You'd need one of those cellarmen – a potboy – they used to have. No. I'll still do it. I'm hoping it'll harden me to embarrassment and, anyway, some of the passengers in the bus would miss me. I get a wave or another gesture most days!'

He was changing, Stan thought. He was confident now.

'What I'd like is a loan.'

'I'm listening.'

'The exam's in March. I'll have to do some re-revision. I'd like to do that. Then, well, I might as well come out with it. When I was at Queen's College there were lads there talking about painting, Impressionism and Post-Impressionism and Cubism and I knew next to nothing, more truthfully nothing at all, about all that, and here's a chance to catch up. Miss Roberts, who teaches art, gives art history classes after school and I'd like to go to those, and the Art Room has a good library. Haven't finished yet! Music. We sang those anthems and so on in church but I don't know anything about the history of it. I talked to Miss Seegar and she said she'd make out a list of the best composers and all I had to do was to buy the *Radio Times* and look up the Third Programme and tick them off. But I can't manage these new things and the rest on what you give me and I don't want any more. But after these next exams it'll be spring and much easier to get a job. I would settle things before the next move. Arnison's have said they would take me on again. And I want to travel a bit. I'll pay you back.'

Stanley leaned back and smiled appreciatively. 'I'm glad you've got that off your chest! How much do you need?'

'Say for twelve weeks. Four pounds a week.'

'I can manage that. And I'm going to do again what I did last time. But this time I'll give you fifty pounds. You'll pay back the forty-eight when you can and I keep on paying for your work in the mornings.'

I had not been prepared to say all of that let alone to meet with such an immediate generous response. I could see in his look the pride he took in being able to do this and I understood the pride.

I went into school the next Wednesday. It was the day we did rugby training after school and I wanted to talk to Miss Roberts and Miss Seegar.

It was dinner time, the place was empty. As I walked through the corridors I felt like a ghost.

I strolled into the library. Mr Blacka was there, alone, reading, a Carr's biscuit tin beside him.

'Ah,' he said. 'We can't seem to get rid of you.'

'Sorry about that.'

'Have a seat.' He nodded at the biscuit tin. 'I never could abide school dinners,' he said. 'I bring my own sandwiches.'

'And you have the place to yourself.'

'That's half the battle,' he said. 'So what brings you here?'

I told him.

'Sensible,' he said. 'We're very bad here in giving music and painting their due. In my opinion, those two women are the best teachers in the school.'

The compliment was ground out, his lips scarcely moving. The thick Yorkshire accent unchanged. I'd missed it.

'What are you reading?'

I pulled it out of my pocket.

'Norman Mailer. *Advertisements for Myself.*'

'Any good?'

'Terrific.'

'I tried to read *The Naked and the Dead.*' He shook his head. 'Over-strained, I thought.'

'I think he's taking on America.'

'Is he now? That's a thought. You'll be seeing Mr James?'

'Yes.'

'He did well by you, but I think you'd have been happier doing English. Your history marks were in the nineties, but English wasn't far behind in the eighties. It strikes me it's easier to get high marks in history. In English there's more interpretation – you weren't bad at that. And you enjoyed it. In history once you've got the facts, that's it. English can carry you through a lifetime.'

'There's interpretation in history. That's the basis of it.'

'But it doesn't ask questions of *yourself.* That's the big difference. Literature lines the mind. I'd better go now before you have me persuading you to change subjects!' He gathered his things together. 'Do you keep reading everything? You were always reading.'

He nodded and, biscuit tin under one arm, books and files under the other, he left.

'This is only a suggestion.' Mr James had taken the small newspaper and magazine room. 'I'm worried about what shape you'll be in.'

I waited.

'You worked yourself up to a pitch for June. Then again for October – without much of a break in between. This has been a longer break and I worry that you'll have slacked off, without realising it. The mind, I was always taught, is a muscle,' said the teacher, firmly, 'and it has to be kept in trim. And I fear the competition may be tougher this time. These are the last batch of colleges. Many of those who failed before will see this as their last chance. And then there are those, like you, who'll feel trapped because of the termination of national service.

'What I'm suggesting, and it's just a suggestion, is that you do a few papers over the next weeks. I'll get hold of previous examination sheets or make up questions and I'm sure we can find one of the smaller rooms and put DO NOT DISTURB on it for three hours and leave you to see what you can do.'

'That's a great idea!'

'I hoped you'd take to it. So what about next Wednesday morning? Start at nine thirty, English history Part One.'

'Yes, sir.'

'I'll mark it overnight and we'll go on from there.'

'It's a really good idea!'

I reorganised myself that night after rugby practice. I adopted the same routine. On the first full night, Thursday, I felt extraordinarily tired after the five-hour stint of homework: so Mr James was right. The muscle was failing.

'You did well,' said the teacher, 'but some distance off your best, I'm afraid. I thought as much. You've relaxed, you see. You achieved what you wanted to achieve so why try again? That's your unconscious mind talking. I'm sorry, but I think this,' he held up the sheets, 'will at best be on the margin.'

It was not what I wanted to hear.

'Shall we try next week with the European history papers?'

This time I even worked on Saturday afternoon after the game.

'Better, but not by much. The problem is you've set yourself a problem by all you've done before.'

'English history again?'

Mr James nodded.

And so it went on. In the break before I went to Oxford for the exam, I spent two days on test papers.

'Just about there,' said Mr James. 'In fact, with that extra bit of adrenalin, back where you were.' He leafed through the papers and smiled. 'They're good, you know.'

I had not only done the work he recommended, but managed to achieve an energising anxiety. I took the papers with me to reread on the train. That soon palled. I'd also taken *The Rainbow.* I asked Sarah not to come to the station to see me off.

It was curious to carry the thought that it wouldn't matter, and might well be better, if I failed.

In Wadham the entrants for the exams were dwarfed by the great oak-beamed hall, the minstrels' gallery, the panelled, almost fortressed splendour of the place, surely not made for anything as ordinary as pork chops, two veg and beer. But we ate it up, drank it up and soon enough talked to each other.

I had taken an alarm clock. Breakfast lacked nothing. We then walked along Parks Road to Keble College, and in its vast Victorian hall we sat at our desks and waited.

'You have three hours. You will find extra sheets of paper on the side tables. Silence is compulsory. You may begin.'

This time I was trapped. The envelope marked Wadham College, Oxford, landed on the mat and my mother brought it upstairs. She grimaced anxiously at my father and handed me the letter. For a moment I felt sick. I took the knife, which had been about to tackle bacon and eggs, and used it to slit open the stiff envelope. My father and mother looked down at their plates.

It was all in slow motion. I read it twice and then put it aside. It was not easy to speak.

'They've given me a scholarship. I can start this October.'

My mother, as if suddenly snapping out of a trance, darted towards me and kissed my cheek.

My father shook his head.

'Well done!' Mr Stowe prided himself on never repeating a phrase. But on this morning he did. 'Well done!'

'My old college,' said Mr James, with a grin that only barely expressed his pleasure. 'Now you have to compose that letter to Queen's turning them down. Very good. Very good.'

'He brought me these,' said Joan, when Mr James got home that afternoon. She pointed to a dozen white roses. 'He delivered them himself.'

'As long as it doesn't make him lose himself,' said my mother, just to say something. She was overcome and doing her best to dampen down the sadness.

'Who'd have credited it?' He shook his head and tapped the new cigarette on the table.

I'd decided to walk to the school the longer way, round by the baths and the church, to show them the letter. I assumed, and wrongly, that as the letter was addressed to me it was for me only. But of course they'd sent a copy to the school.

'I'll announce it at assembly tomorrow morning,' Mr Stowe had said. 'Do you think you could be there?'

'Yes, sir.'

'It gives them something to aim at.' He looked at Mr James and then at me. 'You've done well. Both of you.'

Chapter Forty-nine

After taking the flowers to Mrs James I walked into the country towards the hills. Sarah would not be through work until five thirty. I didn't want to talk to anybody about it. I was making for Ireby, five miles away up country. It was cool, the west wind scudding broken grey clouds, a faint movement in the hedgerows across a landscape budding into spring, scarcely any traffic on the roads, tractors in the fields distantly growling out a soundtrack. Up the long narrow street that was Bolton Low Houses, on to Bolton Gate, where I'd gone to the Christmas Eve service with William, who had friends near the French castellated church, finally to Ireby, an ancient medieval droving town, now a village.

The pub had a small garden at the back looking directly across to the northern fells. I took my light ale and cheese and chutney sandwiches there and pulled out *The Rainbow*. Twenty-four pages to go. Just right. But every so often I put the novel to one side and slipped into a daydream. Now what? The answer came and then retreated, returned to another form, hung around, and then dissolved and I took up the book, but the landscape and my mood blocked an entry.

It was not only the landscape in front of me, it was the landscape inside my mind. The relief at the result released me into a waterfall of recollections, which I later thought had been stored especially for these moments.

Once again I was drawn into a past that I now know would never fade. I saw my father alone in the bar, wreathed in smoke, smiling, the smile saying, 'Life can be good, just don't flinch.' My mother on that low stool in front of the fire in the kitchen, drawing the last warmth from it after a long day, musing and looking into the embers, finding comfort, I think, and peace perhaps. And me, safe upstairs, asleep, the pub quiet, the town emptied into the night.

For the rest of my life I would find these images alive on the screen of my mind, my father moving surely around the cellar, checking the barrels, my mother going from room to room, cleaning in the morning, talking to friends, customers in the evenings, a homing place to which I could always fly.

The mass of those tiny budgerigars of all colours, the smell of the new-mown grass in the park, my grandfather measuring the swathe he had cut as carefully as if it had been a furrow, the winding river full of memories that were already more like dreams.

It was as if the concentration and anxiety that had locked me inside myself had escaped and stood outside me, like a spirit, free as could be, to be blown where the wind blew.

The fells, there for so long before me, to be there long after me and my species. Living on through extreme elements, trees that would far outlive my generation; bridleways and sheep tracks. A vastness in the broad expanse in front of me, fell, river, fields, drystone walls newly replenished over the centuries but not destroyed, above all a landscape not bothered about us however much we spoiled it, cut it, dug it. Yet in our speck of the cosmos we wanted a reaction from it, we still searched for evidence or a sustainable vision, a vision of some grand, mysterious force, whatever it turned out to be. Thoughts not unlike these, from writers who had lined my mind, as Mr Blacka put it, and also from my own attempts to put into thought what I felt in this sweep of monumental serenity as I sat in the pub garden. Why leave this? What more was there? This was surely more than enough.

I walked back to Wigton slowly, even though it was mostly downhill. The weather was settled, scarcely-moving heavy-bellied clouds very stately, the occasional cyclist's or rambler's passing

'Hello'. My mood threatened to persuade me to go into Bolton Gate church, but I walked on by. I would have soon sunk into a sort of holiness or at least solemnity I did not feel or want to feel. After Red Dial, with time in hand, I climbed over a gate and went into the humps and twisting little paths that was Old Carlisle and tried to imagine a thousand soldiers stationed there, cavalrymen, two thousand horses grazing on that turf, drinking from the river. But I could not get into the mood of it.

Through Crozier's field where we had come in the dark to set alight the Highmoor bonfire, past that mad Venetian Tower still drawing attention to itself, something of the town's luck in it.

Stony Banks, the baths, Little Lane, Water Street, Church Street, down King Street to collect my bike and wait for Sarah. I would tell her first.

Without setting out to do so, I had made up my mind.

I looked around and everything I saw I loved.

I would go. But I would never leave.

Acknowledgements

Thanks to Philip Davis, Emeritus Professor of Literature and Psychology at the University of Liverpool, for his early encouragement.

Thanks also for some bare-knuckle discussions to Robert Colls, Professor of Cultural History at the International Centre for Sports, History and Culture, De Montfort University Leicester.

William Ismay, my oldest and best friend who never left the town, died before I could get the book to him. He was a touchstone for the years we spent together in Wigton.

Caroline Michel's strong commitment was always encouraging.

Thanks to Vivien Green, who has been such a support and friend for many years.

The editorial contribution of Carole Welch was, as always, a spur and a pleasure. My lifelong friend Julia Matheson's help was invaluable.

Finally to my wife Gabriel for her constant love and support – many thanks.